THE AIR PILOT'S MANUAL

Volume 4

The Aeroplane – technical

covering Aircraft (General) and Aircraft (Type) for the PPL(A)

Trevor Thom

graphics by
Robert Johnson

Airlife
England

Nothing in this manual supersedes any legislation, rules, regulations or procedures contained in any operational document issued by Her Majesty's Stationery Office, the Civil Aviation Authority, the manufacturers of aircraft, engines and systems, or by the operators of aircraft throughout the world.

Text, Copyright © 1987, 1988 Trevor Thom.
Original Illustrations & Diagrams, Copyright © 1987, 1993
Trevor Thom & Robert Johnson.

Thom, Trevor
    Air pilots manual.—Rev. 2nd ed.
    Vol. 4: The aeroplane technical
    1. Airplanes—Piloting   2. Private
    flying
    I. Title
    629.132′5217   TL710

    ISBN 1-85310-017-X

First edition published 1987
by Airlife Publishing Ltd.

This second revised edition published 1988.
Reprinted with amendments 1989, 1991 and 1993.

Printed in England by Livesey Ltd., Shrewsbury.

Airlife Publishing Ltd.

101 Longden Road, Shrewsbury SY3 9EB, Shropshire, England.

THE AIR PILOT'S MANUAL Vol. 4

The Aeroplane – technical

CONTENTS

PERSONAL PROGRESS TABLE	
Theory	Exercises

(continued)

EDITORIAL TEAM

Trevor Thom.
A current Boeing 757 Captain with a European airline, Trevor has been active in the *International Federation of Airline Pilots' Associations (IFALPA),* based in London, and a member of the *IFALPA Aeroplane Design and Operations Group.* He also served as IFALPA representative to the *Society of Automotive Engineers (SAE) – Aerospace,* a body which makes recommendations to the aviation industry, especially the manufacturers. Prior to his airline positions Trevor worked as a lecturer in Mathematics and Physics, and also as an Aviation Ground Instructor and a Flying Instructor. He is a double degree graduate from the University of Melbourne and also holds a Diploma of Education.

John Fenton.
A Flying Instructor since 1970, John is former joint proprietor and assistant CFI of Yorkshire Flying Services at Leeds/Bradford. He is a PPL Examiner and recently received the Bronze Medal from the Royal Aero Club for his achievements and contributions to air rallying. John has made considerable contributions to the field of flying instruction in this country and pioneered the use of audio tapes for training.

Peter Godwin.
Chief Flying Instructor at Leavesden Flight Centre, Peter has amassed over 10,000 instructional flying hours. As a member of the CAA Panel of Examiners, he is an Instrument Rating and Type Rating Examiner and is currently instructing for the Basic Commercial Pilots Licence and Instrument Rating. Previously he was Chief Flying Instructor at London School of Flying, Elstree and Denham.

Jim Hitchcock.
Supervisor of Pilot Technical Training, Oxford Air Training School, Jim joined the RAF as an apprentice in 1945. Later commissioned as a Navigator, he served in Coastal and Flying Training Commands, and on Photo Reconnaissance. On leaving the RAF he joined CSE in 1967. Jim has organised navigation events for the HCGB, including the 1973 World Championships. He also holds a C Mech E.

Ronald Smith.
A senior Aviation Ground Instructor, Ron's twenty-five years in aviation include considerable time as a flying instructor, specialised flying in remote areas, fish-spotting, and a period operating his own Air Taxi Service. He is an active member of the *International Wheelchair Aviators* and holds a Commercial Pilot's Licence.

Robert Johnson.
An experienced aviator, Bob drew most of the diagrams, designed the cover, and prepared the final sub-edit and layout of the manuals for printing. His aviation experience includes flying a *Cessna Citation* executive jet, a *DC-3* and light aircraft as Chief Pilot for an international University based in Switzerland, and seven years as a First Officer on *Fokker Friendship, Lockheed Electra* and *McDonnell Douglas DC-9* airliners. Prior to this he was an Air Taxi Pilot and also gained technical experience as a Draughtsman on Airborne Mineral Survey work in Australia.

ACKNOWLEDGEMENTS

We greatly appreciate the input that has been made by the following:

The Civil Aviation Authority, Ralph Bryder, Edward Pape and Bill Ryall; Brian Hill, Robyn Hind, Lewis Kiddle, Knut Meyer, Tim Newman, Ian Perry and Lesley Ward; also ARV, Cessna, Gulfstream American, Piper and Slingsby for technical material, and of course Airtour International Ltd. and Robert Pooley Ltd.

'Good, clear Knowledge
minimises
Flight Training Hours'

INTRODUCTION

An **Aeroplane** is a man-made device designed to use natural forces to enable motion through the air – that is, to enable *'flight'.*

Air is that mixture of gases which surrounds the Earth. If any slight pressure is applied to air, it will flow and change its shape, hence it may be classified as a fluid.

Aerodynamics studies the motion of a body through the air or, if you like, the flow of air past a body. It is concerned with the relative motion of air and a body. The basic principles of aerodynamics relevant to the motion of an aeroplane through the air come under the name **Principles of Flight.**

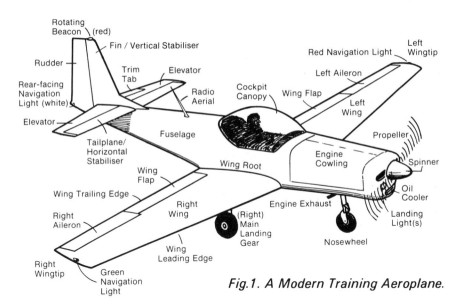

Fig.1. A Modern Training Aeroplane.

In order to control an aeroplane safely and to make correct decisions during the course of a flight, a Pilot must have an understanding of the Principles of Flight.

When actually in flight the Pilot does not have time to analyse in minute detail the effect of everything that he does, or is about to do, or fails to do, however he should be aware of the fundamentals.

The purpose of our course is to provide you with the required understanding and knowledge. Our notes will remain as an adequate reference book on this subject and should be retained throughout your flying career.

As a Student Pilot you are about to commence an exciting hobby or possibly a very rewarding career. To be a good pilot you must have a sound understanding of the principles of flight, the operation of aircraft and the performance that your particular aircraft is capable of.

This book (Volume 4 of The Air Pilot's Manual) is designed to prepare you for the UK Private Pilot's Licence (Aeroplanes) examination in **Aircraft (General)**. You take this examination at your Flying School/Aero Club.

Our course for **Aircraft (General)** is divided into five main sections:

- 1 — **Principles of Flight;**
- 2 — **Airframe, Engines and Systems;**
- 3 — **Instruments;**
- 4 — **Airworthiness and Performance;** plus
- Section on **Safety, First Aid and Survival**, which covers *Aeromedical* items in the CAA Aircraft (General) syllabus; this section is located at the end of Volume 6 of the Air Pilot's Manual series, **Human Factors and Pilot Performance**; (this information was formerly contained in Vol. 2).

NOTE: **Emergencies** — included in the CAA Aircraft (General) syllabus is a requirement to be familiar with the general procedures in handling *a fire in the air or on the ground.* These are covered in the first chapter of 'Flying Training' (Volume 1 of this series). Also, a coverage of *fire extinguishers and their use* is contained in the Safety, First Aid and Survival section at the end of Volume 6.

Exercises and Answers to all the chapters in this book (Sections 1 — 4) can be found in the Exercises Section at the end of Volume 2. Exercises on First Aid and Survival are contained in that Volume (6).

At the end of this volume is an Appendix containing information designed to prepare you for the ground examination: **Aircraft (Type).** This is normally an oral examination which is confined to the type of aeroplane in which you are flight tested, and is usually conducted at the same time as your Private Pilot's Licence flight test.

1

PRINCIPLES OF FLIGHT

1

THE FORCES THAT ACT ON AN AEROPLANE

Like all things, an aeroplane has **Weight,** a force which always acts in a vertical direction towards the centre of the Earth.

Whilst the aeroplane is on the ground, its Weight is balanced by the Reaction Force of the ground on the aeroplane, which acts through the wheels.

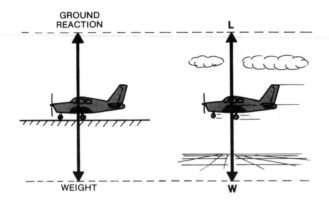

Fig.1-1. The Aeroplane is Supported by the Ground, or by Lift.

Whilst in level flight, the Weight of the aeroplane is balanced by the **Lift** force, which is generated aerodynamically by the flow of air over the wings (also known as the **main aerofoils).** In addition, as the aeroplane moves through the air it will experience a retarding force known as **Drag** and which, unless counteracted (or balanced), will cause the aeroplane to decelerate, i.e. to lose speed.

Fig.1-2. Drag Balanced by Thrust.

In steady **Straight and Level** flight, the Drag (or retarding force) is balanced by the **Thrust,** which is produced by the engine-propeller combination in most smaller aircraft. (In pure jet aircraft the thrust is produced by the turbine engines without the need for a propeller.)

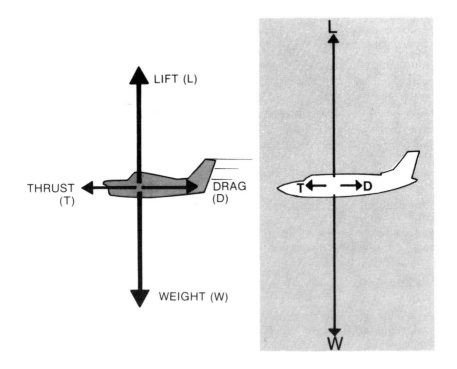

Fig.1-3. The Four Main Forces in Balance.

As the Forces in the above illustration are in balance, the Resultant Force acting on the aeroplane is Zero, and it will neither accelerate nor decelerate. In this situation the aeroplane is said to be in a state of **'Equilibrium'.** In this case (steady straight and level flight):

The WEIGHT Is Balanced By The LIFT,

The DRAG Is Balanced By The THRUST.

The aeroplane will continue flying at the same velocity, i.e. at the same speed and in the same direction, unless, for example, the Pilot or a gust of wind alters this situation.

For the type of aeroplane that you are likely to be flying during your training (and indeed as a licensed Private Pilot) the magnitude (size) of the **Lift** (and therefore the **Weight)** during cruising flight will be approximately 10 times greater than the **Drag** (and **Thrust).** This relationship of Lift to Drag is very important and is referred to as the **Lift/Drag** ratio. The L/D ratio is in this case 10 to 1, i.e. the Lift (to balance the Weight) is 10 times greater than the Drag (which is balanced by the Thrust).

In this Section (Principles of Flight), we will look at each of the four basic forces in turn:

- WEIGHT
- LIFT
- DRAG
- THRUST

Our plan of attack is to discuss **Weight** first of all, because the aeroplane is subject to this force at all times, both in flight and on the ground. This takes only a page or two.

Then we will examine the **Aerofoil** and the production of **Lift** and **Drag**. Lift is produced by the wings, and Drag is produced by the wings and most other parts of the aeroplane, as the entire flying machine moves through the air.

Next, we will discuss how the **Propeller** produces the **Thrust** which moves the aeroplane along.

Straight and level flight at a steady airspeed is a fairly simple situation. Other phases of flight such as **accelerating, decelerating, climbing, descending, gliding, turning, stalling, taking-off** and **landing** are slightly more complicated and are considered in detail further on in this Section.

☐ Before moving on to the next chapter we suggest you complete **Exercises 1 — The Forces That Act On An Aeroplane.**

(All the exercises for this volume are found at the end of Volume 2 of The Air Pilot's Manual.)

2

WEIGHT

Gravity is the downward force attracting all bodies vertically towards the centre of the Earth. The name given to the gravitational force is **Weight** and for our purposes in this study of principles of flight it is the total weight of the loaded aeroplane. This **Weight** may be considered to act as a single force through the **Centre of Gravity (CG)**.

The CG is the point of balance and its position depends upon the weight and position of all the individual parts of the aeroplane and the load that it is carrying. If the aeroplane was suspended by a rope attached to its centre of gravity, the aeroplane would balance.

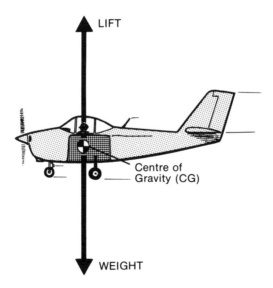

Fig.2-1. Weight Acts Down Through The Centre of Gravity.

The **Magnitude** of the weight is important and there are certain limitations placed upon it, e.g. a Maximum Take-Off Weight (MTOW) will be specified for the aircraft. **Weight limitations** depend upon the structural strength of the components making up the aircraft and the operational requirements that the aircraft is designed to meet.

The **Balance** point **(Centre of Gravity — CG)** is very important during flight because of its effect on the stability and performance of the aeroplane. It must remain within carefully defined limits at all stages of the flight.

The location of the CG depends upon the weight and the location of the load placed in the aeroplane. The CG will move if the distribution of the load changes, e.g. by passengers moving about or by transferring fuel from one tank to another. The CG may move as the weight changes by fuel burning off or by parachutists leaping out. It is usual for the all-up weight to decrease as the flight progresses.

Both of these aspects, **Weight and Balance,** must be considered by the Pilot prior to flight. If any limitation is exceeded at any point in the flight, safety will be compromised. A detailed study of Weight and Balance follows in the section on *Airworthiness and Performance*.

A useful means of describing the load that the wings carry in straight and level flight (when the Lift from the wings supports the Weight of the aeroplane) is **Wing Loading,** which is simply the **weight supported per unit area of wing.**

$$\text{Wing Loading} = \frac{\text{Weight of the Aeroplane}}{\text{Wing Area}}$$

Example: An aeroplane has a Maximum Certificated Weight of 1,220 kg and a wing area of 20 square metres. What is its wing loading?

Wing Loading = Weight/Wing Area = 1220/20 = 61 kg/square metre.

☐ Now complete **Exercises 2 — Weight.**

3

AEROFOIL – LIFT

PRESSURE DISTRIBUTION AND AIRFLOW AROUND AN AEROFOIL.

An aerofoil is a surface designed to help in lifting, controlling or propelling an aircraft by making use of the airflow. Some well-known aerofoils are the wing, the tailplane (or horizontal stabiliser), the fin (or vertical stabiliser), and the propeller blades.

Control surfaces such as ailerons, elevators and rudders form part of the various aerofoils. The Pilot can move these to vary the shape of the aerofoil and the forces generated by the airflow over it. This enables the Pilot to manoeuvre the aircraft and have some semblance of control over it.

The shape of the wings can be changed by extending and lowering flaps to provide better low speed characteristics for take-off and landing.

The production of the **Lift** force by an aerofoil is explained by Bernoulli's Principle ('high flow velocity gives a low static pressure' – also known as the venturi effect). **Daniel Bernoulli** (1700–1782) was the Swiss scientist who discovered this effect.

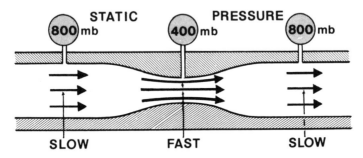

Fig.3-1. The Venturi – High Flow Velocity, Low Static Pressure.

At Private Pilot level we are mainly concerned with aircraft that fly at 200 knots and below. At higher speeds, even well before the speed of sound is reached, there is the complication of the compressibility of air – this is considered at Commercial Pilot level.

AIRFLOW AROUND AN AEROPLANE.

The pattern of the airflow past an aeroplane depends mainly upon the shape of the aeroplane and its attitude relative to the free stream airflow. It is the **Relative Velocity** of the aeroplane and the airflow that matters, not whether it is the aeroplane moving through the air or the air flowing past the aeroplane. Either approach gives us the same answers.

The most important part of the aeroplane is the **Aerofoil**. Airflow past the main aerofoils (wings) generates the **Lift** force that enables the aeroplane to fly. The airflow around an aerofoil may be likened to the airflow through a venturi.

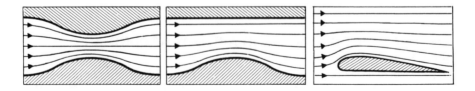

Fig.3-2. The Airflow Around an Aerofoil Resembles a Venturi.

Some other factors apart from the speed of the air past the aerofoil are involved. The size of the aeroplane, the shape of the wings, the density and viscosity (stickiness) of the air – each of these plays a role in determining the characteristics of the airflow around the aeroplane.

The behaviour of the airflow nearest the surface of the aerofoil is most important, and this layer of air is referred to as the **Boundary Layer.**

STREAMLINE FLOW.

If succeeding molecules follow the same steady path in a flow, then this path can be represented by a streamline. There will be no flow across the streamlines, only along them.

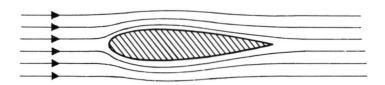

Fig.3-3. Streamline Flow.

At any fixed point on the streamline, each air molecule will experience the same velocity and static pressure as the preceding molecules when they passed that particular point. These values of velocity and pressure may change from point to point along the streamline. A reduction in the velocity of streamline flow is indicated by wider spacing on the streamlines whilst increased velocity is indicated by decreased spacing of the streamlines.

Any molecule following a streamline will experience the same velocities and pressures as the preceding molecules.

Streamline flow is very desirable around an aircraft.

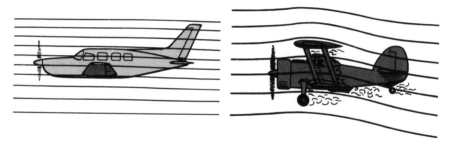

Fig.3-4. Streamline Flow around an Aeroplane is Desirable.

TURBULENT FLOW.

In turbulent flow, succeeding molecules do not follow a streamlined flow pattern. Succeeding molecules may travel a path quite different to the preceding molecules. This turbulent flow is also known as unsteady flow or eddying and is an undesirable feature in most phases of flight.

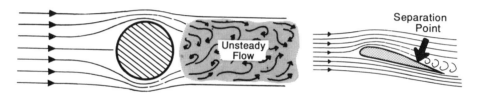

Fig.3-5. Turbulent Flow.

Steady streamline flow is desirable in most phases of flight, and turbulent flow is best avoided. The point where the smooth boundary-layer flow separates from the surface of an aerofoil and becomes turbulent is known as the **separation point**.

BERNOULLI'S PRINCIPLE.

A fluid in steady motion has energy:
• Static Pressure Energy; and
• Dynamic Pressure Energy (Kinetic Energy due to motion).

Daniel Bernoulli showed that for an ideal fluid:

Total Energy in a Steady Streamline Flow Remains Constant

Pressure Energy + Kinetic Energy = constant Total Energy
(static)   (dynamic)

The energy can change from the one form to the other, but the total energy content will remain the same. If the Pressure Energy decreases (lower static pressure) then the Kinetic Energy must increase (higher velocity of flow), i.e. venturi effect.

The **Static Pressure** at any point in a fluid acts equally in all directions. Static pressure of the atmosphere is being exerted at all points on your hand right now.

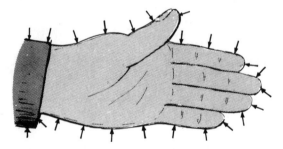

Fig.3-6. Static Pressure Acts in All Directions.

The energy of **Motion** is known as **Kinetic Energy** and is expressed as:

K.E. = ½ x Mass x Velocity-squared.

The Kinetic Energy of a parcel of air in motion relative to an object allows it to exert a force on the object. This force, when calculated per unit surface area, is called **Dynamic Pressure.**

Dynamic Pressure is expressed as '½.Rho.V-squared'.

Dynamic Pressure involves **air density 'Rho',** which is mass per unit volume (rather than just 'mass', which is used in the formula for K.E.). Dynamic Pressure is a more useful quantity than Kinetic Energy when discussing aerodynamics.

If you hold your hand up in a strong wind or out of the window of a moving car, then the wind pressure or moving pressure is felt due to the air impacting upon your hand and flowing around it. This pressure is called Dynamic Pressure, i.e. pressure due to relative movement between your hand and the air.

Just how strong this Dynamic Pressure is depends upon two things:

1. The **Speed** of the body relative to the air – the faster the car drives or the stronger the wind blows, then the stronger the dynamic pressure that you feel on your hand. This is because of the greater number of molecules per second.

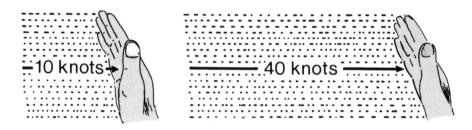

Fig.3-7. Dynamic Pressure Increases with Airspeed.

2. The **Density** of the air – at the same speed, the denser the air, the more molecules per second that will affect you and so the greater the Dynamic Pressure.

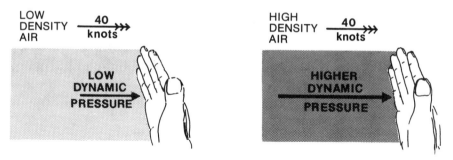

Fig.3-8. Dynamic Pressure is Greater in Dense Air.

Since Dynamic Pressure equals ½.Rho.V-squared – our equation can now be written:

STATIC PRESSURE + DYNAMIC PRESSURE = CONSTANT TOTAL PRESSURE.
        (p)   (½.Rho.V-squared)

The term '½.Rho.V-squared' is one of the most important in aerodynamics. There must be Dynamic Pressure for an aerofoil to produce lift. (Dynamic Pressure is also important when we consider other aerodynamic items such as Drag and Indicated Air Speed.)

Static Pressure + Dynamic Pressure = constant

If the speed (V) of the airflow increases, the Dynamic Pressure increases – this means that the Static Pressure must decrease. (Bernoulli's Principle.)

Increased Velocity Means Decreased Static Pressure.

Note: A further explanation of this effect may be found in Volume 1 (page viii).

Conversely, if the velocity (and therefore the Dynamic Pressure) decreases, the Static Pressure must increase.

Decreased Velocity Means Increased Static Pressure.

THE AEROFOIL AND BERNOULLI'S PRINCIPLE.

All parts of the aircraft contribute towards both Lift and Drag, but it is the aerofoil, or wing, that is specifically designed to provide the Lift force to support the whole of the aircraft.

A study of the variation of static pressure and velocity around the aerofoil, using Bernoulli's Principle, is the easiest non-mathematical way to understand the production of Lift (and Drag) by the aerofoil.

A thin flat plate placed in an airflow at zero angle of attack causes virtually no alteration of the airflow and consequently experiences no reaction (force).

If the angle of attack is altered however, the flat plate experiences a **reaction** that both tends to lift it and to drag it back – the same effect you feel with your hand out of a car window. The amount of reaction depends upon the speed and the angle of attack between the flat plate and the relative airflow.

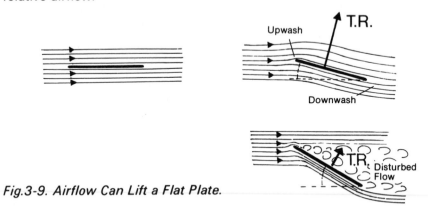

Fig.3-9. Airflow Can Lift a Flat Plate.

Due to the angle of attack, the straight-line streamline flow is disturbed. A slight **Upwash** is created in front of the plate causing the air to flow through a more constricted area, almost as if there were an invisible venturi above the plate. The air, as it passes through this constricted area, speeds up.

The Velocity Increase Means A Decrease In Static Pressure
(Bernoulli's Principle).

The static pressure above the plate is lower than the static pressure beneath the plate causing a net upwards reaction. After passing the plate there is a **Downwash** of the airstream.

The Total Reaction on the plate caused by it disturbing the airflow has two components — one at right angles to the relative airflow known as **Lift**, and one parallel to the relative airflow, and opposing the relative motion, known as **Drag**.

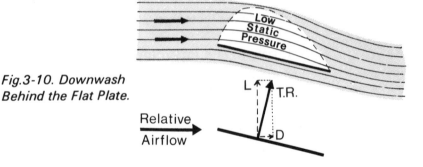

Fig.3-10. Downwash Behind the Flat Plate.

AEROFOIL SHAPES.

Most aeroplanes do not have flat plates for wings. A flat plate is not the ideal aerofoil for a number of reasons – it breaks up the streamline flow causing eddying (turbulence), with a great increase in drag; it is difficult to construct a thin, flat wing.

A curved aerofoil surface not only generates more Lift and less Drag compared to a flat plate, it is also easier to construct in terms of structural strength.

An aerofoil can have many cross-sectional shapes. The aircraft designer chooses that shape which has the best aerodynamic characteristics to suit his purposes. Although most low speed aerofoils are similar in shape, each section (cross-section) is designed to give certain specific aerodynamic characteristics. Our discussion will be only in broad terms that can be generally applied to most aerofoils.

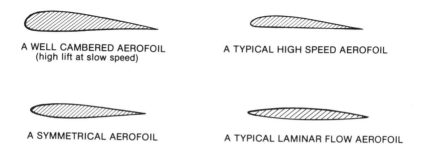

A WELL CAMBERED AEROFOIL
(high lift at slow speed)

A TYPICAL HIGH SPEED AEROFOIL

A SYMMETRICAL AEROFOIL

A TYPICAL LAMINAR FLOW AEROFOIL

Fig.3-11. Various Aerofoil Cross-Sections.

CAMBER.

Camber is curvature.

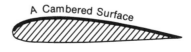

A Cambered Surface

Fig.3-12.

Increasing the camber on the upper surface causes the airflow over it to accelerate more and to generate more lift at the same angle of attack (since a higher velocity means a lower static pressure).

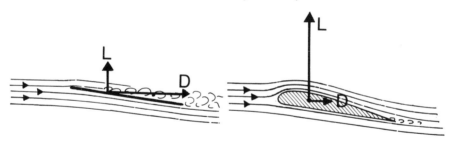

Fig.3-13. More Camber – More Lift.

13

Wings with a large camber give good lift, making them suitable for low speed flight and carrying heavy loads. The position of greatest camber is usually about 30% of the chord back from the leading edge.

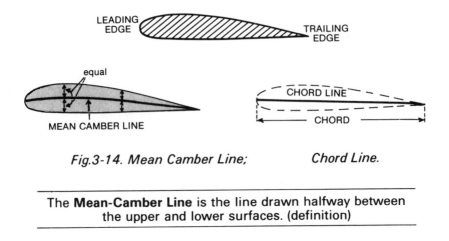

Fig.3-14. Mean Camber Line;   Chord Line.

The **Mean-Camber Line** is the line drawn halfway between the upper and lower surfaces. (definition)

The Mean Camber Line gives a picture of the average curvature of the aerofoil.

The **Chord Line** is the straight line joining the Leading Edge and the Trailing Edge of the aerofoil. Another way of saying this is:

The **Chord Line** is the straight line joining the ends of the (curved) Mean Camber Line. The length of the chord line is called the **Chord**. (definition)

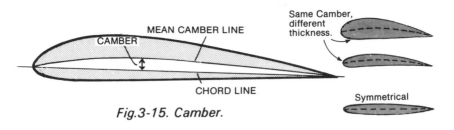

Fig.3-15. Camber.

The **Camber** is the distance between the mean-camber line and the chord line. (definition)

The shape of the mean-camber line is extremely important in determining the aerodynamic characteristics of the aerofoil section. The magnitude and position of the maximum camber relative to the chord of the aerofoil help to define the shape of the mean-camber line and are usually expressed as a percentage of the chord.

Note that a highly cambered wing may be thick or thin and that a symmetrical aerofoil has zero camber.

**The Thickness of an aerofoil is the greatest distance
between the upper and lower surfaces. (definition)**

Fig.3-16. Thickness.

A thick wing with a well-cambered upper surface is ideal for producing
high lift at low speeds. *STOL* aircraft (designed for take-off and landing on
short fields and rough or unprepared strips) are most likely to have well-
cambered and thick wings, e.g. de Havilland Canada Dash 7, Beaver and
Twin Otter, Pilatus Porter and GAF Nomad.

Also, as mentioned earlier, a thick wing is easier to construct than a thin
wing as there is more room for spars and other structural parts. A thick
wing is also advantageous when it comes to installing fuel tanks.

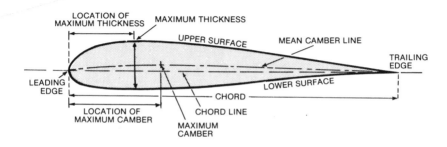

Fig.3-17. Summary of Aerofoil Terminology.

A TYPICAL LOW SPEED, WELL-CAMBERED WING.

At the small positive angles of attack common in normal flight, the static
pressure over much of the top surface of the aerofoil is slightly reduced
when compared to the normal static pressure of the free air stream well
away from the aerofoil. The static pressure beneath much of the lower
surface of the aerofoil is slightly greater than that on the upper surface.

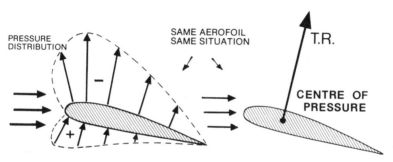

Fig.3-18. Total Reaction Acts Through the Centre of Pressure.

This pressure difference is the origin of the Total Reaction force exerted on the aerofoil, the greatest contribution coming from the upper surface. In the same way that the total Weight can be considered to act through a point called the Centre of Gravity, the Total Reaction of the aerodynamic forces on the aerofoil can be considered to act through the **Centre of Pressure.**

It is convenient for us to consider this **Total Reaction (TR)** in its two components – **Lift** and **Drag.**

Lift is the component of the Total Reaction at right-angles, or perpendicular, to the Relative Airflow. (definition)

Drag is the component of the Total Reaction parallel to the Relative Airflow and opposing motion. (definition)

The **Relative Airflow** refers to the relative motion between a body and the remote airflow, i.e. the airflow far enough away from the body not to be disturbed by it. (definition)

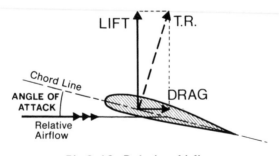

Fig.3-19. Relative Airflow.

The **Angle of Attack** (AoA) is the angle between the **Chord Line** of an aerofoil and the remote **Relative Airflow.** (definition)

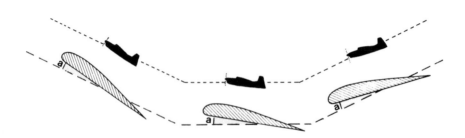

Fig.3-20. Same Angle of Attack, but Different Pitch Angles.

Do not confuse the pitch angle or attitude of the aircraft (relative to the horizontal) with the angle of attack of the aerofoil (relative to the remote airflow).

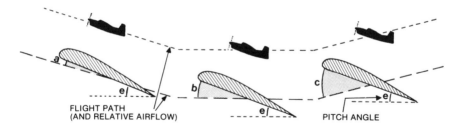

FLIGHT PATH
(AND RELATIVE AIRFLOW)

PITCH ANGLE

Fig.3-21. Same Pitch Angle, but Different Angles of Attack.

Do not confuse **'Angle of Attack'** (relative to the remote airflow) with **'Angle of Incidence'**, the angle at which the wing is fixed to the airframe relative to the longitudinal axis. The **'Angle of Incidence' is fixed,** but the **'Angle of Attack' changes in flight.**

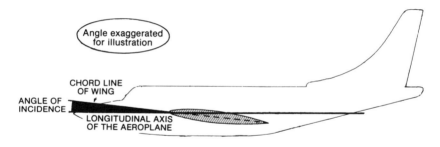

Angle exaggerated
for illustration

CHORD LINE
OF WING

ANGLE OF
INCIDENCE

LONGITUDINAL AXIS
OF THE AEROPLANE

Fig.3-22. The Angle of Incidence is Fixed During Design and Construction.

Bernoulli's Principle associates a decrease in Static Pressure with an increase in Velocity, i.e. a decreasing Static Pressure goes hand in hand with an accelerating airflow. The **Shape of the Aerofoil** and its **Angle of Attack** determine the distribution of velocity and therefore the distribution of the static pressures over the surface.

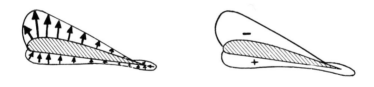

Fig.3-23. Distribution of Static Pressure Around an Aerofoil.

As a means of illustrating different Static Pressures, we will use an arrow away from the aerofoil to indicate a pressure less than the free airstream static pressure (i.e. a 'suction') and an arrow towards the surface to indicate a static pressure greater than that of the free airsream. Elsewhere you may see a '–' to indicate a **lower static pressure** and a '+' to indicate a **higher static pressure**

At the **Leading Edge** of the wing, the airflow actually comes to rest relative to the wing – this point being called the Leading Edge **Stagnation Point**. There is also a Trailing Edge Stagnation Point.

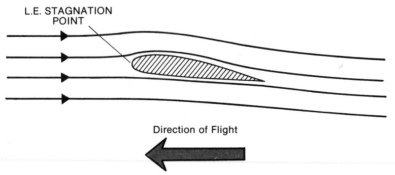

Fig.3-24. Leading Edge Stagnation Point.

At the LE stagnation point the airflow divides to pass over and under the aerofoil section. The positive angle of attack causes an increased velocity on the upper surface and therefore a decreased static pressure (Bernoulli). If the profile produces a continuous acceleration there will be a continuous static pressure reduction.

At other points on the aerofoil the airflow must slow down and this will be accompanied by a corresponding rise in static pressure (Bernoulli). A smoothly contoured surface will produce a smoothly changing pressure distribution.

PRESSURE DISTRIBUTION CHANGES WITH ANGLE OF ATTACK.

It is interesting to consider the pressure distribution around a particular aerofoil as the angle of attack is varied. **In normal flight,** the airflow accelerates over the Leading Edge (LE) of the aerofoil – the rate of acceleration being greater at greater angles of attack. As the velocity increases, the static pressure decreases (Bernoulli) and at the point of highest velocity, the static pressure is least.

The airflow under the aerofoil accelerates much less rapidly than that above and so the static pressure decreases much more slowly. It may or may not decrease to a value less than the static pressure of the free airstream, depending upon the angle of attack.

At small angles of attack there are static pressure reductions over both the upper and lower surfaces, with the Lift force being generated by the pressure differential.

18

The static pressure is reduced to a lower value on the upper surface compared to the static pressure on the lower surface at small angles of attack.

At a small negative angle of attack, about –4 (minus four) degrees for this aerofoil, pressure reductions are about equal and therefore no Lift force results.

At high angles of attack the Lift is due to the decreased pressure on the upper surface and the slightly increased pressure on the lower surface.

Beyond the stalling angle of attack the streamline flow over the upper surface is reduced, with a consequent weakening of the low pressure area due to the formation of eddies. (Bernoulli's Principle only applies to streamline flow.)

What little Lift is left is due mainly to the pressure increase on the lower surface.

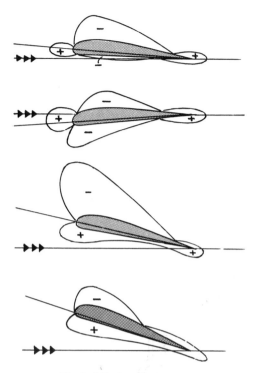

Fig.3-25. Static Pressure Distribution at Various Angles of Attack.

THE CENTRE OF PRESSURE.

Rather than have all these complicated pressure plots it is easier to show the overall effect of these changes in static pressure using the single aerodynamic force **Total Reaction** acting at a single point on the chord line – the **Centre of Pressure.**

As the angle of attack is increased in normal flight two important things happen:

1. The lifting ability of the wing (Coefficient of Lift) increases, allowing the wing to produce the same lift (required to balance the weight) at a lower airspeed.

2. The Centre of Pressure moves forward.

At normal cruising speeds (about 4 degrees angle of attack), the CP is back towards the centre of the wing. As the angle of attack is increased and the airspeed decreases, the CP moves forward. The furthest forward that it moves is to about ⅕th of the chord (20%) aft of the Leading Edge.

Past the **Stalling angle of attack** (about 16 degrees angle of attack), the streamline flow over the upper surface breaks down, and the lower static pressures on the upper surface are not created. The Total Reaction (especially the Lift Component) is reduced and the CP moves back along the chord.

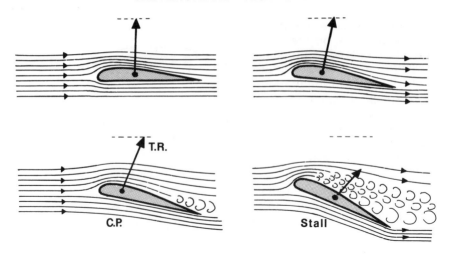

Fig.3-26. Change in Size of Total Reaction and Movement of Centre of Pressure at various Angles of Attack.

LIFT FROM A TYPICAL WING.

The Lift force is perpendicular to the relative airflow.

The Total Reaction is resolved into two components – the Drag force, which opposes motion and acts parallel to the relative airflow, and the Lift force, which is perpendicular to the relative airflow and the flight path of the aeroplane.

Experimentally, it can be shown that the Total Reaction, and therefore the Lift, depends upon:
- wing shape;
- angle of attack;

- air density (Rho);
- free stream velocity (V-squared in fact, i.e. V x V);

- wing surface area (S).

The Lift (and Drag) produced by a wing follows natural laws. We can simplify our understanding of this marvellous natural effect by describing it in a fairly simple formula (one of the very few that a Pilot needs to remember).

Velocity of the airflow and air density (Rho) we combine in the expression for **Dynamic Pressure** '½ x Rho x V-squared', with which we are already familiar. (The Greek letter *Rho* is symbolised by ρ .)

Putting this together with the wing surface area (S) we obtain:
$$\text{LIFT} = (\text{some factor}) \times \tfrac{1}{2}.\text{Rho.V-squared} \times S$$

We use 'some factor' to cover the other variables, especially the **Wing Shape** and the **Angle of Attack** (i.e. the profile the wing presents to the airflow). 'Some factor' is given the more technical sounding name of **Coefficient of Lift (C_Lift)**, which is really the 'lifting ability' of the wing at that particular angle of attack. Therefore: $\text{LIFT} = C_{Lift} \times \tfrac{1}{2}.\text{Rho.V-squared} \times S$

$$\boxed{\text{LIFT} = C_L \tfrac{1}{2} \rho \, V^2 S}$$

Since the wing shape is fixed by the designer, any changes in 'C$_{Lift}$' must be due to changes in angle of attack. If the 'C$_{Lift}$' (lifting ability) of the wing is high at a particular angle of attack, then the same Lift force (L) to off-set the Weight can be generated at a lower speed. This **inter-relationship between 'angle of attack' (C$_{Lift}$) and 'airspeed' is important for the Pilot.**

By using the formula: L = C$_{Lift}$ x ½.Rho.V^2 x S and measuring L, V, Rho and S, we can calculate C$_{Lift}$ and develop a graph or curve of 'C$_{Lift}$' vs 'Angle of Attack', known as the **'Lift Curve'** (Fig.3-27.)

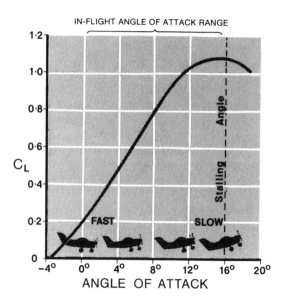

Fig.3-27. The 'Coefficient of Lift' Curve (versus AoA).

Each 'Angle of Attack' Produces a particular 'C$_{Lift}$' Value.

For a given wing, the angle of attack is the major controlling factor in the distribution of the static pressure around the wing. This determines the Lift force that is generated. The actual value of 'C$_{Lift}$' will therefore differ according to the 'angle of attack'.

Each aerofoil shape has its own particular 'Lift Curve' which relates its 'C$_{Lift}$' to 'Angle of Attack'. We consider an average cambered wing like that found on a typical training aircraft like a Cessna 172.

- At zero degrees angle of attack the cambered aerofoil creates some Lift and has a positive C_{Lift}.
- At about –4 degrees angle of attack the Lift is zero and $C_{Lift} = 0$. The aeroplane is rarely flown at the zero lift angle of attack, which occurs in a vertical climb or vertical dive.
- As the angle of attack increases, the C_{Lift} increases proportionally up to about 12 or 13 degrees angle of attack.

At higher angles of attack the curve starts to lean over, until at the stalling angle of attack (about 16 degrees in this case) there is a significant drop in C_{Lift} and the ability of the wing to produce Lift. This occurs when the airflow is unable to remain streamline over the upper surface, separates and breaks up into eddies. This is called **stalling** of the aerofoil. Notice that the maximum C_{Lift} (the maximum lift capability of the wing) occurs just prior to the stall.

The Lift force acts through the Centre of Pressure. At 4 degrees angle of attack the location of the CP is about 40% of the chord back from the LE, and moves further forwards to about 20% as the angle of attack is increased through the normal flight range (from about 4 degrees used in the cruise and glide, up to 16 degrees near the stalling angle).

- At the stalling angle of attack the CP is at the furthest point forward.
- Beyond the stalling angle of attack the CP moves rearwards.

As the magnitude of the Lift force and the location of the Centre of Pressure changes, there will be a different moment or turning effect in the pitching plane of the aircraft. The turning effect (moment) generated by the Lift force depends upon both its magnitude (size) and the distance between the CP and the CG. The Pilot can balance this turning moment, and prevent the aircraft pitching nose-up or nose-down, by varying the amount of the Aerodynamic Force generated by the **tailplane.** He does this by the fore and aft movement of the control column, which controls the elevators. (More of this later.)

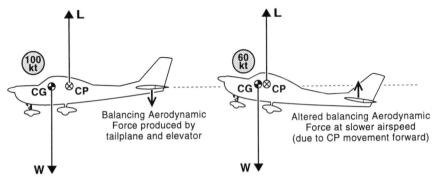

Fig.3-28. The Tailplane keeps the Aeroplane in Balance.

LIFT FROM A SYMMETRICAL AEROFOIL

Typical symmetrical aerofoils are the rudder and some tailplanes. The mean camber line of a symmetrical aerofoil is a straight line because of the identical curvature of the upper and lower wing surfaces. Therefore the chord line and mean camber line are identical.

The Lift curve for a symmetrical aerofoil will give a $C_{Lift} = 0$ (and zero lift) at 0 degrees angle of attack.

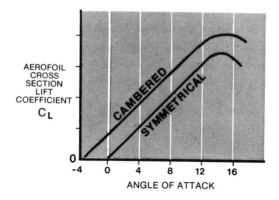

Fig.3-29. Comparison Between 'C_Lift's of a Cambered Aerofoil and a Symmetrical Aerofoil.

THE LAMINAR FLOW WING.

A wing with low curvature allows the air to retain laminar (streamline) flow over more of the surface. The location of maximum thickness is usually about 50% back.

A TYPICAL LAMINAR FLOW AEROFOIL   A TYPICAL CAMBERED AEROFOIL

Fig.3-30. Comparison of Aerofoil Cross-Sections.

A laminar flow wing produces the same lift in the cruising speed range for less drag, when compared to a thicker wing, and are to be found on some high speed aircraft like the Mustang WW II fighter and on some training aircraft like the Piper Cherokee Warrior.

There are some disadvantages of a laminar flow wing. The behaviour near the stall is not as good as a normal aerofoil. The lower value of '$C_{Lift\,max}$' means that the stalling speeds are higher.

To produce the required Lift (to balance the weight) the stalling angle of attack (about 15-16 degrees) is reached at a higher Indicated Air Speed than with a well-cambered wing. The '$C_{Lift\,max}$' for the aerofoil occurs near the stalling angle, but it is a lower value than the '$C_{Lift\,max}$' for a well-cambered aerofoil.

☐ Now complete **Exercises 3** on **Aerofoil – Lift**

4

DRAG

Whilst in flight, each and every part of the aircraft exposed to the airflow will produce an aerodynamic force – some aiding flight, such as Lift, and some opposing flight, such as **Drag.**

Fig.4-1. Drag Has Existed For As Long As Aeroplanes.

Drag is the aeronautical term for the air resistance experienced by the aeroplane as it moves relative to the air. It acts in the opposite direction to the motion through the air, i.e. it opposes the motion and acts parallel to, and in the same direction as, the relative airflow.

Drag is the enemy of high-speed flight. Streamlining of shapes, flush rivetting, polishing of surfaces and many design features are all attempts to reduce the drag force.

The main function of the powerplant-produced **Thrust** is to overcome the **Drag. Obviously:**

The Lower The Drag, The Less The Thrust Required To Balance It.

The advantages of a lower thrust requirement are obvious – smaller engines, possibly even fewer engines, lower fuel flows, less strain on the engines and associated structures, and lower operating costs.

Fig.4-2. Low Drag Requires Only Low Thrust to Balance It.

TOTAL DRAG.

Total Drag is the sum of all of the aerodynamic forces which act parallel to, and opposite to, the direction of flight. Total Drag is the total resistance to the motion of the aircraft through the air.

Note: *'opposite to the direction of flight'* is equivalent to *'in the same direction as the relative airflow'.*

Fig.4-3. Total Drag Is The Total Resistance to Motion.

The total drag is the sum total of the various drag forces acting on the aeroplane. A convenient way of studying these various drags is to break them up into two basic groups:

1. Those drag forces associated with the production of **Lift,** known as **Induced Drag** (manifested as vortices at the trailing edge of the wing and especially at the wingtips).

2. Those drag forces not directly associated with the development of lift – known as **Parasite Drag,** which includes form drag, skin friction and interference drag. (Form drag and skin friction are sometimes classified together under the name Profile Drag.)

PARASITE DRAG comprises Skin Friction, Form Drag and Interference Drag.

Skin Friction Drag results from the friction forces existing between an object and the air through which it is moving. The magnitude of the skin friction drag depends upon:

• The surface area of the aircraft. The whole surface area of the aircraft experiences surface or skin friction drag as it moves through the air.

• Whether the boundary layer airflow near the surface is laminar or turbulent. A turbulent boundary layer mixes more with the air around it, causing more drag.

• Roughness on a surface (including ice accretion) will increase skin friction drag. The transition from a laminar to a turbulent boundary layer may even occur immediately at the point of roughness. **Flush Rivetting** and polishing are attempts to smooth the surface and reduce skin friction drag.

• An increase in airspeed increases skin friction drag.

• An increase in aerofoil thickness increases skin friction drag from the wing.

• An increase in angle of attack increases skin friction.

Form Drag results when the airflow actually **separates** from the surface, eddies are formed and the streamline flow is disturbed. The turbulent wake so formed increases drag.

Perhaps the easiest way to distinguish form drag from skin friction drag is to consider a flat plate in two different attitudes relative to the airflow. At zero angle of attack the drag is all skin friction. When the flat plate is perpendicular to the airflow, the drag is all form drag.

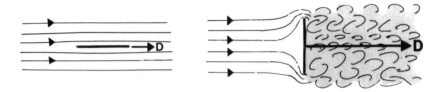

Fig.4-4. Skin Friction;   *Form Drag.*

The point at which the streamline flow separates from the surface and becomes turbulent is known as the **Separation Point.** Behind the separation point the local flow along the upper surface of the wing is forward towards the separation point, i.e. a **flow reversal** aft of the separation point.

Eddies are formed in the wake behind the body (which could be an aerofoil or indeed a whole aeroplane), the size of the wake being an indicator of the magnitude of the form drag. This form drag may be a large part of the total drag and good design should reduce it if possible.

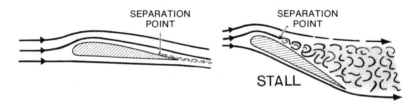

Fig.4-5. A Stalled Wing Increases Form Drag Substantially.

A spectacular case of airflow separation can be experienced when an aerofoil is at a very high angle of attack. This creates a pressure gradient on the upper surface too severe to allow the boundary layer to adhere to the surface and separation may occur well forward near the leading edge.

The low static pressures (i.e. 'suction') needed on the upper surface for lift production are lost and Stalling occurs. To reduce form drag we need to delay separation of the boundary layer from the surface.

Streamlining of Shapes Reduces Form Drag by decreasing the curvature of surfaces, delaying separation of the boundary layer and thereby reducing eddying. The designer may choose an aerofoil of different 'fineness ratio' (thickness/chord) to achieve better streamlining.

Streamlining of other parts of the airframe can be achieved by adding fairings.

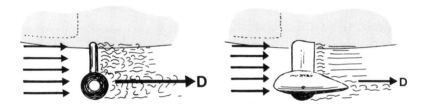

Fig.4-6. An Example of How Streamlining Reduces Form Drag.

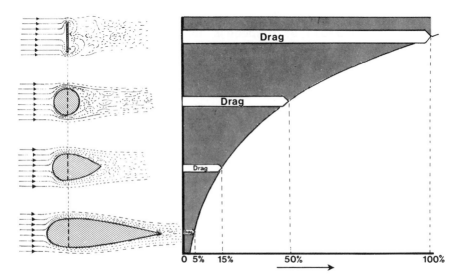

*Fig.4-7. Streamlining, Especially Behind the Shape, Reduces
Form Drag Substantially.*

The streamlining of shapes may be ineffective if ice is allowed to form on them.

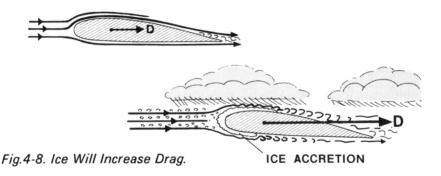

Fig.4-8. Ice Will Increase Drag.   **ICE ACCRETION**

Interference Drag. If we consider the aircraft as a whole, the total drag is greater than just the sum of the drag on the individual parts of the aircraft. This is due to flow 'interference' at the junction of various surfaces, such as at the wing/fuselage junction, the tail section/fuselage junctions and the wing/engine nacelle junctions.

This flow interference creates an additional drag, which we call **Interference Drag.** As it is not directly associated with the production of lift it is a parasite drag. Airflow from the various surfaces of the aircraft meet and form a wake behind the aircraft. The additional turbulence that occurs in the wake causes a greater pressure difference between the front and rear surfaces of the aircraft and therefore increased drag.

Suitable filleting, fairing and streamlining of shapes to control local pressure gradients can aid in minimizing this interference drag. A **Fairing** is part of the skin (external surface) of an aeroplane added to encourage **Streamline Flow,** thereby reducing eddying and decreasing drag.

Parasite Drag Increases as Airspeed is Increased. At zero airspeed there is no relative motion between the aeroplane and the air. Therefore there is no parasite drag. As the airspeed increases the skin friction, the form drag and the interference drag (which together make up Parasite Drag) all increase.

Airspeed has a powerful effect on parasite drag. Doubling the airspeed gives four times (2-squared – i.e. 2 x 2 = 4) the Parasite Drag.

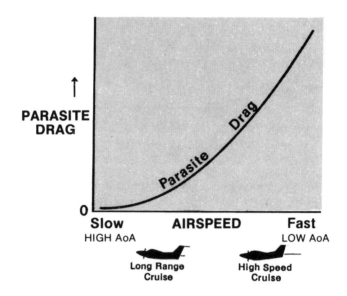

Fig.4-9. Parasite Drag.

Tripling the airspeed would give 3 x 3 = 9 times the Parasite Drag. Mathematically we call this a square rule, with 'Parasite Drag' varying as 'V-squared'. This 'square rule' often occurs in nature.

Parasite Drag is of Greatest Significance at High Speeds and is practically insignificant at low speeds. An aircraft flying at a speed just above the stall may have only 25% of its total drag due to Parasite Drag (most of the total drag being due to Induced Drag resulting from the heavy formation of wingtip vortices and the downwash behind the wing).

At a very high speed the total drag may be due almost entirely to Parasite Drag (with practically no Induced Drag). The predominance of Parasite Drag at high flight speeds shows the need for aerodynamic cleanness to obtain high speed performance.

It may interest you to know that about half of the Parasite Drag on some aircraft is due to the wings. Any reduction in skin friction, form drag and interference drag from the wings can have a significant effect in reducing the overall Parasite Drag.

INDUCED DRAG.

Induced Drag Is A By-Product Of The Production Of Lift.

To produce positive lift, the static pressure on the upper wing surface will be less than that on the lower wing surface. As the air flows rearwards, some airflow will 'leak' or spill around the wingtip from the high static pressure area under the wing to the low static pressure area above the wing. This causes a spanwise flow component of air outwards away from the fuselage on the lower surface and an inwards component towards the fuselage on the upper surface.

At the trailing edge of the wing where these upper and lower flows meet – both moving rearwards but with opposite spanwise (or lateral) components – a sheet of vortices is formed. **At the wingtips,** where the spanwise flow is greatest, by far the strongest vortices are formed. These are known as **Wingtip Vortices.** (A vortex is a whirling or twisting flow of air or some other fluid. The plural of 'vortex' is 'vortices'. In some versions of English the plural is 'vortexes'.)

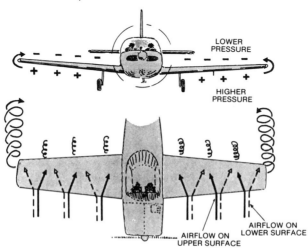

LOWER PRESSURE

HIGHER PRESSURE

AIRFLOW ON LOWER SURFACE

AIRFLOW ON UPPER SURFACE

Fig.4-10. Production of Lift – Induced Drag – Wingtip Vortices.

Fig.4-11. Wingtip Vortex.

More will be heard of wingtip vortices later under the title *'Wake Turbulence'*.

When the wings are producing a high value of C_{Lift} (necessary when supporting an aeroplane in manoeuvres, or at low speed and high angles of attack, as in the approach phase), the pressure difference between the lower and upper surfaces of the wing is greatly increased. In these situations **very strong wingtip vortices result.**

Sometimes, in moist air, the pressure drop in the core of these vortices will cause condensation of the moisture so that the small, twisting vortices are visible as vapour – especially with large passenger aeroplanes on approach and landing in moist conditions.

A similar effect may occasionally be seen near the sharp tips of trailing edge flaps. (These wingtip vortex trails are quite a different phenomenon to the high altitude vapour trails caused by condensation in the jet engine exhaust, so do not confuse them.)

How Induced Drag is Caused.

(This explanation is a little beyond what is required in the Private Pilot syllabus however it will assist your understanding of this very important phenomenon.)

The airflow underneath the wings spills around the wingtips forming a large twisting vortex at each wingtip. The upward flow in the vortex is outside the span of the wing, but the downward flow is behind the trailing edge of the wing, within the span of the wing. The net effect is a downwash behind the wing.

There is an overall downflow of air behind the trailing edge and within the span of the wing.

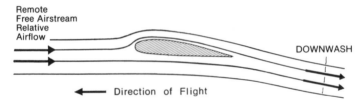

Remote
Free Airstream
Relative
Airflow

DOWNWASH

← Direction of Flight

Fig.4-12. After Encountering a Wing Generating Upwards Lift, the Airflow Will Be Deflected Downwards.

Newton's Third Law of Motion (which states that *'For Every Action There is an Equal and Opposite Reaction')* dictates that, in order for the action of airflow on a wing to generate an upwards Lift force, there will be an equal and opposite reaction of the wing on the airflow – (downwards in this case).

The deflection of the airflow downwards causes the wing to experience a local airflow (i.e. an **average** relative airflow), the direction of which is the average between the remote free airstream well ahead of the wing and the direction of the downwash immediately behind the wing. Since this local or average relative wind experienced by the wing is inclined downwards, the Lift force produced by the wing (perpendicular to the local relative airflow) is inclined backwards by the same amount.

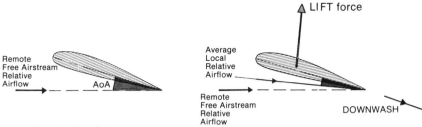

Figs.4-13a & b.

When we consider the **overall effect of Lift and Drag** on an aeroplane, we need to relate their effects relative to the direction of flight, i.e. relative to the **remote** free airstream well away from the influence of the local airflows around various parts of the aeroplane.

By convention:
- the **'Lift'** of a wing is referred perpendicular to the *remote* relative airflow; and
- the **'Drag'** of a wing (or any part of the aeroplane) is referred parallel to the *remote* relative airflow.

Therefore, the Lift force produced by a wing perpendicular to the local airflow will have a component parallel to the **remote** relative airflow. This component of the Lift force that is in the **Drag** direction is the undesirable – but unavoidable – consequence of the production of **Lift**. It is known as **Induced Drag.**

NOTE: The Induced Drag is separate from the Parasite Drag (resulting from Skin Friction, Form Drag and Interference Drag). **Induced Drag is due to the development of Lift.** A wing will have both Induced and Parasite Drag.

A Wing of High Aspect Ratio Can Reduce Induced Drag.

Prandtl, an early pioneer in the study of aerodynamics, discovered that induced drag could be reduced by having a long, narrow wing (i.e. a wing of high aspect ratio).

Compared with a short, stubby wing (low aspect ratio) of the same area, a long, narrow wing of high aspect ratio (and therefore smaller wingtips) has weaker wingtip vortices, less induced downwash and therefore less induced drag. Unfortunately, a high aspect ratio wing (long and narrow) is more difficult to build from the structural strength point of view.

$$\text{Aspect Ratio} = \frac{\text{Span}}{\text{Chord}}$$

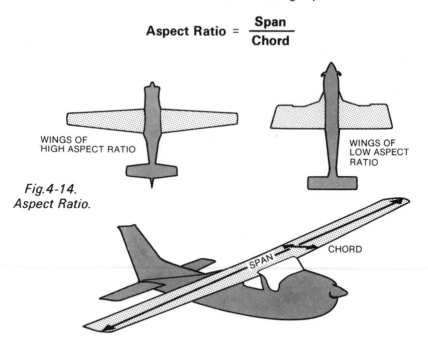

WINGS OF
HIGH ASPECT RATIO

WINGS OF
LOW ASPECT
RATIO

Fig.4-14.
Aspect Ratio.

SPAN

CHORD

Another Way of Expressing 'Aspect Ratio' is:

Aspect Ratio = span/chord
= (span x chord)/chord-squared
= area/(chord-squared)

Reducing Induced Drag by Tapering the Wing.

Fig.4-15. Tapered Wings Reduce Wingtip Vortices and Induced Drag.

A tapered wing has weaker wingtip vortices (because there is less wingtip) and so the induced drag is less.

An Inbuilt Twist in the Wing called 'Washout' Reduces Induced Drag.

The higher the angle of attack, the greater the pressure differences between the upper and lower wing surfaces. If the wing is built with 'washout', the angle of attack at the wingtip is less than the angle of attack at the wing-root near the fuselage. Therefore most of the Lift force is generated on the inner part of the wing, whilst not so much Lift will be generated near the wingtips.

The lower pressure differences between the upper and lower surfaces near the wingtip not only lead to reduced Lift production there, but also to less leakage of the airflow around the wingtip, reduced formation of wingtip vortices and a lower induced drag.

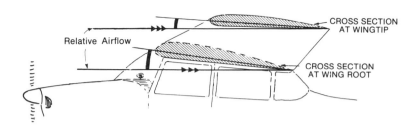

Fig.4-16. Inbuilt 'Washout' on the Wings Decreases Induced Drag Due to the Lower Angle of Attack Towards the Wingtips.

Wingtip Modification Can Reduce Induced Drag.

Wingtip tanks and modified wingtips can reduce the leakage of the airflow around the wingtip and therefore reduce the formation of Induced Drag. Also, the installation of wing fences reduces spanwise flow and thus Induced Drag.

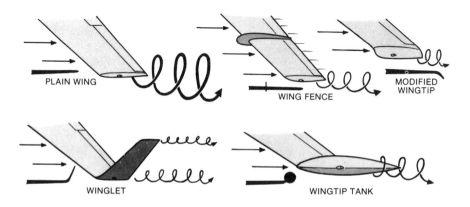

Fig.4-17. Modified Wingtips Can Reduce Formation of Vortices.

Induced Drag Increases at Low Airspeeds and High Angles of Attack.

In straight and level flight at a given weight, the Lift must remain constant (to balance the weight) as the speed changes. As the airspeed reduces, the Pilot increases the angle of attack (and Coefficient of Lift) to achieve the same Lift – hence high angles of attack are associated with low airspeeds.

The slower passage of air rearwards over the wing allows the spanwise flow of air spilling up over the wingtip to form greater wingtip vortices and greater downwash behind the trailing edge of the wing.

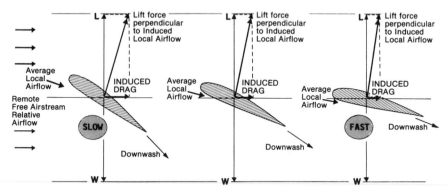

Fig.4-18. Induced Drag is Greatest at Low Airspeeds and High Angles of Attack.

The greater downwash causes the **average local airflow** experienced by the wing to be inclined downwards even more, with the Lift force produced by the wing being tilted further back, resulting of course in a stronger component of this Lift force in the DRAG direction – parallel to the remote free airstream.

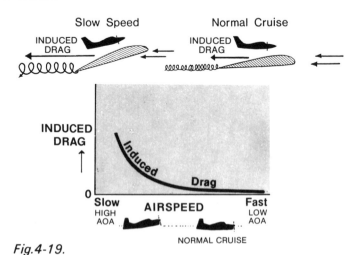

Fig.4-19.

Induced Drag is Most Significant at Low Speeds and High Angles of Attack.

Induced Drag Increases Greatly as the Stalling Angle of Attack is Approached.

Near the stalling speed in level flight, Induced Drag could be 75% of the total drag (Parasite Drag making up the rest), yet at high speed in level flight the Induced Drag might provide only 1% of the total drag.

Increased Lift means Increased Induced Drag.

A heavy aeroplane requires greater Lift to fly straight and level than a light aeroplane. An aeroplane which is manoeuvring requires greater lift than when it is flying straight and level. For example, in a steep turn of 60 degrees bank the wings must generate double the Lift force generated straight and level.

Under conditions of high Lift, the pressure differential between the lower and upper surfaces increases, resulting in stronger wingtip vortices.

The Greater the Lift Produced, The Greater the Induced Drag.

In level flight at high weights more **Lift** is required to balance the higher weight, and in manoeuvres, say a steep turn, an excess of Lift over Weight is required to provide the turning or centripetal force.

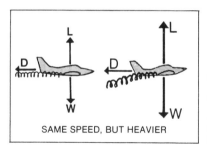
SAME SPEED, BUT HEAVIER

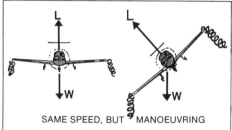
SAME SPEED, BUT MANOEUVRING

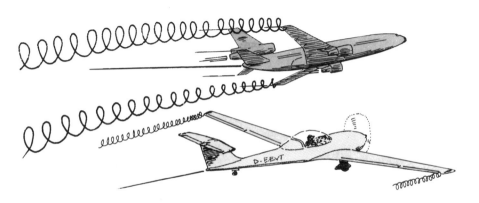

Fig.4-20. Increased Lift Means Increased Induced Drag.

TOTAL DRAG.

Total Drag is the sum total of all the drag forces. On some occasions we may talk of the total drag on an **aeroplane,** while on other occasions we need only refer to the total drag on an **aerofoil** when only the aerodynamics of that aerofoil in isolation are considered. Be clear in your own mind whether the whole aircraft is under discussion or just the wings.

As we have seen, the total drag has two components:
• **Parasite Drag,** and
• **Induced Drag.**

If we combine the graphs of each of these drags as they vary with airspeed, we end up with a graph that illustrates the variation of Total Drag with Airspeed for a given aeroplane in level flight at a particular weight, configuration and altitude.

This curve (Fig.4-21) **'Drag vs Airspeed (Angle of Attack)'** is an extremely important relationship. It is really a summary of all we need to know about Drag. If you understand the message contained in this curve, then you are well on the way to understanding Drag and its importance to flight.

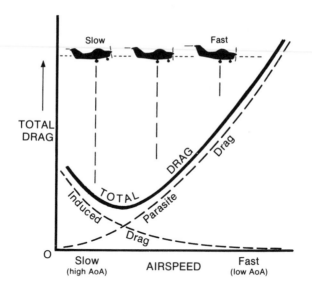

Fig.4-21. 'Total Drag' versus 'Airspeed'.

The Parasite Drag increases with speed. The Induced Drag decreases as the speed increases. The graph shows how Induced Drag is predominant at low speed, whilst at high speed the Parasite Drag predominates. The Total Drag is least at the point where the Parasite Drag and the Induced Drag are equal. Many items of aeroplane performance are related to this **Minimum Drag Speed.**

In straight and level flight, **Lift equals Weight,** therefore at the point of minimum drag the wing will be producing that Lift required to balance the weight, but with the minimum amount of drag possible.

Mainly INDUCED DRAG   MINIMUM DRAG   Mainly PARASITE DRAG

Low Speed, High Drag.   Minimum Drag Speed.   High Speed, High Drag.

Fig.4-22. Minimum Drag Speed.

Thrust is used to balance Drag to achieve steady straight and level flight. It can be seen from the above illustration that high thrust will be required at both very high and very low airspeeds, and less thrust at intermediate speeds.

The **Stall** in level flight under the particular conditions stated on the graph is indicated by a sharp rise in the actual drag, this being contributed by the rapid increase in Induced Drag as the airspeed decays.

The **Total Drag** curve for an aeroplane is a major factor in many items of aeroplane performance, such as landing, take-off, climbing, gliding, manoeuvring, range capability and endurance capability. Combining the Induced Drag (from wingtip vortices, a by-product of the generation of Lift) and the Parasite Drag (the rest of the drag), we obtain the Total Drag curve.

DRAG FROM AN AEROFOIL.

At low speeds the Total Drag from the aerofoil is high (due to Induced Drag) and at high speeds the Total Drag is high (due to Parasite Drag). A formula (similar to that for Lift) can be developed for the Drag produced by an aerofoil:

$$DRAG = C_{Drag} \times \tfrac{1}{2} \text{ Rho V-squared} \times S$$

– where the Coefficient of Drag (C_{Drag}) represents **shape** and **angle of attack**
– Rho is air density
– V is velocity (True Air Speed)
  (Indicated AirSpeed IAS = $\tfrac{1}{2}$ Rho V-squared)
– S is area.

A **Drag Curve** for the aerofoil relating 'C_{Drag}' to 'Angle of Attack' can be developed. This is useful for comparison with the Lift Curve ('C_{Lift}' vs 'Angle of Attack').

Note that at high angles of attack nearing the stalling angle, the Coefficient of Drag for an aerofoil is high and plays a large role in the formula:

$$D = C_{Drag} \times \tfrac{1}{2} \text{ Rho V-squared} \times S$$

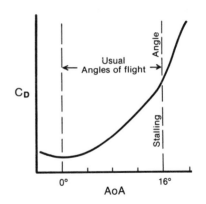

Fig.4-23. Coefficient of Drag versus Angle of Attack.

At low angles of attack near the cruise, the Coefficient of Drag for the aerofoil is small, but the airspeed (V) is higher and this has a large effect in the formula. This is why the Drag force (D) is high at both extremes of angle of attack (and airspeed). In between these extremes is an angle of attack (and airspeed) where the Drag force is a minimum. The minimum C_{Drag} for a typical aerofoil occurs at a small positive angle of attack.

☐ You should now attempt **Exercises 4 — Drag.**

5

LIFT/DRAG RATIO

To determine the performance and efficiency of an aerofoil at a particular angle of attack (and airspeed), both the **Lift** and the **Drag** need to be considered. The relationship of one to the other (the **Lift/Drag ratio**) is very important.

We have already discussed the Lift Curve (C_{Lift} vs Angle of Attack) and the Drag Curve (C_{Drag} vs Angle of Attack).

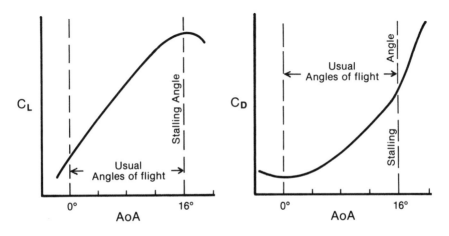

Fig.5-1. 'C_{Lift}' vs 'AoA'; 'C_{Drag}' vs 'AoA'.

The **Lift Curve** shows a steady increase in the Coefficient of Lift as the angle of attack is increased, up to the stalling angle, beyond which C_{Lift} decreases.

The **Drag Curve** shows that Drag increases steadily with change in angle of attack, being least at small positive angles of attack and increasing either side as angle of attack is increased or decreased. As the stalling angle is approached the Drag increases at a greater rate. At the stall the breakdown of streamline flow and the formation of turbulence, or eddies, causes a large increase in Drag.

VARIATION OF THE LIFT/DRAG RATIO WITH ANGLE OF ATTACK.

In a sense, Lift is the benefit you obtain from an aerofoil and Drag is the price you pay for it. For a given amount of Lift it is desirable to have the minimum amount of Drag, i.e. the best possible L/D ratio.

If you require 120 units of Lift and the cost is 10 units of Drag from the aerofoil, then L/D = 120/10 = 12, i.e. the Lift is 12 times greater than the Drag from the aerofoil. If the 120 units of Lift come with 20 units of Drag from the aerofoil, then the **Lift/Drag Ratio** = 120/20 = 6, and the wing is nowhere near as efficient.

An aerofoil has the greatest lifting ability (C_{Lift}) at a high angle of attack, just prior to the stalling angle of attack, in this case approximately 16 degrees. Unfortunately, near the stalling angle, the aerofoil generates a lot of induced drag.

The minimum drag occurs at a fairly low angle of attack, in this case at about 0 degrees AoA. Unfortunately, at low angles of attack, the lifting ability (C_{Lift}) of the wing is low.

Neither of these situations (high angle of attack or low angle of attack) is really satisfactory, because the **Ratio** of Lift to Drag at these extreme angles of attack is low. What is required is the greatest lifting ability compared with the drag at the same angle of attack, i.e. the angle of attack that gives the best lift/drag ratio, and for a normal cambered wing this occurs at about 4 degrees angle of attack.

To get the **Lift/Drag Ratio** we can divide the two equations:

$$\frac{LIFT}{DRAG} = \frac{C_{Lift} \times \frac{1}{2}\, Rho\; V\text{-squared} \times S}{C_{Drag} \times \frac{1}{2}\, Rho\; V\text{-squared} \times S} = \frac{C_{Lift}}{C_{Drag}}$$

For each angle of attack we can calculate the L/D ratio by dividing C_{Lift} by C_{Drag} (and these are obtained off the Lift and Drag curves). We can develop a curve for: **'L/D' vs 'Angle of Attack'**. The resulting 'L/D' vs 'Angle of Attack' curve shows that L/D increases rapidly up to about 4 degrees angle of attack, where the Lift is typically between 10 to 15 times the Drag, depending upon the aerofoil used.

At angles of attack higher than about 4 degrees the L/D ratio decreases steadily. Even though the C_{Lift} is still increasing, the C_{Drag} increases at a greater rate. At the stalling angle of attack the L/D ratio for this particular aerofoil is about 5.

The curve illustrated on the next page shows clearly the specific angle of attack at which the L/D ratio is a maximum, and this angle of attack is where the aerofoil is most efficient – it gives the required Lift for the minimum cost in Drag.

The **Angle of Attack** that gives the **Best Lift/Drag Ratio** is the **Most Efficient Angle of Attack.** (definition)

In most aircraft the Pilot does not have an instrument to indicate angle of attack, but he can read airspeed, which is related to angle of attack. High angles of attack in steady flight are associated with lower airspeeds (and vice versa).

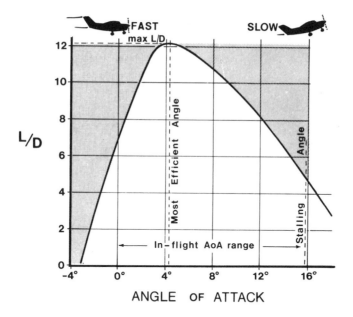

Fig.5-2. 'Lift/Drag Ratio' versus 'Angle of Attack'.

The angle of attack (and airspeed) for the **Best Lift/Drag Ratio** gives the required Lift (to balance the weight) for the minimum cost in Drag. At any other angle of attack there is a greater cost in terms of increased Drag to obtain the same Lift.

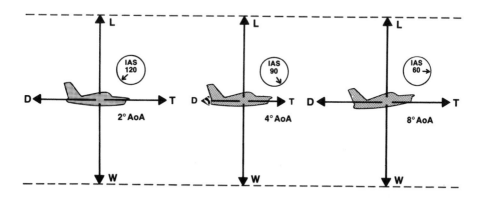

Fig.5-3. Same Lift at a Different Cost in Drag.

In steady flight the Drag is balanced by the Thrust. If the Lift required to balance the Weight is obtained at the minimum Drag cost, then Thrust can be kept to a minimum with the resulting benefits – the engine/propeller can be smaller; better economy through lower fuel and maintenance costs, etc.

Some important in-flight performance characteristics are obtained at the best L/D ratio, such as the maximum cruising range and the maximum power-off gliding range.

LEVEL FLIGHT AT A CONSTANT WEIGHT.

In straight and level flight:

LIFT = WEIGHT = C_{Lift} x ½ Rho V-squared x S

– in which 'C_{Lift}' is a function of angle of attack, and '½ Rho V-squared' is related to the Indicated Air Speed (IAS) that the Pilot sees on the Airspeed Indicator. (V is the True Airspeed or TAS, which the Pilot cannot read directly in the cockpit.)

LIFT = WEIGHT = a function of (Angle of Attack x IAS x S)

- **If the angle of attack is increased,** the required Lift can be generated at a reduced airspeed.
- **If the angle of attack is reduced,** the same required Lift will be generated at a higher airspeed.

Therefore, in normal straight and level flight, high angles of attack permit lower airspeeds, and low angles of attack permit higher airspeeds.

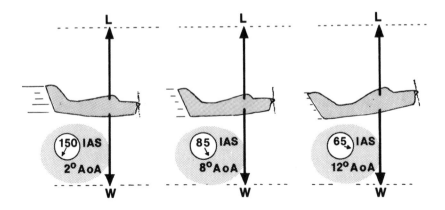

Fig.5-4. Constant Weight, Angle of Attack Increases, Indicated Air Speed Decreases.

DECREASED WEIGHT.

As a flight proceeds and fuel is burnt off the weight decreases. A decreased weight requires less lift to balance it. We can reduce the Lift produced by flying at a lower angle of attack, which will lead to a gradually increasing speed (unless we reduce power).

Notice that the precise relationship between 'angle of attack' and 'airspeed' changes if the Weight changes. At lower weights, the same IAS occurs at a slightly smaller angle of attack.

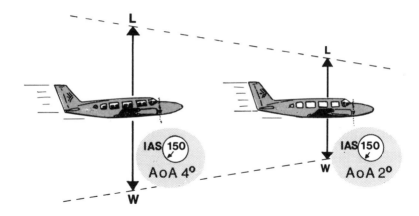

*Fig.5-5. Decreasing Weight, Same IAS, Decreasing AoA
(decreasing power).*

Suppose you want to fly at the same angle of attack (say the most efficient one for the best L/D ratio at about 4 degrees). As the Weight gradually decreases, you should gradually reduce airspeed, so that less Lift is generated.

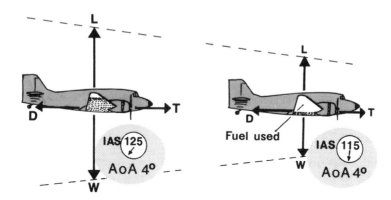

Fig.5-6. Same Angle of Attack, Lower Weight has Lower IAS and Drag.

CHANGING CRUISE ALTITUDES.

Suppose we fly straight and level at a higher altitude, but at the same weight and therefore with the same lift requirement. The relationship between angle of attack and IAS will be the same as before.

At a particular angle of attack, the Indicated Air Speed (a measure of the magnitude of Dynamic Pressure '½ Rho V-squared' and displayed in 'knots') will be the same. Because at higher altitudes the air density Rho is less, to retain the same value of '½ Rho V-squared', the value of V (the True Air Speed) must be greater.

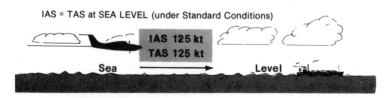

Fig.5-7. Same IAS – A Higher Altitude Gives A Higher TAS.

As you fly at higher altitudes, the same Indicated Air Speed (shown on your Air Speed Indicator) will give you a higher velocity through the air (True Air Speed, which is not usually shown on a cockpit instrument). Remember that it is IAS (related to Dynamic pressure '½ Rho V-squared') which determines the flying qualities of your aeroplane. It is only necessary to calculate the TAS (V) for navigational purposes.

The relationship between IAS and TAS is considered in more detail in Chapter 25 under the heading 'The Air Speed Indicator'. The Air Speed Indicator displays an IAS that differs from the TAS by a factor that depends upon air density.

CHANGING WING AREA.

There is another factor that can be varied and that is the wing area 'S'. If we could increase S, then we would obtain the same lift at an even lower airspeed. Changing S actually changes the shape of the aerofoil and we will consider this later in this Section under the heading of Flaps.

☐ You should now be able to complete **Exercises 5 — Lift/Drag Ratio.**

6

THRUST FROM THE PROPELLER

A piston engine requires a propeller to convert the power output of the engine into thrust. The power is developed by the piston engine, and is transmitted to the propeller, via a shaft, as 'engine torque' or 'turning effect'. This is used to rotate the propeller, which converts most of this turning effect into a pull or push force, called 'thrust'. The propeller does this by generating forces due to its motion through the air.

The propeller pulls the aeroplane through the air by generating a basically horizontal Lift force which we call **Thrust.**

A cross-section taken through a propeller blade is simply an **Aerofoil** section and we can study its aerodynamics in the same terms as any other aerofoil, such as a wing.

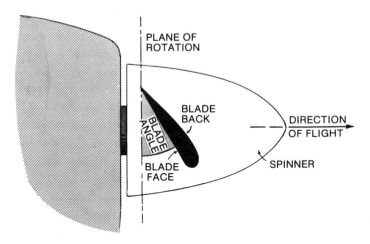

Fig.6-1. Propeller Terminology.

The propeller blade causes the air to flow so that the static pressure ahead of the blade is less than that behind the blade. The result is a forwards **Thrust** force on the propeller blade which pulls the aeroplane along.

Consider just one blade section, or 'blade' element as it is sometimes called, at some radial distance from the hub or the centreline of the propeller rotation. The blade section is an aerofoil and it has a leading edge, a trailing edge, a chord line and a camber just like any other aerofoil.

The angle which the chord line of a propeller section makes with the plane of rotation is called the **Blade Angle.** (definition)

The blade angle, as we shall soon see, varies from a large blade angle at the blade root near the hub, gradually becoming less towards the propeller tip. The cambered side of the blade is called the **Blade Back** and the flatter side is called the **Blade Face.**

ROTATIONAL VELOCITY.

If the aircraft is stationary, the motion of the propeller section under consideration is purely rotational. The further out along the blade the section is, the faster its rotational velocity. Also, the higher the rpm (revolutions per minute) of the propeller, the faster the rotational velocity of the section.

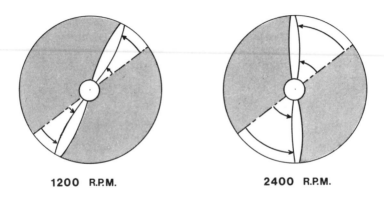

1200 R.P.M.   2400 R.P.M.

Fig.6-2. Speed of Blade Section Depends on Radius and R.P.M.

FORWARD VELOCITY.

As the aircraft moves forward in flight, the propeller section will have a forward velocity as well as the rotational velocity. This forward motion is superimposed upon the rotational motion of the blade section to give it an overall resultant velocity as shown. The angle between the resultant velocity of the propeller blade and the plane of rotation is called the **Helix Angle** or the **Pitch Angle** or the **Angle of Advance.**

HELICAL MOTION.

Each propeller blade section follows a corkscrew path through the air – called a **Helix** – as a result of the combined rotational and forward velocities. The easiest way to picture it is to consider the helix as the path the trailing edge of the propeller section follows.

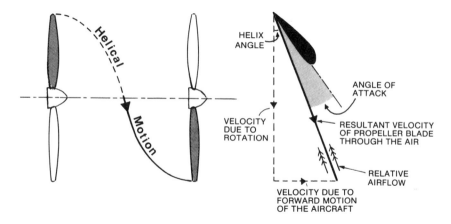

Fig.6-3. Each Propeller Section Follows Its Own Helical Path.

The blade section experiences a relative airflow directly opposite its own path through the air. The angle between the chord line of the propeller blade section and the relative airflow is its **Angle of Attack.** Notice that the angle of attack plus the helix angle (pitch angle) make up the blade angle.

When the aeroplane is in flight each propeller blade section will have the same forward velocity component. What will differ, however, is the rotational component of velocity – the further each blade section is from the propeller shaft the faster it is moving. If the blade angle was the same along the whole length of the propeller (which of course it never is), then the angle of attack would be different at all points.

For a propeller with the same blade angle along its length, the angle of attack would vary with distance from the propeller shaft, and the thrust would not be produced in an efficient manner. The propeller blade could even be stalled near the tip.

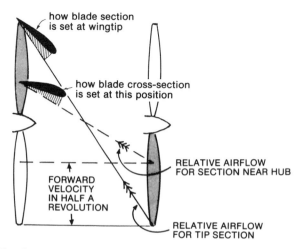

Fig.6-4. The Propeller Blade Angle Is Made Progressively Larger from Tip to Hub to Provide Efficient Angles of Attack Along Its Full Length.

Like all aerofoils, there is a **most efficient angle of attack.** If the propeller is designed to be most efficient at a certain airspeed of the aeroplane and rpm of the propeller, then the designer will aim to have this most efficient angle of attack along the whole length of the propeller blade when it is operating under the design airspeed and rpm conditions.

To achieve this, the blade angle at the hub needs to be much greater than the blade angle at the tip. This is known as **'blade twist'** or 'helical twist'.

THE MOST IMPORTANT SECTIONS OF THE PROPELLER.

There will be aerodynamic losses both near the propeller hub and at the tip. Near the hub the propeller sections must be thick and structurally strong, which may interfere with aerodynamic design. Also, there will be a fair amount of interference to the airflow from the nearby engine and associated structures.

At the propeller tip, there will be tip vortices formed as air spills around from the high pressure area on the flat blade face to the the low pressure area in front of it, forward of the cambered blade back. (The **'back'** of the propeller blade is actually to the **front** of the aeroplane.) The formation of vortices at the propeller tip leads to the usual increase in the induced drag (see *'Induced Drag of an Aerofoil',* Chapter 4) and a consequent weakening of the effectiveness of the thrust at the tip.

The propeller tip is the fastest travelling part of the propeller – indeed of the whole aeroplane, as it has its rotational velocity superimposed upon the forward speed of the aeroplane as a whole.

Only a small part of the whole propeller blade is effective in producing thrust – that part being between about 60% and 90% of the tip radius. The greatest useful thrust is produced at approximately 75% of the tip radius. When the blade angle of a propeller is quoted, it usually refers to the 75% station for this reason.

FORCES ON A BLADE SECTION.

The airflow around an aerofoil, with the consequent pressure changes, causes a **Total Reaction** force on the aerofoil. In the case of a wing, we resolve (break up) this total reaction into one component perpendicular to the relative airflow, this component being called **Lift,** and another component parallel to the relative airflow, called **Drag.** The relative airflow is in the same direction as the direction of flight, but in the opposite sense.

Due to its rotational velocity, the direction of the relative airflow striking the propeller and the direction of flight of the aeroplane are not parallel. Whereas the relative airflow striking all sections of a main wing comes from a constant direction, the relative airflow striking a propeller blade changes its direction depending upon how far that section is from the hub.

Instead of resolving the **Total Reaction** on a propeller blade section into a lift component perpendicular to the relative airflow and a drag component parallel to the relative airflow (which would be very complicated when we came to total up the effects along the length of the blade), it is much more convenient to resolve the total reaction into:

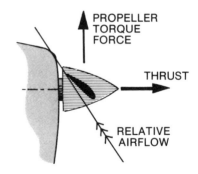

- one component in the plane of rotation called the **Propeller Torque** force; and

- one component in the direction perpendicular to the plane of rotation called **Thrust**.

Fig.6-5. Forces on a Blade.

For our purposes, we can generally assume the direction perpendicular to the plane of propeller rotation to be the same as the direction of flight, and therefore for the thrust to be considered as acting in the direction of flight.

The **Propeller Torque** is the resistance to motion in the plane of rotation. (definition).

For a wing, Drag must be overcome to provide Lift. For a propeller, the propeller torque must be overcome or balanced by the engine torque for the propeller to provide Thrust. Opening the throttle increases the engine power and engine torque, causing the propeller to rotate faster.

NOTE: If the aeroplane is put into a dive, the relative airflow is changed because of the higher forward speed and, as a result, the propeller torque force is reduced. The result is an increase in engine speed (i.e. rpm) even though the throttle may not been moved.

VARIATION OF PROPELLER EFFICIENCY WITH FORWARD SPEED AND WITH RPM.

Consider a well-designed fixed-pitch propeller blade. As most of the thrust (and propeller torque) is produced in the blade sections near the 75% station, reference to blade angle, angle of attack, etc., will refer to this most effective part of the propeller blade. (The term **'fixed-pitch'** means that the blade angle at the section under consideration is fixed and unable to be changed.)

If the propeller rpm is constant, then the direction of the relative airflow and the angle of attack will be determined by the forward speed.

As forward airspeed increases, the angle of attack of a fixed pitch propeller blade at constant rpm will decrease. At some high forward speed, the angle of attack of the blade will be such that little or no thrust will be produced.

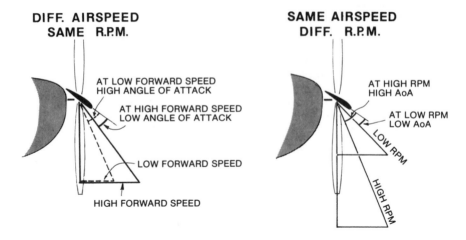

Fig.6-6. Fixed Pitch Propeller: Angle of Attack Varies with Forward Speed, and with RPM.

For a given rpm, there will be only one airspeed at which the propeller will operate at its most efficient angle of attack.

A FIXED-PITCH PROPELLER IS MOST EFFICIENT AT ONLY ONE AIRSPEED AND RPM.

The designer chooses a fixed-pitch propeller whose best-efficiency airspeed/rpm combination fits the tasks for which the aeroplane is designed.

A preferable situation would be to have a propeller whose blade angle could be varied so that at any airspeed it would operate at an efficient angle of attack, i.e. a variable-pitch propeller. Whilst this will not be examined at PPL level, most Private Pilots will fly an aeroplane with a variable pitch propeller and so we have included this topic in our notes.

THE VARIABLE PITCH PROPELLER and THE CONSTANT SPEED UNIT.

An early development in propeller technology was the two-pitch propeller – a fine pitch for take-off and low speed operation, and a coarse pitch for higher airspeeds.

Subsequently the **'Constant Speed propeller'** was developed, with a blade angle that could take up any position (i.e. infinitely variable) between two in-flight limits at the fine and coarse ends of its range. The pitch-changing mechanisms are usually operated electrically or hydraulically.

At low airspeeds, the blade angle needs to be small for the angle of attack to be optimum. This is known as **Fine Pitch.** As the forward speed increases, the blade angle needs to increase, or **Coarsen,** for the angle of attack to remain optimum.

The device used to achieve this is the **Constant Speed Unit** (CSU), sometimes called the Propeller Control Unit (PCU). It contains a governor whose function is to regulate the propeller speed (rpm) to that selected by the pilot. It does this by automatically adjusting the blade angle electrically or hydraulically so that rpm is maintained irrespective of the airspeed and the power delivered by the engine.

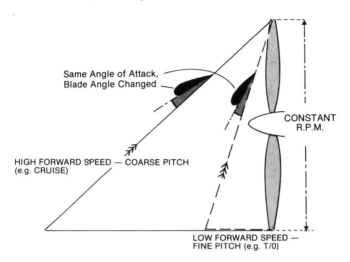

Same Angle of Attack, Blade Angle Changed

CONSTANT R.P.M.

HIGH FORWARD SPEED — COARSE PITCH (e.g. CRUISE)

LOW FORWARD SPEED — FINE PITCH (e.g. T/0)

Fig.6-7. A Constant Speed Propeller Retains an Efficient Angle of Attack Over a Wide Forward Speed Range by Altering Blade Angle Automatically.

The aim is to have the propeller working close to the best angle of attack and maximum efficiency at all times throughout its working range.

In the extreme case of low engine power, the blade angle will fine-off until it reaches the limit, known as the 'fine-pitch stop'. From then on, the propeller acts as a fixed-pitch propeller – further power reductions causing a drop in rpm because the pitch cannot fine-off any more due to the fine-pitch stop.

THE ADVANTAGES OF CONSTANT SPEED OR VARIABLE PITCH PROPELLERS.

A variable pitch (constant speed) propeller adjusts to the most efficient angle of attack over a wide range of rpms and airspeeds. A fixed-pitch propeller only operates efficiently under the one set of rpm and airspeed conditions.

Change of Power.

The pilot selects the desired rpm using the pitch control. The propeller pitch automatically increases to absorb any extra engine power supplied and yet still retain the same rpm, i.e. constant speed. The increased thrust gives the aeroplane better performance and it can accelerate or increase its rate of climb.

If the engine power is decreased, the propeller automatically fines-off to balance the power supplied to it by the engine and the rpm will remain constant (unless the blade comes up against the fine-pitch stop of course), the reduced thrust produced causing a decrease in the aeroplane's performance.

Change of Airspeed.

If the aeroplane is put into a climb, without the pilot making any power adjustments, the blade will automatically fine-off just enough to stop the engine/propeller rpm from reducing and the engine power output will remain unchanged. Similarly, if the aeroplane is put into a dive without the pilot removing any engine power, the airspeed will increase and the blade will coarsen sufficiently to prevent overspeeding of the propeller and engine.

Two other very big advantages of some variable-pitch propellers are:

1. The ability to be put into ground-fine pitch or reverse pitch to provide a braking effect on the ground run.

2. The ability to be feathered in flight to reduce drag and further engine damage following an engine failure.

TAKE-OFF EFFECTS OF PROPELLERS.

Slipstream Effect.

A propeller rotating clockwise (as seen from the cockpit) will impart a clockwise rotation to the slipstream as it flows back over the rest of the aeroplane. This causes an asymmetric flow over the fin and rudder, especially in the case of a single-engined aircraft. Under high power conditions the slipstream would impinge on the left of the fin (an angle of attack would exist between the fin and the slipstream airflow), generating an aerodynamic lift force which pushes the tail to the right and yaws the nose to the left. Some aircraft have an **Off-Set Fin** to help overcome this effect.

Propeller Torque Reaction.

If the propeller rotates clockwise (when viewed from behind), the torque reaction will tend to rotate the aircraft anti-clockwise and roll it to the left. This effect is most pronounced under high power conditions and high propeller rpm, such as during take-off.

On the ground this rolling to the left is stopped by the left wheel, which will have to support more load than the right wheel. This will increase the rolling friction force on the left wheel, tending to slow it down, and consequently the aircraft will tend to yaw to the left. Notice that this effect yaws the aeroplane in the same direction as the slipstream effect. (If the propeller rotates the other way, as in some older aircraft, then the yaw will be in the other direction.)

The next two effects will not be examined, but are included for those of you who will be flying tail-wheel aircraft.

Gyroscopic Effect, Especially on Take-Off in a Tailwheeler.

Early in the take-off run of a tailwheel aircraft (e.g. DHC Chipmunk) the tail is lifted off the ground to place the aeroplane into a low drag and flying attitude. As the tail is being raised, a torque force becomes applied to the rotating propeller in a nose-down sense. Because a rotating body tends to resist any attempt to change its plane of rotation, when such a change is forced upon it, a 'gyroscopic' precession will be superimposed.

(*'Gyroscopic precession'* is covered in more detail in Chapter 26 on Gyroscopic Flight Instruments.)

Gyroscopic precession rotates the applied force 90 degrees in the direction of rotation – this phenomenon being known as **'Gyroscopic Effect'**. When nose-down torque is applied to the aircraft to raise the tail on take-off (which is like a forward force applied to the top of the rotating propeller disc), gyroscopic effect causes a similar force to be applied *90 degrees in the direction of propeller rotation.* This will be like a forwards force acting on the right side of the rotating propeller disc, causing the aircraft to yaw. The direction of yaw depends on the direction of propeller rotation.

The amount of gyroscopic effect depends upon the mass of the propeller, how the mass is distributed along the blades and how fast the propeller is rotating (all of this being combined into a physical quantity called the *'moment of inertia')*. It will also depend upon how fast you try to change the plane of rotation.

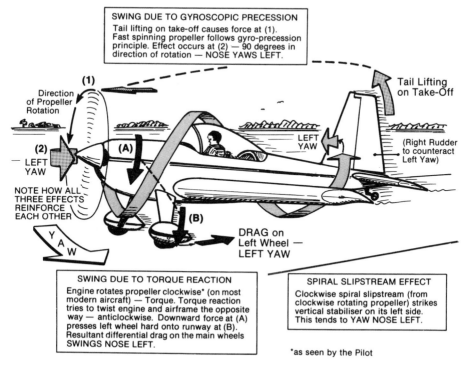

Fig.6-8. Take-Off Swing Resulting from the Combined Effects of: Slipstream Effect, Torque Reaction and Gyroscopic Precession.

Raising the tail of a high-powered aeroplane like a Spitfire on take-off produces a much greater gyroscopic effect than raising the tail of a Tiger Moth.

NOTE: The three effects cause a **Yaw to the Left** in an aeroplane whose propeller rotates clockwise (as seen from the cockpit), which the pilot will counteract with however much right rudder is required to keep straight. For aeroplanes with anti-clockwise rotating propellers (e.g. Merlin-powered Spitfires, Chipmunks, Tiger Moths), the Yaw on take-off will be to the right.

Asymmetric Propeller Blade Effect, especially on Tail-Wheel Aircraft.

At the start of the take-off run of a tailwheel aircraft when the tail is still on the ground, the propeller shaft is inclined upwards and the plane of rotation of the propeller is not vertical.

The aeroplane is travelling horizontally and a down-going propeller blade will therefore have a greater angle of attack than an up-coming blade, causing the down-going blade to produce more thrust and the aeroplane to yaw accordingly.

The down-going blade will also travel further than the up-coming blade in the same time (and we have considered half a rotation), causing the velocity between the down-going blade and the relative airflow to be greater and hence to produce more thrust. Therefore the down-going half of the propeller 'disc' will produce more thrust than the up-going half, causing an aircraft with the propeller rotating clockwise (as seen from behind) to yaw to the left while the tailwheel is still on the ground.

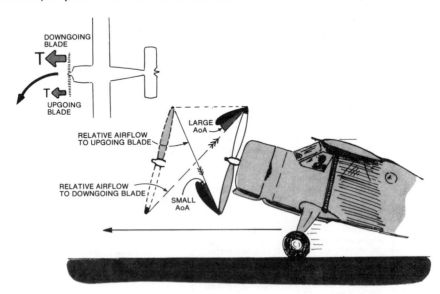

Fig.6-9. Down-Going Blade Produces More Thrust With the Tail on the Ground.

☐ Now tackle the questions in **Exercises 6 — Thrust From The Propeller.**

7

STABILITY

EQUILIBRIUM IN STRAIGHT AND LEVEL FLIGHT.

Four main forces act on the aircraft in flight:

LIFT, WEIGHT, THRUST and DRAG.

- **Lift** acts through the Centre of Pressure, which moves continually with every change in angle of attack.
- **Weight** acts vertically downwards through the Centre of Gravity, which moves as fuel is burned off or as cargo or passengers move.
- **Drag** acts to oppose the motion of the aircraft, therefore is parallel to the relative airflow and in the opposite direction to the flight path. The point through which the total drag may be considered to act varies with angle of attack, airspeed, operation of flaps, landing gear, etc.
- **Thrust** acts through the propeller shaft, or the centre-line of a jet engine. For a single-engined aircraft at least, this is the only constant position that any of the four forces acts through.

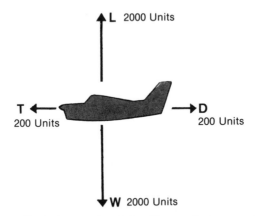

Fig.7-1. Lift Balances Weight, Thrust Balances Drag in Straight & Level Flight.

For the aircraft to remain in equilibrium in straight and level flight, the opposing forces must be equal so that they balance out, leaving no resultant force acting on the aeroplane.

- Lift opposes Weight, and these two must be equal.
- Thrust opposes Drag, and these two must be equal.

The aeroplane is subject to no resultant force and continues in its state of unaccelerated flight – steady motion in a straight and level line.

There is usually a considerable difference between the two pairs of forces, Lift and Weight being much greater in magnitude than the Thrust and Drag in normal flight. For example: Lift and Weight may be each 2,000 units; Thrust and Drag each 200 units (recognisable as a Lift/Drag ratio of 2,000/200 = 10 to 1.)

When in straight and level flight, the Lift and Weight will only decrease gradually as the weight reduces with fuel burn-off. The Thrust and Drag will vary considerably depending upon angle of attack and therefore airspeed.

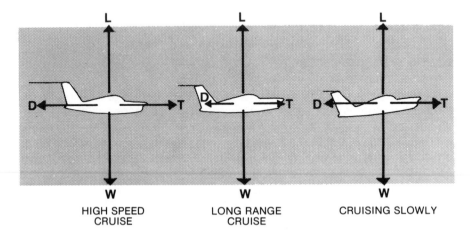

HIGH SPEED   LONG RANGE   CRUISING SLOWLY
CRUISE   CRUISE

Fig.7-2. Drag (and Thrust Requirement) Depends on AoA and Airspeed.

Note the assumption we have made regarding the Thrust. Whilst it acts along the propeller shaft or jet engine centreline and therefore, at the high angle of attacks in straight and level flight, would point slightly up, we have assumed that it points in the direction of flight, directly opposing the drag.

PITCHING MOMENTS.

The positions of the Lift force acting through the Centre of Pressure (CP) and the Weight force acting through the Centre of Gravity (CG) are not constant in flight.

Under most conditions of flight the CP and CG are not coincident, i.e. are not at the one point. The CG will move as passengers or crew move around (this is noticeable in airliners as flight attendants walk down the cabin), if freight is shifted and as fuel burns off. The CP changes position according to the angle of attack (and therefore airspeed).

The outcome is that the opposing forces of Lift and Weight, even though they are equal in magnitude and balance out, will set up a **Couple,** causing a nose-down pitching moment if the Lift (CP) is behind the Weight (CG), or a nose-up pitching moment if the CP is in front of the CG. (Remember that a *'couple'* is a pair of equal, parallel forces acting in opposite directions and tending to cause rotation because they act in different axes.)

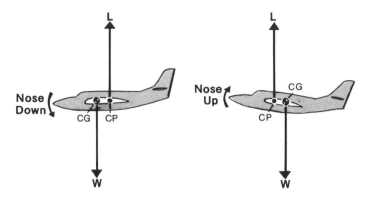

Fig.7-3. Lift and Weight Produce a Pitching Couple.

The different lines of action of the Thrust force and the Drag force produce another **Couple,** causing a nose-up pitching moment if the drag line is above the thrust line, or a nose-down pitching moment if the drag line is below the thrust line.

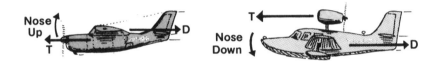

Fig.7-4. Thrust and Drag form a Pitching Couple.

Ideally, the pitching moments from the two couples should neutralise each other in level flight so that there is no resultant moment tending to rotate the aircraft.

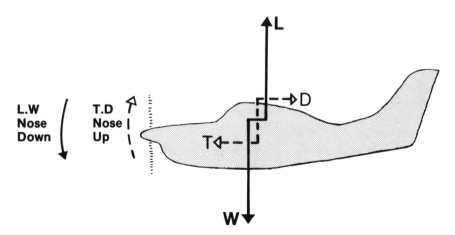

Fig.7-5. 'Lift.Weight' Couple and 'Thrust.Drag' Couple in Balance.

In many aeroplanes the lines of action are designed to be as shown in the above illustration. With this arrangement the Thrust.Drag couple produces a nose-up pitching moment and the Lift.Weight couple produces a nose-down pitching moment. The distances between the lines of action are positioned so that the turning effects of the two couples are equal and opposite, thereby cancelling out.

The turning moment of a couple depends upon the magnitude of the two forces and the distance between their lines of action. Therefore, for the turning moments of these two couples to balance, the larger forces of Lift and Weight should have their lines of action (CP and CG) fairly close, and the significantly smaller forces of Thrust and Drag should have a somewhat greater distance between their lines of action.

There is a very good reason for the 'Lift.Weight' couple to have a nose-down pitching moment balanced by the 'Thrust.Drag' nose-up pitching moment. If Thrust is lost (e.g. engine-failure), the Thrust.Drag nose-up couple is weakened and therefore the Lift.Weight couple will pitch the aircraft nose-down (without any action on the part of the pilot) so that it assumes a gliding attitude without a tendency to lose flying speed.

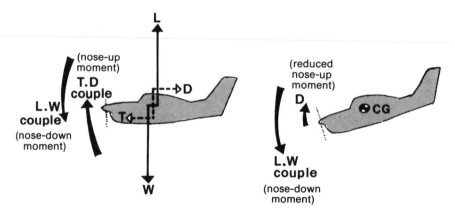

Fig.7-6. A Loss of Thrust: Lift.Weight Couple Pitches the Aeroplane Nose-Down.

Conversely, when power is added causing Thrust to increase, the nose will tend to pitch-up. It is rarely possible to have a perfect balance between these four main forces and the two couples formed by them. The tailplane is used to provide the final balancing force.

THE TAILPLANE.

The ideal balance of the pitching moments of the Lift.Weight couple and the Thrust.Drag couple is difficult to maintain in flight and there is usually a residual pitching moment arising from inequalities in the two main couples.

The function of the tailplane (or Horizontal Stabiliser) is to counteract these residual pitching moments from the two main couples, i.e. it has a stabilising function.

The tailplane is simply another aerofoil that can generate an aerodynamic force, if required, by being at an angle of attack (positive or negative) relative to the local airflow. This force can be up or down, as required by the designer, and because of this **the tailplane usually has a symmetrical aerofoil cross section.**

The aerodynamic force produced by the tailplane can be varied by changing its angle of attack relative to the local airflow, either by moving the elevators and holding them there with pilot force or a trim force, or by moving the entire tailplane, as is possible in some aircraft.

If the residual moment from the four main forces is nose-down (as is usually the case), the tailplane provides a downward aerodynamic force which will produce a nose-up pitching moment to balance the residual nose-down moment from the four main forces.

Because the tailplane is situated some distance from the Centre of Gravity, and its moment-arm is therefore quite long, the aerodynamic force provided by the tailplane needs only to be small to have a significant pitching effect. Hence the area of the tailplane (and its aerodynamic capabilities) is small compared with the mainplanes (main wings).

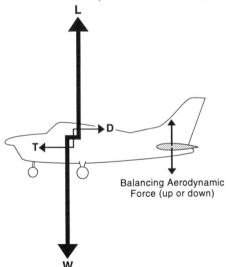

Fig.7-7. The Tailplane provides the Final Balancing Moment.

The turning effect (or turning moment) of a force on the aeroplane depends upon its magnitude and its distance from the Centre of Gravity. If the residual moment from the two main couples is nose-down, then the tailplane can produce a downward aerodynamic force which will have a nose-up pitching moment to balance out the moments.

Many aircraft are designed to operate most efficiently at cruise speed. The four main forces and the two main couples are designed to be at least in approximate equilibrium when on the cruise, with only small balancing forces required from the tailplane. Generally the Centre of Pressure is aft of the Centre of Gravity and the tailplane produces a downwards aerodynamic force.

STABILITY.

An aeroplane in flight is continually being disturbed from steady flight by external forces from small (and large) gusts of wind. The stability of the aeroplane is its natural or in-built ability to return to its original condition without any action being taken by the pilot.

Stability is concerned with the motion of the body after the disturbing force has been removed. **Positive Stability** indicates a tendency to return to the original equilibrium position or state prior to the disturbance. It is usual to call this 'stable'.

Do not confuse 'Stability' with 'Controllability'.

- **Stability** is the natural ability of the aeroplane to return to its original condition after being disturbed without any action being taken by the pilot.

- **Controllability** refers to the ease with which a Pilot can manoeuvre the aircraft using the control surfaces.

There is a significant **contradiction between Stability and Controllability.** A high degree of stability makes the aircraft resistant to change and thereby tends to reduce the controllability, i.e. good stability makes it harder for the pilot to control and manoeuvre the aeroplane.

An aeroplane with some positive stability is a lot easier to fly for a pilot than an unstable aeroplane that shows a natural tendency to diverge from the trimmed flight attitude. The stability must not be so great, however, as to require high control forces for manoeuvring.

An aeroplane is in a state of **Equilibrium** when the sum of all the forces on it is zero and the sum of all the turning moments on it is zero. The aircraft is **'In-Trim'** if all the moments in pitch, roll and yaw are zero. Equilibrium is established in the various phases of flight by use of the surfaces of the aircraft, modified by control surface movement where steady pressures may be held by the effort of the Pilot, by trim tabs or by biassing the surface.

The external force most commonly displacing an aircraft in flight is a gust of wind. A stable aeroplane will return to its original condition naturally – an unstable one will not, unless the pilot takes action.

An unstable aircraft is difficult for a Pilot to fly because he must continually interfere by applying control forces. A stable aircraft can almost fly 'hands-off' and requires only guidance rather than second-to-second control inputs by the pilot.

Our examples so far have been drawn from the pitching plane, but stability in the other planes and about the other axes is just as vital.

THE THREE REFERENCE AXES.

We refer the motion of the aircraft to motion about each of three axes – each passing through the Centre of Gravity and each mutually perpendicular (i.e. at 90 degrees to each other).

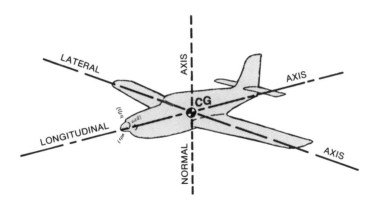

Fig.7-8. Angular Movement Can Occur About Three Axes.

The **Longitudinal Axis** runs fore and aft through the Centre of Gravity. **Movement** around the **Longitudinal Axis** is known as **Rolling.**

Stability around the **Longitudinal Axis** is known as **Lateral Stability,** because it is concerned with movement in the **Lateral** or **Rolling Plane.**

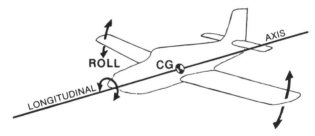

Fig.7-9. Rolling About the Longitudinal Axis.

The **Lateral Axis** passes through the Centre of Gravity across the aircraft from one side to the other.

Movement around the **Lateral Axis** is called **Pitching** (nose-up or nose-down). **Stability** around the **Lateral Axis** is called **Longitudinal Stability,** because it is concerned with stability in the **Longitudinal** or **Pitching Plane.**

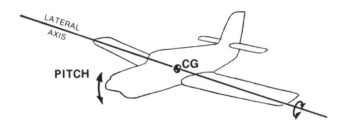

Fig.7-10. Pitching About the Lateral Axis.

The **Normal Axis** passes through the centre of gravity and is normal (perpendicular) to the other two axes. **Movement** around the **Normal Axis** is called **Yawing.**

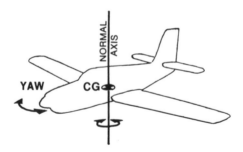

Fig.7-11. Yawing About the Normal Axis.

Stability around the **Normal Axis** is known as **Directional Stability,** because it is concerned with stability in the **Directional** or **Yawing Plane.**

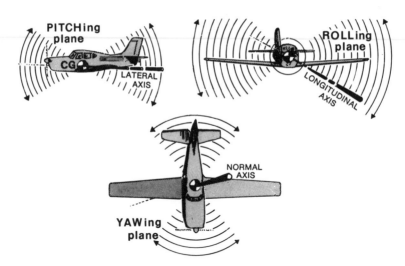

Fig.7-12. Angular Motion Can Occur in Three Planes.

Rotation around a point or axis is called **angular motion** – the number of degrees of rotation being called *'angular displacement'* and the speed with which it occurs *'angular velocity'*.

The motion of an aircraft is best considered in each of the planes (or about each of the reference axes) separately, although (except in straight and level flight) the actual motion of the aircraft is a little more complex. For example: rolling into a level turn the aircraft will not only roll but also pitch and yaw. (More of this later.)

We will consider longitudinal stability (pitching) first, then directional stability (yawing) and lateral stability (rolling). Roll and yaw are closely connected.

LONGITUDINAL STABILITY

Longitudinal Stability is in the pitching plane and about the lateral axis. To be longitudinally stable, an aircraft must have a natural or inbuilt tendency to return to the same attitude in pitch after any disturbance. If the **angle of attack** is suddenly **increased** by a disturbance, then forces will be produced that will lower the nose and decrease the angle of attack.

The longitudinally stable aeroplane tends to maintain the trimmed condition of flight and is therefore easy for a Pilot to fly in pitch.

The Tailplane is the Greatest Longitudinally Stabilising Factor

Let us consider a situation that is constantly occurring in flight. If a disturbance, such as a gust, changes the attitude of the aircraft by pitching it nose-up, the aircraft, due to its inertia, will continue **initially** on its original flightpath and therefore present itself to the relative airflow at an increased angle of attack.

Changes in the Tailplane Force lead to Longitudinal Stability.

With the same initial pitch-up caused by the disturbance and the aeroplane at first continuing in the original direction due to its inertia, the tailplane will be presented to the relative airflow at a greater angle of attack. This will cause the tailplane to produce an upwards, or decreased downwards, aerodynamic force, which is different to before the disturbance.

The altered aerodynamic force of course gives a nose-down pitching moment, tending to return the aeroplane to its original trimmed condition.

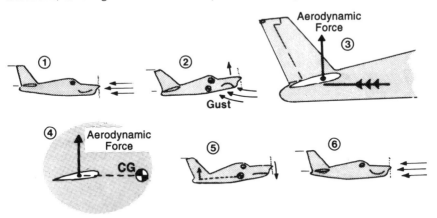

Fig.7-13. Longitudinal Stability Following an 'Uninvited' Nose-up Pitch.

Because of the great length of the moment arm between the centre of gravity and the tailplane, the aerodynamic force produced by the tailplane need not be large for its turning effect to be quite powerful. As the tail is raised and the nose pitches back down, the original angle of attack is restored, the extra upwards, or decreased downwards, aerodynamic force from the tailplane disappears and things are back to where they were prior to the disturbance.

As shown in Fig.7-14, the tailplane has a similar stabilising effect following an uninvited nose-down pitch.

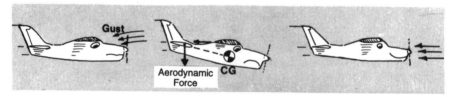

Fig.7-14. Longitudinal Stability following an 'Uninvited' Nose-down Pitch.

A good example of the stabilising effect of a tailplane is the passage of a dart or an arrow through the air, in which the tail-fins act as a tailplane to maintain longitudinal stability.

*Fig.7-15. Longitudinal Stability is provided
by the Tail Fins of a Dart.*

A Forward Centre of Gravity Increases Longitudinal Stability

The further forward the CG of the aircraft the greater the moment arm for the tailplane, and therefore the greater the turning effect of the tailplane lift force. This has a very stabilising effect longitudinally.

The position of the CG can be marginally controlled by the Pilot by the disposition of payload and fuel, usually done prior to flight. A forward CG leads to increased longitudinal stability and an aft movement of the CG leads to reduced longitudinal stability.

Limits are laid down for the range within which the CG must lie for safe flight and a prudent Pilot always loads his aeroplane and checks the trim sheet to ensure that this is so. If the CG is behind the legally allowable aft limit, the restoring moment of the tailplane in pitch may be insufficient for longitudinal stability. The same example of a dart is useful here. A CG further forward leads to more stability.

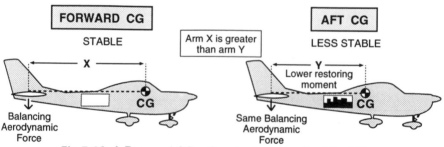

Fig.7-16. A Forward CG – Greater Longitudinal Stability.

The more stable the aeroplane, the greater the control force the Pilot must exert to control or move the aeroplane in manoeuvres, which can become tiring. Also, if the CG is too far forward, the elevator may not be sufficiently effective at low speeds to flare the nose-heavy aeroplane for landing.

Design Features to Aid Longitudinal Stability.

Tailplane design features also play a very large part in longitudinal stability – tailplane area, distance from the centre of gravity, aspect ratio, angle of incidence and longitudinal dihedral are considered by the designer. The aim is to generate a restoring force that is effective because of a long moment arm – leading to an aeroplane that is longitudinally stable.

At high angles of attack the mainplane may shield the tailplane or cause the airflow over it to be turbulent and this will decrease longitudinal stability.

DIRECTIONAL STABILITY.

Directional stability of an aeroplane is its natural or in-built ability to recover from a disturbance in the yawing plane, i.e. about the normal axis. It refers to an aeroplane's ability to *'weathercock'* its nose into any cross-wind, (i.e. a wind with a component from the side).

If the aircraft is disturbed from its straight path by the nose or tail being pushed to one side (i.e. yawed), then, due to its inertia, the aircraft will initially keep moving in the original direction.

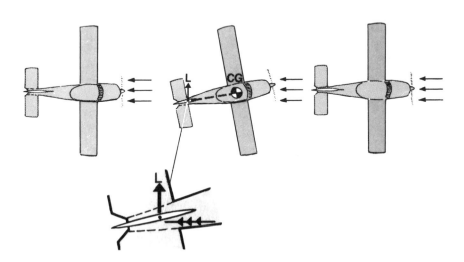

Fig.7-17. Directional Stability Following an Uninvited Yaw.

The aircraft will now be moving somewhat sideways through the air, with its side or keel-surfaces exposed to the airflow. This is known as a **Sideslip.**

The vertical fin (or tail or vertical stabiliser) is simply a symmetrical aerofoil. As it is now experiencing an angle of attack, it will generate a sideways Lift force which tends to take the fin back to its original position. This restores the nose to its original position.

The powerful moment (turning effect) of the vertical fin, due to its large area and the length of the moment arm between it and the Centre of Gravity, restores the nose to its original position. **The greater the fin area and keel surface area behind the CG, and the greater the moment arm, the greater the directional stability of the aeroplane.** Thus a forward CG is preferable to an aft CG as it gives a longer moment arm for the fin or vertical stabiliser.

A secondary effect of power or thrust is that caused by the **slipstream.** Propeller slipstream can affect the airflow over the fin, and therefore the fin's effectiveness as a directional stabiliser.

Changes in power cause changes in the slipstream and can lead to large directional trim changes (see later).

LATERAL STABILITY.

Lateral stability is the natural or in-built ability of the aeroplane to recover from a disturbance in the lateral plane, i.e. rolling about the longitudinal axis without any Pilot input.

A disturbance in roll will cause one wing to drop and the other to rise.

When the aircraft is banked, the lift vector is inclined and produces a sideslip into the turn. As well as the forward motion through the air the aeroplane slips sideways due to the Lift and Weight not being directly opposed, causing a resultant sideways force on the aeroplane.

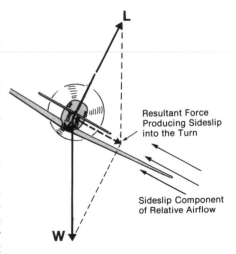

Fig.7-18. A Roll Disturbance Will Cause A Sideslip.

As a result of this **Sideslip,** the aeroplane is subjected to a sideways component of relative airflow and forces are generated that produce a rolling moment to restore the aeroplane to its original wings-level position.

The Main Contributor to Lateral Stability is the Wing.

Dihedral Increases Lateral Stability.

The wing can add to lateral stability if it has **Dihedral,** i.e. each wing is inclined upwards as you proceed from the fuselage to the wingtips.

Fig.7-19. Dihedral.

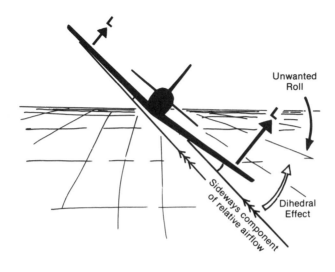

Fig.7-20. Dihedral Corrects Uninvited Rolling.

As the aircraft sideslips, the lower wing, due to its dihedral, will meet the upcoming relative airflow at a greater angle of attack and will produce increased Lift. The upper wing will meet the relative airflow at a lower angle of attack and will therefore produce less lift. It may also be shielded somewhat by the fuselage, causing an even lower lift to be generated.

The rolling moment so produced will tend to return the aircraft to its original wings-level position.

A negative dihedral (which is known as *'anhedral')* would have an unstable effect.

Sweepback Increases Lateral Stability.

The wing can add to lateral stability if it has **Sweepback.** As the aircraft sideslips following a disturbance in roll, the lower sweptback wing generates more lift than the upper wing. This is because in the sideslip the lower wing presents more of its span to the airflow than the upper wing and therefore the lower wing generates more lift and tends to restore the aeroplane to a wings level position.

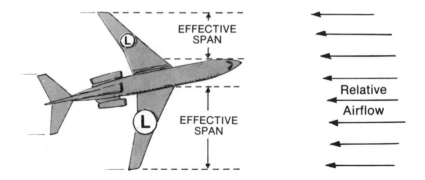

Fig.7-21. Sweepback Corrects Uninvited Roll.

High Keel Surfaces and a Low Centre of Gravity Increase Lateral Stability.

In the sideslip that follows a disturbance in roll, a high sideways drag line caused by high keel surfaces (high fin, a T-tail high on the fin, high wings, etc.), and a low CG will give a restoring moment tending to raise the lower wing and return the aircraft to the original wings-level position.

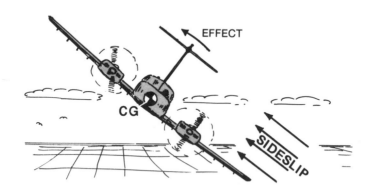

Fig.7-22. High Keel Surfaces and a Low CG Correct Uninvited Roll.

A High Wing Increases Lateral Stability.

If a gust causes a wing to drop, the Lift force is tilted. The resultant force (i.e. the combined effect of the lift and weight) will cause the aircraft to sideslip. The airflow striking the upper keel surfaces (i.e. above the CG) will tend to return the aircraft to the wings level condition. The high wings are above the CG and so are part of the keel surfaces tending to level the wings.

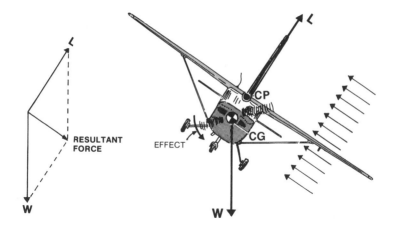

Fig.7-23. Upper Keel Surfaces Tend to Level the Wings.

LATERAL AND DIRECTIONAL STABILITY CONSIDERED TOGETHER.

Roll Followed By Yaw.

For lateral stability it is essential to have the **Sideslip** which the disturbance in roll causes. This sideslip exerts a force on the side or keel surfaces of the aircraft, which, if the aircraft is directionally stable, will cause it to yaw its nose into the relative airflow. **The Roll Has Caused a Yaw** in the direction of the sideslip and the aeroplane will turn further off its original heading in the direction of the lower wing.

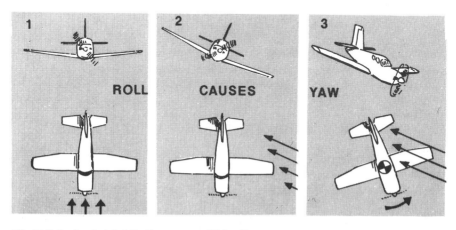

Fig.7-24. An Initial Roll ⟶ Sideslip ⟶ Yaw.

Note the interesting consequence that the greater the directional stability of the aircraft, the greater the tendency to turn away from the original heading in the direction of the lower wing. Also, the nose will tend to drop.

This further turn or yaw due to good characteristics of directional stability causes the higher wing on the outside of the turn to move faster and therefore produce more lift.

The lateral stability characteristics of the aeroplane, such as dihedral, cause the lower wing to produce increased Lift and to return the aircraft to the wings-level position. There are two effects in conflict here:

1. The directionally stable characteristics (large fin) want to steepen the turn and drop the nose further.

2. The laterally stable characteristics (dihedral) want to level the wings.

If the first effect wins out, i.e. strong directional stability and weak lateral stability (large fin and no dihedral), then the aircraft will tend to bank further into the sideslip, towards the lower wing, with the nose continuing to drop, until the aeroplane is in a spiral dive; (and all this without any input from the Pilot). This is called **Spiral Instability.**

Most aircraft are designed with only weak positive lateral stability and have a slight tendency to spiral instability. This is preferable to the reverse situation, which we will now discuss.

If the lateral stability (dihedral) is stronger, the aircraft will right itself to wings-level, and if the directional stability is weak (small fin) the aircraft may have shown no tendency to turn in the direction of sideslip and may have even turned away from the sideslip, causing a wallowing effect known as **Dutch Roll,** which is best avoided.

Yaw Followed by Roll.

If the aircraft is displaced in yaw, it will initially continue in the original direction of flight due to its inertia, and therefore **Sideslip.** This sideslip will cause the lateral stability characteristics of the aircraft's wing, such as dihedral, sweepback, or high-wing, to increase Lift on the forward wing and decrease Lift on the trailing wing.

This causes a rolling moment that will tend to raise the forward wing, resulting in the aircraft rolling towards the trailing wing and away from the sideslip.

Yaw Causes Roll.

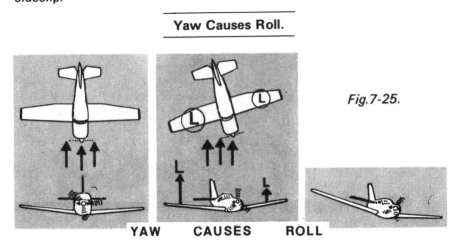

Fig.7-25.

YAW   CAUSES   ROLL

Another point to note is that, as the aircraft is actually yawing, the outer wing will move faster and produce more Lift than the inner wing, giving a tendency to roll towards the inner wing. The aeroplane's inherent directional stability (from the fin) will tend to weathercock or yaw the aircraft in the direction of the sideslip.

Note that **A Roll Causes a Yaw** and **A Yaw Causes a Roll,** and the two effects need to be studied together.

The **Sideslip** is very important, with lateral stability characteristics (dihedral) tending to raise the forward wing in a sideslip and directional stability characteristics (large fin) tending to weathercock or yaw the aircraft in the direction of sideslip and raise the outer wing in the yawing turn (which is the trailing wing).

Some notes follow about control by the Pilot as it is affected by stability characteristics:

- If the directional stability is poor (small fin) and the lateral stability good (dihedral), then a rudder input will cause a significant yaw and sideslip. The dihedral will bank the aeroplane in the direction of yaw (away from the sideslip) and it will enter a banked turn with no aileron input.

- If the directional stability is good (large fin) and the lateral stability not so strong, then if the Pilot banks the aeroplane with the ailerons, but does not touch the rudder, a sideslip towards the lower wing occurs. The good directional stability characteristics very smartly turn the aeroplane's nose into the sideslip and the turn will be fairly balanced even without the Pilot touching the rudder – there will be at least a little sideslip initially as the turn is entered, but this may be so small as to be hardly detected.

STABILITY ON THE GROUND.

The Centre of Gravity (CG) must lie somewhere in the area between the wheels at all times on the ground. The further the CG is away from any one wheel, the less the tendency for the aeroplane to tip over that wheel.

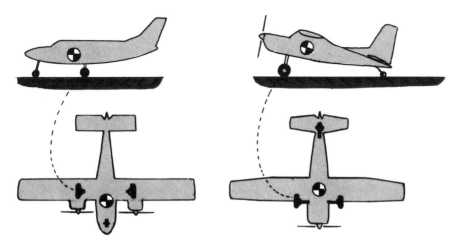

Fig. 7-26. The CG Must Remain Within the Area Bounded by the Wheels.

A low CG and widely-spaced wheels reduces the tendency for the aeroplane to tip over on the ground, e.g. when turning, when brakes are applied to stop, or when high power is applied on take-off.

A low thrust-line lowers the tendency for an aeroplane to pitch over on its nose when high power is applied (especially with brakes on).

High keel surfaces and dihedral allow crosswinds to have a greater destabilizing effect.

AIRCRAFT'S TRACK

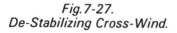
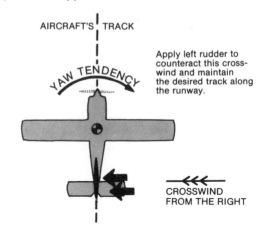

Apply left rudder to counteract this cross-wind and maintain the desired track along the runway.

CROSSWIND FROM THE RIGHT

Fig. 7-27.
De-Stabilizing Cross-Wind.

□ Proceed now to **Exercises 7 — Stability.**

8

CONTROL

All aeroplanes have a control system to allow the Pilot to manoeuvre and trim the aircraft in flight about each of the three axes. The moments (turning forces) required to achieve this are generated by changing the airflow pattern around the aerofoils, by modifying their shape or changing their position.

The control surfaces that the Pilot can move are usually hinged surfaces near the extremities of the aerofoils so that they have a long moment arm from the CG and the greatest leverage effect.

Usually there are three sets of **Primary Control** systems and three sets of control surfaces:

- the **Elevator** for longitudinal control in **Pitch,** operated by fore and aft movement of the control wheel or column;

- the **Ailerons** for lateral control in **Roll,** operated by rotation of the control wheel or sideways movement of the control column;

- the **Rudder** for directional control in **Yaw,** operated by movement of the two interconnected rudder pedals.

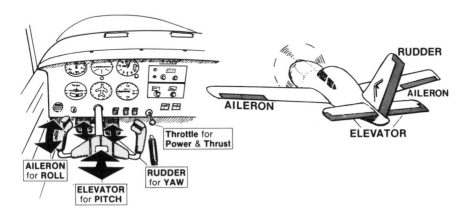

Fig.8-1. The Primary Controls: Elevator, Ailerons and Rudder.

Ideally, each set of control surfaces should produce a moment about only one axis, but in practice moments about other axes are often produced as well, e.g. aileron deflection to start a roll also causes adverse yaw (see later under 'aileron drag').

The control surfaces are connected to controls in the cockpit. The Pilot moves the elevators by fore and aft movement of the control column or yoke, the ailerons by rotating the wheel attached to the control column (or by sideways movement of the stick in older aircraft), and the rudder by the rudder pedals.

The deflection of the control surface changes the airflow and the pressure distribution over the whole aerofoil and not just over the control surface itself. The effect is to change the lift produced by the total aerofoil-control surface combination. The effectiveness of moving these control surfaces is called the *controllability* of the aircraft.

As mentioned earlier, an aeroplane with too much stability designed into it (thereby making it very resistant to change) has poor controllability. Stability opposes controllability. The Designer must achieve a reasonable balance between stability and controllability, bearing in mind the qualities most desirable for the aeroplane's planned use. For instance, a passenger aircraft would require more stability whereas a fighter would benefit from greater controllability and manoeuvrability. In a sense, controls act as *de-stabilisers.*

NOTE: **Excessive movement** of the control surface is prevented by *stops* at the control surface itself and/or at the controls in the cockpit. When the aeroplane is parked in strong winds or overnight, control locks should be fitted to prevent the control surfaces being moved by the wind and suffering damage. The control locks may take the form of a pin that passes through the control column, holding it firmly in place; or they may take the form of *blocks* that fit into the spaces around the control surface itself. It is vital that the control locks are removed before flight. Usually a *flag* is attached to make them very visible.

THE PRIMARY CONTROL IN THE PITCHING PLANE IS PROVIDED BY THE ELEVATOR

The Pilot controls the elevator by fore and aft movement of the control column – forward movement moving the elevator down which has the effect of pushing the nose of the aircraft down, and rearward movement of the control column moving the elevator up and which has the effect of pulling the nose of the aircraft up. These movements are logical and instinctive for a Pilot.

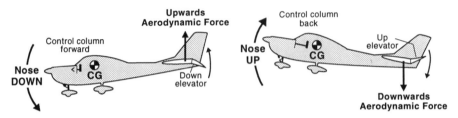

Fig.8-2. The Elevator is the Primary Pitching Control.

When the control column is moved forward, the elevators move downwards, changing the overall shape of the tailplane-elevator aerofoil section so that it provides an altered aerodynamic force. This supplies a reduced downwards, or even an upwards, aerodynamic force on the tail of the aircraft, depending upon the extent of the downwards deflection of the elevator. The effect is to create a pitching moment about the CG of the aircraft that moves the nose down.

Note that, even though the angle of attack of the parent aerofoil may be unaltered, the deflection of the control surface on the trailing edge will alter the aerodynamic force produced. For example, when the control column is pulled back by the Pilot, the elevator moves up and an altered force is produced by the tailplane-elevator aerofoil, causing the nose of the aircraft to pitch up.

The strength of the tail moment depends upon the force it produces and the length of the arm between it and the CG. The force generated by the tailplane-elevator combination depends upon their relative sizes and shape, the tailplane basically contributing to stability and the elevator to control. The larger the relative size of the elevator, the more the control.

To retain satisfactory handling characteristics and elevator effectiveness throughout the desired speed range, the position of the CG must be kept within the prescribed range.

If, for instance, the CG is too far forward, the aircraft will be too stable longitudinally because of the long moment arm to the tailplane. Even with the control column pulled fully back there will be insufficient up-elevator to reach the high angles of attack and low speeds sometimes required in manoeuvres such as flying slowly, and take-off and landing. Therefore, the **forward allowable limit of the CG is** determined by the amount of pitch control available from the elevator. The **aft limit of the CG** is determined by the requirement for longitudinal stability. (Refer to our chapter on Stability.)

Usually, the most critical situation for a nose-up requirement is in the round-out and landing. A forward CG makes the aeroplane nose-heavy and resistant to changes in pitch. This may make it difficult to raise the nose during a landing, especially since the elevator will be less effective because of the reduced airflow over it at landing speeds.

Sometimes action has to be taken to avoid this situation, e.g. the Tiger Moth is flown solo from the rear seat so that the CG is not too far forward – as could be the case if the solo Pilot sat in the front seat. Also, Concorde Pilots alter the position of the CG by transferring fuel from forward tanks to rear tanks and vice versa, depending upon the stability and control qualities desirable in each phase of flight.

With power off and no slipstream effect providing increased air velocities across the tail, the tail is less capable of producing aerodynamic forces. Of course in the final stages of a landing the power is off and the designer must allow for the elevator to produce a sufficient downwards force to raise the nose in this situation.

To reduce landing speeds most aircraft have trailing-edge flaps that can be lowered. As we will see in our discussion on lift augmentation devices, full extension of flaps usually causes a pitching moment, which the Pilot can counteract with the elevator and then trim off the control pressure.

Fig.8-3. Elevator Control In The Landing Flare is Critical.

Steady flight at a low speed and a high angle of attack will require a fairly constant up-deflection of the elevators and backwards pressure on the control column to keep the nose up.

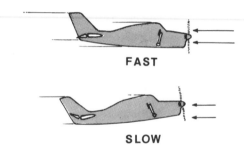

FAST

SLOW

Fig.8-4. Steady Elevator Deflection At Different Speeds.

At a high cruise speed there will need to be a steady down-deflection of the elevators to keep the nose down and maintain a low angle of attack, hence a steady forward pressure on the control column.

Because the elevators must provide differing steady forces when in steady flight at various speeds and angles of attack, trimming devices are provided to carry these steady loads and take the pressure off the Pilot. We look at **Trimming Devices** in more detail later.

The Stabilator (or All-Flying Tail).

Some designers choose to combine the tailplane and elevator into the one surface and have the whole tailplane movable – known as the *all-moving tail,* the *flying tail* or the *slab tail.* As the tailplane is also known as the *horizontal stabiliser* you may find the *'horizontal stabilizer – elevator'* combination referred to as the **'stabilator'.** When the control column is moved the entire *'slab'* moves. Forward movement of the control column will lower the nose (by raising the leading edge of the stabilator, generating a force that causes the tail to rise).

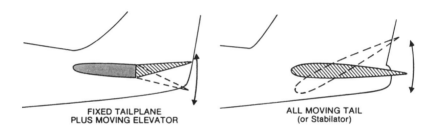

**FIXED TAILPLANE
PLUS MOVING ELEVATOR**

ALL MOVING TAIL
(or Stabilator)

Fig.8-5. Separate Tailplane and Elevator;   All-Flying Tail.

Some aircraft have a
Vee-tail, combining
the functions of the
elevator and rudder.

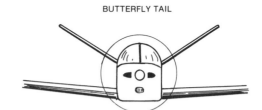

BUTTERFLY TAIL

Fig.8-6. V-Tail.

THE PRIMARY CONTROL IN ROLL IS PROVIDED BY THE AILERONS.

The ailerons are usually positioned on the outboard trailing edge of the mainplanes. The ailerons act in opposing senses, one going up as the other goes down, so that the Lift generated by one wing increases and the Lift generated by the other wing decreases. The Pilot operates the ailerons with rotation of the control wheel or sideways movement of the control column (whichever is fitted).

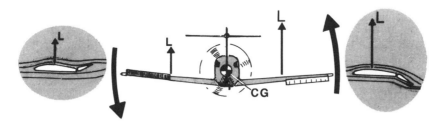

Fig.8-7. Ailerons: One Up, One Down — Rolling Moment.

A resultant rolling moment is exerted on the aeroplane. The magnitude of this rolling moment depends upon the moment arm (the reason the ailerons are outboard, giving a long moment arm to the CG) and the magnitude of the differing lift forces.

Note that for a wing to rise its aileron will be deflected downwards. Conversely, for a wing to go down its aileron will be deflected upwards.
• The down-going aileron is on the up-going wing;
• the up-going aileron is on the down-going wing.

ADVERSE AILERON YAW DUE TO 'AILERON DRAG'.

Deflecting an aileron down causes an effective increase in camber of that wing and an increase in the effective angle of attack. The Lift from that wing increases, but unfortunately so does the Drag. As the other aileron rises, the effective camber of that wing is decreased and its angle of attack is less, therefore Lift from that wing decreases, as does the Drag.

The differing Lift forces cause the aircraft to bank one way, but the differential 'aileron drag' causes it to yaw the other way – neither a comfortable nor convenient effect. This is known as *'aileron drag'* or *'adverse aileron yaw'* and is mainly a low airspeed problem that a Pilot would notice with a turn at low speed shortly after take-off.

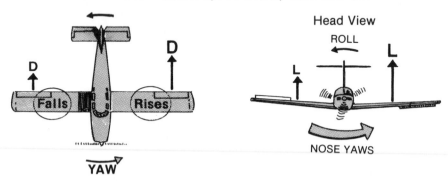

Fig.8-8. Rising Wing Has Increased Aileron Drag – Adverse Yaw.

'Adverse Aileron Yaw' (also known as *'aileron drag')* can be reduced by good design incorporating differential ailerons, frise-type ailerons, or coupling the rudder to the ailerons. To a large extent, aileron drag has been practically eliminated from modern training aeroplanes.

Differential Ailerons Overcome Adverse Aileron Yaw.

Differential aileron movement is designed to increase the drag on the descending wing on the inside of the turn. This design allows the up-going aileron, (which is on the descending wing) to deflect through a greater angle than the down-going aileron (on the rising wing).

The greater deflection of the aileron on the wing that is descending causes it to have increased drag with a tendency to yaw the aeroplane into the bank. The adverse yaw is therefore reduced.

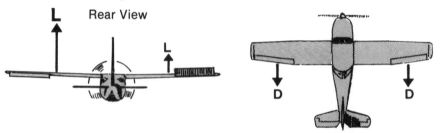

*Fig.8-9. Differential Ailerons Equalise Aileron Drag,
Reducing Adverse Yaw.*

Frise-Type Ailerons Overcome Adverse Aileron Yaw.

Frise-type ailerons increase the drag of the descending wing on the inside of the turn. As the aileron goes up (to drive the wing down), its nose protrudes into the airstream beneath the wing causing increased drag on the down-going wing. On the other wing, which is rising, the nose of the down-going aileron does not protrude into the airstream.

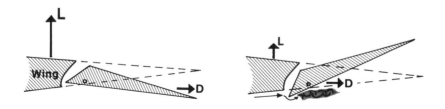

Fig.8-10. Frise-Type Ailerons Equalise Aileron Drag and Reduce Adverse Yaw.

Frise-type ailerons may also be designed to operate differentially, thereby combining both effects.

Coupling of Ailerons & Rudder to Overcome Adverse Aileron Yaw.

On some aircraft, the rudder is coupled into the aileron system so that, when the aircraft is banked with the ailerons, the rudder automatically moves to yaw the aeroplane into the bank and oppose the adverse yaw from the ailerons.

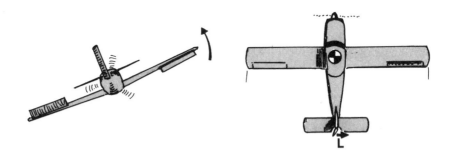

Fig.8-11. Rudder Coupled to Aileron Can Reduce Adverse Yaw.

Note the **interconnection between Roll and Yaw** throughout this discussion. The primary effect of rudder is to yaw the aeroplane, and the secondary effect is to roll it. The primary effect of ailerons is to roll the aeroplane, and the secondary effect is to yaw it.

ROLL IS FOLLOWED BY YAW.

When the aeroplane is banked using the ailerons, the Lift becomes tilted. It now has a horizontal component that is not balanced by any other force and so the aeroplane will slip in that direction. As a result of the slip, an airflow will strike the side of the aeroplane and the large keel surfaces (such as the fin) which are mainly behind the CG, causing the nose of the aeroplane to yaw progressively in the direction of bank. It is in this way that **roll is followed by yaw.**

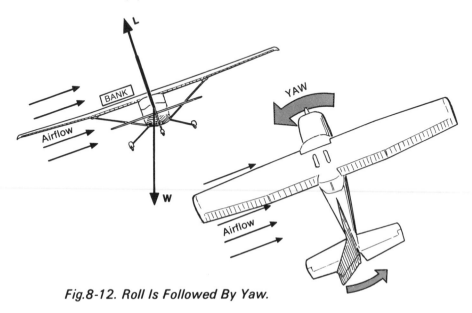

Fig.8-12. Roll Is Followed By Yaw.

NOTE: Whilst the ailerons are deflected, there may be a small amount of adverse aileron yaw opposite to the direction of bank, but, once established in the bank and with the ailerons neutral, the aeroplane will yaw progressively towards the lower wing. It will gradually enter a spiral descent and lose height unless the Pilot does something about it, i.e. levels the wings or exerts back pressure on the control column.

THE PRIMARY CONTROL IN YAW IS PROVIDED BY THE RUDDER.

The rudder is hinged to the rear of the fin (or vertical stabiliser). It is controlled from the cockpit by the rudder pedals attached to the rudder bar.

By pushing the left pedal, the rudder will move left. This alters the fin-rudder aerofoil section and sideways lift is created that sends the tail to the right and yaws the aeroplane to the left about the normal axis. Left rudder, the aeroplane yaws left.

Rudder effectiveness increases with speed, so large deflections at low speeds and small deflections at high speeds may be required to give a particular yaw. In propeller-driven aircraft, any slipstream flowing over the rudder will increase its effectiveness.

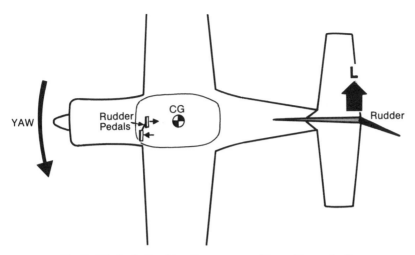

Fig.8-13. Left Rudder Pressure - Nose Yaws Left.

Yaw Is Followed By Roll.

The primary effect of rudder is to yaw the aeroplane. This causes the outer wing to speed up and generate increased lift. Having commenced to yaw, the aeroplane will continue in its original flight path for a brief period due to inertia - any dihedral on the forward wing causing it to be presented to the airflow at a greater angle of attack, therefore generating more lift. Having yawed the aeroplane, the **further effect of rudder is to cause a roll.**

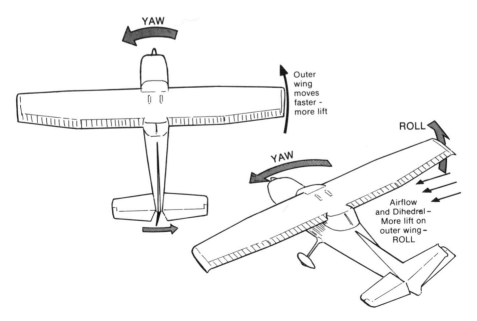

Fig.8-14. Yaw is Followed by Roll.

The Slipstream Effect on the Rudder.

Anything that increases the airflow over the rudder, like a slipstream, makes it more effective. As the slipstream corkscrews around the fuselage, it strikes one side of the fin-rudder at a different angle to the other. The shape of the fin-rudder aerofoil section is usually symmetrical, however in some propeller-driven aircraft the fin may be constructed a little 'off-set' or structured a little asymmetrically to balance the slipstream effect in the cruise condition.

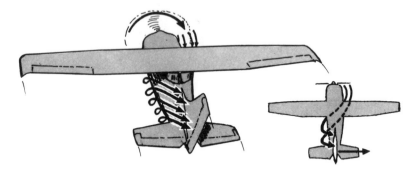

Fig.8-15. The Slipstream Strikes One Side of the Rudder.

If the slipstream over the fin and rudder changes, then the rudder deflection must be changed to balance it. This is especially noticeable at high power and low airspeed, as during take-off.

For example, the propeller in most training aeroplanes, when viewed from the cockpit, rotates clockwise. Its slipstream corkscrews back accordingly, striking the fin on the left side and driving the tail to the right. This causes the nose of the aeroplane to yaw left and so, as he opens up power, the Pilot must therefore apply right rudder to balance the slipstream effect.

The Rudder and Crosswind Take-Offs and Landings.

In ground operations, any crosswind will hit the side of the fin and tend to weathercock the aircraft into wind. The rudder must be used to stop the aircraft yawing into wind and keep it tracking straight along the runway.

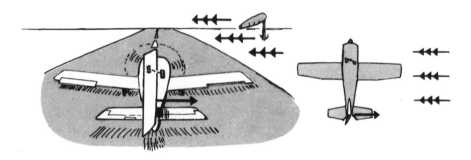

Fig.8-16. Crosswind Take-Off.

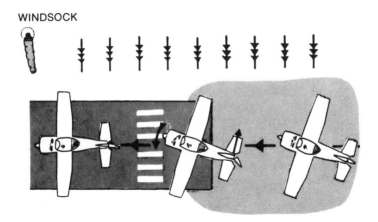

Fig.8-17. Crosswind Landing.

On approach to land the most common technique is to crab the aircraft into wind so that it is flying in balance (i.e. directly into the relative wind and with the rudder ball centred) and tracking somewhat *'crab-wise'* along the extended centre-line of the runway.

Just prior to touchdown the aircraft is yawed with the rudder so that when the wheels touch thay are aligned in the direction of the runway. Another technique in a crosswind landing is the sideslipping approach. On a typical cross wind approach, you would crab the aeroplane into wind so that it is tracking towards the aerodrome along the extended centreline of the runway.

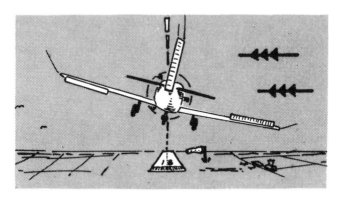

Fig.8-18. Sideslipping Approach.

Near the ground, you would yaw the aeroplane straight (with the rudder) so that it is aligned with the centreline. Unless the wheels touch almost immediately, the wind will cause the aeroplane to drift towards the side of the runway. To avoid this, you would lower (using the ailerons) the into-wind wing sufficiently to stop the aircraft drifting off the centreline prior to touchdown. The aeroplane is now sideslipping and flying a little bit out of balance. Touchdown will be on the up-wind wheel.

Not enough wing down, the aeroplane drifts downwind – too much wing down, it sideslips off the centreline into wind. It takes a little bit of juggling, especially as the wind may be gusting and will certainly change in strength and direction as the ground is approached.

A demonstration by your Flying Instructor will make it look easy.

The strongest crosswind that the aircraft can handle is limited by rudder effectiveness, and the maximum crosswind is specified in the Flight Manual and Pilot's Operating Handbook.

NOTE: This section is a reference text on Principles of Flight, so refer to your Flying Instructor for the correct crosswind landing technique to use with your particular aeroplane. Crosswind operations are fully covered in Volume 1 of this series – Flying Training.

The Power of the Rudder.

Whilst the rudder must be sufficiently powerful to handle the above requirements satisfactorily, it must not be too powerful. Given maximum deflection by the Pilot it should not cause structural damage.

The maximum allowable speed for maximum control deflection is called the manoeuvring speed (V_A).

CONTROL EFFECTIVENESS.

The size and shape of the control surface and its moment about the Centre of Gravity are of great importance in its effectiveness. Since the size and shape are fixed by the designer and the CG only moves small distances, these can be considered constant. The variables in control effectiveness are **Airspeed** and control surface **Deflection** angle.

If an aileron is deflected downwards, the angle of attack and the camber of that wing is increased, thereby increasing the C_{Lift} and the Lift produced. The greater the control surface deflection, the greater the change in Lift from the aerofoil (provided stalling angle of attack is not exceeded). The change in turning moment produced is the 'change in lift x the moment arm to the CG'.

The other aileron is deflected upwards, reducing the angle of attack and the camber on that wing, thereby reducing the Lift produced and reducing the turning moment, hence the aircraft rolls.

As we saw in the sections on Lift and Drag, the aerodynamic forces vary with the dynamic pressure ($\frac{1}{2}$.Rho.V-squared). If the airspeed 'V' is doubled, the effect of this is V-squared ($2 \times 2 = 4$). So, doubling the airspeed quadruples the effect of the same control surface deflection.

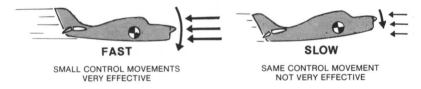

FAST

SMALL CONTROL MOVEMENTS
VERY EFFECTIVE

SLOW

SAME CONTROL MOVEMENT
NOT VERY EFFECTIVE

Fig.8-19. Controls Are More Effective With Increased Airflow.

If the airspeed is halved, the same control surface deflection is only ¼ as effective. Therefore, at low airspeed, to achieve a desired change in attitude requires a much greater control surface deflection (commonly known as 'sloppy controls' or 'less-effective controls'). Conversely, at **Higher Airspeeds, Controls are More Effective.**

Slipstream Increases Effectiveness of Rudder and Tailplane.

At low airspeeds, but with high power set, the slipstream may flow strongly over the tail section, making the elevator and rudder more effective than at the same speed with no power on. The ailerons are not affected by the slipstream and so will remain relatively ineffective.

Approaching the stall with power on, the elevator and rudder would retain more effectiveness than the ailerons, due to the slipstream flowing over them. Use of the slipstream is made when taxying tail-wheel aircraft on the ground – apply power to give rudder effectiveness to turn.

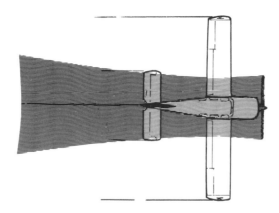

Fig.8-20. Prop-Wash.

CONTROL PRESSURES ON THE PILOT.

When a control surface is deflected, (for example, a down elevator – by pushing forward on the control column), the aerodynamic force produced by the moving control surface itself opposes its (downwards in this case) deflection. This causes a moment to act on the control surface about its hinge line trying to return the elevator to its original faired (i.e. streamlined) position, and the Pilot must overcome this to maintain the desired position. The Pilot feels this as *'stick-force'*.

The stick-force depends upon the turning moment at the hinge-line of the control surface and the means by which the control column is linked to the control surface.

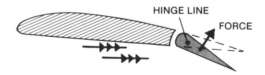

Fig.8-21. Hinge Moment at the Control Surface.

If the control surface is hinged at its leading edge and trails from this position in flight, the stick forces required are very high, especially in heavy or fast aircraft, and the Pilot needs assistance. This assistance is provided by **aerodynamic balance.**

The Designer provides an **inset hinge, a horn balance or a balance tab** to use the aerodynamic forces produced by the deflected control surface to partially balance or reduce the moment, i.e. aerodynamic balance of a control surface is designed to reduce the control forces required from the Pilot. The Designer, however, must be careful not to *'over-balance'* the controls otherwise the Pilot will lose all sense of *'feel'*.

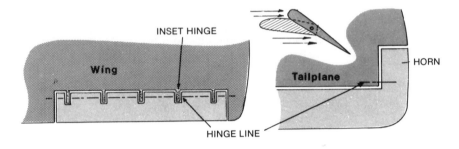

Fig.8-22. Inset Hinge Balance;   *Horn Balance.*

Fixed Balance Tab.

Some older aircraft, if found to have a flying fault (like a tendency to fly one wing low due to faulty rigging, for instance), had a small flexible metal tab on the rear of the appropriate control surface. This could be bent to alter the forces slightly and so correct the flying fault without having to re-rig the aeroplane.

This could only be done on the ground and the effectiveness established through test flying.

Balance Tab.

On conventional tailplanes it is quite common to have a balance tab incorporated as part of the elevator. It is mechanically linked to the elevator by a linkage that causes it to move in the opposite direction.

If the Pilot exerts back pressure on the control column, the elevator is raised and the balance tab goes down. The *'elevator/balance tab'* unit now generates a small upward aerodynamic force that acts to hold the elevator up, thereby reducing the control load required of the Pilot.

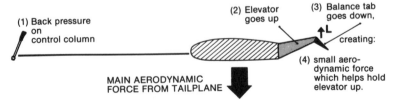

Fig.8-23. The Balance Tab.

NOTE: The balance tab acts automatically as the elevator moves. This movement should be checked in the pre-flight inspection by moving the elevator one way and noting that the tab moves the other way.

Trim Tabs.

An aircraft is in trim in pitch, roll or yaw, when it maintains a steady state of flight without the Pilot having to exert any steady pressure on the particular control surface.

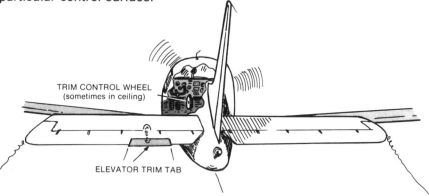

TRIM CONTROL WHEEL
(sometimes in ceiling)

ELEVATOR TRIM TAB

Fig.8-24. Elevator Trim Tab.

An aircraft that the Pilot has trimmed properly is far more pleasant to fly than an untrimmed aircraft. It requires control inputs only to manoeuvre and not to maintain an attitude or a heading. The function of the trim tab is to reduce the moment at the hinge line of the control surface to approximately zero for that condition of flight, so that the aeroplane will maintain it 'hands-off'.

Almost all aircraft have an elevator trim, many light singles and all multi-engined aircraft have a rudder trim, and the more sophisticated aeroplanes have an aileron trim.

Trim tabs can differ in sophistication – from metal strips that can only be altered on the ground, or springs that can apply a load to the control column, to trim tabs that the Pilot can operate from the cockpit, usually by a trim-wheel or trim-handle, and which may be mechanical or electrical. Simple metal strips can be found on an aileron of some aircraft types and may be altered after a test flight to make wings-level flight more easily achievable, without steady pressure being required on the control column.

In most light aircraft trim systems are mechanical and operated by a trim-wheel that acts in a natural sense. For example, if the pilot is pressing forward on the control column to maintain a desired attitude, then, by moving the top of the elevator trim-wheel forward, he can gradually release the stick force until the aircraft maintains the desired attitude without any steady pressure from him.

If the trim is electrical, then the switch will be spring-loaded to the central *OFF* position. To remove a steady load that he is holding on a control surface, the Pilot will move the switch in the natural and instinctive sense and then release it, when it will return to the *OFF* position.

The method of trimming is to hold the aircraft exactly how you want it with **Control Pressures** and then trim these pressures out to zero. As you trim the relevant control pressure is gradually relaxed until it is zero.

Do not use the trim to change the attitude of the aeroplane. Change attitude with the elevators – and then trim-off steady control pressures once stable flight has been achieved.

Although the control surface may be moved by the Pilot to manoeuvre the aircraft, the trim tab itself will remain in the same fixed position relative to the control surface until the Pilot decides to re-trim. There is a small proviso to this – **some tabs perform a dual function,** both as a trim tab and as an aerodynamic balance as the control surface moves. Its *'average'* position will be trimmed in by the Pilot and it will vary about this mean position automatically to serve its other function of balancing control surface movements. This is typical with a **balance tab.**

The aircraft will stay in trim until the power changes, or the airspeed changes, or the position of the Centre of Gravity changes. The Pilot should then re-trim. Aircraft with all-flying tailplanes (i.e. stabilators) usually have the elevator trim incorporated so that trimming moves the entire slab.

Mass Balancing.

At high speeds some control surfaces have a tendency to *'flutter'*. This is a vibration that results from the changes in pressure distribution over the surface as its angle of attack is altered.

If part of the structure starts to vibrate (and control surfaces are particularly susceptible to this) then these oscillations can quickly reach dangerous proportions. To avoid this tendency to flutter, the designer needs to alter the mass distribution of the surface.

The aim of mass-balancing is not for the control to be balanced in the sense of remaining level, but to alter the mass-distribution of the control to avoid any 'flutter' or vibration.

The **'mass balance'** is placed forward of the hinge-line to bring the CG of the control surface up to the hinge-line or even slightly ahead of it. On the *'inset hinge'* or *'horn balance'* this mass can easily be incorporated in that part ahead of the hinge line, but on others the mass must be placed on an arm that extends forward of the hinge-line. The distribution of mass on control surfaces is very important.

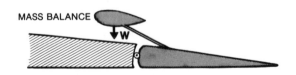

Fig.8-25. Mass-Balance to Avoid Control 'Flutter'.

Anti-Balance Tab.

Because of their combined function, stabilators have a much larger area than elevators and so produce a more 'powerful' response to control input, i.e. small movements can produce large aerodynamic forces. To prevent a Pilot from moving the stabilator too far and overcontrolling (especially at high airspeeds), a stabilator often incorporates an 'anti-balance tab'.

An anti-balance tab moves in the **same** direction as the stabilator's trailing edge and generates an aerodynamic force which makes it harder to move the stabilator further, as well as providing 'feel' for the Pilot.

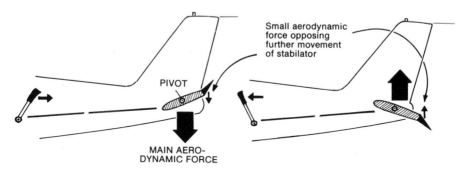

Fig.8-26. The Anti-Balance Tab Opposes Further Movement and Provides 'Feel'.

Correct movement of the anti-balance tab can be checked in the pre-flight inspection by moving the trailing edge of the stabilator and noting that the anti-balance tab moves in the **same** direction.

SUMMARY OF CONTROLS.

The **Primary Controls** are the Elevator, Ailerons and Rudder.

Ancillary Controls (extra controls) may include the throttle, pitch lever (for variable pitch propellers), mixture control, carburettor heat, flaps, undercarriage lever (for aircraft with retractable undercarriage), etc. These are covered in a later section of this Volume.

PLANE	AXIS	CONTROL	INITIAL EFFECT	FURTHER EFFECT
pitch	lateral	ELEVATOR	pitch	airspeed change
roll	longitudinal	AILERONS	roll	yaw
yaw	normal	RUDDER	yaw	roll

Although the **Throttle** is an ancillary control, it does affect the aeroplane in flight sufficiently for us to consider it briefly here. The initial effect of applying throttle is to increase the power and thus the Thrust – this increases the Thrust.Drag nose-up turning moment and pitches the nose up. It will also increase the slipstream effect, causing the aeroplane to yaw unless counteracted by rudder.

With a propeller rotating clockwise as seen from the cockpit, applying power will raise the nose and yaw the aeroplane to the left (counteracted by the Pilot applying forward pressure on the control column and right rudder).

When the power is removed, the nose will tend to drop and yaw to the right (counteracted by holding the attitude with a back pressure and applying left rudder).

CONTROL ON THE GROUND.

Directional Control is by use of the rudder, nose-wheel steering (which may be connected to the rudder pedals), power and brakes. Airflow over the rudder increases its effectiveness. Do not turn too sharply, especially when taxying fast – a high CG, a narrow wheel-base, or an unfavourable wind-effect, may all combine to roll you onto the outer wingtip. Any wind will tend to weathercock the aeroplane into wind – so take care when taxying in crosswinds and tailwinds.

Speed is controlled by power and brakes. Applying power with the throttle is generally used to accelerate the aeroplane and, once moving, the power can usually be reduced. Air resistance, ground friction and wheel brakes will slow the aeroplane. **It is good airmanship not to use power against brakes.** Hard braking, especially in a tailwheel aircraft, may cause it to nose-over. Braking a 'tailwheeler' may de-stabilise it directionally – the CG (due to inertia) will try to move ahead of the main wheels on which the brakes are being applied. In a nosewheel (tricycle undercarriage), braking will not cause the aircraft to yaw.

Crosswind Effect. A side wind will tend to lift the up-wind wing, especially if it has dihedral. The wings can be kept level with aileron. There will also be a weathercock tendency to turn the nose into wind.

Tailwind Effect. A tail wind will assist fast taxying, which is not good. It will also decrease directional stability by trying to blow the large tail surfaces forward and a turn, once commenced, may be difficult to control. In a strong tailwind, your Flying Instructor may advise you to hold the control column forward – this deflects the elevator down and avoids the tailwind creating a lifting force on the tailplane.

☐ Now complete **Exercises 8 — Control.**

AILERON CONTROL SYSTEM

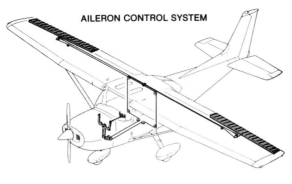

RUDDER AND RUDDER TRIM
CONTROL SYSTEMS

ELEVATOR CONTROL SYSTEM

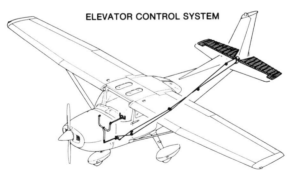

ELEVATOR TRIM
CONTROL SYSTEM

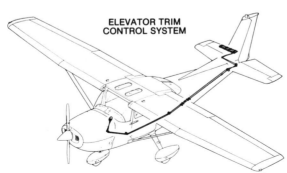

CESSNA MODEL 172N

9

FLAPS

In some phases of flight it is desirable to have a wing that has an increased lifting capability (increased 'Coefficient of Lift maximum') so that slower speeds are possible (take-off and landing).

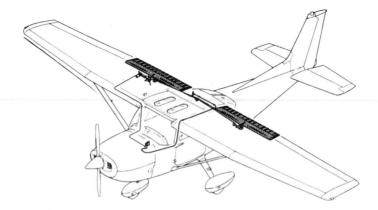

Fig.9-1. Cessna Wing Flap System – Typical of Light Aircraft.

The primary purpose of flaps is to give the required Lift at a lower airspeed. At other times it is convenient to have increased Drag to slow the aeroplane up or increase its rate of descent. Devices that do this come under the headings of *'Lift Augmentation'* and *'Drag Augmentation'*.

Producing more lift from a wing has obvious benefits. In straight and level flight the Weight is balanced by the Lift:

$$\text{LIFT} = \text{WEIGHT} = C_{\text{Lift}} \times \tfrac{1}{2} \text{ Rho V-squared} \times S$$

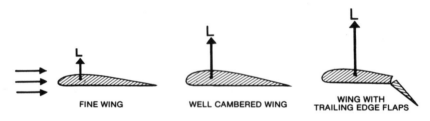

FINE WING   WELL CAMBERED WING   WING WITH TRAILING EDGE FLAPS

Fig.9-2. Same Airspeed: Camber and/or Flaps Give Higher Lift.

If some means of changing the basic aerofoil into a shape that has an increased 'CLift maximum' and possibly an increased wing area (S) is used, then the required lift can be generated at much lower speeds.

At the 'CLift max', reached near the stalling angle of attack, the required lift will be generated at a much lower airspeed. When the stalling angle is finally reached, the airspeed is much lower than for the 'clean' wing. This means that all the other speeds which are factored on the stall speed, such as take-off speed, approach speed, landing speed, etc., will be lower – a safer situation allowing the use of shorter take-off and landing distances.

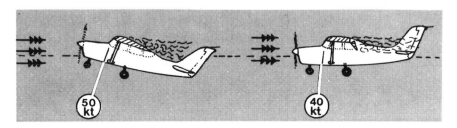

Fig.9-3. Flaps Lower the Stalling Speed.

INCREASING 'CLift Maximum' WITH HIGH-LIFT DEVICES.

There are two main types of high-lift devices that are capable of augmenting (increasing) 'CLift max':
- **Slats and Slots** — either automatic or controlled by the Pilot, e.g. Tiger Moth, Boeing 727.
- **Flaps** (Pilot controlled), which may be trailing edge or leading edge – most aircraft having trailing edge flaps.

THE FLAP CONTROL IN THE COCKPIT.

The wing flaps are controlled from the cockpit usually by either:
- an electrical switch spring-loaded to *OFF,* and which allows any degree of flap between full up and full down to be selected, with the precise degree being displayed on a cockpit indicator; or
- a mechanical lever or handle, which usually allows the flap to be selected in set stages, with the stage displayed on an indicator at the base of the handle.

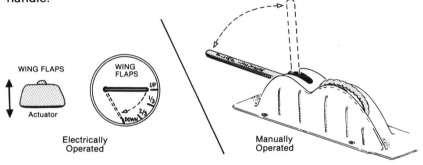

Fig.9-4. The Flap Control and Indicator.

As the flap lever is operated, the flaps on both wings move identically. It is usual to check the flaps carefully during the pre-flight external inspection to ensure that they are securely attached, that they both extend to the same degree and that the flap (and wing) surfaces are free from damage.

TRAILING EDGE FLAPS.

Flaps alter the camber of the aerofoil section. An aerofoil designed to give high lift has a curved mean camber line (the line equi-distant between the upper and the lower surfaces) – and the greater the mean camber line, the greater the lift capability (the 'maximum C_{Lift}' possible) of the wing. By a *'high lift'* wing we mean one that can produce the required lift at a lower airspeed.

Most high speed aerofoils, however, have a mean camber line that is fairly straight and hardly curved at all. If the trailing edge or the leading edge can be hinged downwards, then a more highly-cambered aerofoil section results – which means it can produce the required lift at a lower airspeed, i.e. it has become more of a high lift wing.

Virtually all aircraft have trailing edge flaps. (Larger aircraft, especially those with swept-back wings, often have leading edge flaps as well. These have a similar function to trailing edge flaps in that they increase the camber of the wing and thus increase its effectiveness in producing Lift.)

Trailing Edge Flaps Give Increased Lift.

The increased camber will give increased Lift (more Lift at the same airspeed or the same Lift at a lower airspeed).

The initial effect of lowering the flaps is to give increased Lift (C_{Lift} increases and at the same speed 'V' this gives a greater Lift force). Unless the Pilot lowers the nose to decrease angle of attack (and C_{Lift}), the aeroplane will experience a short-lived and unpleasant climb – a 'balloon'. It is only short-lived because the increased Drag soon slows the aeroplane down, reducing airspeed and consequently the Lift force is reduced.

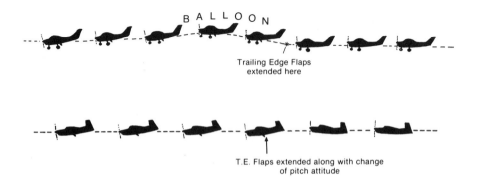

B A L L O O N

Trailing Edge Flaps
extended here

T.E. Flaps extended along with change
of pitch attitude

Fig.9-5. Lowering Flap Can Cause A 'Balloon' Unless The Pilot Adjusts The Pitch Attitude.

Extending Trailing Edge Flaps May Cause the Nose to Pitch.

Because the increased camber due to extending trailing edge flaps occurs at the rear of the wing, the centre of pressure moves aft as the flaps are lowered, thereby altering the L.W couple. The T.D couple may also be altered due to the change in drag. The resultant pitching effect will vary between aircraft types depending upon whether the nose-down L.W couple or nose-up T.D couple predominates.

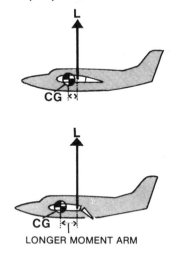

LONGER MOMENT ARM

Fig.9-6. Extending Flap May Cause The Nose To Pitch.

Trailing Edge Flaps Decrease the Lift/Drag Ratio.

When the flaps are lowered the lift increases, but so too does the drag. When we consider the angles of attack giving the best Lift/Drag ratio, the drag increase is proportionately much greater than the lift increase, i.e. the L/D ratio is less with flap extended.

As a result of a lower L/D ratio, the aeroplane will not glide as far with flap as it would when clean, nor will it climb out at as steep an angle. Also, it will require more fuel to travel the same distance – if you cruise with flaps down.

Trailing Edge Flaps Give Increased Drag.

As flap is extended, the Drag, as well as the Lift, increases. In the early stages of the extension the lift increases quite markedly (sometimes causing the aircraft to 'balloon'), with some increase in Drag. In the later stages of flap extension, the increase in Drag is much greater.

It is of value to the Pilot to think of the trailing edge flaps at their early extension as *'lift flaps'* (when the lifting capability of the wing is increased significantly for little cost in drag), and when fully extended as *'drag flaps'*. The latter stages of Trailing Edge flap extension give only a small increase in lifting capability for a large increase in Drag.

When the flaps are extended, because the drag increases, the speed will commence to decrease unless power is added or the rate of descent increased – or both.

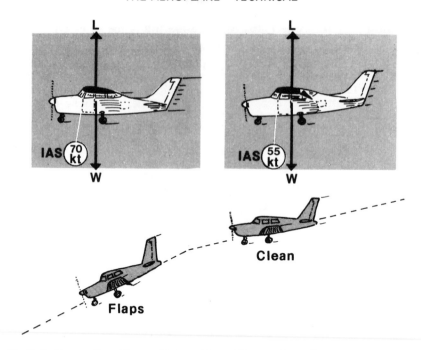

*Fig.9-7. Extending Flap – Either More Thrust Or A Steeper Descent Is
Required To Balance The Increased Drag.*

**Trailing Edge Flaps give a Lower Stalling Angle of Attack, (when
referred to the chord line of the original un-flapped aerofoil).**

The angle of attack is measured against the chord line of the original
'unflapped' wing. This means that there is a **constant** reference line
against which to measure angle of attack in all stages of flight.

The trailing edge flaps do not extend along the whole of the trailing edge,
but usually only along the inner sections. The flaps are lowered
simultaneously and symmetrically on each side of the aircraft.

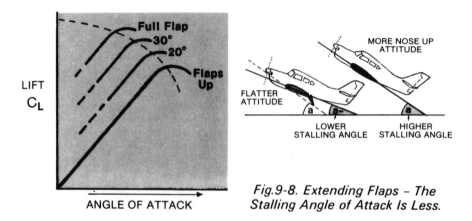

*Fig.9-8. Extending Flaps – The
Stalling Angle of Attack Is Less.*

With the flaps down, the **stalling angle of attack** (referred to the chord of the unflapped wing) is less than the stalling angle of attack when the wing is clean. The Pilot will see this as a lower nose attitude when stalling with flaps down compared to flaps up.

Do not confuse angle of attack with attitude as they are two different things. The attitude has no fixed relationship to the angle of attack while the aircraft is manoeuvring. The attitude is the angle of the aircraft with respect to the horizontal and the angle of attack is the angle with respect to the relative airflow.

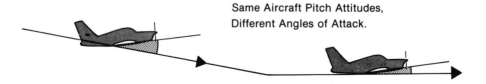

Same Aircraft Pitch Attitudes, Different Angles of Attack.

Fig.9-9. Same Attitudes But Different Angles Of Attack.

Trailing Edge Flaps in the Take-Off.

By partially lowering the flaps to the recommended take-off position (specified in the Operations Manual for your aircraft), you can obtain a lift advantage for a small drag penalty. The increased lift coefficient (C_{Lift}) means that the required amount of lift can be obtained at a lower airspeed and that the stalling speed is lowered. This allows the aircraft to fly at a lower speed and the take-off run to be shortened, even though the drag may be slightly increased.

The variation between the climb-out gradients with and without flaps will vary from aircraft to aircraft, and for the one aeroplane will vary according to the amount of flap selected.

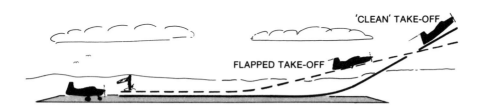

'CLEAN' TAKE-OFF

FLAPPED TAKE-OFF

Fig.9-10. Flaps Allow A Shorter Take-Off Ground Run.

If you set the flaps at an angle greater than that recommended for take-off, then you are taking on increased drag with very little improvement in lift. This greatly increased drag at the larger flap extensions will decrease your rate of acceleration on the ground take-off run and diminish your climb-out performance.

FLAP MANAGEMENT ON TAKE-OFF.

Choose an appropriate flap setting for take-off bearing in mind Take-Off Run Available (TORA) and obstacle clearance in the take-off path.

In flight, prior to retracting the flaps, ensure that you have sufficient flying speed for the new configuration. If the flaps are retracted at too low a speed, the clean wing (or the less-flapped wing if you are retracting in stages) produces less lift and, if insufficient to support the aeroplane, causes it to sink or stall.

As you raise the flaps the aeroplane will tend to sink because of the reduction in lift that the wing is producing. To counteract this sinking, the Pilot needs to raise the nose and increase the angle of attack (and the C_{Lift}). If he does not raise the nose to make up the loss of lift as the flaps come in, the aircraft will sink until it has gained sufficient airspeed to make up the reduced lift.

When you retract the flaps, the reduction in camber at the rear of the wing moves the CP forwards and there is also a change in drag. There is usually a tendency for the nose to pitch, in which case re-trimming would be necessary. If you are accelerating towards a higher climb speed or cruise speed, further re-trimming will be necessary as speed increases.

To achieve the same lift at the same speed clean (as compared to flapped) your nose attitude must be higher. By the Pilot raising the nose slightly as the flaps are retracted the C_{Lift} generated remains about the same, and so the aircraft does not sink. Even though the C_{Lift} is the same, the C_{Drag} will be reduced with the flaps retracted, and this drag reduction allows the aircraft to accelerate faster.

TRAILING EDGE FLAPS ON APPROACH AND LANDING.

Lowering the flaps for landing allows the wing, because of the increased C_{Lift}, to generate the required lift at a lower speed and therefore makes a lower approach speed possible. The stall speed is lowered significantly by the increased C_{Lift} and hence the landing speed, which must be at least 1.3 V-Stall in the approach configuration (i.e. a 30% buffer above the stall), is lowered.

There are a number of things to consider when about to lower the flaps:

- Ensure you do not lower them at too high a speed – the Flight Manual (and the Pilots Operating Handbook) specify the maximum flap extension speed (V_{FE}).

- As the trailing edge flaps are extended, the C_{Lift} will increase and the aircraft will tend to 'balloon' unless counteracted with a lower attitude.

- When lowering the flaps there is usually a tendency for the nose to pitch. The Pilot should set and hold the desired attitude. Any pressure held on the control column in steady flight should then be trimmed off.

Note also that the increase in drag (with lowered flaps) will require higher power settings to maintain airspeed and altitude or to maintain a steady rate of descent. If you want a steeper angle of descent, then lowering the flaps (and not applying any power) will achieve that.

TRAILING EDGE FLAPS INCREASE THE PILOT'S VISIBILITY.

With Trailing Edge flaps extended, the aeroplane's required nose attitude is lower. This improves the visibility for the Pilot — especially important during approach and landing.

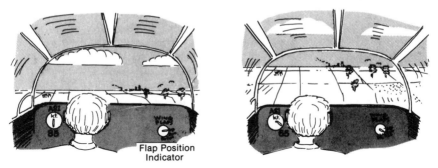

Flap Position
Indicator

Fig.9-11. Extended Flaps Improve The Pilot's Forward Field of Vision.

Sometimes a *'precautionary cruise'* is required. This is a low speed cruise used, for example, when you want to inspect the ground, or when finding your way in poor visibility (which should have been avoided). Partially lowering the flaps allows a slower cruise, the adequate margin above the stall, and increased visibility from the cockpit.

TYPES OF TRAILING EDGE FLAPS.

There are various types of flap that may be found on light aircraft. They include:

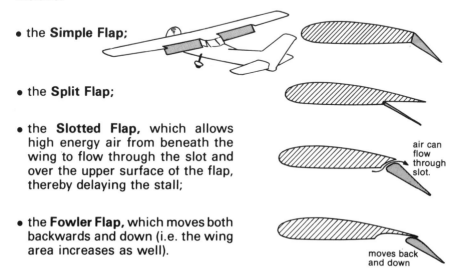

• the **Simple Flap;**

• the **Split Flap;**

• the **Slotted Flap,** which allows high energy air from beneath the wing to flow through the slot and over the upper surface of the flap, thereby delaying the stall;

air can
flow
through
slot.

• the **Fowler Flap,** which moves both backwards and down (i.e. the wing area increases as well).

moves back
and down

Fig.9-12. Different Types of Trailing Edge Flaps.

LEADING EDGE DEVICES.

At high angles of attack the airflow breaks away (or 'separates') from the upper surface of the wings and becomes turbulent. This leads to a stalled condition which destroys much of the lifting ability of the wing.

Some aircraft have leading edge devices that cause some of the high energy air from beneath the wing to flow through a slot and over the upper surface of the wing, thereby delaying separation and the stall, **allowing the aeroplane to fly at a higher angle of attack and a lower airspeed.** This can be achieved with slats which form part of the upper leading edge of the wing in normal flight, but which can be extended forward and/or down to form a slot.

Some wings have fixed-slots actually built-in to the wing leading edge but this is less common because they generate high drag at cruising speeds. On a high performance aircraft this would be unacceptable and so the more complicated *'extendable slat'* would be fitted.

Fig.9-13. Slots Delay the Stall.

SPOILERS.

Most advanced jet transports and most gliders have **spoilers** on the upper surfaces of their wings. These are hinged control panels which, when extended, disturb the airflow over the upper lift-producing part of the wing, thereby decreasing (or "spoiling") lift and increasing drag.

Pilots use spoilers to reduce airspeed and/or steepen the descent path without increasing airspeed.

On large jet aircraft, pilots deploy the spoilers after touchdown to dump the lift and get all of the weight onto the wheels, thus making the wheel brakes more effective.

☐ Now complete **Exercises 9 – Flaps.**

10

STRAIGHT AND LEVEL

In steady straight and level flight the aeroplane is in equilibrium. This means that all the forces acting on it are in balance and there is no resultant force to accelerate or decelerate it. Acceleration is a change in velocity, which means a change in speed or a change in direction, or both. In straight and level flight, the aeroplane is not forced to change either speed or direction.

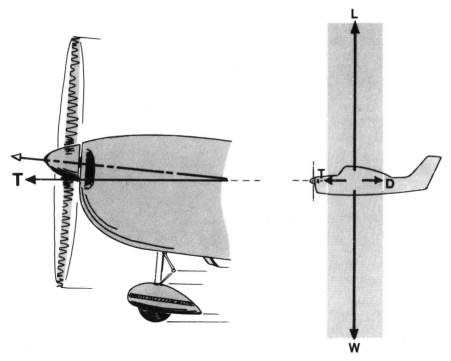

Fig.10-1. The Four Main Forces.

The **four main forces** acting on the aeroplane are **Lift, Weight, Thrust and Drag.** We assume that Thrust acts in the direction of flight, as indicated in Fig.10-1 above.

Each of the four main forces has its own point of action:
• the **Lift** through the **Centre of Pressure;**
• the **Weight** through the **Centre of Gravity;**
• the **Thrust** and the **Drag** in opposite senses, parallel to the direction of flight, through points that vary with aircraft attitude and design.

We make the assumption that the Thrust force from the engine/propeller is acting in the direction of flight, even though this is not always the case. For instance, at a high angle of attack and slow speed the aircraft has a nose-high attitude with the propeller shaft inclined upwards to the horizontal direction of flight. This assumption that **thrust acts in the direction of flight** simplifies our discussion considerably.

In straight-and-level flight:

LIFT = WEIGHT   and   THRUST = DRAG.

The Lift-Weight forces are much larger than the Thrust-Drag forces.

For in-depth study and revision of each of these forces you should refer back to their individual chapters.

PITCHING MOMENTS

The CP and the CG vary in position – the CP changing with angle of attack and the CG with fuel burn-off and passenger or cargo movement. The result is that the Lift.Weight combination sets up a couple which will cause a nose-down or a nose-up pitching moment, depending upon whether the Lift acts behind or in front of the CG.

Similarly the effect of the Thrust.Drag couple depends upon whether the Thrust line is below the Drag line (as is usually the case) or vice versa.

The usual design is to have the CP behind the CG, so that the L.W couple is nose-down, and the thrust line lower than the drag line, so that the T.D couple is nose-up. Any loss of power will weaken the nose-up couple, and consequently the nose-down Lift.Weight couple will pitch the aeroplane into a descent, thereby maintaining flying speed – a fairly safe arrangement.

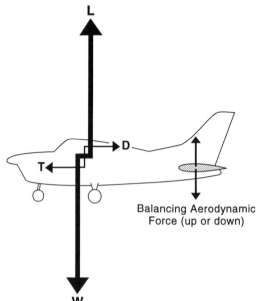

Balancing Aerodynamic
Force (up or down)

Fig. 10-2. The Tailplane provides the Final Balancing Moment.

The Lift.Weight couple and the Thrust.Drag couple should balance each other in straight and level flight so that there is no residual moment acting to pitch the aeroplane either nose-up or nose-down.

This ideal situation rarely exists between the four main forces and so the tailplane/elevator is designed into the aeroplane to produce a balancing force. This force may be an up or down force, depending upon the relationship that exists at the time between the Lift.Weight nose-down couple and the Thrust.Drag nose-up couple.

If you have to exert a steady pressure on the control column, so that the elevator produces the required balancing force, then you can trim this pressure off with the elevator trim wheel. Hold the desired attitude, and then trim to relieve the load.

VARIATION OF SPEED IN LEVEL FLIGHT.

For level flight, Lift = Weight. From our now (hopefully) familiar lift formula:
$$L = C_{Lift} \times 1/2 \text{ Rho V-squared} \times S$$

 – we can see that if the speed factor V (the TAS) is reduced, then the lift coefficient 'C$_{Lift}$' (angle of attack) must be increased to retain the balance of Lift = Weight.

V is the True Air Speed – the speed of the aeroplane relative to the air mass that it is passing through – TAS is not shown on a cockpit instument. What can be read in the cockpit, however, is Indicated Air Speed – and this depends upon the dynamic pressure '½ Rho V-squared'.

We need to be careful in our discussion not to become confused between TAS and IAS. Where you see V, think of True Air Speed (TAS), and where you see the formula '½ Rho V-squared', think of Dynamic Pressure and Indicated Air Speed (IAS).

• **TAS** determines the distance travelled through the air.

• **IAS** determines the aerodynamic effects – the Lift and the Drag.

ATTITUDE IN LEVEL FLIGHT.

To obtain the required Lift, at low speed a high angle of attack (high C$_{Lift}$) is required; while at high speed only a small angle of attack (low C$_{Lift}$) is needed.

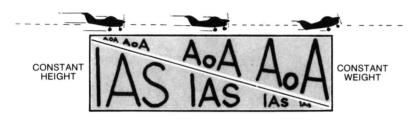

INDICATED AIRSPEED DECREASES
AS ANGLE OF ATTACK INCREASES

Fig.10-3. Indicated Air Speed Varies Inversely with Angle of Attack.

Since we are considering level flight, the Pilot *'sees'* these angles as an aeroplane pitch attitude relative to the horizon – nose-up at low speeds and fairly nose-level at high speeds.

THE EFFECT OF WEIGHT ON LEVEL FLIGHT.

In a normal flight the Weight gradually reduces as fuel is burned-off. If the aeroplane is to fly level, the Lift produced must gradually decrease as the weight reduces.

If there is a sudden decrease in Weight, say by half a dozen parachutists leaping out, then to maintain straight and level flight the Lift must reduce by a corresponding amount. The C$_{Lift}$ (angle of attack) or the airspeed must be reduced so that Lift generated is less.

Suppose that the aeroplane is flying at a particular angle of attack, say at that for the best L/D ratio (about 4 degrees). To maintain this most efficient angle of attack (C$_{Lift}$ for best L/D ratio) as the weight reduces, the velocity factor 'V' must be reduced to lower the Lift produced so that it still balances the Weight.

So, if the height and the angle of attack are kept constant, then the airspeed will have to be reduced. The power (Thrust) will be adjusted to balance the Drag. For most efficient flying (best L/D ratio), the cruising speed will decrease with decreasing Weight.

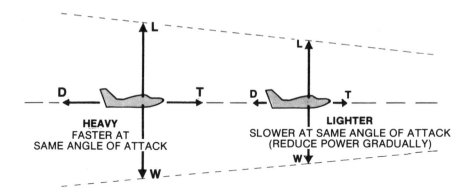

Fig.10-4. For Same AoA – Lighter Aeroplane Must Fly Slower.

If the power is kept constant and you want to maintain height as the weight decreases, the lift must be decreased by lowering the angle of attack (decreasing the C$_{Lift}$). Therefore the speed will increase until the power produced by the engine/propeller is equalled by the power required to overcome the drag.

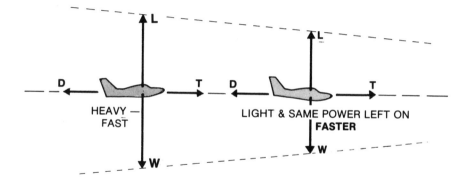

Fig.10-5. Same Power – Lighter Aeroplane Has Lower Angle of Attack and Flies Faster.

If you want to keep the speed constant and maintain height, then as the weight reduces you must reduce the lift produced, and you do this by decreasing C$_{Lift}$ (angle of attack). In cruising flight this will mean less drag, and therefore the power required from the engine/propeller is less. If the power is not reduced as the weight decreases, the airspeed will tend to increase.

If your aim is to maintain a constant airspeed, then you would raise the nose a little to avoid the airspeed increasing. Without any reduction in power, the aeroplane would commence a climb and gradually a new set of equilibrium conditions (balance of forces) would establish themselves for a steady climb – no longer level flight. (This is covered in the next chapter – *'Climbing'.)*

A very practical relationship for a Pilot to remember is that:

POWER + ATTITUDE = PERFORMANCE
(airspeed or rate of climb)

If you have excess power, then you can adjust the attitude so that the height remains the same and the airspeed increases; or you can hold the attitude for the same airspeed and accept an increase in the rate of climb.

Sometimes the Weight increases in flight, for instance by the formation of ice on the structure. An increased Weight will mean that increased Lift is required to maintain level flight – and once again the above discussion applies, but in reverse.

Ice-accretion means more than just a Weight addition. If ice forms on the wings, especially on the upper surface near the leading edge, it will cause a drastic decrease in the lift-producing qualities (C$_{Lift}$ for a particular angle of attack) of the wing. There will also be a significant increase in drag. The aeroplane must be flown at a greater angle of attack to return C$_{Lift}$ to its original value and so the speed will decrease unless power is added.

If ice forms on the propeller blades, it diminishes their thrust producing qualities. Icing means reduced performance all round, so avoid it if at all possible.

The Remainder of this Chapter Goes A Little Beyond What Is Required For The Aeroplane – Technical Exam But Is Included Here as Useful Reference Material.

PERFORMANCE IN LEVEL FLIGHT.

The **'Thrust Required'** for steady (unaccelerated) straight and level flight is of course equal to the drag (i.e. T = D) and so the *'Thrust Required'* curve is identical to the familiar Drag Curve (shown opposite).

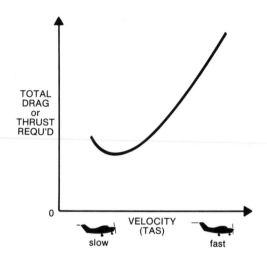

Fig.10-6. The Thrust Required Curve (or The Drag Curve).

Points to be noted from the *'Thrust Required'* or *Drag Curve* (Fig.10-6) are:

- High thrust is required at high speeds and low angles of attack to overcome what is mainly parasite drag;
- Minimum thrust is required at the minimum drag speed (which is also the best L/D ratio speed, since L = W in straight and level flight and D is at its minimum value);
- High thrust is required at low speeds and high angles of attack to overcome what is mainly induced drag (caused in the production of Lift).

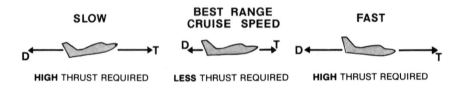

Fig.10-7. Both Low Speed and High Speed Require High Thrust.

The engine-propeller combination is a 'power-producer' (rather than a 'thrust-producer' like a jet engine). The fuel flow (in litres/hr or gallons/hr) of an engine-propeller combination is a function of power produced (rather than thrust).

Power is defined as the rate of doing work, i.e. the speed at which an applied force moves a body. Therefore the power required for flight depends on the product of:
- **thrust required;** and
- **flight velocity** (True Air Speed).

We can develop a *'Power Required'* Curve from the *'Thrust Required'* curve (shown previously) by multiplying:

the thrust required at a point on the curve x the TAS at that point,

– to give us the **Power Required** to maintain level flight at that speed. The graph will appear as shown.

These graphs are easy to understand if you take it slowly. If you want to fly at a particular velocity (TAS) then, by reading up from that TAS on the airspeed axis, the Power Curve will tell you the power that the engine-propeller must deliver. This power will supply sufficient thrust to balance the drag and maintain speed straight and level.

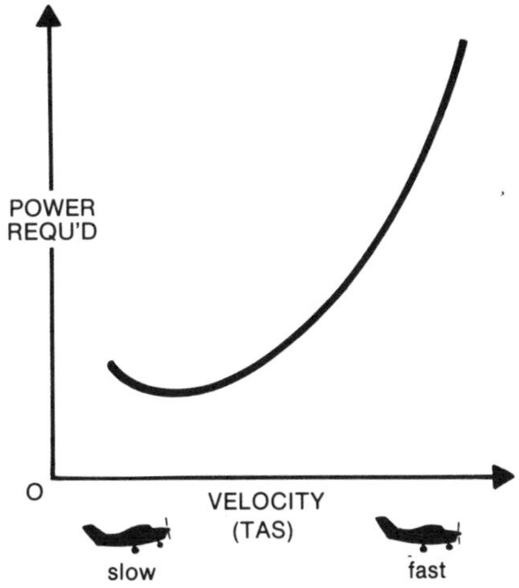

Fig. 10-8. The Power Required Curve.

In **straight and level** flight you would set the attitude for the desired airspeed (different airspeeds require different angles of attack) and adjust the power to maintain this speed.

MAXIMUM LEVEL FLIGHT SPEED.

Maximum level flight speed for the aeroplane occurs when the power available from the engine-propeller matches the power required to produce enough thrust to balance the drag at the high speed. At higher speeds, there is insufficient power available.

MINIMUM LEVEL FLIGHT SPEED.

At low speeds (slower than the minimum drag speed), higher power from the engine-propeller is required to provide thrust to balance the higher drag (mainly induced drag).

The **minimum** level flight speed is usually **not** determined by the power capabilities of the powerplant, but rather by the aerodynamic capabilities of the aeroplane. As airspeed reduces, the stalling angle is reached, or some condition of instability or control difficulty usually occurs, prior to any power limitation of the powerplant.

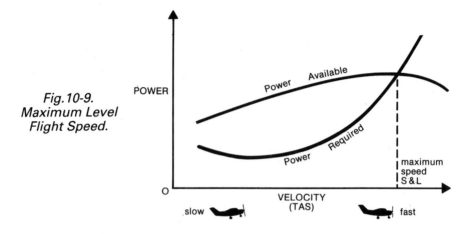

*Fig.10-9.
Maximum Level
Flight Speed.*

MAXIMUM RANGE SPEED

Maximum Range in still air is achieved at the TAS which allows:

- maximum air distance for a given fuel burn-off or, conversely,
- minimum fuel burn-off for a given air distance (i.e. the lowest 'fuel burn-off / air distance' ratio).

By converting burn-off and air distance to rates, this ratio becomes 'fuel burn-off per unit time / air distance per unit time', i.e. 'fuel flow/TAS'. Since fuel flow depends on power, the ratio becomes 'power/TAS', and maximum range will be achieved at the TAS for which this ratio is least. This occurs at the point on the Power vs TAS Curve where the tangent from the origin meets the curve. At all other points, the ratio 'power/TAS' is greater.

Power is defined as force x velocity, so:

Power Req'd = Thrust Req'd x TAS = Drag x TAS (since Thrust = Drag).

Therefore the 'Power/TAS' ratio

$= \dfrac{\text{Drag x TAS}}{\text{TAS}} =$ Drag, and will of course

have a minimum value when Drag is a minimum, i.e. Maximum Range TAS is the TAS for minimum Total Drag.

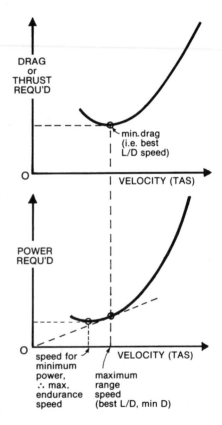

Fig.10-10. Maximum Endurance Speed and Maximum Range Speed.

THE REQUIRED PERFORMANCE IS OBTAINED USING POWER PLUS ATTITUDE.

Whilst in flight the Pilot of course does not refer to these graphs. Instead he adjusts both the power from the engine-propeller and the pitch attitude of the aeroplane to achieve the desired performance.

POWER + ATTITUDE = PERFORMANCE

To sum up, the maximum range speed shows up on the Drag Curve at the **minimum drag** point (which, as explained earlier, is also the point of **maximum L/D ratio**).

MAXIMUM ENDURANCE SPEED.

Maximum endurance means either:
- the maximum **time** in flight for given amount of fuel; or
- a given **time** in flight for the minimum amount of fuel.

It is appropriate to fly at maximum endurance speed when (for instance):
- holding overhead or near an aerodrome waiting to land; or
- carrying out a search in a specific area.

Since fuel flow for an engine-propeller combination depends upon **power** set, minimum fuel flow (and therefore maximum endurance) will occur when minimum power is required.

SPEED STABILITY IN THE HIGHER SPEED RANGE.

In the higher speed range above minimum drag speed, any minor speed fluctuation (due to say a gust or wind variation) is corrected for without any action by the Pilot. This is called 'speed stable'.

An increase in airspeed will increase the total drag, as can be seen from the Drag Curve, mainly due to an increase in parasite drag. This drag increase is not balanced by the thrust from the powerplant and so the aeroplane slows down.

A decrease in airspeed due to a gust will decrease the total drag (due mainly to a decrease in parasite drag) and the thrust, which now exceeds the drag, will cause the aeroplane to accelerate back to its original speed.

In the normal flight range (above the minimum drag speed) the Pilot does not have to be too active on the throttle since the aeroplane is 'speed stable' and, following any disturbance, will tend to return to its original equilibrium airspeed without aid from the Pilot.

LACK OF SPEED STABILITY IN THE LOWER SPEED RANGE.

At low airspeeds towards the stalling angle it is a different matter however. **If a gust causes airspeed to decrease,** the total drag increases (due to an increase in induced drag) and D now exceeds T, causing the aeroplane to slow down even further unless the Pilot responds with more power.

If a gust causes airspeed to increase, the total drag decreases (due to a decrease in induced drag) and D is now less than T, causing the aeroplane to accelerate further away from the original speed unless the Pilot reacts by reducing power.

In low speed flight (near the stalling angle), the Pilot needs to be fairly active on the power lever(s) to maintain the desired speed (e.g. in a precautionary approach to land in a short field).

The 'thrust required' for steady straight and level flight is of course equal to the 'drag', and so the curve is identical to the familiar Drag curve – which is a graph of Drag vs Speed.

STRAIGHT AND LEVEL FLIGHT AT A HIGHER ALTITUDE.

At any altitude, if the aeroplane is in steady straight and level flight the Lift must balance the Weight.

$$\text{LIFT} = C_{Lift} \times \tfrac{1}{2} \text{ Rho V-squared} \times S$$

As altitude is increased, air density Rho decreases. One way to generate the required lift and compensate for the decreased density (Rho), is for the Pilot to increase the True Air Speed 'V' so that the value of '½ Rho V-squared' remains the same as before, i.e. the decrease in Rho with altitude can be compensated for with an increase in V (the TAS) so that '½ Rho V-squared' remains the same.

The term '½ Rho V-squared' (known as Dynamic Pressure) is related to the Indicated Air Speed and the Pilot can read it in the cockpit on the Air Speed Indicator. If '½ Rho V-squared' remains the same, the Indicated Airspeed (IAS) remains the same. (A further explanation of the difference between IAS and TAS is given later in Chapter 25, *Pressure Instruments.*)

To Produce The Same Lift At A Different Altitude, You Still Fly At The Same Indicated Airspeed.

LESS DENSE AIR

IAS = TAS at SEA LEVEL (under Standard Conditions)

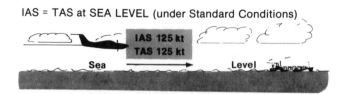

Fig.10-11. Same IAS (and Lift) At A Higher Altitude Means Higher TAS.

At higher altitudes the maximum power available from the engine/propeller will be less than at sea level.

☐ You should now tackle **Exercises 10 — Straight and Level.**

11

CLIMBING

As an aeroplane climbs, it is gaining potential energy (the energy of position, in this case due to altitude). There are two ways in which an aeroplane can do this:
- by 'zooming' (transient only, providing a temporary gain in height for a loss in airspeed);
- by a steady climb.

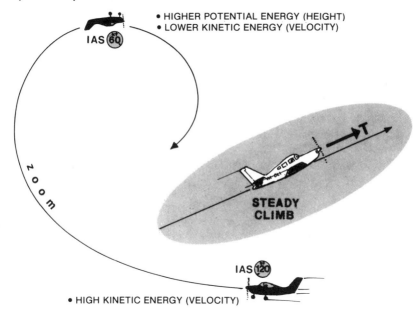

Fig.11-1. We Study The Steady Climb In Detail.

Climbing can be a temporary gain in height for a loss in airspeed, or it can be a long term steady climb.

1. Climbing by exchanging the kinetic energy of motion ($\frac{1}{2}mV^2$) for potential energy (mgh), i.e. by converting a high velocity 'V' to an increase in height 'h' by 'zooming' the aeroplane. 'Zooming' is only a transient (temporary) process, as the velocity cannot be decreased below flying speed.

    Of course, the greater the speed range of the aeroplane and the greater the need for a rapid increase in altitude, the greater the value and capability of zooming, e.g. a jet fighter being pursued at high speed can gain altitude rapidly with a zoom, or an aerobatic glider that converts the kinetic energy of a dive into potential energy at the top of a loop.

2.   Climbing by converting propulsive energy in excess of that needed for straight and level flight to potential energy. The propulsive energy of course comes from fuel energy which is converted to propulsive energy via the engine and propeller. In this way a **Steady Climb** can be maintained. It is the steady climb that is of importance to us.

FORCES IN THE CLIMB.

We make the assumption that, for the normal steady en route climb, the Thrust force acts in the direction of flight, directly opposite the Drag force.

The Lift force acts perpendicular to the direction of flight.

The Weight force acts vertically, but note how, in the climb, it has a component that acts in the direction opposing flight.

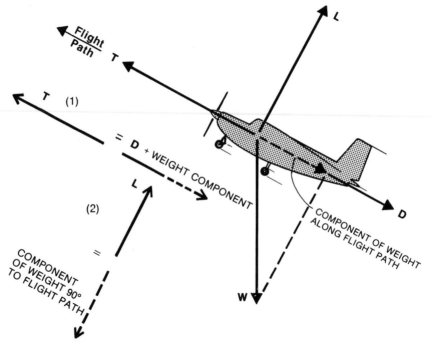

Fig.11-2. The Four Forces In A Steady Climb.

If the Pilot maintains a **Steady Climb** at a constant Indicated Air Speed, the engine-propeller must supply sufficient thrust to:
(a) overcome the Drag force;
(b) help lift the Weight of the aeroplane at a vertical speed (known as rate of climb).

In a steady climb there is no acceleration. The system of forces is in equilibrium and consequently the resultant force acting on the aeroplane is zero. An interesting point is that, when climbing, the Lift force (developed aerodynamically by the wing at 90 degrees to the direction of flight) is marginally *less* than the Weight.

The equilibrium is possible because the excess force of 'Thrust minus Drag' has a vertical component to help balance the Weight force.

In a Climb: Thrust is Greater than Drag; Lift is Less than Weight.

ANGLE OF CLIMB — (GRADIENT OF CLIMB).

The angle of climb depends directly upon the 'Excess Thrust' (the Thrust force in excess of the Drag force) and the Weight. **A heavy aeroplane** will not climb as well as when it is lighter. The higher the Weight, the poorer the climb performance.

The lower the Weight (W), the greater the angle of climb. A light aeroplane can climb more steeply than a heavy one. Thrust is used to overcome Drag. If the engine/propeller can provide Thrust in excess of that needed to balance the Drag, then the aeroplane is capable of climbing.

The greater the Thrust (T), the greater the angle of climb. The lower the Drag (D), the greater the angle of climb. For good climb-gradient capability, the aeroplane should generally be kept in a low drag configuration, e.g. flaps up. This is a very important consideration for take-off. Flap for take-off decreases the take-off run prior to lift-off, but once in flight the angle of climb may be less due to the higher Drag with flaps down.

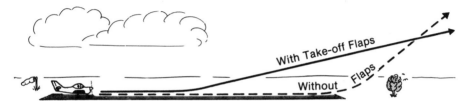

Fig.11-3. Climb Gradient May Be Less With Flaps Extended.

Since the Pilot normally cannot vary the weight significantly in flight, the only way he can improve the angle of climb is to make sure the aeroplane is 'clean' (low drag), and to fly at the speed which gives the maximum 'excess thrust' force.

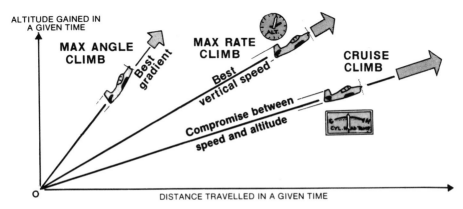

Fig.11-4. Max Rate Climb, Max Angle Climb, Cruise Climb;
Use The One That Fits The Situation.

RATE OF CLIMB.

The vertical velocity is given the name 'rate of climb'. It is usually expressed in 'feet per minute'. A Rate of Climb (RoC) of 500 fpm means that the aeroplane will gain 500 ft of altitude in one minute. Rate of Climb is shown in the cockpit on the Vertical Speed Indicator (VSI).

The greater the 'excess power', the greater the rate of climb. The lower the weight, the greater the rate of climb. The **maximum rate of climb** usually occurs at a speed somewhere near that for the best Lift/Drag ratio, and is faster than the speed for maximum angle of climb (gradient).

The **best rate** of climb speed will gain altitude in the shortest **time.**

THE VARIOUS CLIMB SPEEDS.

When mention is made of climb performance, then you must think of both angle (gradient) and rate. The Pilot will decide which type of climb he wants:

- a **Maximum Gradient (Angle) Climb** to clear obstacles – height gained for horizontal distance travelled is the consideration here. **Maximum gradient speed** (also known as **Vx**) is the lowest of the three climb speeds. It is usually carried out at high power and for only sufficient time to clear obstacles. The low speed leads to less cooling and consequently higher engine temperatures.

- a **Maximum Rate Climb** to gain height in the shortest time – to get to cruise altitude as soon as possible. **Max rate climb speed (Vy)** is usually somewhere near the speed for the best Lift/Drag ratio.

- a **Cruise Climb** is a compromise climb that allows for a high speed (to hasten your arrival at the destination) as well as allowing the aeroplane to gain height and reach the cruise altitude without too much delay. It also allows for better engine cooling due to the higher speed. The cruise climb will be a shallower climb at a higher airspeed.

Refer to your Pilot's Operating Handbook or Flight Manual for the various climb speeds for your particular aeroplane. Typically, Max Gradient Climb speed (Vx) is about 10kt less than Max Rate Climb speed (Vy).

CLIMB PERFORMANCE.

Increased Weight decreases Climb Performance.

High Temperatures decrease Climb Performance because of lower air density.

Increasing Altitude decreases Climb Performance. *'Power Available'* from the engine/propeller decreases with altitude. Even though sea-level performance can be maintained to high altitudes with supercharging, sooner or later power available starts to fall off. The climb performance, the rate of climb, and the angle of climb capability, will therefore all decrease with altitude.

The altitude at which the climb performance falls close to zero and a steady climb can no longer be maintained is known as the **'ceiling'.** In technical terms, the **Service Ceiling** is the altitude at which the steady rate of climb has fallen to just 100ft/min; the **Absolute Ceiling** is the slightly higher altitude at which the steady rate of climb achievable at climbing speed is zero (and therefore almost impossible to climb to).

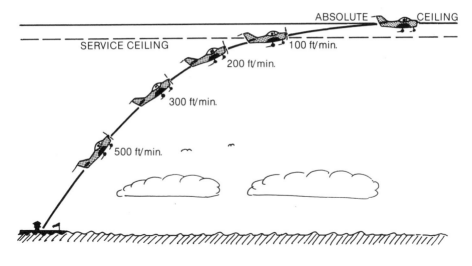

Fig.11-5. Climb Performance Decreases with Altitude.

The aeroplane's Flight Manual and Pilot's Operating Handbook will normally contain a table or graph with climb performance details.

MAXIMUM RATE OF CLIMB

CONDITIONS:
Flaps Up
Full Throttle

NOTE:
Mixture leaned above 3000 feet for maximum RPM.

WEIGHT LBS	PRESS ALT FT	CLIMB SPEED KIAS	RATE OF CLIMB - FPM			
			-20°C	0°C	20°C	40°C
1670	S.L.	67	835	765	700	630
	2000	66	735	670	600	535
	4000	65	635	570	505	445
	6000	63	535	475	415	355
	8000	62	440	380	320	265
	10,000	61	340	285	230	175
	12,000	60	245	190	135	85

Note that RoC decreases with temperature

Note that climbing IAS for best RoC decreases with altitude

Note that RoC decreases with altitude

Fig.11-6. A typical Climb Performance table.

Note that:
- Climb performance decreases as air density decreases (i.e. at high altitudes and high air temperatures); and
- Climbing IAS for best performance decreases as altitude is gained.

Flying Too Fast Decreases Climb Performance. If you fly faster than the recommended speeds, say at the speed where the Thrust = Drag, and the power available = power required, then there is no *excess thrust* to give you an angle of climb, and no *excess power* to give you a rate of climb. The aeroplane can only maintain level flight. At higher speeds, there would be a thrust deficiency and a power deficiency, causing the aeroplane to have an angle of descent and a rate of descent, rather than a climb.

Flying Too Slowly Decreases Climb Performance. Flying slower than the recommended speeds will cause the *excess thrust* and *excess power* to be less than optimum (due to the high drag and high angles of attack that it must overcome) and so climb performance will be decreased. At low speed the engine/propeller loses efficiency and produces less thrust. The aeroplane at low speed has a high drag (mainly induced drag). Eventually the aeroplane will come up against the stall if flown too slowly.

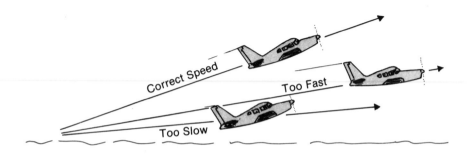

Fig.11-7. Fly At The Correct Climb Speed For The Best Performance.

Climbing flight is possible in the speed range where the engine-propeller can produce sufficient power to provide *excess thrust* (i.e. Thrust in excess of Drag). On the low speed side you may be limited by the stalling angle.

High Ambient Temperatures Decrease Climb Performance. If the temperature is high then the air density (Rho) is less. The engine/propeller and the airframe will both be less efficient and so the performance capability of the aeroplane is less on a hot day than on a cold day.

THE EFFECT OF A STEADY WIND ON THE CLIMB.

The aeroplane flies in the medium of air and it 'sees' only the air. Rate of climb will not be affected by a steady wind. Similarly, the angle of climb through the **air** will not be affected by a steady wind.

However, if we consider the angle of climb (or the gradient of climb) over the **ground**, i.e. the **flight path,** a headwind increases the effective climb gradient over the ground and a tailwind decreases the effective climb gradient over the ground.

Taking-off into wind has obvious advantages for obstacle clearance – it improves your clearance of obstacles on the ground.

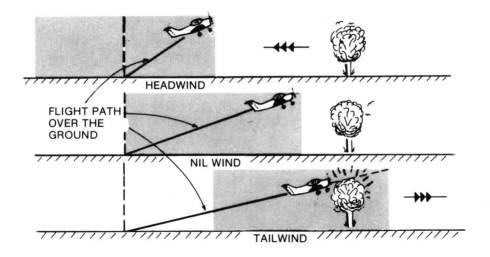

Fig.11-8. Wind Affects Flight Path Achieved Over the Ground.

THE EFFECT OF WINDSHEAR.

A windshear is defined as a change in wind direction and/or speed in space. A windshear is a **changing** wind. This can mean a wind whose speed alters as you climb or descend to a different altitude. It can mean a wind whose direction changes from place to place or it can mean an updraft or a downdraft that an aircraft has to fly through. Windshear is generally understood to mean a wind change within a short distance or a short space of time.

Overshoot Effect.

Flying into an updraft will increase the rate of climb and will increase the angle of climb relative to the ground. **Flying into a downdraft** will have the opposite effect.

Due to its own inertia (or resistance to change) an aeroplane **flying into an increasing headwind** will want to maintain its original speed relative to the ground. Thus the effect of flying into an increasing headwind will be to increase the airspeed temporarily.

Attempting to maintain the correct climbing speed by raising the nose will lead to increased climb performance (only transient as the shear is flown through).

In this way, the climb performance will increase when flying into an increasing headwind, a decreasing tailwind or into an updraft. The aeroplane has a tendency to *overshoot* the original flight path, i.e. go above it, or to gain airspeed temporarily – hence the term *Overshoot Effect*.

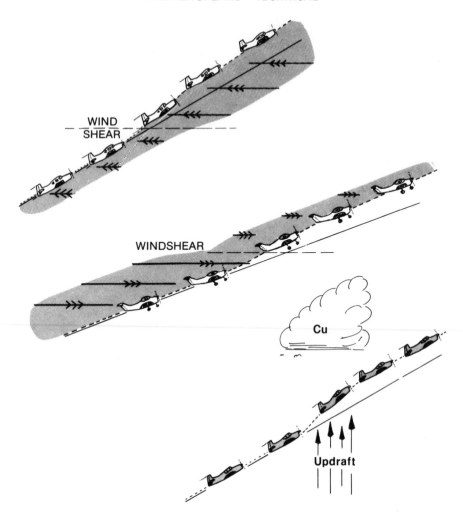

Fig.11-9 Overshoot Effect is a (Temporary) Gain in Performance.

Once again, the advantages of taking-off into wind are seen. Wind strength usually increases as you climb away from the ground, so you would normally expect an aircraft taking-off into wind to climb into an increasing headwind. This leads to increased climb performance over the ground, i.e. a steeper climb-out gradient over ground obstacles.

Undershoot Effect.

Taking-off downwind, the aeroplane would normally climb into an area of increasing tailwind. Due to its inertia, the aeroplane would temporarily tend to maintain its original speed over the ground, leading to a decreased airspeed. To maintain the target climb speed, the Pilot would have to lower the nose. Climb performance, both rate and gradient, would fall off.

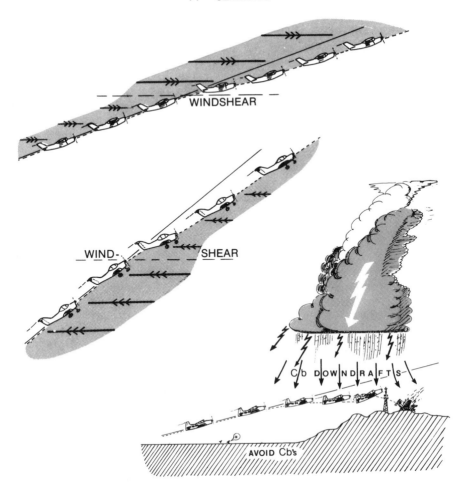

Fig.11-10. Undershoot Effect is a Decrease in Performance.

Exactly the same effect of decreased climb performance will occur flying into an increasing tailwind, a decreasing headwind, or a downdraft. The aeroplane will tend to fall below the original flight path, or to lose speed, hence the term *Undershoot Effect*.

An **Initial Overshoot Effect** (for example, when flying into an increasing headwind coming out of the base of a cumulonimbus storm cloud) may be followed by a **Severe Undershoot Effect** as you fly into the downdraft and then the rapidly increasing tailwind. So **Avoid Flying Near Cb clouds**.

☐ Now attempt **Exercises 11 — Climbing**.

12

DESCENDING

If the aeroplane is descending, with no Thrust being produced by the engine/propeller, only three of the four main forces will be acting on the aeroplane – **Weight, Lift** and **Drag** – and in a steady glide these three forces will be in equilibrium as the resultant force acting on the aeroplane is zero.

Suppose that the aeroplane is in steady straight and level flight and the Thrust is reduced to zero. The Drag force is now unbalanced and will act to decelerate the aeroplane – unless a descent is commenced where the component of the Weight force acting in the direction of the flight path is sufficient to balance the Drag. This effect allows the aeroplane to maintain airspeed by descending and converting potential energy due to its altitude into kinetic energy (motion).

Resolving the forces in the flight path direction shows that a component of the Weight force acts along the flight path in a descent, balancing Drag and contributing to the aeroplane's speed.

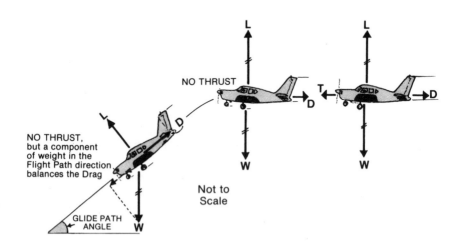

Fig.12-1. In a Glide, a Component of Weight Balances the Drag.

Resolving the forces vertically, the Weight is now balanced by the Total Reaction (i.e. the resultant of the Lift and Drag).

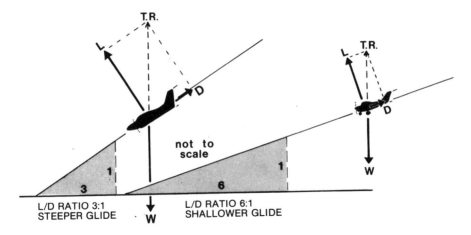

Fig.12-2. Lift and Drag Balance the Weight in a Steady Glide.

Notice that the greater the Drag force, the steeper is the glide. The shallowest glide is obtained when, for the required Lift, the Drag is least, i.e. at the best Lift/Drag ratio.

If the L/D is high, the angle of descent is shallow, i.e. a flat gliding angle and the aeroplane will glide a long way.

If the L/D is poor (low), with a lot of Drag being produced for the required Lift, then the aeroplane will have a large angle of descent, i.e. a steep glide angle and will therefore not glide very far.

Two points can be made here:

1. An 'aerodynamically efficient' aeroplane is one which can be flown at a high Lift/Drag ratio. It has the capability of gliding further for the same loss of height than an aeroplane that is flown with a lower L/D ratio.

2. The same aeroplane will glide furthest through still air when it is flown at the angle of attack (and airspeed) that gives its best L/D ratio. This angle of attack is usually about 4 degrees.

Because the Pilot cannot read angle of attack in the cockpit, flying at the recommended gliding or descent speed (in the Pilot's Operating Handbook) will ensure that the aeroplane is somewhere near this most efficient angle of attack.

If the aeroplane is flown at a smaller angle of attack (and therefore faster), the L/D ratio will be less and the aeroplane will not glide as far – it will 'dive' towards the ground faster and at a steeper angle.

If the aeroplane is flown at a greater angle of attack (lower airspeed) than that for the best L/D ratio, the L/D ratio will be less and therefore the optimum glide angle will not be achieved. This may be deceptive for the Pilot – the nose attitude may be quite high, yet the aeroplane is descending steeply.

The Wrong Airspeed (too fast or too slow) Steepens the Glide.

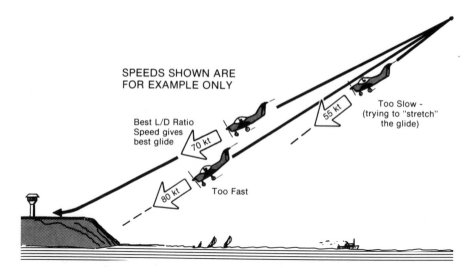

Fig.12-3. The Flattest Glide is Achieved at Best L/D Airspeed.

To Glide the Furthest in Still Air, Fly at the Recommended Airspeed (and therefore Angle of Attack) that Gives the Best Lift/Drag Ratio.

If you are gliding at the recommended airspeed and it looks like you will not reach the desired point, **do not** raise the nose to increase the glide distance. **It will not work!** The higher nose attitude may give the appearance of stretching the glide, but in fact it will **decrease** your gliding distance.

FLAPS STEEPEN THE GLIDE (i.e. increase the Glide Angle).

Any flap settings will increase the Drag more than the Lift and consequently the L/D ratio is lower. This gives a steeper glide.

The **Smaller Flap Settings** increase Lift significantly, with only a small increase in Drag – hence the name *'Lift Flaps'* sometimes given to low flap settings.

The **Larger Flap Settings** give large increases in Drag with only a small increase in the Lift – hence the name *'Drag Flaps'* for the larger flap settings. Large flap settings will give a much steeper glide. (The lower nose attitude required with flap extended give the Pilot much better visibility.)

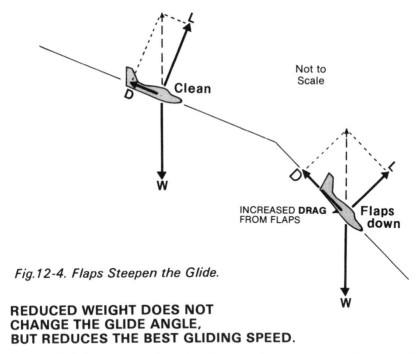

Fig.12-4. Flaps Steepen the Glide.

REDUCED WEIGHT DOES NOT CHANGE THE GLIDE ANGLE, BUT REDUCES THE BEST GLIDING SPEED.

If the weight is less, the aircraft will have a lower airspeed at any particular angle of attack compared to when it is heavy.

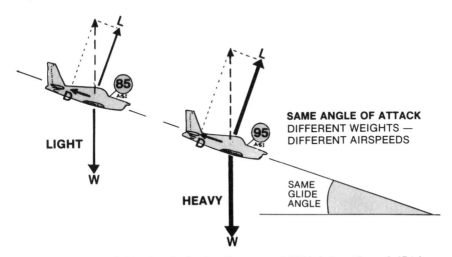

Fig.12-5. Best Glide Angle is the Same at All Weights (Best L/D) but Airspeed Must be Lower at Lower Weights.

At the angle of attack for the best L/D ratio (and therefore for the best glide), the airspeed will be lower but the glide angle the same. This also means that the rate of descent for the aeroplane when it is lighter will be less.

123

The recommended gliding speed (stated in the Flight Manual and the Pilot's Operating Handbook) is based on **maximum all-up-weight.** The variation in weight for most training aircraft is not sufficiently great to significantly affect the glide if the recommended glide speed is used at all times – even though, theoretically, a slightly lower glide speed could be used when lightly-loaded.

The recommended descent speed in your Pilots Operating Handbook will be suitable for all normal weights of your light training aircraft.

GLIDING DISTANCE OVER THE GROUND.

A Headwind Reduces the Gliding Distance Over the Ground, even though it does not affect the gliding distance through the air, nor does it affect the rate of descent.

- **'Glide Angle'** means **'relative to the air mass';**
- **'Flight Path'** means **'relative to the ground'.**

The aeroplane 'sees' only the air in which it is flying. In the case illustrated below we can see three identical glides through an air mass – same airspeed, same nose attitude, same angle of attack, same rate of descent (therefore same time taken to reach the ground) in all three cases. The only difference is that the air mass is moving over the ground in three different ways and carrying the aeroplane with it. **The Ground Distance covered differs.**

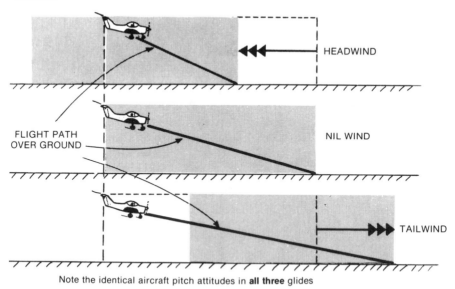

HEADWIND

FLIGHT PATH
OVER GROUND

NIL WIND

TAILWIND

Note the identical aircraft pitch attitudes in **all three** glides

Fig.12-6. More Ground is Covered Gliding With a Tailwind and Less With a Headwind.

A Tailwind Increases the Gliding Distance Over the Ground (even though it does not affect the gliding distance relative to the air mass nor the rate of descent).

ESTIMATION OF GLIDING DISTANCE IN STILL AIR.

If you refer to the diagram of the forces acting in a glide you will see that, for the best L/D ratio, the gliding distance is furthest.

If the L/D ratio is 5:1, the aeroplane will glide 5 times as far as it will descend. If you are 1 nautical mile high (about 6,000 ft), you will glide for about 5 nautical miles. If you are at about 12,000 ft (2 nm), you will glide approximately 10 nm.

An aeroplane with a L/D ratio of 12:1 will glide 12 times further horizontally **in still air** than the height it descends.

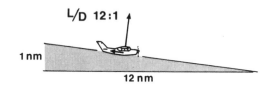

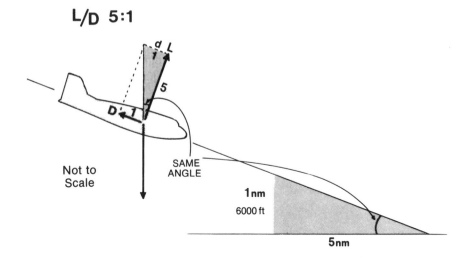

Figs.12-7a & b. 'Air Distance/Altitude' is the Same Ratio as 'Lift/Drag'.

POWER FLATTENS THE DESCENT.

If the engine/propeller is producing power, then the Thrust force will help overcome part of the Drag force. The result is that the aeroplane will have a shallower descent angle and a lower rate of descent than in the power-off glide. Of course, with sufficient power, the descent angle may be zero, i.e. the aeroplane will fly level. With even more power, the aeroplane may climb.

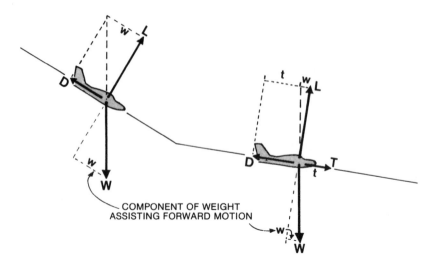

COMPONENT OF WEIGHT
ASSISTING FORWARD MOTION

Fig.12-8. Adding Power Will Flatten the Descent.

FLAPS STEEPEN THE DESCENT.

If you are sinking beneath your desired flight path, the correct procedure is to apply some power and not to just raise the nose (which, as we saw, simply worsened the situation by steepening the glide). Any change in power will require some small adjustments to the nose attitude for the desired airspeed to be maintained.

If you are descending above your desired descent path, there are two things that you can do:
• reduce the Thrust, and/or
• increase the Drag (extend the flaps, lower landing gear). Usually when you extend the flaps, a lower nose attitude is required.

☐ Now attempt the **Exercises 12 — Descending.**

126

13

TURNING

A moving body tends to continue moving in a straight line at a constant speed (as stated in Newton's First Law of Motion). To change this state (either to change the speed or to change the direction, i.e. to accelerate the body) a force must be exerted on the body (Newton's Second Law of Motion).

A body constrained to travel in a curved path has a natural tendency to travel in a straight line (and therefore to fly off at a tangent). To keep it on its curved path, a force must continually act on the body forcing it towards the centre of the turn. This force is called the **Centripetal Force.**

Holding a stone tied to a string, your hand supplies a *'Lift'* force equal and opposite to the Weight of the stone. If you swing the stone in a circle, your hand supplies not only a vertical force to balance the Weight but also a centripetal force to keep the stone turning. The total force exerted through the string is greater and you will certainly feel the increase.

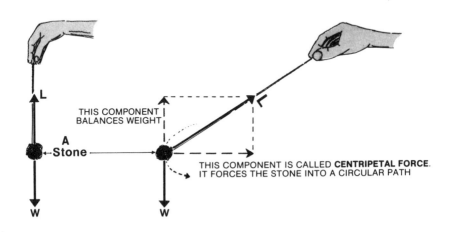

Fig.13-1. Centripetal Force Pulls A Body Into A Turn.

To turn an aeroplane, some sort of force towards the centre of the turn needs to be generated. This can be done by banking the aeroplane and tilting the Lift force so that it has a sideways component.

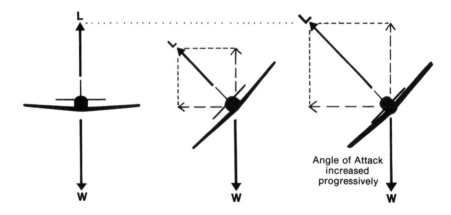

Fig.13-2. By Banking, Lift from the Wings Provides a Centripetal Component.

Flying straight and level, the Lift force from the wings balances the Weight of the aeroplane. If you turn the aeroplane, the wings still need to supply a vertical force to balance the Weight (unless you want to descend) plus a centripetal force towards the centre of the turn to keep the turn going.

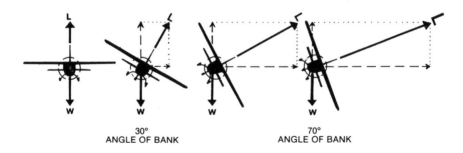

Fig.13-3. To Maintain Altitude - the Steeper the Bank, the Greater the Lift Force Required from the Wings.

The Lift force in a level turn will be greater than the Lift force when flying straight and level. To develop this increased Lift force at the same airspeed, the angle of attack of the aerofoil must be increased by backward pressure on the control column.

The steeper the level turn, the greater the Lift force required. Note that a Pilot turns the aeroplane using **Ailerons** (to put the bank on) and **Elevator** (to increase the angle of attack and increase the lift generated). The Pilot uses the ailerons to maintain the desired bank angle and the elevator to maintain the desired altitude. The rudder (as yet) has not been necessary.

The stability designed into the aeroplane may make it resist turning, and the application of a little rudder (left rudder for a left turn and vice versa) helps bring the tail around and turn the nose into the turn, i.e. the rudder is used to *'balance'* the turn.

The Pilot of course is forced into the turn along with the aeroplane and he feels this as an increase in the force exerted on him by the seat – it feels like an *'apparent'* increase in his weight.

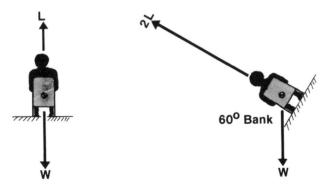

Fig.13-4. The Steeper The Bank, the Greater The 'G-Forces'.

THE LOAD FACTOR ON THE WINGS IS INCREASED IN A TURN.

Straight and level, the wing produces a Lift force equal to the Weight, i.e. L = W. The load factor is said to be 1. The Pilot experiences a force from the seat equal to his normal weight. He feels it as '1g'.

In a banked turn of 60 degrees, the wings produce a Lift force equal to double the Weight, i.e. L = 2W. This means the loading on the wings is doubled when compared to straight and level flight, i.e. each square metre of wing has to produce twice as much lift in a 60 degree banked turn as it does in straight and level flight. The Pilot experiences a force from the seat equal to twice his weight, i.e. 2g. The load factor is said to be 2.

The load factor is the ratio of the Lift force produced by the wings compared to the Weight force of the aeroplane.

LOAD FACTOR = LIFT/WEIGHT

= WING LOADING IN MANOEUVRE/WING LOADING S & L

At angles of bank beyond 60 degrees, the Lift force generated by the wings must increase greatly so that its vertical component can balance the weight – otherwise height will be lost.

Increased Lift from the wings means increased wing loading and an increased **Load Factor**. We can show this in a curve of *'load factor'* vs *'bank angle'*.

NOTES:

- In a 30 degree banked turn you will experience 1·15g load factor, i.e. the wings will produce 15% more lift than when straight and level, and the Pilot will feel 15% heavier.

- At 60 degrees bank angle, the load factor is 2, i.e. the wings have to produce a lift force equal to double the weight to maintain height. The 'g-force' is 2g, and the Pilot will feel twice as heavy.

- A 70 degrees bank, the load factor is 3.

- At 80 degrees bank angle, the load factor is 6. The wing is required to produce 6 times the lift as in straight and level flight for the aeroplane to be capable of an 80 degree banked turn without losing height – this requires a very high performance aeroplane.

- In a 90 degree banked turn, the Lift force is horizontal, and, even if of infinite size, would have no vertical component to balance the weight. Therefore height cannot be maintained.

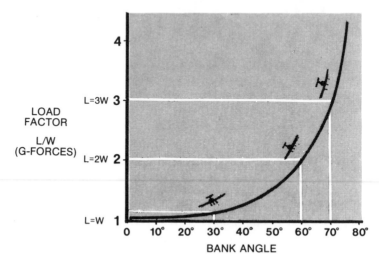

Fig.13-5. 'Load Factor' versus 'Bank Angle'.

EXTRA THRUST IS REQUIRED IN A TURN TO MAINTAIN HEIGHT AND AIRSPEED.

In a turn, an **increased Lift** from the wings is required to maintain height. This is achieved by the Pilot applying back-pressure on the control column to increase the angle of attack.

The steeper the bank angle, the greater the angle of attack and back-pressure required. As we saw in our discussion on Drag, an increase in the angle of attack will lead to an increase in the induced drag. If a constant airspeed is to be maintained in a level turn, an increase in thrust to balance the increased drag in a turn is required.

If extra thrust is not added the airspeed will reduce in a level turn. Airspeed could be maintained by allowing the aeroplane to lose height, i.e. to trade potential energy for kinetic energy.

STALLING ANGLE OF ATTACK OCCURS AT HIGHER AIRSPEEDS IN A LEVEL TURN.

In a turn, the angle of attack has to be greater than at the same speed in straight and level flight. This means that the stalling angle of attack will be reached at a higher speed in a turn – the steeper the angle of bank, the higher the airspeed at which the stalling angle of attack is reached.

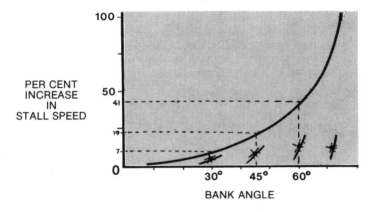

Fig.13-6. 'Percentage Increase in Stall Speed' versus 'Angle of Bank'.

- At 30 degrees bank angle, the stall speed is increased by 7% over the straight and level stall speed.
- At 45 degrees bank angle, the stall speed is increased by 19%.
- At 60 degrees bank angle, the stall speed is increased by 41%.
- At 75 degrees bank angle, the stall speed is increased by 100%.

If your aeroplane stalls at 50 kt straight and level, then in a 60 degree banked turn it will stall at (141% of 50 kt =) 71 kt – quite a significant increase. In steep turns, you will feel the onset of the stall buffet at these high speeds.

THERE IS A TENDENCY TO OVERBANK IN LEVEL AND CLIMBING TURNS.

To commence a level turn, the Pilot applies bank with the ailerons. Once the aircraft starts turning, the outer wing travels faster than the inner wing and so generates more lift. The tendency is for the bank angle to increase.

To overcome the tendency to overbank in a level turn, once in the turn the Pilot may have to hold-off bank.

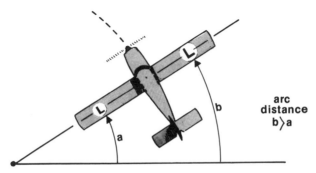

Fig.13-7. Outer Wing Moves Faster and Generates More Lift – Hold-Off Bank In A Level Or Climbing Turn.

In a climbing turn, the outer wing travels faster and produces more Lift than the inner wing.

There is a second effect to consider also: that as the inner and outer wings climb through the same height, the outer wing travels a greater horizontal distance as it is on the outside of the turn.

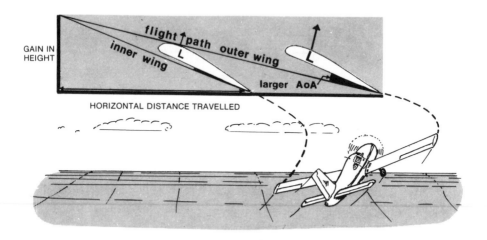

Fig.13-8. Tendency to Overbank In A Climbing Turn.

The angle of attack of the outer wing is greater than that for the inner wing and so the Lift produced by the outer wing in a climbing turn will be even greater. Once in a climbing turn, the Pilot may have to hold-off bank to avoid the turn becoming too steep – there is no need to plan this, just observe what is happening and hold the desired bank angle with the ailerons.

UNDERBANK/OVERBANK IN A DESCENDING TURN.

In a descending turn, the outer wing travels faster and wants to produce more lift than the inner wing, but, due to the descent, the inner wing travels a smaller horizontal distance for the same height loss when compared to the outer wing and so has a larger angle of attack. Therefore, the inner wing tends to produce more Lift – and the two effects may cancel out.

In a descending turn, the pilot may have to hold bank on (or off), depending upon the aircraft. There is no need for the Pilot to plan this – just keep your eyes open and hold the desired bank angle with the ailerons.

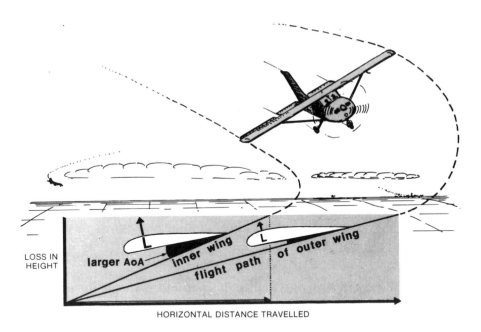

Fig.13-9. Underbanking Tendency – Due to Larger AoA on Inner Wing in a Descending Turn. (Higher Speed of Outer Wing May Compensate.)

BALANCING THE TURN.

The Pilot banks the aeroplane using the **Ailerons,** and exerts back pressure on the control column, using the **Elevator** to increase the angle of attack and the lift produced. The natural stability of the aeroplane will cause it to turn its nose into the turn, due to the sideslip effect on keel surfaces behind the Centre of Gravity.

There is an effect that tends to turn the nose away from the turn – known as **Aileron Drag.** As the outer aileron goes down into the high pressure area under the wing, it not only causes increased Lift (to bank the aeroplane by increasing the angle of attack of the up-going wing), but also suffers increased induced drag.

This increase in Drag on the up-coming wing causes the nose to yaw in the direction opposite to the turn – and this is neither comfortable nor efficient. The aircraft is said to be *'slipping'* into the turn. The rudder ball will be on the down-side of the turn. The Pilot will feel as though he is slipping down to the low side of the aircraft – (see Fig.13-10).

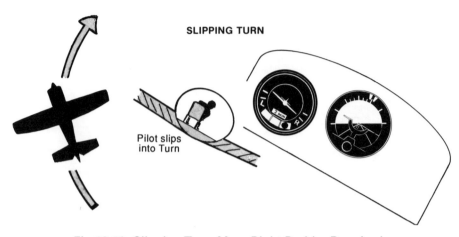

Fig.13-10. Slipping Turn: More Right Rudder Required.

By pressuring the rudder ball back into the centre with the appropriate foot, the nose of the aircraft (and the tail) is yawed so that the longitudinal axis of the aeroplane is tangential to the turn. The rudder ball will be in the centre and the turn will be balanced. The Pilot will feel comfortable in the seat and not feel as though he is slipping down into the turn.

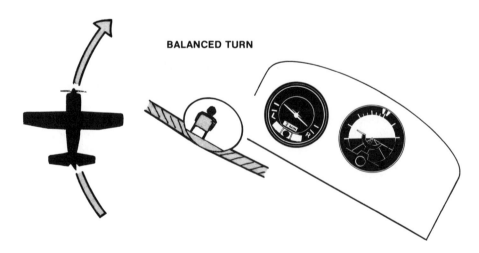

Fig.13-11. A Comfortable and Balanced Turn.

If the tail tends to *skid* onto the outside of the turn, the rudder ball (and the Pilot) will also be thrown to the outside. If the ball is out to the left, use left rudder pressure to move it back into the centre.

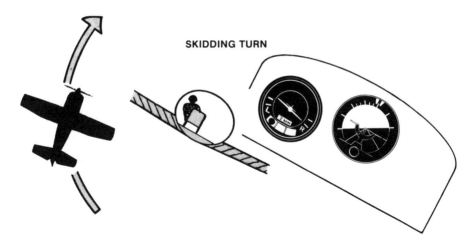

Fig.13-12. Too Much Right Rudder in this Case – a Skidding Turn.

CONSTANT ANGLE TURN

An aeroplane in a 30° banked turn will travel around different circular paths depending upon its airspeed. At low speed the turn is tighter (the radius of turn is smaller) than at high speed.

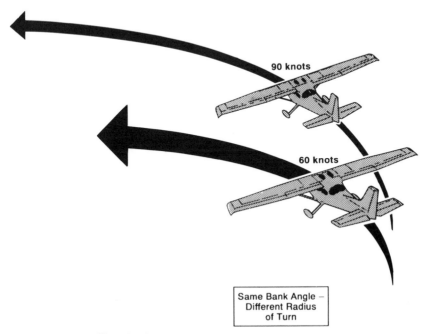

Same Bank Angle –
Different Radius
of Turn

Fig.13-13.

CONSTANT RADIUS TURN.

To fly a turn of the same radius at a higher speed requires a greater bank angle.

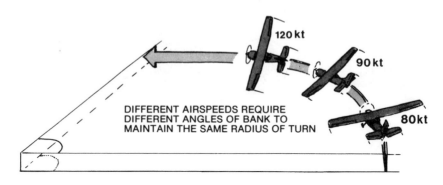

Fig.13-14.

CONSTANT SPEED TURN.

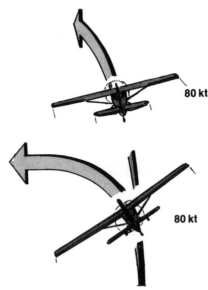

Fig.13-15.

At a constant airspeed, the greater the bank angle, the tighter the turn (the smaller the radius of turn) and the greater the rate of turning (in degrees per second).

CONSTANT RATE TURN

The rate of turning of an aircraft in degrees per second is important. Instrument Flying usually requires Rate 1 turns, which means the turns are made at a rate of 3 degrees per second:
- 180° in 1 minute;
- 360° in 2 minutes.

A Rate 1 turn at a higher airspeed requires a steeper angle of bank.

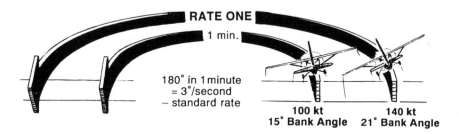

Fig.13-16. A Rate 1 Turn requires Steeper Bank at Higher Speed.

An easy way to estimate the bank angle (in degrees) required for a Rate 1 turn is: $^1/_{10}$ of the airspeed in knots, plus $^1/_2$ of this.

For example, *the required bank angle for a Rate 1 turn at 120 kt* is 120/10 = 12, plus $^1/_2$ of this (12 ÷ 2 =) + 6 = 18°.

A Rate 2 turn is 6°/second.

❏ You now have the knowledge to make **Exercises 13 – Turning**, seem easy.

14

STALLING

The airflow around an aerofoil varies as the angle of attack is increased. For most conditions of flight this flow is **Streamline** flow and Bernoulli's Theorem applies – 'increased velocity goes hand in hand with decreased static pressure'. The increased flow velocity (especially over the upper surface of the wings) leads to decreased static pressure – and so a **Lift** force is generated. Drag is also present.

The **Lifting Ability (or Coefficient of Lift)** of the aerofoil increases as the angle of attack increases – but only up to a 'Critical Angle'.

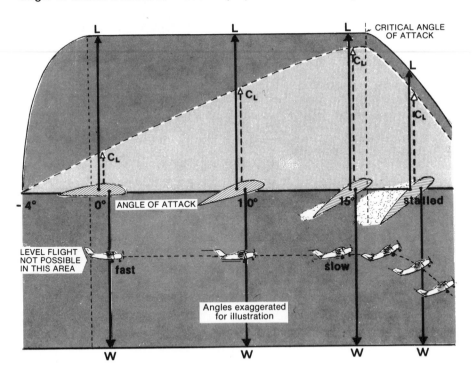

Fig.14-1. An Aerofoil reaches 'C$_{Lift\ max}$' at the Critical Angle.

Ideally the airflow around an aerofoil is streamline. In real life the streamline flow breaks away (or separates) at some point from the aerofoil surface and becomes turbulent. At low angles of attack this separation point is towards the rear of the wing and the turbulence is not significant.

At higher angles of attack the separation point moves forwards. As the angle of attack is increased, a critical angle is reached beyond which the separation point will suddenly move well forward causing a large increase in the turbulence over the wing.

The formation of low Static Pressures on the upper surface of a wing (the main contributer to the generation of the Lift force) is reduced by the breakdown of streamline flow. Turbulent flow does not encourage the formation of low static pressure areas.

The lifting ability of a wing (i.e. Coefficient of Lift, C_L) decreases markedly beyond this critical angle of attack as a result of the breakdown of streamline flow.

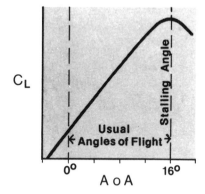

Fig.14-2. The 'C$_{Lift}$' Curve.

The significant breakdown of streamline flow into turbulence over a wing is called **stalling** of the aerofoil. The **critical angle** or **stalling angle** of attack is where C_L reaches its maximum value and beyond which C_L decreases markedly.

Beyond the stalling angle the Centre of Pressure (which has been gradually moving forward as angle of attack increases) suddenly moves rearwards and there is also a rapid increase in Drag.

RECOGNITION OF THE STALL.

Approaching the stalling angle of attack, the streamline flow breaks down over parts of the wing and turbulent air flows back over the tailplane. The airframe may shake or *'buffet'* as a result – known as **Pre-Stall Buffet or Control Buffet.**

At the stall, the decrease in Lift will cause the aeroplane to **Sink.** The rearwards movement of the Centre of Pressure will cause the **Nose to Drop.**

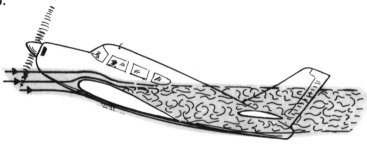

Fig.14-3. Turbulent Flow Over the Tailplane.

Stalling Is Associated With A Particular Angle Of Attack.

For most training-type aircraft, the stalling angle of attack is somewhere about 15-16 degrees. 'C_Lift maximum' occurs at the stalling angle of attack, but beyond it 'C_Lift' decreases.

To recover from a stall, the angle of attack must be reduced. This is accomplished by moving the control column forward.

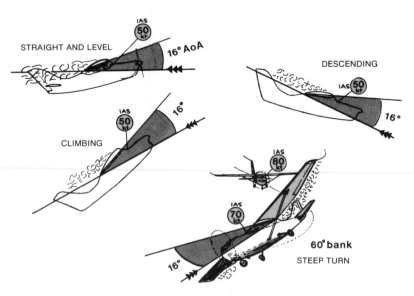

Fig.14-4. Stalling Occurs at the Same Stalling Angle in all Phases of Flight.

Fig.14-5. High Speed Stall.

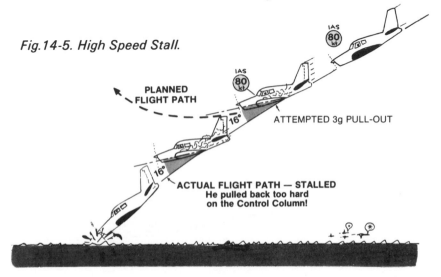

'STALLING ANGLE' AND THE ASSOCIATED 'STALLING SPEED'.

The (hopefully now familiar) Lift Formula is:

$$\text{LIFT} = C_{\text{Lift}} \times \tfrac{1}{2} \text{ Rho V-Squared} \times S$$

Of the factors that determine the value of the **Lift** force, the Pilot can only readily change **Angle of Attack (C_{Lift})** and **Indicated Air Speed** ($\tfrac{1}{2}.\text{Rho}.V^2$). He can change these by altering the attitude and/or the power. For a given aerofoil:

Stalling Occurs at a Particular Angle of Attack.

When the Aerofoil reaches this Critical Angle of Attack – IT WILL STALL.

It does not matter what the airspeed is. If the stalling angle is 16 degrees for that aerofoil, it will stall at 16 degrees – irrespective of the airspeed.

A specific aerofoil will stall at a particular angle of attack, however the stall may occur, for example, at:

- 50 kt straight and level for an aeroplane at maximum weight;
- 45 kt straight and level when it is light;
- 54 kt in a 30 degree banked turn;
- 70 kt in a 60 degree banked turn;
- 80 kt if you experience 3g pulling out of a dive.

(Do not bother learning these figures.)

Stalling depends directly upon Angle of Attack and **not** upon airspeed.

There is, however, some connection between *'Angle of Attack'* and *'Indicated Air Speed'*. Their precise relationship depends upon:
- lift produced by the aerofoil;
- weight;
- load factor;
- bank angle;
- power;
- flap (changes aerofoil shape and C_{Lift}).

'STALLING SPEED' VARIES WITH 'THE SQUARE ROOT OF LIFT'.

On a number of occasions we have mentioned that 'square laws' are common in nature. The natural principles involved in the production of Lift by an aerofoil are no exception:

$$\text{LIFT} = C_{\text{Lift}} \times \tfrac{1}{2} \text{ Rho } \textbf{V-squared} \times S.$$

Indicated Air Speed (IAS) is directly proportional to True Air Speed (TAS or V) and can be written as 'IAS = k x TAS' or 'IAS = k x V', where k is a constant at a particular altitude and whose value depends upon the ratio of air density (Rho) at sea level to the ambient air density at the aircraft's altitude. (There is no need for you to remember this – it is discussed in more detail under the heading of 'The Air Speed Indicator'.)

We can now write our familiar Lift equation as:

LIFT is a function of C_L x $(IAS)^2$.

At the **stalling angle,** the Coefficient of Lift reaches its maximum value, written as C_{Lmax} and so the relationship at the stall becomes:

LIFT **at the stall** is a function of C_{Lmax} x $(IAS\ stall)^2$

Since C_{Lmax} will be constant for the particular aerofoil, the relationship can be simplified even further to:

LIFT **at the stall** is a function of $(IAS\ stall)^2$.

In other words, the square of the Indicated Stalling Speed depends upon the Lift that the wing has to generate. Then, taking the square root of each side of this relationship, we can say:

Indicated Air Speed **at the stall** depends on the square root of the Lift.

This really means that:

---

anything that requires the generation of extra Lift (such as extra weight or 'pulling g' in a manoeuvre like turning) will cause an increase in the Indicated Stalling Speed.

Mathematically these two statements may be written:

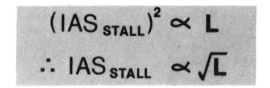

$$(IAS_{STALL})^2 \propto L$$
$$\therefore IAS_{STALL} \propto \sqrt{L}$$

$\propto$ means "IS PROPORTIONAL TO" or "VARIES DIRECTLY WITH".

The airspeed that the performance of the aeroplane depends upon, and the airspeed that the Pilot can read in the cockpit, is the Indicated Air Speed (IAS). At the stall:

Stalling Speed Depends Upon The Square Root Of The Lift Required And The Lift Required Depends On The Weight And The Load Factor.

If the Lift required is increased by 44% to $1 \cdot 44$ times the original Lift, then the stalling speed will increase by 'the square root of $1 \cdot 44$', i.e. $1 \cdot 20$ times the original S & L stalling speed – an increase of 20%. A straight and level stall speed of 50 kt would become 60 kt (a 20% increase) if, for some reason, a 44% increase in Lift were required.

An increased Lift (over and above that needed for straight and level flight, where L = W) is required for a steep level turn, or for pulling out of a dive or, indeed, whenever there is an increased load factor (L/W) and 'g forces' are experienced. Another name for 'load factor' or 'g-forces' is **Dynamic Loading.**

The stalling angle of attack remains the same (as always for a particular aerofoil), but the stalling speed increases whenever the dynamic loading or load factor increases.

Now, of course, a Pilot cannot sit in the cockpit and calculate the 'square root' of this and that – but he **does** need to be aware that:

Stalling Speed Increases When Load Factor Increases.

If You Feel 'g-forces', then Stalling Speed Is Increased.

ESTIMATING THE STALLING SPEED WHEN 'g' IS BEING PULLED (i.e. when the Load Factor is greater than 1).

If the Load Factor is greater than 1, then the stalling speed will be increased. Whilst the Pilot performing manoeuvres in flight does not have time to carry out precise calculations, he must be aware of the fact that stall speed will be increased quite significantly on occasions.

Pulling 4g (outside the limit of most training aeroplanes), the stalling speed is doubled, i.e. it increases by a factor equal to the square root of 4, which is 2.

Pulling 2g (say in a 60° banked turn), the stalling speed is increased by a factor equal to the square root of 2, i.e. 1·41, which is an increase of 41%. This is illustrated on the graph below.

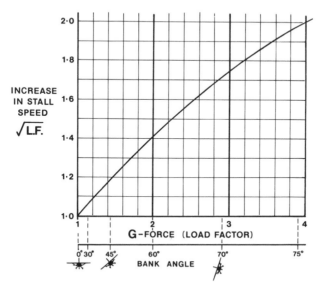

EXAMPLES FOR USE OF CHART:

1. AT 2-G (LOAD FACTOR 2) THE STALL SPEED INCREASES BY 1.41, AND AT 3-G BY 1.73 TIMES THE LEVEL STALL SPEED FOR THE AEROPLANE

2. IN A 60° BANK TURN THE LOAD FACTOR IS 2 AND THE STALL SPEED INCREASE IS BY 1.41.

Fig.14-6. 'Increase In Stall Speed' is a Function of 'g'; Stalling Speed Increases in a Turn (at which time Load Factor Increases).

As increased Lift is required in a turn (because the Lift force is tilted and yet a vertical component equal to Weight must still be produced), the Lift in a turn must exceed the Weight, and therefore the Load Factor exceeds 1.

The steeper the turn, the greater the load factor ('g forces') and the higher the stalling speed. It is very useful and practical for the Pilot to know the percentage increase in straight and level stalling speed at a few bank angles.

In a 30 degree bank, lift must be increased from 100% to 115% of the straight and level value, i.e. to 1·15 times the original value. Therefore the stall speed will increase to (the square root of 1·15 =) 1·07 times its original straight and level value, i.e. a 7% increase.

A 50 kt stalling speed S & L becomes 54 kt in a 30 degree banked turn.

- **In A 30 degree Banked Turn, Stalling Speed Increases by 7%.**

In a 45 degree banked turn, Lift is 1·41 times greater than the Lift when straight and level. The Load Factor is 1·41. Therefore the stalling speed will increase to (the square root of 1·41 =) 1·19 times its original value. A 50 kt stall speed S & L becomes 60 kt in a 45 degree banked level turn.

- **In A 45 Degree Banked Level Turn, Stalling Speed Increases By 19%.**

In a 60 degree banked turn, Lift must be doubled to retain altitude, i.e. L is increased to 2 times its original value. The Load Factor is 2. Therefore the stalling speed will increase to (the square root of 2=) 1·41 times its original straight and level value. A 50 kt S & L stalling speed becomes 71 kt in a 60 degree banked turn.

- **In A 60 Degree Banked Turn, Stalling Speed Increases By 41%.**

STALLING SPEED VARIES WITH SQUARE ROOT OF THE LOAD FACTOR, for a given weight.

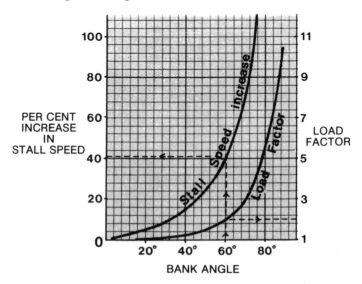

Fig.14-7. Stall Speed Increases With Load Factor.

Any time the **Lift** force from the wings is increased, the **Load Factor** increases and the **Stalling Speed** increases. This will occur in turns, when pulling out of dives, in gusts and in turbulence.

What happens to stall speed can be represented graphically as in Fig.14-7. (There is no need to remember these graphs, but you should be able to interpret them. You may be presented with them in exams.) Just enter the graph with the information you have, and read off what you want to find.

STALLING SPEED INCREASES WITH WEIGHT,
(stalling angle of attack stays the same).

In straight and level flight, sufficient **Lift** must be generated to balance the **Weight.** A heavier aeroplane means an increased Lift force is required.

We saw earlier that:

'stalling speed' varies with the 'square root of lift'.

If the weight decreases 20% to only 0·8 of its original value, then the stall speed will decrease to (the square root of 0·8=) 0·9 times its original value (9 x 9 = 81, so the square root of 80 is close to 9, and the square root of 0·8 is close to 0·9).

If the stalling speed at maximum all-up-weight (say 2,000 kg) was stated in the Flight Manual to be 50 kt, then at 1,600 kg (20% less, and only 80% of the max. weight), the stalling speed is only 90% of the original stalling speed (a drop of 10%), i.e. 45 kt.

Similarly, an increase in weight will give an increase in stalling speed.

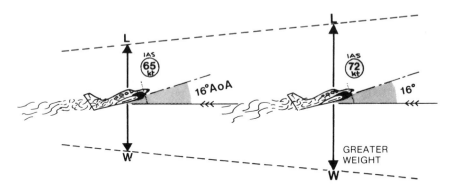

Fig.14-8. Stall Speed Is A Function Of Weight.

The Flight Manual States The Stalling Speed Straight and Level, Power-Off, at Maximum Allowable All-Up-Weight.

STALLING INDICATED AIR SPEED (IAS) DOES NOT VARY WITH ALTITUDE.

Stalling speed is a function of 'C$_{Lift\,max}$' (which occurs at the stalling angle) and 'Indicated Air Speed' (which is related to '½.Rho.V-squared').

A variation in altitude will not affect 'C$_{Lift\ max}$' and so the stalling angle will be reached (straight and level) at the same stalling Indicated Air Speed.

STALLING SPEED IS LESS IN A POWER-ON STALL.

With power-on, the slipstream adds kinetic energy (of motion) to the airflow.

The separation of the airflow from the upper surface of the wing is delayed, and so the stall occurs at a lower Indicated Air Speed.

As the stalling angle is approached with power on, the high nose attitude allows the Thrust to have a vertical component which will partially support the Weight. Therefore, the wings are off-loaded a little and less Lift is required from them. Less Lift means a lowered stalling speed.

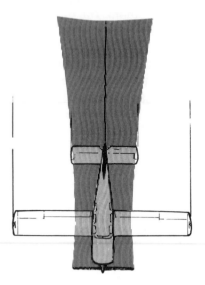

Fig.14-9. Slipstream Can Lower Stalling Speed.

As the power-on stall is approached, the slipstream will provide a fast airflow over the tailplane – the rudder and elevator will remain effective, but the ailerons, not being affected by the slipstream, will become 'sloppy' or less-effective.

A POWER-ON STALL MAY BE MORE DEFINITE AND ACCOMPANIED BY A WING-DROP.

If the slipstream encourages the generation of Lift from the inner parts of the wing, then the outer sections of the wing may stall first. Any uneven production of Lift from the outer sections of the two wings will lead to a rapid roll.

STALLING FIRST AT THE WING ROOT IS PREFERABLE TO STALLING AT THE WING-TIP.

If there is an uneven loss of lift from the outer sections of the wings near the tips by one of them stalling first, then a strong rolling moment is set up due to the long moment arm from the outer sections of the wing to the CG. Also, the effectiveness of the ailerons is affected.

Stalling at the wing-roots is preferable – it allows the control buffet over the tailplane (due to the turbulent air from the inner sections of the wing) to be felt, whilst the outer sections of the wings are still producing Lift and the ailerons may still be effective. An uneven loss of Lift on the inner sections, if one wing stalls ahead of the other, does not have as great a rolling moment.

The wing can have **Washout** – a lower angle of incidence (and therefore a lower angle of attack) at the wing-tip when compared to the wing-root. This means that the wing-root will reach the stalling angle prior to the wing-tip. (Washout also helps to reduce the induced drag from wingtip vortices.)

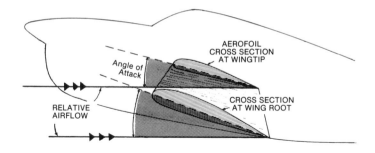

Fig.14-10. In-built Washout Causes the Wingtip to Stall Later than the Root.

Stalling at the wing-root first can be achieved in a number of ways by the designer. For instance, small metal plates can be placed at the inboard leading edges to encourage the early onset of the stall at the wing-root.

FLAP EXTENSION DECREASES THE STALLING SPEED.

Extending flaps gives us a new aerofoil shape with an increased 'CLift max', i.e. the 'new' aerofoil has a greater lifting ability and can support the same load at a lower speed. The airspeed can decrease to a lower value before 'CLift max' is reached and the wing stalls.

The lowering of stalling speeds is the main advantage of flaps. It makes for safe flight at lower speeds – very useful for take-offs, landings (shorter fields) and low speed searches. Extending of trailing edge flaps allows lower nose-attitudes. Not only is visibility increased, but the stalling angle will be reached at a lower nose-attitude also.

The stall with flaps extended may be accompanied by a wing-drop. Use rudder to pick it up, not aileron. Because of the increased drag with flaps extended, any speed loss, especially with power-off, could be quite rapid, with little advance warning to the Pilot of an impending stall.

In the stall with flaps down, turbulence over the tailplane may cause very poor control from the elevator – known as 'blanketting' of the elevator. Some training aircraft have a T-tail with the tailplane high on the fin to avoid blanketting of the elevator in the stall.

STALL WARNING DEVICES.

Most aircraft are fitted with a device such as a horn, flashing red light or a whistle to warn of an impending stall. Such a device is only secondary to the aerodynamic 'stall warnings' that you must learn to recognise, such as stall buffet, decreasing speed, 'g forces' or load factor, less-effective controls, etc.

ICE-ACCRETION INCREASES STALLING SPEED.

Ice accretion has two effects:

1. Ice increases weight, and so the stall speed will be increased.

2. Much more significantly, ice-accretion on the wings (particularly the front half of the upper surface where most of the Lift is generated) will cause a breakdown of streamline flow at angles of attack well below the normal stalling angle. Therefore stalling will occur at higher speeds.

Any ice at all, even if only the texture of very fine sandpaper, should be removed from the wing prior to flight. It pays to remove any accumulation of such things as insects and salt from the wing leading edges for the same reason.

THE SPIN

The spin is a condition of stalled flight in which the aeroplane describes a spiral descent path, following a yaw with a wing drop on the point of stall. In a spin the aeroplane is:
- stalled;
- rolling;
- yawing;
- pitching;
- sideslipping; and
- rapidly losing height.

HOW A SPIN DEVELOPS.

A Spin is a condition of stalled flight, so the first prerequisite is that the wings be at a high angle of attack. This is achieved by moving the control column progressively back, as in a normal stall entry.

A wing drop is essential to enter a spin and this may occur by itself or (more likely) be induced by the Pilot yawing the aeroplane with rudder or 'misusing' the ailerons just prior to the aeroplane stalling. **During a premeditated spin entry,** as the Pilot yaws the aeroplane near the point of stall:

- **the outer wing speeds up and generates more Lift,** causing it to rise; its angle of attack decreases, taking it further from the stalling angle; and

- **the inner wing slows down and generates less Lift,** causing it to drop; its angle of attack increases and the dropping wing stalls (or, if already stalled, goes further beyond the stalling angle).

'Autorotation' will commence through the dropping wing becoming further stalled, with a consequent decrease in Lift and increase in Drag. The aeroplane will roll, a sideslip will develop and the nose will drop. If no corrective action is taken, the rate of rotation will increase and a spin will develop. It will be an unsteady manoeuvre with the aeroplane appearing to be very nose-down. The rate of rotation may increase quite quickly and the Pilot will experience a change of g-loading.

An aeroplane will not usually go straight from the stall into a spin. There is usually a transition period which may vary from aeroplane to aeroplane, typically taking two or three turns in the unsteady and steep autorotation mode, before settling into a fully-developed and stable spin.

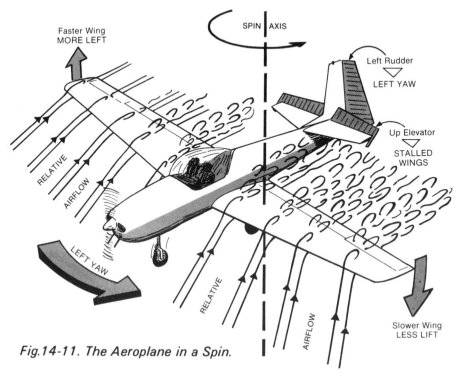

Fig.14-11. The Aeroplane in a Spin.

ON SOME AEROPLANES, 'MISUSE' OF AILERONS CAN CAUSE A SPIN.

Trying to raise a dropped wing with opposite aileron may have the reverse effect when the aeroplane is near the stall. If, as the aileron goes down, the stalling angle of attack is exceeded, instead of the wing rising it may drop quickly, resulting in a spin. This is the spin entry technique on some aircraft types.

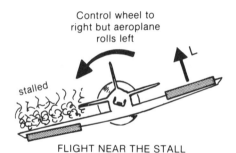

Fig.14-12. Inducing a Spin With Opposite Aileron.

It is not a requirement that full spins be carried out in Private Pilot training, although they will be practised to the incipient spin stage before the wings pass through 90°. Pilots training in approved aeroplanes may have the opportunity to practise fully-developed spins.

☐ Now tackle **Exercises 14 — Stalling,** prior to moving on (eagerly) to the next Section.

2

AIRFRAME, ENGINES AND SYSTEMS

15

THE AIRFRAME

The major components of an aeroplane are:
- the fuselage;
- the wings;
- the tail assembly;
- the flying controls;
- the landing gear (or undercarriage);
- the engine and propeller.

The **fuselage** forms the body of the aeroplane to which the wings, tail, engine and landing gear are attached. It contains a cabin with seats for the Pilot and passengers, plus the cockpit controls and instruments, and may also contain baggage lockers.

The fuselage of many modern training aircraft is of **semi-monocoque** construction, a light framework covered by a skin (usually aluminium) that carries much of the stress. It is a combination of the best features of a strut-type structure, in which the internal framework carries almost all of the stress, and a monocoque structure which, like an egg-shell, has no internal structure, the stress being carried by the 'skin'.

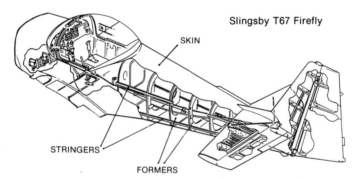

Slingsby T67 Firefly

SKIN

STRINGERS

FORMERS

Fig.15-1. Typical Semi-Monocoque Construction.

The **wings** are designed to generate lift and are exposed to heavy loads, well in excess of the total weight of the aeroplane in manoeuvres. Wings generally have one or more internal **spars** attached to the fuselage and extending to the wingtips. The spars carry the major loads, which are upward bending where the lift is generated and downward bending where they support the fuselage and the wing fuel tanks.

152

In addition to the spar(s), some wings also have external **struts** to provide extra strength by transmitting some of the wing loads to the fuselage.

Ribs, roughly perpendicular to the spar(s), assisted by stringers running parallel to the spars, provide the aerofoil shape and stiffen the skin which is attached to them. The ribs transmit loads between the skin and the spar(s).

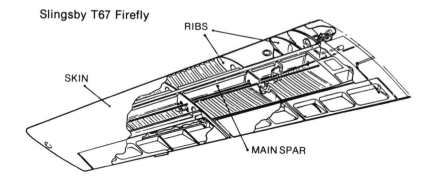

Slingsby T67 Firefly

RIBS

SKIN

MAIN SPAR

Fig.15-2. Spars, Ribs and Formers in the Wing.

Ailerons are fitted at the outer trailing edge of each wing, and move in opposite directions to allow the Pilot to control roll. **Wing Flaps** are fitted on the inner trailing edges and are lowered in unison to increase the lifting ability of the wing, or to increase its drag. The wings in most aeroplanes also contain **fuel tanks.**

The **tail unit** is generally built similar to the wings and consists of a vertical and horizontal stabiliser to which the **rudder** and **elevator** are attached. There are variations in design, some aeroplanes having a stabilator *(all-flying tailplane),* others having a *ruddervator* (combined rudder and elevator) in the form of a *butterfly tail,* and yet others having a high T-tail. The elevator (and, on some aircraft, the rudder) will have a trim tab. This enables the Pilot to remove prolonged loads on the controls aerodynamically.

The main flight controls (elevator, ailerons and rudder) are operated from the cockpit, usually via an internal system of cables and pulleys. Turnbuckles may be inserted in the cables to allow adjustment of their tension. This should only be done by qualified personnel.

To protect the control surfaces from excessive movement in flight and on the ground, there are usually *'stops'* fitted to the structure as well as stops in the flight control system itself, (e.g. to physically limit the control column movement).

The **landing gear** (or *undercarriage*) supports the weight of the aeroplane when it is on the ground and may be of either the tricycle type with a nosewheel or the tailwheel type. Most tricycle landing gear aeroplanes are fitted with nosewheel steering through the rudder pedals and almost all aeroplanes have main wheel brakes. Advanced aeroplanes have a retractable landing gear; most training aeroplanes have a fixed landing gear. The landing gear and brakes are considered in detail in Chapter 24.

The **engine** is usually mounted on the front of the aeroplane, and separated from the cockpit by a **firewall**. In most training aeroplanes, the engine drives a **fixed-pitch propeller.**

TIE-DOWN

At the end of a flight, consideration should be given to the safety of the aeroplane if it is to be left outside overnight or if strong winds or a weather change for the worse is forecast. A normal procedure is to chock the wheels and to tie the aeroplane down.

Ensure that a **Tie-Down Kit** is carried on overnight flights or whenever you think a tie-down might be necessary. A typical tie-down kit will contain at least:
- 3 tie-down ropes of adequate length;
- 3 pegs;
- a hammer or mallet;
- a minimum of two wheel chocks.

Park the aeroplane into wind or facing into an expected wind, **set the brakes to 'Park'** (refer to the Flight Manual to check if this is recommended for your aeroplane) and **chock the wheels.** Chock both in front of and behind the wheels to prevent movement in any direction.

On some aeroplanes the nosewheel or the tailwheel can be locked straight, (e.g. the *Dakota DC-3* and an agricultural aircraft called the *Thrush Commander*). As well as assisting in directional control on the ground during take-off and landing, having the wheel locked straight helps prevent the tail from swinging around when parked in a wind – so lock the tail-wheel when parking, if your aeroplane has this facility.

Lock the Control Surfaces. Some aircraft have a control column lock (e.g. *Cessna 172*), which, by locking the control column, holds the control surfaces firm. Other aircraft have external locks that can be fitted to prevent control surface movement, (e.g. aileron locks for a *Fokker Friendship*). **Care must be taken pre flight to ensure the removal of any control surface lock** – locked control surfaces are not an aid to worry-free flight and may lead to disaster!

Tie the Aeroplane Down. There are tie-down rings designed into the modern aeroplane somewhere along the wings, at the tail and possibly at the nose. **In a field** you may have to drive pegs into the ground and attach the tie-down ropes to them. The ropes attached to the wing should be angled forward and out, and the pegs driven in in such a manner as to provide the best anchor. Some operators prefer **two ropes** from each wing point, one angled forward and out at 45° and the other angled rearward and out at 45°.

At permanent tie-down points on aerodromes, there are often tie-down anchors – large concrete blocks with metal rings or, better still, tie-down points already installed in the tarmac itself.

Nylon rope is better than manila rope, as it is more elastic and will not shrink when wet. **Tie the aircraft down 'loosely, but not too loosely',** using a 'non-slip' knot. **With manila tie-down ropes, leave a bit of 'slack'.** If the ropes are too tight, especially if it rains and the ropes shrink, stresses are placed on the airframe.

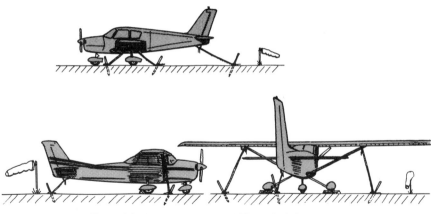

• Parked facing into-wind.   • Wings tied-down.
• Chocks prevent aircraft moving back due to wind.
• Tail rope stops aircraft moving forward.

Fig.15-3. How to Tie-Down the Aircraft.

If the ropes are too loose, a wind could lift the aeroplane over the wheel-chocks, or cause it to jerk against the rope, placing stress on the airframe or pulling the peg out of the ground. Ensure that the **tie-down ropes are of adequate strength.**

Cover the Pitot Head. Any contamination, (e.g. wasps) in the pitot tube or static vent can cause erroneous readings of the pressure instruments (air speed indicator, altimeter). Once again, a pre-flight inspection should ensure their removal prior to flight.

Cover the engine or the engine-openings to prevent birds making a nest around the oil cooler and so on. Birds can build a complete nest within a matter of hours – and they will. Over-heating, possibly even an in-flight fire, can result.

Lock the doors and windows after securing any loose equipment in the cockpit or in the cabin.

NOTE: For full instructions on tie-down, etc., of your particular aeroplane, refer to the Pilot's Operating Handbook.

CABIN FIRE.

Although a rare event, cabin fire is a possibility, especially if passengers are careless with cigarettes. As well as causing distress to the Pilot and passengers, fire can damage the aeroplane structure. A cabin fire should be quickly extinguished with the fire extinguisher and the cabin window or air vents opened to ensure that there is adequate ventilation and to remove the fumes from the fire and the extinguisher.

CABIN VENTILATION, HEATING AND DEMISTING.

Pilot comfort is very important for safe and efficient operations and, for this reason, most aeroplanes have built-in ventilation and heating systems. Clear forward vision is also important, so provision is usually made for hot air to be directed onto the windshield by the Pilot when necessary to demist or defrost it.

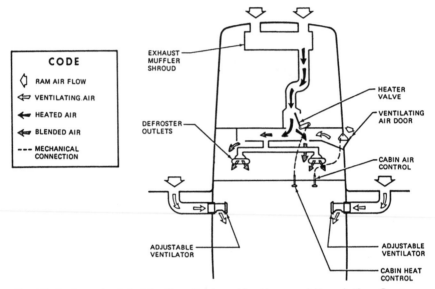

CODE

◊ RAM AIR FLOW

⇐ VENTILATING AIR

⬅ HEATED AIR

⬅ BLENDED AIR

- - - MECHANICAL CONNECTION

EXHAUST MUFFLER SHROUD

DEFROSTER OUTLETS

HEATER VALVE

VENTILATING AIR DOOR

CABIN AIR CONTROL

ADJUSTABLE VENTILATOR

ADJUSTABLE VENTILATOR

CABIN HEAT CONTROL

Fig.15-4. A typical Cabin Ventilation, Heating and Demisting System.

Good **ventilation** is essential to ensure that the Pilot has an adequate supply of fresh air. Directing flow from the cabin air vents over passengers is also very useful in preventing and combatting motion sickness.

Cabin heating should be used to keep the cockpit environment comfortable enough to be able to fly in shirt sleeves. Many cabin heating systems use warm air from around the engine and exhaust manifold (where the air is heated) and allow the Pilot to direct it to various points in the cabin. Temperature control can be achieved by mixing the heated air with the cooler ventilating air. Cabin heating is necessary in cold climates, but it may also be necessary in warm climates when flying at high altitudes (since, on average, temperature decreases by about 2°C per 1000 ft gain in altitude).

There is a risk in using cabin heating that the Pilot should be aware of. Any leaks in the heat exchanger/exhaust manifold area could allow **carbon monoxide** from the engine to enter the cabin in the heating air. Carbon monoxide is produced during combusion and is a **colourless, odourless, but very dangerous, gas.** It displaces oxygen from the blood and may cause:

- headache;
- dizziness;
- nausea;
- deterioration in vision;
- a slower breathing rate;
- unconsciousness; and
- death.

'Engine Smells' from other exhaust gases associated with the carbon monoxide are a warning and, if carbon monoxide is suspected in the cabin, shut off all cabin heat, stop all smoking and increase the supply of fresh air through vents and windows. If oxygen masks are operational, then don them. Under normal conditions, a Pilot should always ensure some fresh and cool ventilating air is mixed with the heated air.

Demisting and/or Defrosting of the windscreen may be necessary from time to time when the aeroplane has been flying in cool and moist conditions. Hot air directed onto the inside of the windshield should clear at least some of it from mist or, in icing conditions, frost or ice.

☐ Now complete **Exercises 15 — The Airframe** please.

16

THE AEROPLANE ENGINE

Aeroplanes can be powered by a variety of engines, the two fundamental types being **Piston Engines** and **Gas Turbines** (jets). The jet engine will not be considered in this manual. The piston engine can be designed in various ways, many of which are suitable for aircraft.

Older types of engines often had the **cylinders arranged radially** around the crankshaft, e.g. the Pratt and Whitney radial engine in the *Dakota (DC-3)*, the *de Havilland Beaver* and the *Harvard,* and the Bristol Centaurus engine in the *Tempest MkII* fighter.

The *de Havilland Beaver* and the *Grumman Ag-Cat* are two types with radial engines, which are still in use today, because these engines have an excellent power/weight ratio in the high power range required in aircraft of this type, i.e. agricultural work.

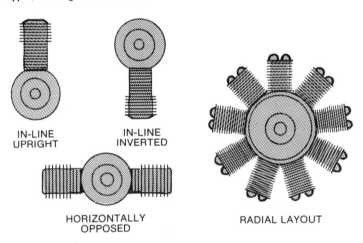

IN-LINE
UPRIGHT

IN-LINE
INVERTED

HORIZONTALLY
OPPOSED

RADIAL LAYOUT

Fig.16-1. Common Cylinder Layouts in Aircraft Engines.

Some aircraft have in-line engines, where the cylinders are arranged in one line – the same basic design as in many cars. Some of the earliest aeroplanes had upright, in-line engines, with the cylinder head at the top of the engine and the crankshaft/propeller shaft at the bottom, e.g. the *de Havilland Cirrus Moth.*

Raising the thrust line to a suitable position, due to design requirements, put the cylinders and the main body of the engine in a very high position. This obscured the Pilot's vision and prevented effective streamlining.

Another problem with a low crankshaft/propeller shaft is the ground clearance of the propeller, requiring long struts for the main wheels. The easiest way to solve this problem is to invert the engine and have the crankshaft/propeller shaft at the top of the engine, quite different to automotive engine design where the crankshaft is always at the bottom. Many aircraft have inverted in-line engines, e.g. *Tiger Moth, Chipmunk.*

There are other possibilities as well, such as the **V-engines** and the **H-engines** (V and H describing the layout of the cylinders) which were used in military aircraft (e.g. *Spitfires,* early model *Tempests*) requiring high horsepower (2–3,000 horsepower) from a compact engine.

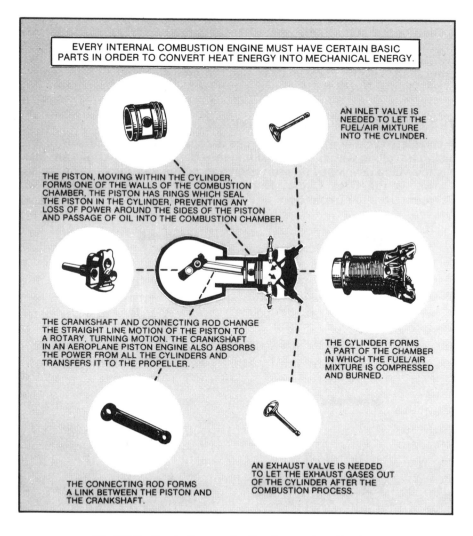

EVERY INTERNAL COMBUSTION ENGINE MUST HAVE CERTAIN BASIC PARTS IN ORDER TO CONVERT HEAT ENERGY INTO MECHANICAL ENERGY.

AN INLET VALVE IS NEEDED TO LET THE FUEL/AIR MIXTURE INTO THE CYLINDER.

THE PISTON, MOVING WITHIN THE CYLINDER, FORMS ONE OF THE WALLS OF THE COMBUSTION CHAMBER. THE PISTON HAS RINGS WHICH SEAL THE PISTON IN THE CYLINDER, PREVENTING ANY LOSS OF POWER AROUND THE SIDES OF THE PISTON AND PASSAGE OF OIL INTO THE COMBUSTION CHAMBER.

THE CRANKSHAFT AND CONNECTING ROD CHANGE THE STRAIGHT LINE MOTION OF THE PISTON TO A ROTARY, TURNING MOTION. THE CRANKSHAFT IN AN AEROPLANE PISTON ENGINE ALSO ABSORBS THE POWER FROM ALL THE CYLINDERS AND TRANSFERS IT TO THE PROPELLER.

THE CYLINDER FORMS A PART OF THE CHAMBER IN WHICH THE FUEL/AIR MIXTURE IS COMPRESSED AND BURNED.

THE CONNECTING ROD FORMS A LINK BETWEEN THE PISTON AND THE CRANKSHAFT.

AN EXHAUST VALVE IS NEEDED TO LET THE EXHAUST GASES OUT OF THE CYLINDER AFTER THE COMBUSTION PROCESS.

Fig.16-2. Basic Parts of a Reciprocating Engine.

The usual engine found in the modern light aeroplane is the reciprocating piston engine, with the cylinders (4, 6 or 8 of them) laid out in a **horizontally-opposed manner.**

BASIC PRINCIPLES OF THE PISTON ENGINE.

The reciprocating engine has a number of cylinders in which pistons move up and down (hence the name *reciprocating engine*). In each cylinder a fuel/air mixture is burned, the heat energy causing the gases to expand and drive the piston down the cylinder. This is a conversion of chemical energy (in the fuel) to heat energy to mechanical energy.

The piston is connected by a rod to a shaft, which it turns. This *connecting rod*, or *conrod*, converts the up-down motion of the piston into a rotary motion of the crankshaft, which transmits the power generated by the engine to the propeller. Light aircraft with fixed-pitch propellers (and most with constant speed propellers) have the propeller directly coupled to the crankshaft, i.e. the crankshaft is also the propeller shaft. The propeller produces the *Thrust* force so necessary for powered flight.

THE CYCLES OF A FOUR-STROKE ENGINE.

A complete cycle of this sort of engine is comprised of four strokes of the piston travelling within the cylinder, hence the name **four-stroke engine.** Nicholas *Otto* developed this sort of engine, so the four-stroke cycle is also known as the **Otto Cycle.** The four strokes are: **(1) Induction; (2) Compression; (3) Expansion** (or Power Stroke); **(4) Exhaust.**

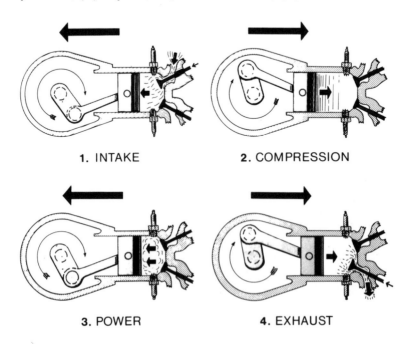

1. INTAKE   2. COMPRESSION

3. POWER   4. EXHAUST

Fig.16-3. The Four Strokes of a Reciprocating Engine.

160

In the **Intake (or Induction) Stroke,** the fuel/air mixture is 'sucked' or induced to flow into the cylinder. The piston, moving from the top to the bottom of the cylinder, decreases the pressure in the cylinder which causes air to flow in through the induction system, through the carburettor, where fuel is metered into the airflow to give a fuel/air mixture, and on into the cylinder via the inlet manifold and (open) inlet valve.

The higher pressure in the manifold(s) from the carburettor forces the fuel/air mixture to flow through the inlet valve, which has been opened, into the cylinder, where the pressure is decreasing due to the increasing volume.

Early in the **Compression Stroke,** the inlet valve is closed and the piston moves back towards the top (or the head) of the cylinder. This increases the pressure of the fuel/air mixture – and because of the compression, the temperature of the fuel/air mixture rises.

As the piston is completing the compression stroke, the fuel/air mixture is ignited by an electrical discharge between the electrodes of a spark plug and a controlled burning commences. This causes the gases to expand and exert a pressure on the piston. The piston, which has now passed the top of its stroke, is driven back down the cylinder in the **Power Stroke.**

Just prior to the completion of the power stroke, the exhaust valve opens and then, as the piston returns to the top of the cylinder in the **Exhaust Stroke,** the burned gases are forced out of the cylinder to the atmosphere via the exhaust manifold.

As the piston is approaching the cylinder head again, whilst the last of the burned gases is being exhausted, the inlet valve opens in preparation for the next induction stroke. And so the cycle continues . . .

Note that, in this one complete Otto cycle of the engine, of the four strokes of the piston, only one stroke provided power but the crankshaft (which carries this power to the propeller) has rotated twice.

To increase the power developed by the engine and to allow smoother operation, the engine has a number of cylinders whose power strokes occur at different positions during the revolution of the crankshaft. The spacing of these power strokes is equal, so that evenly spaced impulses are imparted to the crankshaft. Thus, in a full Otto cycle of a six cylinder engine the crankshaft would, in two revolutions, receive the power from six different power stokes – one per cylinder.

In an engine with four cylinders (quite common in light aircraft), in two revolutions the crankshaft would receive four impulses of power. The more evenly these impulses of power from each of the cylinders are spread, the more efficient the transfer of power, and the smoother the running and the less the vibration.

VALVES AND VALVE TIMING.

The *inlet valve*, through which the fuel/air mixture is taken in, and the *exhaust valve*, through which the burned gases are exhausted, must open and close at the correct times with respect to the movement of the individual piston.

To achieve this there is a **Camshaft** which is gear-driven by the crankshaft. The camshaft rotates at half crankshaft speed and operates *rocker arms* and *push rods* which push the appropriate valve open (against spring pressure) at what has been determined by the designer to be the most suitable time in the cycle.

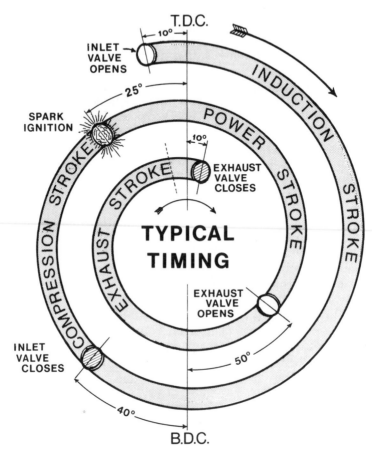

Fig.16-4. Typical Valve Timing in the Four Stroke Cycle.

A typical engine speed while cruising is 2400 *revolutions per minute* – abbreviated to *rpm* (or maybe *rev/min*).

Each inlet valve will open once in the four strokes of the piston, i.e. once in every two revolutions of the the crankshaft. The same will apply to each exhaust valve.

The inlet valve, and the exhaust valve, must open and close once in every two revolutions of the crankshaft. Therefore the camshaft rotates at half engine speed. At 2400 rpm, each valve will have to open and close 1200 times – 1200 times in 60 seconds means 20 times a second – quite amazing.

The power that the engine can develop depends upon how much fuel/air mixture can be induced through the inlet valve during the intake stroke – and the time involved is, as you can see, extremely short.

By opening the inlet valve just prior to the piston reaching *top-dead-centre* (TDC), and by not closing it until the piston has gone just past *bottom-dead-centre* (BDC) following the induction stroke, allows maximum time for the intake of the fuel/air mixture to occur. This is called **valve lead** and **valve lag.** Similarly, the exhaust valve opens just prior to the piston reaching BDC on the power stroke and remains open until a little after the piston passes TDC for the exhaust stroke and commences the induction stroke.

Notice that, for a brief period at the start of the induction stroke, the burned gases are still being exhausted through the still-open exhaust valve while a fresh slug of fuel/air is commencing induction through the just-opened inlet valve. This brief period when both the inlet and the exhaust valves are open together is called **valve overlap.**

IGNITION.

A high voltage (or *high tension*) spark occurs in the cylinder just prior to the piston reaching top-dead-centre shortly before it commences the power stroke. This slightly advanced spark is to enable a controlled flame front to start moving through the fuel/air mixture that has been compressed in the cylinder.

The burning gases can expand and exert a very high pressure on the piston during its downwards power stroke. The purpose of the ignition system is to provide this correctly-timed spark.

Most aircraft engines have dual (and independent) ignition systems running *in parallel* with one another, with each supplying one of the **two spark plugs per cylinder**. As well as being safer in the event of failure of one ignition system, more even and more efficient fuel combustion results. The necessary *high tension* electrical current for the spark plugs comes from **self-contained generation and distribution units** – the **Magnetos**. Each of the dual ignition systems has its own Magneto. One of the functions of the engine, once it is running, is to mechanically drive each Magneto.

The Magneto consists of a magnet that is rotated (within the magneto housing) near a conductor which has a **Coil** of wire wound around it. The rotation of the magnet induces an electrical current to flow in the coil. Around this (primary) coil is wound a secondary coil of many more turns of wire – a transformer – which transforms the primary voltage into a much higher voltage. The higher voltage is fed to each **spark plug** at the appropriate time, causing a spark to jump between the two electrodes. This spark ignites the fuel/air mixture.

The timing of the spark is critical. The magneto has a set of **Breaker Points,** which are forced to open and shut by a small cam that is part of the rotating magnet shaft, which is connected indirectly to the crankshaft. The *points* are in the circuit of the primary coil and, when they open, the electrical current in the primary coil stops flowing. This sudden collapse of the primary current (aided by a condenser or capacitor placed across the points) induces a high voltage in the secondary coil.

The **spark plug** is in the circuit of the secondary coil and the large voltage, something like 20,000 volts, across its electrodes causes a spark to jump between them.

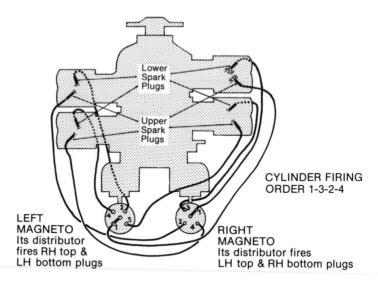

Fig.16-5. A Typical Ignition System.

As each cylinder is operating out of phase with the others, the current must be distributed to each spark plug at the correct moment (just prior to commencement of the power stroke). The **Distributor,** which is part of the magneto, does this.

Each cylinder fires once in every two revolutions of the crankshaft and the distributor has a rotor which is geared to the crankshaft in such a way that it turns once only for every two turns of the crankshaft, i.e. the distributor finger (rotor) turns once in every complete four-stroke cycle. **Once during each turn the distributor rotor transfers the high tension secondary current to each cylinder, in the correct firing order.**

Separate leads to each of the spark plugs belonging to that ignition system (one per cylinder) emanate from different terminals of the distributor case. These leads are often bound together, forming an *ignition harness.* **Leakage of current from the ignition harness** will lead to rough running. (This may occur at high altitudes, even if there is no leakage at sea-level.) One item of the pre-flight inspection is a visual check for chafing and heat cracking of those parts of the ignition harness easily seen.

THE STARTER.

Most modern training aircraft have an electric starter motor that is powered by the battery and activated by turning the ignition key to the *START* position in the cockpit.

Starting the engine causes a very high current to flow between the Battery and the Starter Motor, and this requires heavy duty wiring. If the Ignition Switch in the cockpit in its *START* position were directly connected into the starter circuit, **heavy duty cabling** to the cockpit switch would be required. This would have a number of disadvantages, including the additional weight of the heavy cable, a significant loss of electrical energy over the additional length, and high electrical currents through the cockpit environment (which would introduce an unnecessary fire risk). To avoid these disadvantages, **the starter circuit connecting the Battery to the Starter Motor is remotely controlled from the cockpit using a solenoid-activated switch.**

By moving the Ignition Key to *START*, the Pilot causes a small current to flow through the Starter Key circuit and energise a solenoid (an electromagnet with a movable core). The energised solenoid operates a heavy duty switch that closes the heavy duty circuit between the Battery and the Starter Motor. High current flows through this circuit, activating the Starter Motor which then turns the engine over.

Electric starters often have an associated **starter warning light** in the cockpit that glows while the starter is engaged. It should extinguish immediately the Pilot releases the starter. If by any chance the starter relay sticks (so that electrical power is still supplied to the starter motor even though the starter switch has been released from the *START* position) the warning light will remain on. The engine should be stopped (Mixture Control to *IDLE CUT-OFF)* to avoid damage to the engine and/or starter motor.

NOTE: On start-up of a cold engine, an oil pressure rise should be indicated on the Oil Pressure Gauge within 30 seconds to ensure adequate lubrication (sooner if the engine, and its oil, is warm) – if an oil pressure rise is not indicated within this approximate time, shut the engine down to avoid possible damage.

Only one spark per cylinder is necessary for start-up, so the Left magneto only is provided with a device called an Impulse Coupling (see later). When the ignition key is in the *START* position, the right magneto system is automatically de-energised and only the left magneto system provides a *high tension* supply to the spark plugs. After the start-up, the ignition key being returned to *BOTH* activates the right magneto system as well.

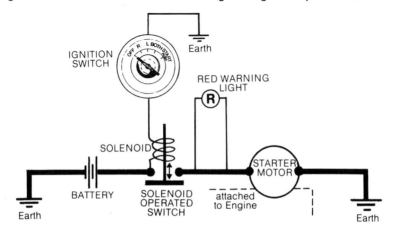

Fig.16-6. The Electric Starter System.

Older aircraft with the starter switch separate to the magneto switches, should only have the Left magneto switch on for start-up. Once the engine is started, the Pilot should ensure that the engine is running on both magnetos.

There are two design difficulties with magnetos that significantly affect starting an Engine. They are:

1. When you turn the engine over (either by hand-swinging the propeller or by an electric starter motor powered by the aircraft's **Battery)**, the engine rotates comparatively slowly, (approximately 120 rpm as against 800 rpm at idle speed). Because the magneto rotates at half crankshaft speed (to supply one spark per cylinder every two revolutions of the crankshaft) magneto speed at start-up is therefore about 60 rpm or less. To generate a spark of sufficiently high voltage to ignite the fuel/air mixture requires a magneto speed of about 100–200 rpm. Thus some device must be incorporated in the system to overcome this.

2. When the engine is running (800–2400 rpm is a typical operating range) the spark occurs at a fixed number of degrees **prior** to the piston reaching top-dead-centre at the commencement of the power stroke. This is known as **Spark Advance.** On start-up, with only very low revs occurring, unless the spark is retarded (delayed) until the piston is at or past top-dead-centre, ignition of the gases could drive the piston down the cylinder prematurely, causing the crankshaft to turn in the wrong direction. This is called **Kick-back.**

To overcome these two difficulties some devices have been developed for installation in the magneto, and most common in small aero engines is the *Impulse Coupling.* (In other engines a component called the *Induction Vibrator* is used, but this is not covered until Commercial Pilot level.)

The Impulse Coupling has two functions:
1. To accelerate the rotating magnet momentarily to generate a high voltage.
2. To effectively retard the ignition timing at low cranking rpm, and then, immediately after start-up, allow the timing of the spark to return to its normal position.

The Impulse Coupling initially prevents the magnet from rotating as the engine is turned over. Energy from the early part of the engine rotation is stored by winding up a coiled spring. When a certain amount of energy is stored, the coupling releases and the spring accelerates the magnet rapidly. This generates a current of sufficient strength to create a spark across the electrodes of the spark plug. It also retards the spark sufficiently to allow the burning fuel/air mixture to drive the crankshaft in the correct direction.

Once the engine is started and is running at its usual rpm, the magnet accelerates away from the coiled spring, which has no further effect. The spark is then produced normally (by the engine rotating the magnet), and the timing is no longer retarded but operates normally, with the spark occurring just prior to commencement of the power stroke.

Notice that, **as the impulse coupling does not depend on any electrical power source, you can start the engine by swinging the propeller.** However, if you did use an electric starter powered by the aircraft battery then, once the engine is running, disconnecting the battery will have no effect (except that the battery will not be re-charged).

Use of the Ignition Switch.

There are two separate ignition systems for safety in the event of failure of one of them, as well as for more efficient burning of the fuel/air mixture with two sparks in the cylinder instead of one. Older aircraft often have separate switches for each magneto, while most modern aircraft have rotary switches operated by the **Ignition Key.** With these, you can select the Left system *'L'*, the Right system *'R'*, or *'BOTH'*. *BOTH* is selected for **normal engine operation.**

The aircraft will run on just one magneto, but not as smoothly as on two, and with a **slight drop in rpm.** With one spark instead of two, there will be only one flame front advancing through the fuel/air mixture in the cylinder instead of two. This increases the time for full combustion to occur and decreases the efficiency of the burning.

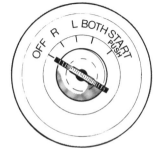

Fig.16-7. The Ignition Switch in the Cockpit.

If *L* is selected, only the left magneto system supplies a spark. The *R* magneto is earthed, i.e. its current runs to earth and no spark is generated. Therefore, going from *BOTH* to *L* should cause a drop in rpm and possibly slightly rougher running. If a slight drop in rpm does not occur, then either the *R* system is still supplying a spark or else the *R* magneto was not working previously when *BOTH* was selected.

Just prior to take-off, the Pilot will normally check both left and right magneto systems in this way as part of a power check, switching from *BOTH* to *L,* noting the rpm drop and returning to *BOTH,* when the rpm originally set should be regained. Then the Pilot will switch from *BOTH* to *R,* noting the rpm drop, and back to *BOTH.*

Comparisons are made between the two rpm drops, which should be within certain limits (see Operating Handbook for your particular aeroplane). Some typical figures are: check at 1600 rpm on *BOTH,* magneto drop 125 rpm maximum on either *L* or *R,* with a difference between these two drops not to exceed 50 rpm.

A Very Important Point to Remember is that placing the ignition switch to *OFF* earths the primary winding of the magneto system so that it no longer supplies electrical power, i.e. with a particular magneto's ignition switch *OFF,* that system is supposed to be earthed and unable to supply a spark. With a loose or broken wire, or some other fault, **switching the ignition off may not earth both of the magnetos.** Therefore, any person swinging the propeller may inadvertently start the engine, even though the ignition is switched off. It has happened – often with fatal results – and is still happening.

If you want to re-position the propeller when the engine is stopped, rotate it opposite to its normal motion so that you are protected against an inadvertent start.

ALWAYS TREAT A PROPELLER AS 'LIVE'.

The Pilot has no visual method of checking that the magneto sytems, although switched off, are de-activated. Just before shutting an engine down, some Pilots do a system function test at IDLE rpm, checking *BOTH, L, R* followed by a **'dead cut'**, i.e. to *OFF,* when a sudden loss of power should be apparent, and rapidly back to *BOTH* to allow the engine to run normally, prior to being shut down normally using the *idle cut-off* function of the mixture control. Some instructors advise against a *dead-cut* check as it may do damage to the engine. Refer to your Pilot's Operating Handbook.

THE EXHAUST SYSTEM.
The burned gases leave the engine and are carried out to the atmosphere via the exhaust system. It is important that there is no leakage of exhaust fumes into the cabin because they contain carbon monoxide, a colourless and odourless gas that is difficult to detect but which can cause unconsciousness and death.

ENGINE FAILURE IN FLIGHT.
Due to improved manufacture and operating procedures, engine failure is becoming a rare event.

Fuel starvation will of course stop any engine and this can be due to:
• insufficient fuel;
• mishandling of the fuel tank selection;
• incorrect use of the Mixture Control;
• ice forming in the carburettor; or
• contaminated fuel (i.e. water in the fuel).

If the **mixture control** is left in *LEAN* **for descent** (instead of being moved to *RICH*), the fuel/air mixture will gradually become more and more lean as the aeroplane descends into denser air, possibly resulting in the engine stopping. **Carburettor ice can also be a problem on descent** when the engine is idling and not producing much heat.

Electrical failure in both magneto systems will also cause the engine to stop.

In all these cases, the airflow past the aeroplane may cause the propeller to windmill and turn the engine over, even though it is not producing power.

Mechanical failure, such as the break-up of pistons or valves, will probably be accompanied by mechanical noise and the engine and propeller may be unable to rotate. In such cases any attempt to restart the engine is not advisable.

Irrespective of whether a Pilot decides to glide down for a landing or attempt to restart the engine, he must **ensure that flying speed is maintained.**

Some obvious items to be considered in an attempted restart of the engine are:

- **a fuel problem:**
  - change fuel tanks;
  - fuel pump on (if fitted);
  - mixture *RICH;*
  - primer locked;

- **an ignition problem:**
  - check magneto switches individually *(BOTH - LEFT - RIGHT).* If the engine operates on one magneto as a result of a fault in the other magneto system, then leave it there, otherwise return to *BOTH;*

- **an icing problem:**
  - carburettor heat *FULL HOT.*

ENGINE FIRE IN FLIGHT.

Engine fire is also a rare event, but a Pilot should be prepared to cope with it. The firewall is designed to protect the structural parts of the airframe from damage and the cockpit occupants from injury if a fire breaks out in the engine bay, provided the fire is extinguished without delay.

The initial reaction to an engine fire in flight should be to turn off the fuel (Fuel Selector *OFF* or Mixture Control to *IDLE CUT-OFF*) and allow the engine to run itself dry of fuel and stop. The engine and induction system will then be purged of fuel and the fire should extinguish. At this point, the ignition should be switched-off and a forced landing carried out.

☐ Now complete **Exercises 16 — The Aeroplane Engine.**

17

THE CARBURETTOR

Gasoline (petrol) needs to be mixed with oxygen in the correct ratio to burn properly. The oxygen is provided by mixing the fuel with air and so the **Fuel/Air** ratio must be kept reasonably correct at about 1 part of fuel to 12 parts of air, by weight. The device normally used to mix fuel with air in an engine is called the **Carburettor.**

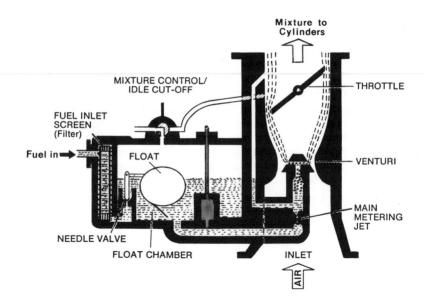

Fig.17-1. Cross-Section of a Simple Float-Type Carburettor.

Combustion can occur in the cylinders when the fuel/air ratio is between approximately 1:8 (rich mixture) and 1:20 (lean mixture). The *'ideal'* or *'chemically correct mixture'* (sometimes called 'ccm') of fuel/air is one in which the fuel and the oxygen are perfectly matched so that, after burning, all of the fuel and all of the oxygen has been used.

If the mixture is *'rich',* there is excess fuel. After burning, some unburned fuel will remain, i.e. **rich = excess fuel.** If the mixture is *'lean',* there is a shortage of fuel in the sense that, after all of the fuel has burned, there is still some oxygen remaining, i.e. **lean = excess oxygen.**

170

A simple carburettor has a venturi through which the amount of airflow is controlled by a **Throttle Valve (or butterfly).** The venturi has fuel jets positioned in it so that the correct amount of fuel by weight is metered into the airflow. The butterfly valve is controlled by the Pilot moving the throttle lever in the cockpit.

It is important that the Pilot moves the throttle smoothly so that unnecessary stress is not placed on the many moving parts in the engine. To open or close the throttle fully should take about the same time as a *'1 - 2-3'* count.

A simple **Float-type Carburettor** has a small chamber that requires a certain level of fuel. If the level is too low, the float-valve opens and allows more fuel from the fuel tanks to enter. This is happening continually as fuel is drawn from the float chamber into the venturi of the carburettor. The air pressure in the float chamber is atmospheric.

The acceleration of the airflow through the carburettor venturi causes a decreased static pressure; (Bernoulli's Principle – increased velocity, decreased static pressure). The higher atmospheric pressure in the float chamber forces fuel through the main metering jet into the venturi airflow. The faster the airflow, the greater the differential pressure and the greater the quantity of fuel discharged to the airflow, i.e. the mass of fuel that flows through the carburettor is controlled by the airflow through the carburettor venturi.

As the level of fuel in the chamber decreases the float falls, causing the needle-valve operated by the float to open and allow more fuel to enter. The required level of fuel in the float chamber is continually maintained.

THE ACCELERATOR PUMP.

When the Pilot opens the throttle, the butterfly valve is fully opened and does not restrict the airflow through the venturi. The airflow therefore increases.

If the throttle is opened quickly, the airflow initially increases at a rate greater than the fuel flow, producing an insufficiently-rich mixture. This would cause a lag in the production of power if it were not for the **Accelerator Pump,** i.e. the accelerator pump is used to prevent a *weak-cut* when the throttle is rapidly opened.

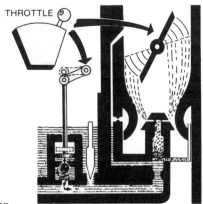

Fig.17-2. The Accelerator Pump.

The accelerator pump is a small plunger within the float chamber, connected to the throttle linkage so that it gives an extra spurt of fuel as the throttle is opened.

THE IDLING SYSTEM.

When the engine is idling with the butterfly valve almost closed, the pressure differential between the venturi and the float chamber is not great enough to force fuel through the main jet.

To allow for this, there is a small **Idling Jet** with an inlet near the butterfly valve, where a small venturi effect is caused when the valve is almost closed. This provides sufficient fuel to mix with the air to keep the engine idling at low rpm.

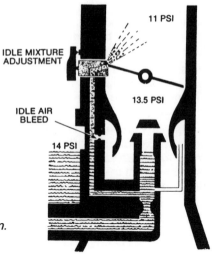

Fig.17-3. The Idling System.

MIXTURE CONTROL.

The carburettor is designed to operate under *'mean sea level conditions in the International Standard Atmosphere (ISA)'*. This is at a pressure altitude of zero (Mean Sea Level, QNH 1013 mb/hPa) and +15 degrees Celsius.

The size of the main metering jet which controls the fuel flow from the carburettor is designed for these ISA MSL conditions. The aeroplane will not operate under these conditions at all times (in fact, most in-flight conditions will differ markedly from ISA MSL), and any significant deviation from these conditions will require a change of fuel flow.

(The terms *'pressure altitude'*, *'QNH'*, and *'ISA MSL'* are explained later, in the chapter on Flight Instruments.)

Use of The Mixture Control.

At a given throttle setting and rpm, the carburettor will process the same volume of air per second, irrespective of the density or weight of the air.

At higher altitudes and/or higher temperatures, the density of the air is less, i.e. there are fewer air molecules per unit volume. Therefore, the volume of air passing through the carburettor will contain fewer molecules and weigh less. However, the density of the liquid fuel will not change. The same volume and weight of fuel will be drawn into the carburettor venturi.

The same number of fuel molecules, but fewer air molecules, means too much fuel by weight for the amount of air – the mixture is too RICH, leading to rough running and excessive fuel consumption.

To maintain a correct mixture, i.e. the correct fuel/air ratio, the Pilot must reduce the amount of fuel entering the carburettor venturi and mixing with the less-dense air as the altitude increases – called *'leaning'* the mixture. This is done using the **Mixture Control** – usually a red knob somewhere near the throttle. The mixture control moves a small needle to restrict the fuel flow through the main jet, thereby restoring the correct fuel/air mixture.

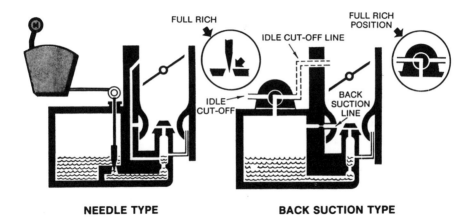

NEEDLE TYPE   **BACK SUCTION TYPE**

Fig.17-4. Mixture Control Systems.

For normal operations in the United Kingdom where most aerodromes are within 2,000 feet of sea-level, the temperature moderate and the air fairly dense, the mixture control is in **full-rich for the Take-off.**

Usually the mixture is kept in full-rich for the climb, unless the climb is an extended one to a cruising altitude in excess of 5000 ft, where the cruise power will most likely be less than 75% Maximum Continuous Power in standard conditions. The excess fuel is used as a cooling agent for the cylinder walls and piston tops to assist in the prevention of detonation. Some of the more sophisticated engines require leaning during the climb, but for training aeroplanes this is not usually the case.

As the aircraft climbs, the fuel/air mixture becomes over-rich causing a loss of power, indicated by a drop in rpm for a fixed-pitch propeller, and by rougher running.

On the cruise and with cruise power set, you should consider leaning the mixture to regain a more chemically-correct fuel/air ratio, which gives more efficient burning of the gases in the cylinders, more efficient operation of the engine (slightly higher rpm for a fixed-pitch propeller) and better fuel economy. In some light aircraft, correct leaning can reduce the fuel consumption by over 25% compared to full-rich – allowing greatly improved range and endurance.

The mixture should be slightly **on the Rich side** of the chemically correct mixture, provided the cruise power setting is less than 75% – (normal cruise for most aircraft is about 55–65% for normal cruise, when leaning the mixture is advisable).

NOTE: Above 5000 feet density height, an unsupercharged engine can **not** achieve more than 75% Maximum Continuous Power (even at full throttle).

At high power settings (in excess of 75%) rich mixture is necessary to provide excess fuel as a coolant. The Pilot's Operating Handbook for the specific aircraft type contains information on how to achieve the *'best power'* mixture and how to achieve the 'best economy' mixture.

To lean the mixture, you slowly move the mixture control towards the lean position. As a chemically-correct fuel/air ratio is regained, the rpm will increase. Eventually, with further leaning, the rpm will decrease slightly and the engine will show signs of running a little roughly. The mixture control is gently pushed back in a little to regain the best rpm, indicating a chemically-correct mixture, and smoother running. The mixture control is then moved to a slightly richer position to:

Ensure that the Engine Is Operating On the Rich Side of the Chemically-Correct Mixture.

This procedure must be repeated when either your cruising altitude or power-setting is changed significantly. Some aeroplanes are fitted with an Exhaust Gas Temperature (EGT) gauge which indicates peak EGT when there is a chemically-correct mixture and can assist the Pilot in leaning the mixture correctly.

During take-off (and landing, when high power in case of a go-around should be anticipated), the mixture control should be in **full-rich.** The mixture is rich to protect against detonation, pre-ignition and overheating in the cylinders. These are more likely to occur at power settings above 75% METO (Maximum Except for Take-Off, or Maximum Continuous Power) than at the normal cruise power settings (55–65%), when leaning is advisable.

For a constant-speed propeller, the leaning is done with reference to a fuel flow gauge, to obtain minimum fuel flow for smooth running. Refer to your aircraft handbook.

An over-rich mixture will cause a loss of power, high fuel consumption, fouling of the spark plugs and formation of carbon (from unburnt fuel) on the piston heads and valves. The extra fuel in a rich mixture causes cooling within the cylinders by its evaporation – this absorbs some of the heat produced in the combustion chamber. A lean mixture will therefore have higher cylinder head temperatures.

An excessively-lean mixture will cause excessively high cylinder head temperatures, leading to **detonation.**

Severe Detonation Can Damage an Engine Very Quickly. The Pilot is then faced with a loss of power and quite possibly complete engine failure. Having adjusted the mixture, check that the Cylinder Head Temperature (if fitted) and the Oil Temperature are still within the operating limits. It may take about five minutes for these temperature readings to stabilise.

Operations at Very High Density Altitudes, where the air density (Rho) is low (i.e. hot, high, or both), may require leaning prior to take-off. Aerodromes at high elevation, aerodromes at sea-level with temperatures approaching 40 degrees Celsius, and aerodromes that are both hot and high, such as at Nairobi, Kenya, require some thought about the mixture control setting for take-off.

Example : Aerodrome elevation 3,000 ft, QNH 1013 mb(hPa), Air Temperature 34 degrees Celsius.
The Density Altitude can be worked out and is in fact 6,000 ft, i.e. the engine/propeller and the airframe will perform as if the aeroplane is at 6,000 feet in the International Standard Atmosphere.

Refer to your Operating Handbook and seek the advice of your Flying Instructor.

IDLE CUT-OUT or IDLE CUT-OFF.

The idle cut-off is the normal means of shutting the engine down. In a typical system, when the mixture control is moved right out to the idle cut-off position by the Pilot, a small needle moves to cut off the fuel flow between the float chamber and the venturi. All the fuel jets are cut-off.

The engine will continue running until all of the fuel/air mixture in the inlet manifold and the cylinders is burned. This leaves no combustible fuel/air mixture anywhere in the system, which would not be the case if the engine was stopped by turning the ignition *OFF.*

DETONATION.

Correct progressive burning of the fuel/air mixture should occur as the flame-front advances through the combustion chamber. This causes an increase in pressure which smoothly forces the piston down the cylinder in the power stroke.

When a gas is compressed, it experiences a rise in temperature. (You can feel this if you hold your hand over the outlet of a bicycle pump during the *'compression stroke'.)* If the pressure and the temperature rise is too great for the fuel/air mixture in the engine cylinders, the burning will not be progressive, but **explosive,** spontaneous combustion.

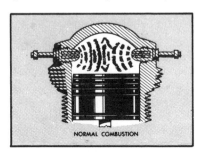
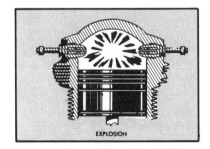
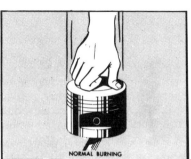
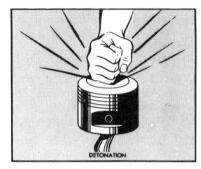

Fig.17-5. A Comparison Between Normal Combustion and Detonation.

This explosive increase in pressure is called **Detonation** and, as mentioned earlier, can cause severe damage to the pistons, the valves and the spark plugs, as well as causing a decrease in power and quite possibly **complete engine failure.**

Using a lower fuel grade than recommended, a time-expired fuel, an over-lean mixture, too high a Manifold Pressure, or an over-heated engine can cause detonation.

Aircraft engines are normally designed to operate a little on the rich side, the extra fuel acting as a coolant to prevent the mixture becoming too hot and to cool the cylinder walls by evaporation.

If **detonation** is suspected (i.e. **rough running and high Cylinder Head Temperatures):**
• enrichen the mixture;
• reduce pressures in the cylinders (throttle back);
• increase airspeed to assist in reducing cylinder head temperatures.

PRE-IGNITION.

Pre-ignition is a progressive burning of the fuel/air mixture but is a burning that commences before the spark from the plug. This early or pre-ignition can be caused by a hot-spot in the cylinder (e.g. a carbon deposit) becoming red-hot and igniting the mixture. The result is rough running, possibly back-firing, and a sudden rise in the cylinder head temperature.

Pre-ignition can be caused by a 'carboned-up' engine, or a use of high power when the mixture is too lean (hence no extra fuel for cooling). It may occur in one cylinder only, where a hot-spot exists, whereas detonation will normally appear in all cylinders.

Pre-ignition is a function of the condition of a particular cylinder or cylinders – detonation is a function of the fuel/air mixture/temperature being supplied to all cylinders.

Both detonation and pre-ignition can be prevented – provided the correct fuel and operating limitations of the engine are observed. This information is available to you in the Pilot's Operating Handbook.

CARBURETTOR ICING.

The expansion of the air as it accelerates through the carburettor venturi causes it to drop in temperature. Quite warm air can cool to below zero and, if there is moisture in the air, ice can form. This will seriously degrade the functioning of the carburettor, even to the point of stopping the engine!

Impact Ice will occur when super-cooled (below freezing point) water droplets in the intake air impact on the metal surfaces of the inlet air scoop and ducting to the carburettor – immediately forming into ice. (This can happen even in a fuel-injection system as well as in a normal float-type carburettor.)

Impact ice can occur when the Outside Air Temperature is near or below zero and the aeroplane is in cloud, rain or sleet – i.e. **visible moisture** and the water droplets are at or below zero, or if the inlet surfaces themselves are below zero, e.g. an aircraft descending from levels above the freezing level into visible moisture.

Fuel Ice can form downstream of the jet where the fuel is introduced into the carburettor airstream, where it vaporises, causing a substantial lowering of the temperature due to latent heat absorption on vaporisation.

If the temperature of the fuel/air mixture drops to between 0 and –8 degrees Celsius, water will precipitate from the incoming air if it is moist, and will freeze onto any surface it encounters, e.g. the inlet manifold walls and the throttle valve (or butterfly). This will seriously restrict the airflow and thus reduce the engine's power output.

Fuel Ice can occur even in ambient air temperatures well above freezing (+20 to +30 degrees C) when the **relative humidity** is above 50% or so.

In some texts, fuel icing may be called **'refrigeration icing'**, as it is caused by the vaporising of a liquid – the same process as that used in most refrigerators.

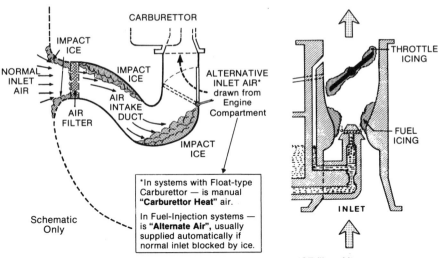

NOTE: As Carb Heat/Alternate Air is **NOT filtered** its use on the ground must be kept to a minimum.

Fig.17-6. Carburettor Icing.

Throttle Ice.

As the fuel/air mixture of gases accelerates past the throttle valve, there is a decrease in static pressure and a consequent drop in temperature. This process can cause icing on the throttle valve. The acceleration and resulting temperature drop is greatest at small throttle openings because the throttle butterfly restricts the airflow most at these power settings, creating a substantial pressure drop. Therefore, there is a **greater likelihood of carburettor icing at low throttle settings.**

NOTE: **Visible moisture is not necessary for the formation of Throttle Ice.**

Carburettor Icing can Occur when the Outside Air Temperature is HIGH!

Both fuel ice and throttle ice can occur when the Outside Air Temperature is high. It is expansion that causes the cooling to freezing point, and just because it is 35 degrees Celsius in Casablanca does not mean that you will not get carburettor icing if the humidity is high enough. In high humidity keep an eye out for carburettor icing – it can form very easily.

All of this carburettor icing can have a very serious effect on the running of the engine. The size and shape of the carburettor passages are altered, the airflow disturbed, the fuel/air mixture ratio affected – leading to rough running, a loss of power and possibly a total stopping of the engine unless action is taken.

The Pilot should notice a drop in rpm (fixed pitch propeller), rough running and a decrease in power showing itself as a loss of airspeed or, if airspeed is maintained, a fall in the rate of climb or an increase in the rate of descent.

The Remedy for Carburettor Icing is **Carburettor Heat.**

Most modern aircraft have a carburettor heat system to counteract icing. This usually involves the air prior to intake into the carburettor being heated by passing near the hot exhaust system. Being hotter, its density will be less, and the initial effect of its introduction will be to decrease the power from the engine (seen as a decrease in rpm for a fixed-pitch propeller), possibly as much as 10–20%.

As the hot air passes through the carburettor venturi, it will melt the ice. There may be some rough running if there has been a large ice build up and a lot of the melted ice (now water) is fed through the cylinders, but this will quickly disappear.

Clearing ice from the carburettor will allow better running of the engine and the power to increase (and the rpm of a fixed-pitch propeller to rise as the ice is cleared).

If you suspect that carburettor icing is present: APPLY **FULL CARBURETTOR HEAT.**

A fixed-pitch propeller will show an initial drop in rpm (power), due to the lower density of the hot air, which enrichens the fuel/air mixture, followed quickly (hopefully) by an increase in rpm (power) as the ice is melted and cleared. Following this, carburettor heat may be removed and cold air again used.

If carburettor ice re-forms then this operation will have to be repeated. **Full Carburettor Heat** will be re-applied until the carburettor ice melts, after which you may elect to set only partial carburettor heat to prevent the further formation of ice.

If carburettor ice forms again, immediately apply full heat to remove it, and then try a higher setting of partial heat to prevent its formation. Of course, you may find under some conditions that full heat is required not only to remove carburettor ice, but also to prevent its formation.

(A Word of Caution – partial use of carb heat may raise the temperature of the induction air into the temperature range which is most conducive to the formation of carburettor icing.)

On descent with low power and shortly before landing, particularly in high humidity (e.g. coastal areas), it is usual to apply carb heat to ensure that no carburettor icing forms or is present. Small throttle butterfly openings increase the chance of carburettor ice forming.

On final approach to land, the carb heat is returned to cold just in case full power is required in the event of a go-around.

Some engines have a **Carburettor Air Temperature Gauge,** and use may be made of this to keep the carburettor air temperatures out of the icing range.

Avoid using carburettor heat on the ground because the hot air is (in most aeroplanes) taken from around the engine exhaust and, unlike the normal inlet air, is **unfiltered**. This will avoid introducing dust and grit into the carburettor and the engine itself, with obvious benefits to both performance and wear.

FUEL INJECTION SYSTEMS.

More sophisticated engines have fuel directly metered into the induction manifold and then into the cylinders without using a carburettor. This is known as **Fuel Injection.**

A venturi system is still used to sense the pressure differential. This is coupled to a **Fuel Control Unit** (FCU), from which metered fuel is piped to the **Fuel Manifold Unit** (fuel distributor). From here, a separate fuel line carries fuel to the **discharge nozzle** in each cylinder head, or into the inlet port prior to the inlet valve.

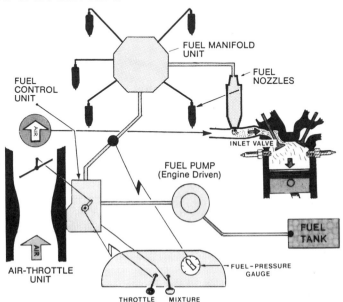

Fig.17-7. A Fuel Injection System.

179

The mixture control in this system also controls the idle cut-off.

With fuel injection, each individual cylinder can be provided with a correct mixture by its own separate fuel line. (This is unlike the system where a carburettor supplies the fuel/air mixture to all cylinders – a slightly richer-than-ideal mixture will need to be supplied to most of the cylinders by the carburettor to ensure that the leanest-running cylinder does not run too lean.)

Advantages of Fuel Injection Systems.

- Freedom from vaporisation ice (fuel ice), thus making it unnecessary to use carburettor heat except in the most severe atmospheric conditions.
- More uniform delivery of the fuel/air mixture to each cylinder.
- Improved control of fuel/air ratio.
- Fewer maintenance problems.
- Instant acceleration of the engine after idling with no tendency for it to stall, i.e. instant response.
- Increased engine efficiency.

Disadvantages of Fuel Injection Systems.

- Starting an already hot engine that has a fuel injection system may be difficult due to vapour locking in the fuel lines. Electric boost pumps that pressurise the fuel lines can help alleviate this problem.
- Having very fine fuel lines, fuel injection engines are more susceptible to any contamination in the fuel such as dirt or water.
- Surplus fuel provided by a fuel injection system will pass through a **return line** which may be routed to only one of the fuel tanks. If the Pilot does not retain an awareness of where the surplus fuel is being returned to, it may result in fuel being vented overboard (thus reducing flight fuel available). A secondary effect could be assymetric (uneven) fuel loading in some early model single-engined aeroplanes.

Correct fuel management is imperative! Know the fuel system of your particular aeroplane!

ENGINE FIRE ON START-UP.

If a fire starts in the engine air intake during start-up, a generally accepted procedure to minimise the problem is:
- continue cranking the engine with the starter (to keep air moving through);
- move the Mixture Control to *IDLE CUT-OFF* (to remove the source of fuel); and
- open the throttle (to maximise the airflow through the carburettor and induction system and purge the system of fuel).

The fire will probably go out, but if it does not, then further action would be taken:

> Fuel – *OFF*
> Switches – *OFF*
> Brakes – *ON*

> Evacuate the aircraft, taking the Fire Extinguisher.

☐ Now do **Exercises 17 — The Carburettor.**

18

THE FUEL SYSTEM

The function of a fuel system is to store fuel and deliver it to the carburettor (or fuel injection system) in adequate quantities at the proper pressures. It should provide a continuous flow of fuel under positive pressure under all normal flight conditions:

• change of altitude;
• change of attitude;
• sudden acceleration; or
• deceleration of the engine.

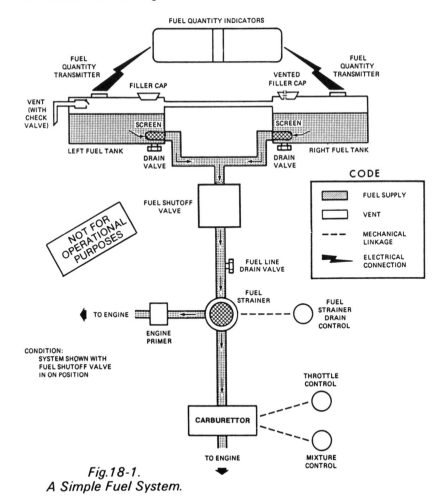

Fig.18-1.
A Simple Fuel System.

Fuel is stored in **Fuel Tanks,** which are usually installed in the wing. A sump and a drain point at the lowest point of the tank allows heavy impurities (such as water) to gather, be inspected and drained off.

The tanks often contain **Baffles** to stop the fuel surging about in flight – especially with large attitude changes or in turbulence.

The fuel supply line commences higher than the sump to avoid any impurities (water or sludge) entering the fuel lines to the carburettor, even though there is a **Fuel Filter** in the line to catch any small quantity of impurities. Because of the fuel supply line to the engine not being right at the bottom of the fuel tank, there will always be some unuseable fuel in the tanks.

The top of the fuel tank is vented to the atmosphere to allow atmospheric pressure to be retained in the tank as altitude is changed and as fuel is used up. Any reduced pressure (due to ineffective venting) in the tank could reduce the rate of fuel flow to the engine and also cause the fuel tanks to collapse inwards. **Fuel vents** should be checked in the pre-flight external inspection to ensure that they are not blocked or damaged.

As well as allowing for reduced pressure, there must be some allowance for an increased pressure. If the fuel volume increases due to the fuel in the tanks warming up in the sun, there must be a space left for it to expand into or to overflow.

A high-wing aircraft with the tanks in the wings will generally allow the fuel to be **gravity-fed** to the carburettor with no need for a fuel pump. If there is no carburettor but a fuel injection system, then electric boost pump assistance is necessary.

In a low-wing aircraft, the tanks, being lower than the engine, need a fuel pump to lift the fuel to the carburettor. Prior to start-up, an electric auxiliary (boost) pump is used to prime the fuel lines and to purge any vapour from the fuel lines. Once the engine is started, the engine-driven mechanical **Fuel Pump** takes over. Correct functioning of the pump can be monitored with a fuel pressure gauge.

It is usual to have the electric fuel pump switched on for critical manoeuvres such as the take-off, landing and low level flying in case the mechanical fuel pump fails and the engine is starved of fuel.

It is important, especially on low-wing aircraft with fuel carried in tanks below the level of the engine, that the **fuel strainer drain valve** is checked closed during the pre-flight external inspection. If it is not closed, the engine-driven fuel pump may not be able to draw sufficient fuel into the engine (sucking air instead), and the engine may be starved of fuel if the electric fuel pump is not used.

THE PRIMING PUMP.

The fuel primer is a hand-operated pump in the cockpit which the Pilot uses to pump fuel into the induction system of the engine in preparation for start-up. This fuel does not pass through the carburettor.

The primer must be locked during flight to avoid excessive fuel being drawn into the cylinders, especially at low power settings, which could stop the engine due to the fuel/air mixture being too rich.

FUEL SELECTION BY THE PILOT.

A fuel line will run from each tank to a selector valve in the cockpit, which the Pilot uses to select the tank from which fuel will be taken or to shut the fuel off. Incorrect selection by the Pilot has led to numerous incidents and accidents, so read this section of the Operations Manual for your particular aircraft carefully. **The sounds of silence** whilst you still have fuel in a tank somewhere can be very loud indeed!

It is advisable when changing tanks to switch on the electric auxilliary or booster fuel pump (if fitted) to guarantee fuel pressure to the carburettor and to positively monitor the fuel pressure as the tanks are changed.

Any sudden and unexpected loss of power should bring two possible causes immediately to mind:
• lack of fuel to the engine, or
• carburettor icing.

If the cause is **incorrect fuel selection** your actions should include:
• closing the throttle (to avoid a sudden surge of power as the engine re-starts);
• setting the mixture control to full-rich;
• turning the electric fuel pump on; and
• checking fuel tank selection/content.

If it is **carburettor ice,** then apply **full carburettor heat.**

FUEL BOOST PUMPS (OR AUXILIARY PUMPS).

The reasons for installing electric fuel boost pumps are:
• to provide fuel at the required pressure to the carburettor or to the fuel metering unit of a fuel injection system;
• to purge the fuel lines of any vapour;
• to prime the cylinders for start-up;
• to supply fuel if the engine-driven pump fails.

If an electric fuel pump is fitted, it is usual to also have a fuel pressure gauge to monitor its operation.

FUEL GAUGES.

Most light aircraft have fuel gauges in the cockpit which may be electrical (in which case the Master Switch will have to be *ON* for them to register) or direct-reading. It is good airmanship not to rely on them, since they can read quite inaccurately, especially when the aeroplane is not straight and level.

Always carry-out a visual check of the contents in the fuel tanks during the pre-flight external inspection by removing the fuel caps, looking into the tanks and then securely replacing the caps.

The fuel consumption rate specified in the Pilot's Operating Handbook assumes **correct leaning of the mixture** which, if not done, could lead to a fuel burn 20% in excess of the 'book-figures' and the fuel gauges reading much less than expected.

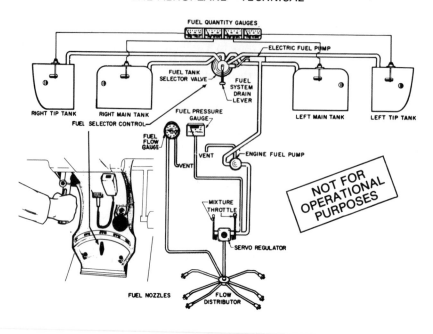

Fig.18-2. A More Sophisticated Fuel System.

REFUELLING.

The most important thing is to ensure that you are loading the correct fuel type. Kerosene (AVTUR) is required for gas turbine engines (jets), and **petrol (AVGAS) for piston engines.** Kerosene is straw-coloured and has a distinctive smell.

DO NOT USE AVTUR (KEROSENE) IN PISTON ENGINES.

NOTE: There are moves afoot to arrange it so that AVTUR refuelling nozzles will not fit into tank openings of AVGAS aeroplanes, and for all AVGAS fittings to be painted red and AVTUR fittings to be painted black.

AVGAS (AViation GASoline) comes in various grades to cater for the requirements of different types of piston engines – some high performance and some low performance. These various grades of AVGAS are colour coded to aid you in checking that the correct fuel is on board. Normal fuel for light aircraft is 100LL (Low Lead), which is coloured blue.

Fuel should possess anti-detonation or *'anti-knock'* qualities which are described by the octane rating or performance numbers quoted above. The higher the rating or grade, the greater the compression that the fuel/air mixture can take without detonating.

The higher number indicates the power possible (compared to the standard reference fuel) before a rich mixture would detonate and the lower number indicates the power possible before the same fuel leaned-out would detonate. Certain engines require certain fuel – make sure you know which one and use it, and make sure that the fuel already in the tanks is the same as that being loaded.

The higher octane or performance number fuels have lead added to improve their anti-detonation qualities.

- If you use fuel of a **LOWER GRADE** than specified, or fuel that is **DATE-EXPIRED,** detonation is likely to occur, especially at high power settings, with a consequent loss of power and possible engine damage.

- If you use fuel of a **HIGHER GRADE** than specified, the spark plugs could be fouled by lead and also the exhaust valves and their sealing faces could be eroded by the higher performance fuel exhausting.

BE WARY OF MOGAS AND DO NOT USE MOTOR GASOLINE.
*see note below.

'AVGAS' (AViation GASoline) comes in batches with tight quality control. Ordinary car petrol from the service station does **not** have such tight quality control and has different burning characteristics to 'AVGAS'. In an aeroplane engine, car petrol would cause a lower power output, lead fouling of the spark plugs and a strong possibility of detonation. Motor gasoline does not come in batches (like AVGAS) and there is no verification of its purity.

Motor fuel is more volatile and vaporises more readily than AVGAS, thus it can cause vapour locks in the fuel system and thus starve the engine of fuel.

'MOGAS' is motor fuel produced in batches to certain specifications and quality, and is not available from motor service stations (*see note below).

FUEL CHECKS (especially for water and other contaminants).

Fuel which is about to be loaded should be checked first for contamination. The most common contamination is water. It can leak into ground fuel tanks and from there be loaded into the fuel truck and into the tanks of an aeroplane quite easily.

Fuel naturally contains a small amount of water and this can condense out, say with a drop in temperature, contaminating the fuel system and possibly resulting in a loss of engine power. However, what we need to check for is a large quantity of water which, if introduced into an engine cylinder, would interrupt the combustion process, causing the engine to stop due to lack of fuel. Water may also block the fuel passages within the carburettor through the formation of water globules, thereby causing an interruption to power.

There are certain pastes and papers available which react when water is present and the fuelling agent will use these on a regular basis to guarantee the purity of the fuel in his storage tanks.

* Reference to the use of **MOGAS** is made in the CAA Airworthiness Notice No.98.

4   LABELLING AND COLOUR CODING

4.1   All tanks should be labelled and colour coded to identify the grade of fuel they contain. Pipelines should also be similarly labelled and colour coded. The form and dimensions of labelling and colour coding are illustrated in Fig 1. The overall dimensions of the grade labels should not be less than illustrated, but the dimensions of the coloured segments on both labels and pipelines may be varied provided that the primary indicator colours for the grades (Red for AVGAS, and Black for Jet A-1) predominate. The grade wording as illustrated should always be used.

4.2   As an additional measure to avoid refuelling errors it is recommended that the appropriate grade markings or a band of the appropriate primary grade indicator colour referred to in 4.1 should be painted on delivery hoses or pipes as close as practicable to the delivery nozzle, but not on the nozzle itself. Any colour coding on the delivery nozzle should be provided by a material which will not flake or separate from the nozzle in general use, for example a securely attached plastic sleeve or ring.

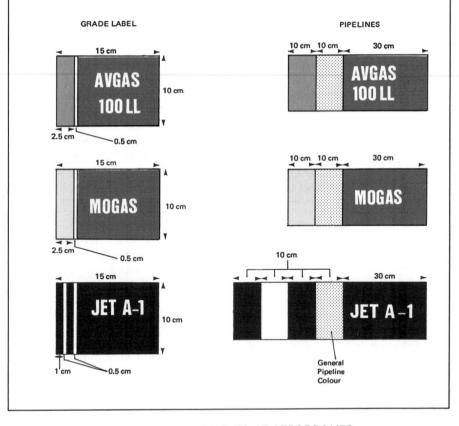

from CAP 434 - AVIATION FUEL AT AERODROMES

FUELLING OF AIRCRAFT

6.1 Introduction

In spite of well known and well publicised procedures to avoid loading of incorrect fuel, cases continue to occur from time to time mainly with general aviation aircraft. The most critical case is the piston-engined aircraft refuelled with turbine fuel, since piston engines will invariably stop as soon as pure turbo fuel reaches the engine; alternatively a mixture of the two fuels reaching the engine can lead to detonation and the consequent risk of destruction of the engine. Either circumstance can easily coincide with a critical stage of flight and in recent years there have been a number of serious accidents resulting from this error.

6.2 Refuelling Procedures

6.2.1

It is the aircraft commander's responsibility to ensure that the aircraft is refuelled with the correct type and quantity of fuel and refuelling crews should not commence to refuel an aircraft until they have established the precise requirements from the aircraft commander or his authorised representative.

6.2.2

The following minimum precautions should always be observed:

6.2.2.1

The aircraft commander or his authorised representative should ensure that the refuelling crew is in no doubt as to the type and quantity of fuel required.

6.2.2.2

The commander should satisfy himself that steps have been taken to check that the correct type of fuel is being supplied and correct delivery should be verified from the supplier's delivery note.

6.3 Marking of Aircraft Refuelling Points

6.3.1

Most regulatory authorities require that aircraft filler points be marked with the word 'FUEL' and the appropriate type. In addition to these markings it is strongly recommended that all 'over-wing' type filler points are further identified by means of a coloured circle or square either around or immediately adjacent to the filler point using the following colours:

Gasoline filler Points — RED

Turbine fuel filler points — BLACK

Ideally these markings should also incorporate the words 'AVGAS' for gasoline points and 'AVTUR' or 'JET A-1' for turbine fuel points.

NB Red and black are respectively the primary colours used for gasoline and turbine fuel in the internationally accepted colour coding scheme for aviation fuel ground installations and piping.

6.3.2

If it is necessary to achieve adequate differentiation between the identification colour and the aircraft colour scheme the above markings should be outlined in white. The precise size of such markings may be varied as required, but it is important that they do provide prominent identification of the filler points. All such markings should be maintained in a legible condition.

6.3.3

Where the actual filler cap is beneath a hinged cover panel, the above markings may, if desired, be applied to the undersurface of the cover panel provided always that they become and remain prominently visible with the panel in its normal 'open' position for refuelling.

from Pooley's PILOTS INFORMATION GUIDE

There is usually a drop in air temperature overnight and, if the airspace above the fuel in the aircraft's fuel tanks is large (i.e. the tanks are fairly empty), the fuel tank walls will become cold and there will be a lot more condensation than if the tanks were full of fuel. If the tanks are kept full when the aircraft is not being used for some days, or overnight if low temperatures are expected, this will help minimise condensation.

Full Tanks Overnight (Especially If Cold) Will Minimise Condensation.

The disadvantages of refuelling overnight include the following:
- If the aircraft has a take-off weight restriction the following day, it will have to be partially defuelled to reduce the weight or adjust the balance.
- If the tanks are full and the temperature rises, the fuel will expand and possibly overflow the tank a little. This could be a fire hazard.

There can be other impurities besides water. Rust, sand, dust and micro-organisms can cause problems just like water. Filtering or straining the fuel should indicate the presence of these and hopefully remove them prior to refuelling.

Be especially careful when refuelling from drums which may have been standing for some time. Always check drum fuel with water-detection paste, for date of **expiry** and for correct grade of fuel. Filter the fuel through a chamois prior to loading.

Water, being more dense than fuel, will tend to gather at the low points in the fuel system. Once in the aeroplane tanks, a small quantity of fuel should be drained regularly from the bottom of each tank and from the fuel strainer drain valve to check for impurities, especially water which will sink to the bottom of the glass. **Fuel drains** are usually spring-loaded valves at the bottom of each fuel tank and the fuel strainer drain is usually found at the lowest point in the whole fuel system.

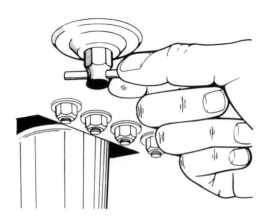

Fig.18-4. Fuel Drains are Located at the Lowest Point of the Fuel Tanks.

What Do You Do If You Find Water In The Fuel Tanks?

**This is an operational matter and guidance
will be given by your Flying Instructor.**

In general terms, if there was found to be a large quantity of water in the tanks, the following procedures should be included in your actions:
- the ground engineer should be informed;
- drain the tanks until all the water has been removed;
- positively rock the wing to allow any other water to gravitate to the water trap;
- drain off more fuel and check for water at ALL drain points.

FUEL MANAGEMENT.

- Ensure that the aircraft has the correct grade of fuel on board and that it is free of impurities.
- Ensure that sufficient fuel for the flight plus adequate reserves is on board. Do not rely only on the fuel gauges as they are often inaccurate. Calculate the fuel required, inspect visually and measure the fuel on board prior to flight. Remember that some of the fuel in the tanks will be unusable fuel.
- Carry out a fuel drain if required or if you think it is advisable.
- Ensure there are no leaks, that fuel caps are replaced and that tank vents are clear and unobstructed.

Fuel tank caps are usually on the upper surface of the wing, which is a low pressure area in normal flight. Fuel will be siphoned out very quickly if the tank caps are forgotten. With high wing aircraft especially, where the tank caps are not visible easily from the ground or when in flight, extra care should be taken.

Be familiar with, and follow, the procedures recommended in the aircraft handbook. Understand the fuel system, especially the functioning of the fuel selector valves. When selecting a new tank, ensure the selector valve is moved firmly and positively into the correct detent.

Do not change tanks unnecessarily immediately prior to take-off or landing. If possible, verify prior to take-off that fuel is being drawn from the appropriate tanks. If operation is possible from more than one tank at the one time, this is usually preferred for operations near the ground. If boost pumps are fitted, their use for take-off is generally advised. (Refer to your Pilot's Operating Handbook for correct procedures.)

When changing tanks, check that there is indeed fuel in the tank about to be selected, if an electric fuel pump is fitted, switch it on and, if a fuel pressure gauge is fitted, monitor during and after the transfer.

☐ You should now be able to answer **Exercises 18 — The Fuel System** without too much trouble.

19

THE OIL SYSTEM

If a small film of oil separates two metal surfaces it will prevent them from rubbing together. Without oil there would be high friction forces, causing very high temperatures to develop quickly in the metal, with extreme wearing of the metal surfaces, and, very likely, mechanical failure.

Consequently:
Sufficient Oil Of The Correct Type In An Engine Is Vital.

The oil film will allow the two metal surfaces to slide one over the other without actually touching each other. There will be only low friction forces and, consequently, high temperatures in the metal are avoided. **The metallic friction is replaced by internal friction in the lubricating oil.**

A thin layer of oil will adhere to each metal surface and, as the metal surfaces move relative to each other, there will be shearing of the layers of oil between the two surfaces, (i.e. sliding of one layer over the other). Heat generated in the oil film due to this shearing is removed by the oil continually being circulated – the hot oil being carried away and cooled in a component known as the **Oil Cooler,** which is exposed to the airflow.

Engine components subjected to high loads, such as the bearings at either end of the connecting rods, especially the crankshaft (or 'big end') bearings, are cushioned by a layer of oil and the mechanical shock on them reduced.

The pistons absorb a lot of heat from the combustion chamber and are cooled by oil splashed or sprayed onto them from below, (i.e. from the connecting rod area). **Lubrication and cooling of the bearings and pistons is very important — and this is the main function of the oil.**

Oil circulating through an engine can carry away dirt and other foreign material, thereby reducing abrasive wear on the moving parts of the engine. This contamination is removed by the **Oil Filter.** If the filter is not kept clean (by correct maintenance or replacement at the recommended service intervals) it may block, causing dirty oil to bypass the filter and circulate within the engine's lubrication system. Dirty oil has poorer cooling and lubricating qualities and so the engine will suffer – there will be an increased wear rate which will shorten the life of the engine.

Oil also provides a seal, e.g. between the cylinder wall and the piston as it moves up and down. This prevents the compressed gases (fuel/air) escaping past the piston rings into the crankcase.

Some of the necessary **Properties of Oil** are:

1. Oil must be sufficiently viscous over the operating temperature range of the engine – it must flow freely, but not be too thin. An oil of high viscosity (stickiness) flows slowly; an oil of low viscosity flows more easily. High temperatures make oil less viscous and cause it to flow more freely.

    Excessively High Temperatures Affect the Lubricating Qualities of Oil, Impairing Its Effectiveness, so Keep An Eye on the Oil Temperature Gauge.

    The oil must remain sufficiently viscous under the wide range of operating temperatures and bearing pressures found in aviation engines.

    The Owner or Operator of the aeroplane may decide to use an oil of lower viscosity than normal in a severely cold climate. Likewise an oil of higher viscosity could be used if the aeroplane is to be operated in a continually hot climate. As the Pilot, be aware of the oil grade being used and **Do Not Mix Oil Grades.**

2. The oil must have a sufficiently high flash point and fire point to ensure that it will not vapourise excessively or catch fire easily.

3. The oil must be chemically stable and not change its state or characteristics.

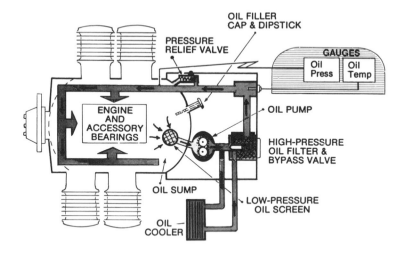

Fig.19-1. A Typical Oil System.

After doing its work in the engine, the oil gathers in the **Sump** which is a reservoir attached to the lower part of the engine casing.

A Wet Sump engine has a sump in which the oil is stored. Most light aircraft engines are wet sump engines.

A Dry Sump engine has scavenge pumps that scavenge the oil from the sump attached to the lower part of the engine casing and pump it back into the oil tank, which is separate from the engine. It is usual to have a dry sump on aerobatic aircraft that commonly find themselves in unusual attitudes. The de Havilland Tiger Moth and Chipmunk have dry sump engines. Radial engines such as in the Dakota (DC-3) and the Beaver have dry sump oil systems.

There is usually an **engine-driven Oil Supply Pump** that supplies oil from the sump or the tank through oil lines, passages and galleries to the moving parts of the engine. Within the oil pump is a spring-loaded **Oil Pressure Relief Valve.** If the pressure set on the pressure relief valve is exceeded, it will open and relieve the pressure by allowing oil to be returned to the pump inlet.

An **Oil Pressure Gauge** in the cockpit indicates the oil pressure provided by the oil pump, i.e. the oil pressure sensor is situated after the oil pump and before the oil does its work in the engine.

Oil Filters and screens are placed in the system to remove any foreign matter such as dirt or carbon particles from the circulating oil. The oil filters should be replaced at regular intervals, as required in the Maintenance Schedule, and inspected, as the foreign matter collected may give an indication of the condition of the engine, e.g. small metal particles might indicate an impending engine failure.

Within the oil filter housing is the **Oil Filter Bypass Valve.** This permits the oil to bypass the filter in the event of the filter becoming clogged. Dirty and contaminated oil is preferable to no oil.

The oil circulates around the moving parts and through the engine, lubricating, cooling and cleaning as it goes, and is then returned to the wet sump by gravity, or to a separate oil tank by scavenge pumps (Dry Sump system).

The **Oil Cooler.** Because the oil absorbs heat, the cooling that occurs in the sump is often insufficient and so most engines have an **Oil Cooler.** The oil is pumped from the sump through the oil filter to the oil cooler.

If the oil is already cool, a thermally-operated valve allows it to bypass the oil cooler, as further cooling is unnecessary. If the oil is hot (as it is when the engine has warmed-up), the thermally-operated valve directs the oil through the cooler. Should the cooler become blocked, a **Pressure Bypass Valve** allows the oil to bypass the cooler.

The oil cooler is commonly placed in the system so that the oil cools a little in the sump and then passes through the oil cooler for further cooling just prior to entering the main parts of the engine.

As part of your **Daily/Pre-Flight Inspection** you should check the condition of the oil cooler for:
- freedom from insects, birds' nests and other contamination, i.e. free air passages;
- any oil leakage or fatigue cracks.

An **Oil Temperature Gauge** is placed in the cockpit. It is connected to a temperature probe that senses the temperature of the oil after the oil has passed through the oil cooler and before its use within the hot sections of the engine.

Some aeroplanes have a **Cylinder Head Temperature (CHT) Gauge** to provide another indication of engine temperature to the Pilot, this time in the area surrounding the cylinder heads.

Oil Changes are necessary periodically. As the same oil is continually used, over a period of time it will become dirtier because the filters cannot clean it perfectly.

Chemical changes will also occur in the oil in the form of:
(a) oxidation caused by contamination from some of the by-products of the fuel combustion in the engine; and
(b) absorption of water that condenses in the engine when it cools after being shut down. Therefore the oil must be changed at regular intervals, as required by the Maintenance Schedule.

Use Only Recommended Type and Grade of Oils and Do Not Mix Grades.

Hint: The Pilot's Operating Handbook will usually show the oil grade as an SAE rating – Society of Automotive Engineers – however commercial aviation oil has a *'commercial aviation number'* which is **double** the SAE rating:

80 grade oil – SAE 40
100 grade oil – SAE 50

There are different types of oils designed for different operating conditions. Use only the correct type of oil as directed in the Pilot's Operating Handbook and **do not use turbine (jet) oil in piston engines.**

MALFUNCTIONS IN THE OIL/LUBRICATION SYSTEM.

Oil Type.

The incorrect type of oil will possibly cause poor lubrication, poor cooling and engine damage. Oil temperature and oil pressure indications may be abnormal.

Oil Quantity.

The oil level should be checked prior to flight. There will be an Oil Dip-Stick in the tank for this purpose. The dip-stick is calibrated to show maximum and minimum oil quantities.

If the oil quantity is **below** the minimum, then you will find that the oil overheats and/or the oil pressure is too low or fluctuates. If the oil quantity is **too great,** then the excess oil may be forced out through various parts of the engine, such as the front shaft seal.

The oil quantity needs to be checked before each flight, as it gradually decreases due to:
• burning with the fuel/air mixture in the cylinders;
• loss as a mist or spray through the oil breather;
• leaks.

Low Oil Pressure.
At normal power, a low oil pressure may indicate a lack of oil and an impending engine failure. Low oil pressure could mean:
● a lack of oil due to a failure in the oil system;
● insufficient oil;
● a leak in the oil tank or oil lines;
● a failure of the oil pump;
● a problem in the engine, such as failing bearings;
● the Oil Pressure Relief Valve (PRV) stuck open.

On start-up, the oil pressure gauge should indicate a rise within approx 30 sec.

High Oil Temperature.
Too little oil being circulated will also be indicated by a high oil temperature, i.e. a rising oil temperature may indicate a decreasing oil quantity. **Prolonged operation at excessive Cylinder Head Temperatures** will also give rise to a High Oil Temperature indication. This would be most likely to occur in situations of **'High Power, Low Airspeed'** (climbing), especially in high ambient air temperatures.

Faulty Oil Pressure Gauge.
Sometimes of course, the oil pressure gauge may be faulty. A low oil pressure indication may be recognised as a faulty indication – and not a genuine low pressure – by noting that the oil temperature remains normal over a period of time. Keep your eye on both gauges.

High Oil Pressure.
A pressure relief valve in the system should ensure that the oil does not reach an unacceptably high oil pressure. A **High Oil Pressure** may cause some part of the system to fail, rendering the whole oil system inoperative.

Low or Fluctuating Oil Pressure.
Where an indication of low or fluctuating oil pressure occurs and is associated with a rise in oil temperature whilst in flight – play it safe and land as soon as possible, as it could indicate a serious problem in the lubrication system.

No Oil — Engine-Seizure — No Power Very Quickly.

Gradual Loss of Oil.
If the engine was gradually losing oil, then the oil temperature would gradually rise due to less oil having to do the same amount of work – cooling and lubricating the engine. In such a situation the oil pressure would probably be maintained, but with the oil temperature rising, until the oil quantity reaches a critically low level when a sudden drop in oil pressure (and consequent engine problems) could occur.

If you suspect a problem concerning oil, then you should plan a landing before the time you estimate the oil problem will become serious. This is a matter of judgement for the Pilot, especially if the choice of nearby landing areas is not great.

☐ Now tackle the slippery questions on **Oil** in **Exercises 19.**

20

THE COOLING SYSTEM

The piston engine converts the chemical energy of the fuel into heat and pressure energy by combustion with air, and this is further converted into mechanical energy to drive the propeller. The transfer to mechanical energy is of course not complete and perfect. Energy losses as heat, noise, etc., may total more than half the original energy of the fuel. The engine will heat up.

High Engine Temperatures are best avoided as they will:
• reduce the efficiency of the lubrication system;
• affect the combustion of the fuel/air mixture;
• cause detonation in the cylinders;
• weaken engine components and shorten the life of the engine.

Most modern light aircraft engines are air-cooled by exposing the cylinders and their cooling fins to an airflow.

The fins increase the exposed surface area to allow better cooling.

As the airflow passes around a cylinder it may become turbulent and break away in such a manner that uneven cooling occurs, forming local poorly-cooled hot-spots.

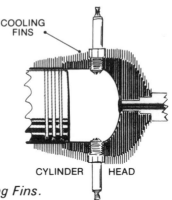

Fig.20-1. Cooling Fins.

To avoid this uneven cooling, cowling ducts at the front of the engine capture air from the high-pressure area behind the propeller and baffles distribute it as evenly as possible around the cylinders. After cooling the engine, the air flows out holes at the bottom and aft-end of the engine compartment.

Air cooling is least effective at high power and low airspeed, e.g. on take-off or go-around. The high power produces a lot of heat and the low airspeed provides only a reduced cooling airflow. At high airspeed and low power, e.g. on descent, the cooling might be too effective.

Some aircraft have moveable **Cooling Cowl Flaps** that can be operated (electrically or manually) from the cockpit, giving the Pilot more control over the cooling of the engine.

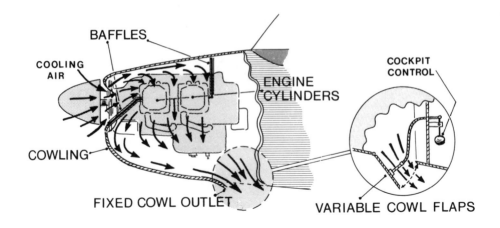

Fig.20-2. Cowl Flaps and Cooling of the Engine.

Open cowl flaps permit more air to escape from the engine compartment. This causes increased airflow over and around the engine. The open cowl flaps cause the parasite drag to increase (sometimes referred to as *'cooling drag'*). Closed or *'faired'* cowl flaps will reduce the airflow compared to when they are open, thereby reducing the cooling.

Cowl flaps are normally open for take-off, partially open or closed on climb and cruise, and closed during a power-off descent. They will be open on final in readiness for a go-around, when high power at a low airspeed will be required. **Cowl flaps should be open when taxying,** to help dissipate the engine heat.

The deciding factor for the Pilot in where to position the cowl flaps is the cylinder head temperature, or the anticipated cylinder head temperature, and this may be indicated to him in the cockpit by a **Cylinder Head Temperature (CHT) gauge.**

The Pilot should monitor the cylinder head temperature gauge throughout the flight and also on the ground, when cooling will be poor. The Pilot's Operating Handbook will give advice on satisfactory temperatures.

If excessive cylinder head temperatures are noted in flight, the cooling of the engine can be improved by:
- opening the cowl flaps fully (to allow greater airflow around the engine);
- making the mixture richer (extra fuel has a cooling effect in the cylinders due to the greater amount evaporated, so a rich mixture cools better than a lean mixture);
- reducing the engine power (so that less heat is produced);
- increasing the airspeed (for greater air cooling).

Just how the Pilot achieves the latter two is a matter for his judgement. On a climb he could reduce power and increase speed and climb with a reduced rate of climb. On a cruise (straight and level) at normal cruise speeds, he could not reduce the power and increase the airspeed except by commencing a descent, however **terrain** may prevent this.

Other factors influencing engine cooling and which the Pilot has little control over during flight include:

• Condition of the oil cooler. A dirty and inefficient oil cooler will not allow the best cooling of the circulating oil. The oil, being warmer than desired, will be unable to carry as much heat away from the engine, as well as having its viscosity and lubricating qualities reduced, which may lead to the creation of higher temperatures in the engine.

• Outside Air Temperature. Obviously, warm air will not cool the engine as well as cool air.

NOTE: On some aircraft the propeller **spinner** is part of the *'airflow director'* for the cooling air, and so these aircraft should *not* be flown without the spinner fitted. If you find yourself in such a situation, reference to the Operator or the CAA will establish what is allowable for your aeroplane.

□ Now complete **Exercises 20 — The Cooling System.**

21

HANDLING

Extreme care must be taken when operating an aeroplane. The Pilot has many things on his or her mind and, especially in the early stages of learning to fly, it is not unusual to feel unable to cope with all aspects of flying.

Your instructor will lead you through each procedure several times and then monitor your actions the next few times. Build up, by repetition, good safe procedures so that they become second nature.

Good **Airmanship** is perhaps the most important quality of a Pilot and its most important component is **Common Sense.** It involves careful pre-flight inspection of the aircraft, verifying that any required maintenance has been completed, ensuring the brakes are on and the area near the propeller is clear prior to starting the engine, correct procedures and checks, and well-placed confidence in yourself and your ability – confidence that you can complete the required flight without undue worries.

'Confidence' is not *'over-confidence',* which has caused many a Pilot (and his/her passengers) grey hairs. Having the confidence in yourself to make correct decisions firmly, as is necessary throughout the course of every flight, is a skill you should develop.

Understanding this theory side of aviation is a necessary preparation – and look at the full-time professional Pilots – they never stop studying and reading.

'Flying the Aeroplane' should always be the primary concern of the Pilot. Navigation calculations, radio work, operating the engine within the defined limitations, handling engine problems – all these are secondary to maintaining the aeroplane on a safe flight path.

KEEP YOUR PRIORITIES RIGHT.

A controlled descent, whilst you sort out an engine problem, shows far better airmanship than a quick solution of the engine problem, with no attention being given to the flight path and airspeed, allowing a spiral dive to develop.

Some incredible accidents have occurred – a trivial problem, a faulty globe in the landing gear indicator, once diverted the attention of a three-man crew long enough for a large aeroplane to descend several thousand feet into the ground. Never divert your attention from the flight path of the aeroplane for more than a few seconds.

A mistake in loading 20,000 **Pounds** of fuel instead of the required 20,000 **Kilograms** caused a modern wide-body airliner to actually run out of fuel in flight. So, **Keep a Fuel Awareness.** Occasional reference to the source of your engine power shows good airmanship. Ensure that the fuel selection is correct and that sufficient fuel remains for completion of your flight, plus reserves.

ENGINE HANDLING.

At all times, follow recommended procedures found in the manufacturer's handbook. This will ensure correct operation of the engine, thereby avoiding spark plug fouling, avoiding over-stressing the engine components, achieving best fuel economy and so on. Know the manufacturer's engine limitations and do not exceed them – for reasons of **Safety.**

Monitor the **Oil Temperature Gauge** (and the Cylinder Head Temperature Gauge if fitted) to help guard against high temperatures which are damaging to the engine. Avoid running the engine on the ground for prolonged periods if possible, but if unavoidable, face the aircraft into wind for better cooling and, if they are fitted, open the cowl flaps. If the limiting red-line temperatures are approached during ground operations, consider taxying clear of the runway and shutting the engine down to allow cooling.

Prevent spark plug fouling by avoiding operating the engine at very low rpm for long periods. At low idling rpm, deposits can form on the spark plugs which will increase their electrical conductivity and may lead to mis-firing.

Do not taxi over rough ground that could cause the propeller to hit long grass or other obstructions or even the ground itself. A sudden burst of high power on the ground, say when taxying on rough ground or to get out of a small ditch or gutter, can compress the nosewheel oleo and lower the propeller. If the propeller blades strike the ground (or even long grass), there may be propeller damage and possibly a bent engine crankshaft – a very costly lack of common sense.

Avoid engine run-ups on stony or gravel surfaces. The strong airflow and vortices around a propeller can easily pick up stones, etc. Damage, such as nicks to the blades, degrade the propeller's performance considerably. Nicks are liable to cause cracks in the blade as it flexes and can ultimately lead to blade failure in flight, with disastrous results. Propeller nicks and other damage should be brought immediately to the attention of the ground engineer.

The normal remedy is to *'dress them out'* with a file, i.e. blend the nick in. This will reduce the life of the propeller, so taxying over loose stones, etc., which are likely to cause nicks in the blades, is best avoided.

Stones thrown back by the propeller or the airflow around it can also do damage to other parts of the aircraft. If you want to remain friends with other users of the airfield, avoid taxying near open hangar doors resulting in stones, dirt and dust being blown into the workshop area – good airmanship includes thinking of others.

CROSS-CHECKING ENGINE INSTRUMENTS.

If one engine instrument indicates a problem, verify this, if possible, by checking against another instrument, e.g. an oil pressure gauge that suddenly shows zero could indicate that all the oil has been lost out of the system or it could be just a faulty gauge.

Cross-reference to the oil temperature gauge should establish the fault – a continuing normal oil temperature would indicate sufficient oil is still circulating, a rapidly increasing oil temperature approaching the maximum limit would indicate that a loss of oil has occurred and that the oil remaining cannot cope. In this case remedial action would have to be initiated fairly quickly.

If you are in flight, a serious loss of oil will mean an engine shut-down, so in a single-engine aeroplane prepare to land as soon as possible. With a faulty gauge, the engine will continue to operate normally.

An aeroplane with a constant speed (rpm) propeller will have a 'manifold pressure gauge' to indicate the air-pressure in the manifold between the carburettor and the cylinders. At a constant rpm, the manifold pressure will decrease as the aircraft climbs into air of lower density. Another cause of a decrease in manifold pressure is carburettor icing. Reference to the 'carburettor air temperature gauge' can aid you in determining if the decrease in Manifold Pressure is due to an increase in altitude and/or carburettor ice.

DO NOT MIS-USE THE ENGINE CONTROLS.

Mis-use of controls can lead to engine damage. Advance and retard the throttle smoothly. Opening the throttle by ramming it forward can induce an incorrect fuel/air mixture and cause the engine to cut-out or it can encourage detonation. Opening the throttle from idle to full in about three seconds is usually about as fast as you should go.

When reducing power, especially from high settings such as after take-off, do it slowly. Rapid changes of engine loading are best avoided – engine-failures often occur at changes of power setting, both decreasing as well as increasing the power.

On a prolonged descent at low power, to avoid the engine becoming too cool, it is good airmanship to slowly open the throttle for brief periods. Closing cowl flaps, if fitted, also helps. This will avoid a sudden temperature shock to the engine when it is returned to high power.

Use the mixture control correctly. A too-lean mixture at high power and low altitudes can cause detonation. It is usual to lean the mixture when cruising at altitude, depending upon the manufacturer's recommendations. On a very hot day, even 1,000 ft above mean sea level may have a density altitude of several thousand feet, and leaning may be required for efficient operation.

ROUGH RUNNING.

Vibration or rough running usually indicates a problem or impending problem. An **Out-of-Balance Propeller Can Cause Vibration.** If the vibration is due to a damaged propeller, possibly an out-of-balance propeller due to nicks, etc., then a change of rpm or a change of airspeed might reduce the vibration. This, of course, is only a temporary remedy until the aeroplane is landed.

If the vibration does not diminish, but worsens, it could indicate a loosening of the bolts attaching the propeller to the shaft. In this case, a shutting down of the engine is advisable. If you suspect this defect in a single-engine aeroplane, a landing as soon as possible (a forced landing, if necessary) should be contemplated.

If the out-of-balance condition is caused by ice on the propeller blades, then removal of the ice will remedy the vibration.

Engine Roughness can be continuous or intermittent. If the engine starts running roughly, refer immediately to the engine instruments to see if they indicate the cause.

An Inadequate Fuel Supply Can Cause Rough Running. A fuel quantity gauge showing empty and a fuel selector positioned to that tank would require immediate selection of a new fuel source if the rough running is not to end up as a total loss of power. With any change of tanks or any suspected problem with the supply of fuel to the engine, the Pilot should switch on the fuel boost pumps (if fitted) to ensure a steady fuel pressure.

Carburettor Ice Can Cause Rough Running. The presence of moisture, even as high humidity, could indicate the formation of ice in the carburettor. This causes a loss of power and possibly rough running. A carburettor air temperature gauge can aid you in determining this as the cause.

Application of Full Carburettor Heat will cause an initial decrease in performance (a drop in rpm for a fixed-pitch propeller), followed by an increase in power and smoother running as the ice is removed. The initial decrease in power is caused by the hot air entering the carburettor being less dense, mixing with the same weight of fuel as before application of carb heat and therefore enrichening the mixture. As the ice melts and the airflow improves, the power increases and the rough running disappears (hopefully).

If there is no carburettor ice present to begin with, then application of carburettor heat will still cause a decrease in rpm for a fixed-pitch propeller – but of course there will be no consequent rise in rpm as there is no carburettor ice to be melted.

Unless the aircraft is fitted with a carburettor air temperature gauge, 'carb heat' should be either full hot or full cold. Intermediate settings could worsen the situation by only changing the temperature marginally and allowing the formation of even more ice. Read again our notes on carburettor icing in Chapter 17.

Because the hot air provided when carburettor heat is applied is usually unfiltered (unlike the normal air induced into the carburettor), it is advisable to **avoid use of carb heat during ground operations** since it may introduce dust and grit into the carburation system and engine.

An Incorrect Mixture Can Cause Rough Running. A prolonged climb will gradually lead to a richening of the mixture as the air density falls, with consequent rough running – unless the mixture is leaned out correctly. A prolonged descent will require the Pilot to move the mixture control towards the rich position.

A Faulty Magneto/Ignition System Can Cause Rough Running. Select a low cruise power and select each magneto individually. If the engine runs smoothly on one particular magneto, but roughly on 'both' or on the other magneto, then select the single magneto system that gives smoother running. Consideration should be given to landing at the nearest suitable aerodrome – the aeroplane engine will still operate satisfactorily, but you now have all your eggs in one basket, and a failure of the second magneto system may leave you with none.

- **Fouling Of The Spark Plugs** can cause faulty ignition. Sometimes this can be cured by leaning the mixture to raise the temperature and perhaps burn the residue off the plug, or by changing the power setting.

- **Leakage Of The Ignition Current,** which can sometimes occur around the ignition harness (the ignition leads that carry the 'spark' to the cylinders), could be the cause, however this cannot be remedied in flight. This leakage from the ignition harness may be worse at high altitude/high power settings and in wet weather.

Excessive Consumption of Fuel and Oil Can Indicate a Problem. Whilst this may not cause rough running or a noticeable decrease in the short-term performance, it certainly indicates a decrease in the performance of the engine that should be investigated.

Inspect for leaks and check fuel and oil caps. Bring excessive consumption to the attention of a ground engineer.

STARTING THE ENGINE.

Ensure that adequate safety precautions are always taken. Position the aircraft prior to start so that it is clear of obstructions, other aircraft, open hangar/workshop doors, refuelling installations and that a clear taxi path is available.

Set the park brakes on or have the aircraft chocked, to avoid the embarassing and dangerous situation of the aeroplane commencing its own taxying. Chocking the nosewheel is not advisable due to its proximity to the propeller. Chocking the main wheels is safer for a single-engine aeroplane.

Be aware of the availability of fire-fighting equipment – just in case. Ensure no naked flames (cigarettes) or fuel spillages in the vicinity.

Be prepared to discontinue the start immediately if a problem develops or if someone approaches the danger area near the propeller.

Starting the Engine in Cold Temperatures.

Starting under these conditions usually requires some priming (providing an initial charge of fuel to the cylinder). Many aircraft have a priming pump (electrical or manual) in the cockpit for this purpose.

In extremely cold conditions (approaching zero or below, or with frost or ice), it is good airmanship to turn the engine through 2 or 3 revolutions (magneto switches checked *OFF* of course, and possibly rotation in the reverse direction should be considered). This will break the oil seal on moving parts, thereby reducing the frictional drag within the engine. The electrical load on the starter motor and battery is therefore reduced – this might mean the difference between starting or not, as well as not draining the battery.

Starting a Hot Engine or One that Has Been Over-Primed.

Start the engine with the mixture control in *IDLE CUT-OFF* so that no more fuel enters the cylinders. As the mixture in the cylinders reaches the right balance the engine should fire, at which stage the mixture control should be moved to the rich position to provide a continuing fuel supply.

If the engine does not fire, then when you feel the cylinders have been cleared after several rotations, move the mixture control to rich to allow fuel to be drawn into the cylinders.

Know the procedures recommended in your aircraft's handbook. These differ from aeroplane to aeroplane and engine to engine. You should understand the reasons why a certain procedure is recommended and when it is appropriate to vary them slightly – an over-primed (flooded) engine or re-starting a hot engine may require a different technique to starting a cold engine in a cold climate.

Starting a Fuel-Injected Engine.

This may require a slightly different technique, especially when the engine is hot. Hot air and vapour in the fine fuel lines of a fuel-injected engine may disturb the fuel supply when starting.

One technique is to switch on the fuel boost pumps. This will pressurise the fuel lines up to the fuel control unit, removing any vapour in that part of the system. Leave the mixture control in *IDLE CUT-OFF* so that fuel does not reach the cylinders but is re-cycled back into the tank.

Some engines require the throttle to be opened for the boost pumps to work in *HIGH*. After 15 to 20 seconds, the narrow fuel lines to the fuel injectors should have been purged of vapour and now be full of fuel. A little bit of fuel will probably have found its way into the fuel nozzles near the cylinders and so a start, with the throttle in idle, can be made without priming.

Hand-Swinging a Propeller.

Do Not Attempt This Procedure Without Adequate Instruction.

Brakes and chocks should be checked. Follow the normal starting procedures to the point of actually engaging the starter. Verify that the throttle is in idle or close to it. Do not touch the propeller until you ensure the ignition switches are *OFF*. Position the propeller into a suitable position for swinging – the aim is to swing it, (i.e. firmly pull it) through the compression stroke.

Immediately prior to attempting a start, check that you have no loose clothing that could become caught in a spinning propeller, that you have a firm footing such that, after the swing and follow through, your body will have a natural tendency to move out of the plane of rotation of the propeller.

The propeller should be held near the tip, the ignition switched *ON*, and pulled in such a manner with a follow through, that, if the engine fires, your body has a natural swing away from the arc of propeller rotation. At all times **Treat the Propeller As Live.**

STOPPING THE ENGINE AND LETTING IT RUN DOWN.

A brief cooling period at idle rpm is usually recommended to allow gradual cooling. This also allows the Pilot to consider the condition of the engine, any abnormal indications, and to perform a systems check of the ignition system for *OFF*, if so desired. (This is mentioned in our description of the magneto/ignition system in Chapter 16.)

Most engines are shut down from a low power position by moving the mixture control to *IDLE CUT-OFF*, thus allowing the cylinders to be purged of fuel. All switches are usually moved to *OFF*.

It is a good practice to:
- leave the mixture control in the idle cut-off position;
- leave the throttle in the closed position in case someone turns the propeller and firing occurs due to a 'live' magneto system.

CHANGING POWER SETTINGS WITH A CONSTANT SPEED UNIT (CSU).

Whilst almost all training aeroplanes are fitted with a fixed-pitch propeller whose rpm is controlled with the throttle, slightly more advanced aeroplanes which you may soon fly have a propeller with a **Constant-Speed-Unit'.**

A CSU allows additional power from the engine to be absorbed, not by increased rpm, but by an increased blade angle which enables the propeller blades to take a larger 'bite' of the air.

The engine controls for a CSU are:
- **The Pitch Lever,** which controls the propeller (for rpm);
- **The Throttle,** which controls the fuel flow, determining the manifold pressure (MP).

The desired engine **Power** is provided by various combinations of rpm and manifold pressure.

Change RPM with the Pitch Lever — Change MP with the Throttle.

Manifold pressures higher than desired can lead to Detonation — to be avoided at all costs. In changing power, the aim is to ensure that MP is **not** increased as a first step, so that **increased MPs at reduced rpm are avoided.**

Increasing Power:
- Increase rpm with pitch lever first (MP will drop automatically – as a result of less time per cycle being available for the fuel/air mixture to be induced into the cylinder, hence a smaller charge in the cylinder for combustion).
- Increase MP to desired value with throttle.

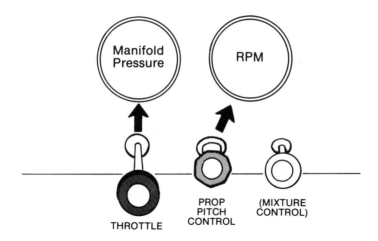

Fig.21-1. With a CSU, the Pitch Lever Controls RPM and the Throttle Determines the Manifold Pressure.

Decreasing Power:
- First reduce MP with throttle.
- Follow by reducing rpm with pitch lever (MP will rise a little automatically – as a result of more time per cycle for the fuel/air mixture to be induced into the cylinder, hence a larger charge in the cylinder for combustion).

After the reduction of rpm, some minor readjustment of MP will be necessary.

☐ Now attempt **Exercises 21 — Engine Handling.**

22

THE ELECTRICAL SYSTEM

Most aeroplanes have a requirement for an electrical system to operate such things as cabin lights, landing lights, instrument lights, navigation lights, beacons or anti-collision lights, starter motors, electric flaps, radios, radar, pitot heaters, fuel gauges, fuel boost pumps, electrically retractable landing gear and so on.

Your Pilot's Operating Handbook will contain information on the electrical system of your particular aircraft. A typical modern light aircraft has a **Direct Current (DC) electrical system.** The current is produced by an **Alternator** when the engine is running, or from a battery or external power source when the engine is not running.

The current runs through wires and the **'Bus Bar'** to the electrical unit requiring power, does its work there and then runs to **'Ground'** through an **Earthing Wire** attached to the aircraft structure (the return path of the electrical current).

THE BUS BAR.

The bus bar is a metal bar which allows electrical current to be supplied to various electrical circuits or units.

The bus bar is the distribution centre of the electrical system. Electrical power is usually supplied to the bus bar by an alternator (or generator) and a battery, and is distributed, via the bus bar, to the circuits and electrical components that require power.

THE BATTERY PROVIDES INITIAL POWER AND EMERGENCY POWER.

A **Battery** provides the initial electrical power to start the engine with an electric starter motor and provides a back-up source of electrical power.

Most light aircraft have a **Lead-acid Battery** that creates an electrical current (amps) by a chemical reaction between lead plates immersed in weak **sulphuric acid** that acts as an electrolyte. To prevent corrosion from any spillage of the acid, the battery is usually housed in its own compartment. The battery needs to be vented to exhaust the hydrogen and oxygen formed when it is being charged.

The battery is classified according to the voltage across its terminals (usually 12 or 24 volts) and its capacity to provide a current for a certain time (amp-hours).

A 30 amp-hour battery is capable of steadily supplying a current of 1 amp for 30 hours (or 6 amps for 5 hours, or 3 amps for 10 hours, etc.). If its electrical energy is depleted, e.g. by an engine start, the battery needs to be recharged. This normally occurs after the engine is running, when it absorbs power produced by the alternator. The largest current draw on the battery is during start-up, when it supplies electrical power to the starter motor to turn the engine over, so the greatest rate of battery recharging will normally occur immediately after the engine is started.

Periodically check the electrolytic level in the battery, to ensure that the plates are covered. If the level is well below the top of the plates, the battery will not retain its full charge for very long, and the ammeter will indicate a high charging rate in flight. Leaks, connections and security of the battery should also be checked. This is carried out in the regular maintenance schedule by ground engineers.

Do not start a flight with a 'flat' battery – it could result in having no electrical power in flight. If the battery is flat, replace it or have it recharged before flight.

Do not start the engine with radios and other unnecessary electrical equipment switched on. Large voltage fluctuations when the starter is engaged may severely damage sensitive electronic circuits. Turn on this ancillary electrical equipment after the engine is started, and after you have checked that the alternator is charging the battery. For the same reasons, **turn off ancillary electrical equipment before shutting down the engine.**

THE ALTERNATOR OR GENERATOR PROVIDES NORMAL IN-FLIGHT ELECTRICAL POWER.

The electrical power in most modern light aircraft is usually supplied by an **alternator.** They are mechanically-driven by the engine and produce a current. On older aircraft, the electrical power may be produced by a **generator,** which is completely self-supporting because it has its own permanent magnetic field. Once the rotor is mechanically turned the generator will produce electrical current.

Both alternators and generators initially produce alternating current (AC) – an electric current that flows in alternate directions. Since most aircraft require direct current (DC) – electric current that flows in only one direction – the AC has to be *rectified* to DC. The AC within the alternator is rectified into DC electronically with diodes, whereas within the generator an electromechanical device known as the commutator performs this function. Also, the **diodes** in the alternator **prevent any reverse current flow** out of the battery, whereas a generator requires a **Reverse Current Relay.**

As well as providing the power for lights, radios and other services, **a very important function of the generator/alternator is to recharge the battery** and ensure that it is ready for further use. Most aircraft electrical systems are Direct Current of 14 or 28 volts. Note that these voltages are marginally higher than the battery voltages to allow the battery to be fully recharged.

The Advantages of an Alternator.

Alternators:
- are lighter than generators because alternators do not contain as heavy electro-magnets and casings, and have a simpler and lighter brush assembly compared to generators;
- have a relatively constant electrical voltage output, even at low rpm;
- are easier to maintain (because of their simpler brush assembly and absence of a commutator).

The Disadvantage of an Alternator.

Unlike a generator, an alternator requires an initial current from the battery to set up a magnetic field, which is necessary before the alternator can produce an electrical current. Therefore **an aircraft with an alternator must have a serviceable battery,** and a flat battery must be replaced.

Even if you hand-swing the propeller to start the engine, the alternator will not come on-line unless the battery has at least some residual voltage. The advantages of an alternator outweigh this disadvantage.

VOLTAGE REGULATOR.

The correct output voltage from the generator/alternator is maintained by a **voltage regulator,** over which the Pilot has no direct control.

OVERVOLTAGE PROTECTOR.

Some aircraft have overvoltage protectors. Refer to your Pilot's Operating Handbook for information.

THE AMMETER MEASURES ELECTRICAL CURRENT (AMPERES).

An **Ammeter** measures the current (amperes) flowing into or out of the battery. (In some aircraft a **Voltmeter** is provided to measure the electromotive force available to deliver the current.)

There are two quite distinct types of ammeter presentation and as a Pilot you should understand exactly what this important instrument is telling you.

The Left-Zero Ammeter.

A left-zero ammeter measures only the output of the alternator or generator. It is graduated from zero amperes on the left end of the scale and increases in amperes to the right end of the scale, or it may be shown as a percentage of the alternator's rated load.

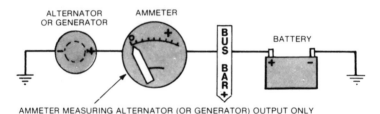

AMMETER MEASURING ALTERNATOR (OR GENERATOR) OUTPUT ONLY

Fig.22-1. The Left-Zero Ammeter.

As the left-zero ammeter indicates the electrical load on the alternator, this type of ammeter can be referred to as a **'Loadmeter'**.

With the battery switch *'ON'* and the engine **not running, or, with the engine running and the alternator switch** *'OFF'*, the ammeter will show zero. If the engine is started and the alternator is turned *'ON'*, the ammeter will then show the **alternator output.**

During start-up, the battery discharges electrical power, so immediately after start-up the ammeter indication will be quite high during the initial battery recharging.

When the battery is fully charged, and the alternator is operating, the ammeter should show a reading slightly above the zero graduation if all the other electrical circuits are switched off. As these extra circuits are switched on (lights, radios, etc.), the ammeter reading will increase.

If the ammeter reading drops to zero in flight, it probably means an **alternator failure.** Some electrical systems have a red warning light that illuminates when the alternator fails to supply electrical power. You should be familiar with the procedures for electrical failure in your Pilot's Operating Handbook, which may allow you to restore electrical power.

Generally, it is advisable to reduce electrical load to a minimum, as only the battery will be supplying electrical power. **Land as soon as possible** to have the problem corrected.

The Centre-Zero Ammeter.

The centre-zero ammeter measures the flow of current (amperage) **into** and out-of the **battery.**

- Current **into the battery** is **'charge'**, with the ammeter needle deflected **right** of centre.

- Current **out of the battery** is **'discharge'**, with the ammeter needle deflected **left** of centre.

- **No current flow either into or out of the battery** is shown by the needle being in the **centre-zero** position.

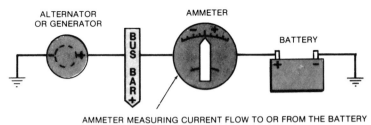

AMMETER MEASURING CURRENT FLOW TO OR FROM THE BATTERY

Fig.22-2. The Centre-Zero Ammeter.

1. With the battery switch *'ON'* and no alternator output, the ammeter will indicate a **discharge** from the battery, i.e. the battery is providing current for the electrical circuits that are switched on. The ammeter needle is to the left (discharge) side of centre-zero.

2. With the alternator 'ON' and supplying electrical power, if the electrical load required to power the circuits switched on is less than the capability of the alternator, the ammeter will show a **charge,** i.e. there will be a flow of current to the battery.

3. If the alternator is 'ON', but incapable of supplying sufficient power to the electrical circuits, the battery must make up the balance and there will be some flow of current from the battery. The ammeter will show a discharge. If this continues, the battery could be drained or 'flattened' – unload the electrical system by switching off unnecessary services until the ammeter indicates a charge, i.e. a flow of current from the alternator into the battery.

THE 'MASTER SWITCH' (or the 'BATTERY SWITCH/ALTERNATOR SWITCH').

The **master switch** controls all of the aeroplane's electrical system, with one very important exception – the ignition system which gets electrical power directly from the engine-driven magneto. (This is not completely true if the aircraft has an electric clock, which will draw a very small amount of electrical power at all times.)

The master switch needs to be 'ON' for any other electrical system to receive power or for the battery to be re-charged when the engine is running. It should be turned 'OFF' after stopping the engine, to avoid the battery discharging via services that are connected to it.

In **aircraft fitted with an alternator,** the master switch is a split switch (with two halves that can be switched on and off separately):

• One half for operating the **battery switch** (or master relay for the electrical systems), which connects battery power to the bus bar (electrical load distribution point or bar);

• The other half, the **alternator switch,** for energising the alternator. It connects the alternator field to the bus bar, thus providing the alternator with battery power for field excitation.

Both switches must be 'ON' for normal operation of the electrical system. If either switch has to be turned 'OFF' in flight then you should consider terminating the flight as soon as possible.

They can be switched on separately, but only the alternator can be switched off separately – switching the battery 'OFF' will automatically switch the alternator off as well.

Fig.22-3. The Master Switch (Battery Switch/ Alternator Switch).

FUSES, CIRCUIT BREAKERS AND OVERLOAD SWITCHES.

These are provided to protect the equipment from any electrical current overload. If there is an electrical overload or short-circuit, a fuse-wire will melt or a circuit breaker (CB) will *pop*, i.e. pop out, and break the circuit so that no current can flow through it. It may prevent the circuit from overheating, smoking or catching fire.

It is normal procedure (provided there is no smell or other sign of burning or overheating) to **reset a circuit breaker once only,** by pushing it back in or re-setting it. If a circuit breaker pops again, you can be fairly sure there is an electrical problem and so it should **not** be reset a second time. Similarly, **a fuse-wire should not be replaced more than once** (with the correct amperage first checked on the replacement fuse-wire). Spare fuses of the correct type and rating should be available in the cockpit.

Do not replace a blown fuse with one of a higher rating (e.g. 15 amp is a *higher rating* than 5 amp) as this may allow excessive current to flow through the electrical circuit that it is supposed to protect. An electrical fire could result.

Overload switches are combined *ON–OFF* switches and overload protectors. Overload switches will switch themselves off with an electrical overload. The Pilot can switch them back on like a resettable Circuit Breaker.

Some aircraft handbooks recommend a delay of a minute or two prior to re-setting, to allow for cooling of the possibly overloaded circuit. If you detect fire, smoke or a burning smell, then caution is advised and a reluctance to re-set the CB or replace the fuse would be the normal reaction of an experienced Pilot.

RELAY.

A 'relay' is a device in one electrical circuit that can be activated by a current or a voltage to produce a change in the electrical condition of another electrical circuit.

Instead of having high currents and heavy wiring running to where the switches are in the cockpit (with consequent current losses, fire danger from arcing, etc.), a low amperage current operated by a switch can be used to close a remote relay and complete the circuit for a much higher amperage circuit, such as for the starter motor.

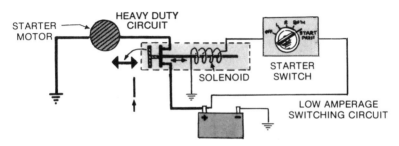

Fig.22-4. Low Amp Relay Circuit Activates High Amp Starter Circuit.

A relay is usually operated on the **solenoid** principle. A solenoid is a metal bar or rod with a coil of wire wound around it. If a current passes through the coil, it establishes a magnetic field that can move the metal rod, which can then perform some mechanical task, such as making or breaking a contact in another electrical circuit.

A typical relay consists of a contact held open by a spring, thereby interrupting an electrical circuit. Around the stem of the relay is wound a coil of wire. If a current is made to pass through this coil, a magnetic field is set up that will move the relay to the closed position, thereby completing the circuit and allowing current to flow in it.

The current that activates the relay is in a completely different circuit to the relay.

Occasionally a relay will stick even though its activating current has been removed, and an unwanted current will flow through the circuit. Many electric starters have an associated red warning light that will stay illuminated to warn the Pilot of the starter relay sticking and the starter motor still operating even though he has switched the starter switch to *OFF.* (In this situation, the engine would be stopped by starving it of fuel – Mixture Control to *IDLE CUT-OFF.)*

EXTERNAL POWER SOCKET or GROUND SERVICING RECEPTACLE.

The more sophisticated light aircraft and most large aircraft have provision for a suitable external power source to be plugged into the aeroplane's electrical system – either to provide ground power over an extended period when the engine or engines are not running or to conserve the aircraft battery during an engine start.

On some aircraft types, with an unserviceable battery, external power can be plugged in but will not connect in to the aircraft electrical system – a small current from the battery is needed to operate the relay that connects the plugged-in external power to the aircraft circuit. There are other systems that operate differently to this, and we refer you to your Pilot's Operating Handbook. Ensure a Ground Power Unit (GPU) of the correct voltage is used. (Putting a 28V GPU on a 12 volt aircraft will damage the radios and electrics.)

ELECTRICAL MALFUNCTIONS.

An electrical overload will normally cause a fuse-wire to melt or a circuit breaker to pop. This protects the affected circuit. Allow two minutes to cool and, if no indication of smoke, fire or a burning smell, replace the fuse or re-set the circuit breaker – but **reset once only.**

If the CB pops or the fuse melts again – do not reset or replace a second time.

The ammeter should be checked when the engine is running to ensure that the alternator is supplying sufficient current (amps) for the electrical services and to recharge the battery. The ammeter usually indicates the rate at which current is flowing into the battery and recharging it.

With the engine running, the ammeter can indicate two faults:
1. Insufficient current to charge the battery.
2. Too much current.

With insufficient current from the alternator, or none at all, electrical services activated should be reduced to a minimum to conserve the battery, and thought should be given to making an early landing. Most batteries cannot supply all electrical services for a long period.

With too much current and an excessive charge rate, the battery could overheat and the electrolyte (which may be sulphuric acid) begin to evaporate, possibly damaging the battery. If the cause of the excessive current is a faulty voltage regulator, equipment such as the radio could be adversely affected. Many aircraft have an *overvoltage sensor* that would, in these circumstances, automatically shut-down the alternator and illuminate a red warning light in the cockpit to alert the Pilot.

NOTE: Operations of an alternator-powered electrical system with a partially-charged battery (e.g. unable to turn the engine over) are not recommended for the above reasons.

If the Alternator fails (indicated in most aircraft by either the ammeter indication dropping to zero or by a red warning light), the battery will act as an emergency source of electrical power. To extend the period for which the battery can supply power following failure of the alternator the electrical load should be reduced. This can be done by switching off non-essential services such as unnecessary lighting and radios. Consideration should be given to terminating the flight at a nearby suitable aerodrome while electrical power is still available.

TYPICAL ELECTRICAL SYSTEMS.

The Pilot's Operating Handbook for each aeroplane will contain a diagram of its electrical system and the services to which electrical power is supplied. It is good airmanship for a Pilot to be aware of what powers vital services and instruments in his particular aeroplane. The arrangement varies greatly between aeroplanes, but certain important services that could be powered by the electrical system include:

- some, or all, Gyroscopic Flight Instruments (Turn Co-ordinator, Attitude Indicator and Direction Indicator) – a common arrangement is electrically-powered Turn Co-ordinator with vacuum-driven AI and DI to reduce the possiblity of all gyroscopic instruments failing simultaneously; (note that the pitot-static instruments – ASI, Altimeter, VSI – are not electrically powered);
- usually the Fuel Quantity Indicators, and perhaps an Oil Temperature Gauge, or Carburettor Air Temperature Gauge (if fitted);
- the Starting system;
- Landing Lights, Beacon, Strobe, Cabin Lights, Instrument Lights;
- Radios.

Check the electrical system diagram for your particular aeroplane. The following two Figs. show examples of typical light aircraft electrical systems.

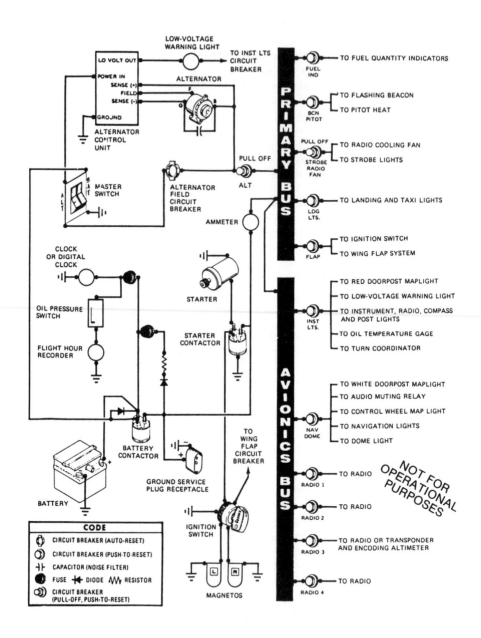

Fig. 22-5. A Typical Light Aircraft Electrical System.

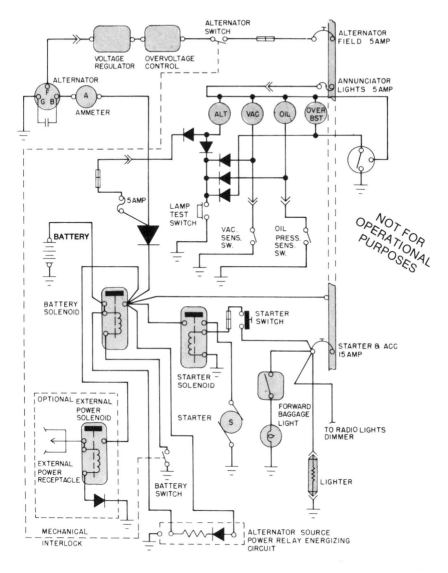

Fig.22-6. Schematic Diagram of another Typical Light Aircraft Electrical System.

☐ Now attempt **Exercises 22 — The Electrical System.**

23

THE VACUUM SYSTEM

The gyroscopes in the Flight Instruments may be spun electrically or by a stream of high-speed air directed at buckets cut into the perimeter of the rotor. The vacuum system (which **draws,** or **induces,** this high-speed air into the gyro instrument cases and onto the gyro rotors, causing them to spin very fast) needs a little explaining.

ENGINE-DRIVEN VACUUM PUMP.

Most modern vacuum systems use an engine-driven suction pump. This evacuates the cases of the gyroscopic-driven instruments creating a *'vacuum'* (low pressure).

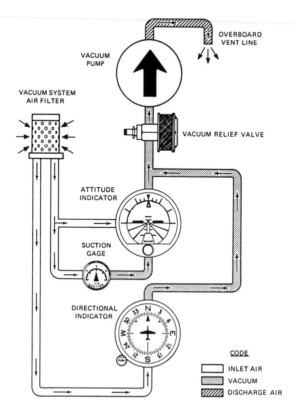

Fig.23-1. A Typical Vacuum System.

216

The required suction is 3–5 inches of mercury (i.e. a pressure 3–5 inches of mercury **less than atmospheric),** indicated in the cockpit on a suction gauge. Filtered air is continuously drawn in at high speed through a nozzle directed at the gyro buckets, causing the gyro to spin at high rpm, often in excess of 20,000 rpm. This air is continuously being sucked out by the suction pump and exhausted into the atmosphere.

If the air filter blocks, or the vacuum system fails, the reduced airflow may allow the gyroscopes to gradually run down and the air-operated instruments will eventually indicate erratically or incorrectly, or respond slowly. A lower suction will be indicated on the gauge. **Failure of the vacuum pump** will be indicated by a zero reading on the suction gauge. With luck, the gyroscopes may have sufficient speed to allow the instruments to read correctly for a minute or two before the gyros run down following failure of the vacuum pump. **A zero reading on the suction gauge** could also mean a failure of the gauge (rather than the vacuum pump), in which case the instruments should operate normally.

If the vacuum pressure is too high, the gyro rotors may spin too fast and suffer mechanical damage. To prevent this, a vacuum relief valve (or vacuum regulator) in the system will admit air from the atmosphere to reduce the excessive suction.

When the gyros are not being used, they should normally be *caged* (if provision is made to do this), i.e. locked in a fixed position. This is also recommended in the Pilot's Operating Handbook of some aircraft when performing aerobatic manoeuvres.

VACUUM PROVIDED BY A VENTURI TUBE.

Some aircraft (especially older ones) have their vacuum system operated by a **venturi-shaped tube** on the outside of the airframe. When air flows through the tube and speeds up due to its shape, the static pressure decreases (Bernoulli's Principle). This low pressure area, if connected to the gyro instrument cases, will cause air to be drawn through each instrument via an internal filter and spin the gyroscopes, as in the engine-driven system.

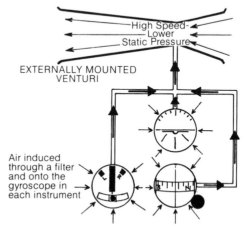

Fig.23-2. Air Flowing through a Venturi Tube can create a 'Suction', and Power a Vacuum System.

Before the Venturi-powered Vacuum System can work there must be an appreciable airflow through the Venturi tube. This is normally created by the forward motion of the aeroplane through the air – sufficient airflow being provided at flying speeds. **It may be several minutes after take-off before the gyroscopes are spinning fast enough for the instrument indications to be reliable.** This is a significant disadvantage compared to the engine-driven system.

Other disadvantages are the increased Drag caused by the externally mounted Venturi-tube, and the possibility of ice affecting it (like a carburettor).

□ **Exercises 23 — The Vacuum System.**

24

LANDING GEAR, TYRES AND BRAKES

The typical training aeroplane has a fixed tricycle landing gear consisting of two main wheels, which incorporate brakes, and a nosewheel, which can be steered by moving the rudder pedals. A typical pre-flight check by a Pilot will include:
- check landing gear and its support points for damage, such as cracks, corrosion or distortion;
- check oleo struts for cleanliness, leaks and correct extension;
- check tyres for inflation, damage and creep;
- inspect brake installation for external evidence of leaks, and for damage and security.

LANDING GEAR.

The **main wheels** carry most of the load when the aeroplane is on the ground, especially during the take-off and landing, and so are more robust than the nosewheel. They are usually attached to the main aircraft structure with legs in the form of:
- a very strong spring leaf of steel or fibre-glass;
- struts and braces; or
- an oleo-pneumatic unit.

The **nosewheel** is of lighter construction than the main wheels and is usually attached to the main structure of the aircraft (often near the engine firewall) with an oleo-pneumatic unit.

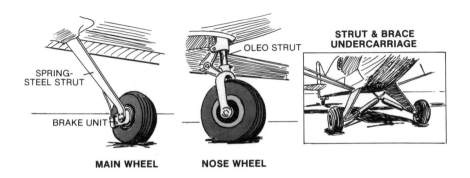

Fig.24-1. Various Means of Attaching the Undercarriage.

The landing gear legs or struts and their attachment points must carry heavy stresses, especially during landings and take-offs, or when taxying over rough surfaces, hence the need to inspect them carefully prior to flight. Obvious damage should be inspected by a qualified Engineer before the aeroplane flies again.

The **oleo-pneumatic unit** is of *telescopic* construction, with a piston that can move within a cylinder against an opposing pressure of compressed air. The piston is attached to the wheel by an *oleo-strut* and the cylinder is attached to the airframe. The nosewheel attachment is often near the firewall directly behind the engine.

The greater the load on the strut, the more the air is compressed by the piston. Whilst the aeroplane is running along the ground, the load will be varying and so the strut will move up and down as the compressed air absorbs the loads and shocks, preventing jarring of the main aeroplane structure.

Special oil is used as a **damping agent** to prevent excessive in and out telescoping movements of the oleo-pneumatic unit and damp its rebound action.

When the aircraft is stationary, a certain length of *polished* oleo strut should be visible (depending of course to some extent on how the aeroplane is loaded) and this should be checked in the pre-flight external inspection. Items to check are:
- correct extension when supporting its share of the aeroplane's weight.
- the polished section of the oleo strut is clean of mud or dirt (to avoid rapid wearing of the seals during the telescoping motion of the strut); and
- there are no fluid leaks.

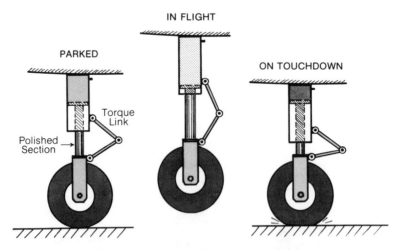

Fig.24-2. The Oleo-Pneumatic Unit.

A **torque-link** is used on nosewheel assemblies to correctly align the nosewheel with the airframe. It links the cylinder assembly attached to the aeroplane structure with the nosewheel assembly, and is hinged to allow for the telescopic extension and compression of the oleo.

Some aircraft have **nosewheel steering,** achieved by moving the rudder pedals which are attached by control rods or cables to the nosewheel assembly, thereby allowing the Pilot greater directional control when taxying.

Other aircraft have **castoring nosewheels** which are free to turn, but are **not** connected by controls to the cockpit. The Pilot can turn the aeroplane by using the rudder when it has sufficient airflow over it (due to either slipstream or airspeed) or with differential braking of the main wheels. **Most tailwheels castor,** allowing the Pilot to steer by differential braking, or by using the rudder if it has sufficient airflow over it.

Nosewheel oleo-pneumatic units are prone to **nosewheel shimmy,** an unpleasant and possibly damaging vibration set up when the nosewheel oscillates a few degrees either side of centre as the aeroplane runs along the ground. To prevent this, most nosewheel assemblies are fitted with a **shimmy-damper,** a small piston-cylinder unit that dampens out the oscillations and prevents the vibration. If nosewheel-shimmy does occur, it could be because the shimmy-damper is insufficiently pressurised or the torque link has failed.

Fig.24-3. The Shimmy-Damper

TYRES.

Aeroplane tyres are pneumatic and must be operated at approximately the correct pressure for them to function as designed. Vibration during taxying, uneven wear and burst tyres may result from a pressure that is too high; damage to the tyre structure and a tendency for the tyre to *creep* with respect to the rim will occur if the pressure is too low. **Correct inflation** is important in achieving a good service life from a tyre.

Creep will occur in normal operations because of the stresses during landing, when a stationary tyre is forced to rotate upon touching the ground and has to 'drag' the wheel around with it, and when the aeroplane is braking or turning. If the tyre creeps too far, the inner tube may suffer and the valve may become unusable or even break.

To monitor creep, there are usually paint marks on the wheel flange and on the tyre which should remain aligned. If any part of the two creep marks is still in contact, that amount of creep is acceptable; but if the marks are separated, then the inner tube may suffer damage and the tyre should be inspected and serviced. This may require removal and re-fitting, or replacement.

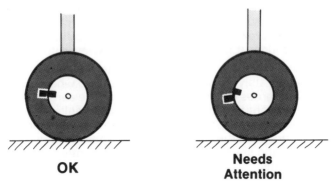

OK   **Needs Attention**

Fig.24-4. 'Creep' Marks on the Tyre and Wheel Flange enable Visual Checks for Creep.

The strength of a tyre comes from its carcass which is built up from *casing cords* and then covered with rubber. The *Ply Rating* is a measure of its supposed strength. Neither the rubber sidewalls nor the tread provide the main strength of the tyre; the sidewalls protect the sides of the tyre carcass, and the rubber tread provides a wearing surface at the contact points between the tyre and the runway.

Shallow cuts or scores in the sidewalls or on the tread, or small stones embedded in the tread, will **not** be detrimental to tyre strength. However, any large cuts (especially if they expose the casing cords) or bulges (that may be external indications of an internal casing failure) should cause a Pilot to reject the tyre prior to flight.

The condition of the tyres should be noted during the pre-flight external inspection, especially with respect to:
- inflation;
- creep;
- wear, especially flat spots caused by skidding;
- cuts, bulges (especially deep cuts that expose the casing cords);
- damage to the structure of the sidewall.

WHEEL BRAKES.

Most training aeroplanes are fitted with **disc brakes** on the main wheels. These are hydraulically operated by the **toe brakes** which are situated on top of the rudder pedals. Pressing the left toe brake will slow the left main wheel down and pressing the right toe brake will slow the right main wheel down. Used separately, they provide **differential braking,** which is useful for manoeuvring on the ground; used together, they provide normal braking.

A typical system involves a separate master cylinder for each brake containing hydraulic fluid. As an individual toe brake is pressed, this toe pressure is transmitted by the hydraulic fluid to a **slave cylinder** which closes the brake friction pads (like calipers) onto the brake disc. The brake disc, which is part of the wheel assembly, has its rotation slowed down.

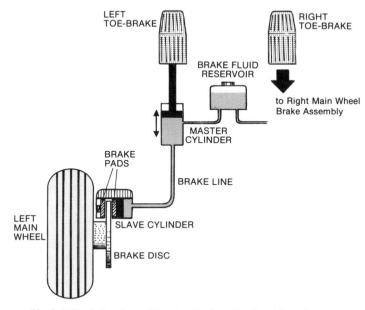

Fig.24-5. A Typical Simple Hydraulic Braking System.

Most aircraft have a parking brake (usually hand-operated, sometimes in conjunction with the toe-brakes) that will hold the pressure on the wheel brakes and can be used when the aeroplane is parked.

During the pre-flight external inspection, the Pilot should check the brakes to ensure that they will function when he needs them, noting especially that:
● there are no leaks of hydraulic brake fluid from the brake lines;
● the brake discs are not corroded or pitted;
● the brake pads are not worn-out;
● the brake assembly is firmly attached.

A severely corroded or pitted disc will cause rapid wear of the brake pads, as well as reducing their effectiveness, and, in an extreme case, the disc may even fail structurally. Fluid leaks from the brake lines or cylinders indicate a faulty system that may in fact provide no braking at all when it is needed. Any brake problems should be rectified prior to flight.

Following a satisfactory external inspection, the Pilot should still test the brakes immediately after the aeroplane first moves, by closing the throttle and gently applying toe brake pressure. **Brake wear** can be minimised by judicious use of the brakes during ground operations.

☐ Now complete **Exercises 24** on The Landing Gear, Tyres and Brakes.

Intentionally Blank

3

FLIGHT INSTRUMENTS

25

PRESSURE INSTRUMENTS

The first impression most people have of an aeroplane cockpit or flight deck is of the number of instruments. When you analyse the instrument panels of even the largest jet transport aeroplanes, you will find that the instrumentation is not all that complicated. In fact, the basic instruments will be very similar to those found in the smallest training aeroplane.

Aircraft Flight Instruments fall into two basic categories:
- those which use **variations in air pressure;** and
- those using **the properties of gyroscopic inertia;**
- to produce information useful to the Pilot.

This chapter covers the 'Pressure Operated Instruments'.

The basic flight instruments informing the Pilot of airspeed (Air Speed Indicator), altitude (Altimeter) and rate of change of altitude (Vertical Speed Indicator) are **pressure instruments.**

As we saw in our study of Principles of Flight there are two aspects of air pressure that need to be considered – **static pressure** and **dynamic pressure.**

Static Pressure.

In the atmosphere at any point **static pressure** is exerted equally in all directions. It is the result of the weight of all of the molecules composing the air above that point pressing down. Static pressure of the atmosphere is being exerted at all points on the skin of your hand right now. As its name implies, static pressure does not involve relative movement of the air. Static Pressure is measured on the surface of an aeroplane by a *'static vent'.*

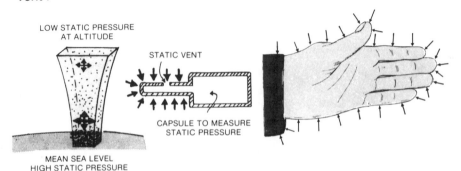

LOW STATIC PRESSURE
AT ALTITUDE

STATIC VENT

CAPSULE TO MEASURE
STATIC PRESSURE

MEAN SEA LEVEL
HIGH STATIC PRESSURE

Fig.25-1. Static Pressure.

Dynamic Pressure.

If you hold your hand up in a strong wind or out of the window of a moving car, then an extra wind pressure is felt due to the air impacting your hand.

This extra pressure, over and above the static pressure which is always present, is called **Dynamic Pressure** or pressure due to relative movement. It is felt by a body which is moving relative to the air, i.e. it could be moving through the air or the air could be flowing past it.

Just how strong this dynamic pressure is depends upon two factors:

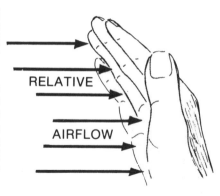

Fig.25-2. Dynamic Pressure.

1. **The Speed of the Body Relative to the Air.**
   The faster the car drives or the stronger the wind blows, then the stronger the extra dynamic pressure that you feel on your hand. This is because of the more molecules of air that impact upon it per second.

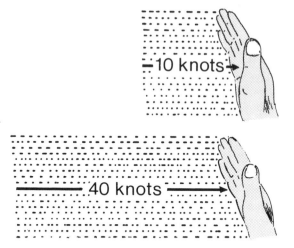

Fig.25-3. Dynamic Pressure Increases with Airspeed.

2. **The Density of the Air.**
   In outer space no matter how fast you travelled you would not feel this dynamic pressure because there are practically no molecules to impact upon you.

   At sea level, where the atmosphere is densest, your hand would be struck by many molecules per second, certainly many more than in the upper reaches of the atmosphere. So, even though you might be travelling at the same speed, you will feel a much lower dynamic pressure in the higher and less dense regions of the atmosphere.

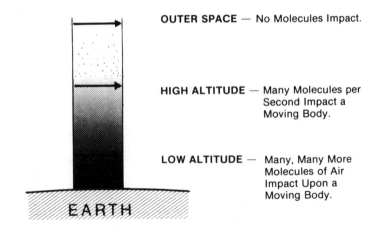

OUTER SPACE — No Molecules Impact.

HIGH ALTITUDE — Many Molecules per Second Impact a Moving Body.

LOW ALTITUDE — Many, Many More Molecules of Air Impact Upon a Moving Body.

EARTH

Fig.25-4. Dynamic Pressure Depends upon Air Density.

At higher altitudes, you would feel less dynamic pressure than at lower altitudes where the atmosphere is denser, even though you were moving through the air at the same speed.

The actual measure of this **Dynamic Pressure** is written:

Dynamic Pressure = ½ Rho V-squared

– where **Rho** is air density, decreasing with altitude, and **V** is the speed of the body relative to the air (i.e. it does not matter whether the body is moving through the air, or the air blowing past the body, or a combination of both – as long as they are moving relative to one another there will be a dynamic pressure).

Dynamic Pressure varies directly with *'V-squared'*. It is one of the *'square laws'* quite common in nature.

TOTAL PRESSURE.

In the atmosphere, some static pressure is always exerted, but, for dynamic pressure to be exerted, there must be motion of the body relative to the air. **Total Pressure** consists of **Static Pressure** plus **Dynamic Pressure.**

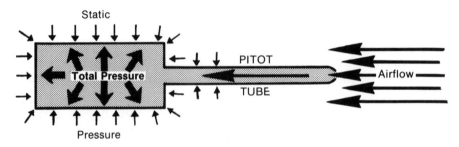

Static

Total Pressure

PITOT

TUBE

Airflow

Pressure

Fig.25-5. Total Pressure is Measured by a Pitot Tube.

NOTE: Total Pressure is also known as Pitot Pressure, Ram Pressure or Impact Pressure.

Much of **Airflow Theory** was developed by **Bernoulli** and is expressed as:

STATIC PRESSURE   +   DYNAMIC PRESSURE   =   TOTAL PRESSURE
measured by static line   ½ Rho V-squared   measured by
(barometer or altimeter)   Pitot Tube

Subtracting Static Pressure from both sides:
DYNAMIC PRESSURE = TOTAL PRESSURE – STATIC PRESSURE

NOTE: The Air Speed Indicator (ASI), which we will shortly discuss, indicates **Dynamic Pressure** (i.e. the difference between Total Pressure and Static Pressure). The ASI scale is calibrated to read in units of Speed **(Knots)** rather than units of pressure.

THE PITOT-STATIC SYSTEM.

Three flight instruments make use of pressure readings:
- the **Altimeter** relates static pressure to height;
- the **Vertical Speed Indicator** relates the rate of change of static pressure to a rate of climb or descent; and
- the **Air Speed Indicator** relates the difference between total (or pitot) pressure and static pressure to the speed through the air.

A **pitot tube** provides the measurement of total pressure and a **static vent** provides the measurement of static pressure. There are two common arrangements of the pitot-static system:
- a combined pitot-static head; or
- a pitot tube (possibly on the wing) and a static vent (or two) on the side of the fuselage.

The pitot tube must be mounted on the aeroplane in a position where the airflow is not greatly disturbed; often forward of or beneath the outer section of one wing. Otherwise the Air Speed Indication system will suffer from significant errors.

Pitot heaters are sometimes provided as a precaution against ice blocking the pitot tube. These are electrical elements built into the Pitot Tube, operated by a switch from the cockpit. It is important that a pitot heater is switched *OFF* when the aeroplane is not in flight or overheating damage could result.

Some aircraft have two static vents, one on each side of the fuselage, so that the reading for static pressure, when evened out, is more accurate, especially if the aeroplane is slipping or skidding (i.e. is being flown out-of-balance).

There is often an **alternative static source** fitted in the cabin in case of ice or other matter obstructing the external vents. Cabin pressure is often slightly less than the external atmospheric pressure and will cause the instrument readings to be slightly in error when the alternate static source is being used.

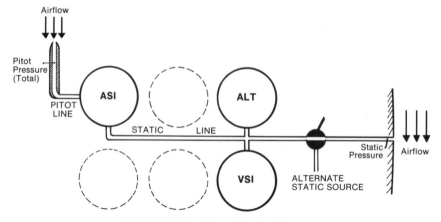

Fig.25-6. The Pitot-Static System.

It is vital that the pitot tube and static vent(s) are not damaged or obstructed, otherwise false readings from the relevant flight instruments could degrade the safety of the flight. They should be carefully checked in the pre-flight external inspection. The pitot cover, used to prevent water or insects accumulating in the tube, should be removed. They should **not** be tested by blowing in them, since very sensitive instruments are involved.

THE AIR SPEED INDICATOR.

The Air Speed Indicator shows the Pilot an airspeed referred to as the Indicated Air Speed (IAS). It is related to the *'dynamic pressure'*.

We can find dynamic pressure by subtracting the static line measurement from the pitot tube measurement. This is easily done by having a diaphragm with Total Pressure from the pitot tube being fed onto one side of it and Static Pressure from the static line being fed onto the other side of it.

The diaphragm will position itself and a pointer connected to it, according to the difference between the Total Pressure and the Static Pressure, i.e. according to the Dynamic Pressure, ½ Rho V-squared.

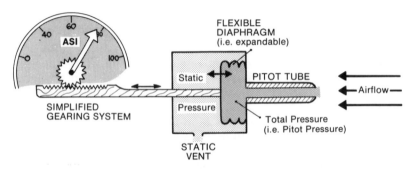

Fig.25-7. The Air Speed Indicator Measures Dynamic Pressure.

In practice we assume that the density of air remains constant at its mean sea level value, which of course it does not, but this allows us to graduate the scale around which the pointer moves in units of speed (usually **knots**). This does however give us an Air Speed Indicator that reads accurately the airspeed on an ISA standard day at MSL – (i.e. Mean Sea Level in the International Standard Atmosphere is 15 degrees Celsius, Pressure Altitude 0 ft.)

As airspeed increases, the dynamic pressure increases, but the static pressure remains the same. The difference between the Total Pressure (measured by the pitot tube) and the Static Pressure (measured by the static vent or static line) gives us a measure of the Dynamic Pressure (which is related to Indicated Air Speed). This difference between total and static pressures causes the diaphragm to reposition itself, and the pointer to indicate a higher airspeed.

Colour Coding on the Air Speed Indicator.

To assist the Pilot, ASIs in modern aircraft have certain speed ranges and certain specific speeds marked according to a **conventional colour code.**

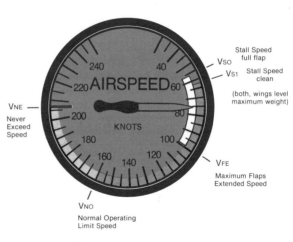

Fig.25-8. Indicated Air Speed is What We Read on the ASI.

- **Green Arc**: denotes the **normal operating speed range,** from stall speed at maximum all-up weight (flaps up, wings level) up to V_{NO} ('normal operating limit speed' or 'maximum structural cruising speed') which should not be exceeded except in smooth air. Operations at IASs in the green arc should be safe in all conditions, including turbulence.

- **Yellow Arc:** denotes the **caution range,** which extends from V_{NO} (normal operating limit speed) up to V_{NE} (the never exceed speed). The aircraft should be operated at IASs in the caution range **only in smooth air.**

- **White Arc:** denotes the **flap operating range,** from stall speed at maximum AUW in the landing configuration (full flap, landing-gear down, wings level, power-off) up to V_{FE} (maximum flaps extended speed).

- **Red Radial Line:** denotes V_{NE}, the **never exceed speed.**

Note   1.   Some ASIs have blue radial lines to denote certain important speeds, (e.g. best single-engine speed for a light twin-engined aeroplane).

2. All ASI markings refer to **Indicated** Air Speed (IAS) and **not** True Air Speed (TAS). Where weight is a factor in determining the limit speed (e.g. stall speeds) the value marked is for the **Maximum All-Up Weight** (max AUW) situation in all cases.

THE DIFFERENCE BETWEEN INDICATED AIR SPEED AND TRUE AIR SPEED.

The fact that Indicated Air Speed (IAS) and True Air Speed (TAS or V) are usually different seems to worry many inexperienced Pilots, but it need not. IAS is an aerodynamic airspeed which is closely related to dynamic pressure – ½ Rho V-squared.

The dynamic pressure (½ Rho V-squared) is a vital aerodynamic quantity because the amount of Lift produced is a function of dynamic pressure:

$$\text{Lift} = C_{\text{Lift}} \times \tfrac{1}{2} \text{ Rho V-squared} \times S$$

– the amount of Drag created also being a function of dynamic pressure: Drag = $C_{\text{Drag}} \times \tfrac{1}{2}$ Rho V-squared $\times$ S.

When we discuss the **flight performance** of the aeroplane – (Lift, Drag, Stalling Speed, Take-Off Speed, Maximum Speeds, Climbing Speed, Long Range Cruise Speed, etc.) – we talk in terms of **Indicated Air Speed** (IAS).

The IAS is vital performance information for the Pilot, as the aerodynamic qualities of the aeroplane depend upon it.

Indicated Air Speed (IAS) Is Important Aerodynamically.

The **True Air Speed** (TAS) is the actual speed of the aeroplane relative to the air. TAS (or V) is important for navigational purposes, such as describing speed through the air (TAS) from which can be found speed over the ground (GS).

True Air Speed (TAS) Is Important For Navigation.

True Air Speed (TAS) Usually Exceeds Indicated Air Speed (IAS).
We will consider the situation in a climb: it is usual for the Pilot to maintain the same climbing Indicated Air Speed throughout the climb, i.e. a constant reading on the ASI. As the aeroplane gains height it climbs into less dense air because air density (Rho) decreases with increasing altitude.

For IAS to remain the same, then the value of the dynamic pressure (which is '½ Rho V-squared') must remain the same. Therefore, because air density (Rho) is decreasing with altitude, to retain a constant '½ Rho V-squared' (and consequently a constant Indicated Air Speed) the value of V (the True Air Speed) must be greater. So if you are climbing to a higher altitude with the Air Speed Indicator showing a constant IAS, the TAS will be gradually increasing.

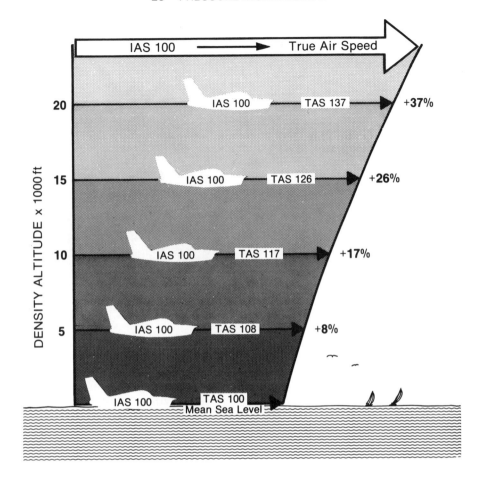

Fig.25-9. With IAS Constant, TAS Increases with Increase in Altitude.

On a hot day and at high aerodromes, to generate sufficient Lift for take-off the aeroplane must be accelerated to a higher V (i.e. TAS) to compensate for the decreased air density. (IAS shown on the ASI will remain the same.) This, coupled with possibly poorer performance from the engine/propeller, will mean a **longer take-off distance.**

NOTE: ● At 5,000 ft your TAS exceeds the IAS by about 8%.

● At 10,000 ft your TAS exceeds the IAS by about 17%.

These are handy figures to remember for rough mental calculations and also for when experienced Pilots are talking about the speeds that their aeroplanes "true-out at". If you are cruising at 5,000 ft with IAS 180 kt showing on the Air Speed Indicator, then your True Air Speed will be approximately 8% greater (8% of 180 = 14), i.e. 194 kt TAS.

Some Air Speed Indicators, As Well As Showing IAS, Can Be Made To Show TAS Also.

Some Air Speed Indicators have a manually rotatable scale attached to them (known as the *tempera-ture/altitude correction* scale), which allows the Pilot to read TAS as well as IAS and which is valid up to speeds of approximately 220 knots TAS. (Above this speed the compressibility of the atmosphere needs to be allowed for – this is considered in the Professional Pilot Licences.)

Setting the *temperature/altitude* scale on the Air Speed Indicator performs exactly the same function as setting the same scale on the Navigation Computer.

Fig.25-10. IAS (and TAS) Indicator.

It allows the Indicated Air Speed read on the ASI to be matched up with the True Air Speed, which is of navigational value when cruising. For performance purposes (take-off, landing and stalling speeds), it is IAS that is important, and not TAS. For this reason, some TAS scales do not extend into the low speed area.

PROBLEMS WITH A BLOCKED STATIC VENT OR PITOT TUBE.

A blockage or icing over will cause the pressure to be trapped in that particular line to the pressure instruments.

If you are **climbing** and the static vent ices over, then the static pressure trapped in the line will be higher than the actual static pressure where the aeroplane has climbed to. The measured difference between pitot (total) pressure and static pressure will be less than actual – therefore the ASI will under-read, i.e. show a lower IAS than actual.

On a **descent,** the reverse would be the case – a blocked static vent would cause the ASI to over-read, i.e. show an IAS higher than actual. This is a dangerous situation if the Pilot does not recognise it and reduces the speed, because the aeroplane will be flying at a speed less than that indicated.

If you commence a **take-off** with a completely blocked pitot tube only the static pressure trapped in the pitot tube will be fed to the ASI to be compared to the static pressure from the static vent. The ASI will indicate zero.

THE ALTIMETER

A Pilot needs to know how high he or she is for three basic reasons:

1. For **terrain clearance**, i.e. to ensure that the aircraft will not collide with terrain or fixed obstacles.

2. For **traffic separation**, i.e. to allow pilots to cruise at different altitudes and ensure safe vertical separation.

3. To be able to calculate the **performance capabilities** of the aircraft, and to operate it safely and efficiently.

The pressure altimeter is a barometer (*baro* – pressure, *meter* – to measure). It makes use of the fact that in the atmosphere:

Air Pressure Decreases with Altitude,
i.e. the higher you are in the Earth's atmosphere,
the **lower** is the static air pressure.

There are various **types of pressure altimeter**. The most compact and robust type for installation in an aircraft is the **aneroid** barometer, similar to those seen hanging on living-room walls.

As an aircraft climbs, the pressure in its immediate vicinity drops (usually about 1 millibar for every 30 ft gain in altitude). The aneroid, which is an expandable and compressible metal capsule containing a fixed amount of air, is able to expand. This movement is transmitted via a linkage system to a pointer which moves around the altimeter scale.

The altimeter scale is graduated, not in units of pressure (millibars, hectopascals, or inches of mercury), but in **feet** (ft).

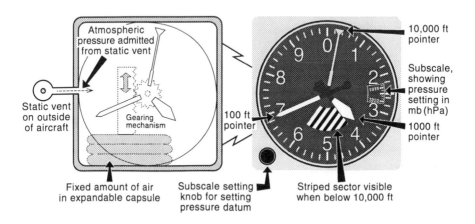

*Fig.25-11. The Altimeter converts Variations in
Static Pressure into Indications of Height;
(the Altimeter is reading 3690 ft).*

As the aircraft descends, the aneroid compresses due to the increasing pressure, and drives the pointer to indicate a lower altitude.

Errors In The Altimeter.

A number of errors are evident in altimeters:

- **Instrument Errors** – imperfections in the design, manufacture, installation and maintenance of the individual altimeter.

- **Instrument Lag** – the altimeter takes a second or two to respond to rapid pressure changes.

- **Position Error** – poor design may place the static vent in a position where the static pressure is not representative of the free atmosphere in that vicinity.

- **Blockages of the Static Vent** – if ice or wasps (or anything) blocks the static vent completely, then that static pressure will remain fixed in the line to the altimeter. A constant altitude will be indicated, even though the aircraft may be changing altitude.

If **ice** forms over the static vent on a climb-out, the altimeter will continue to read the altitude at which the static vent blocked, and not indicate the higher altitude that the aeroplane is actually at, i.e. it will under-read the actual altitude.

Similarly, on a descent, a blocked static vent will cause the altimeter to indicate a constant altitude, i.e. show an altitude higher than the actual altitude the aeroplane has descended to, i.e. it will over-read (dangerous, if terrain clearance is a problem).

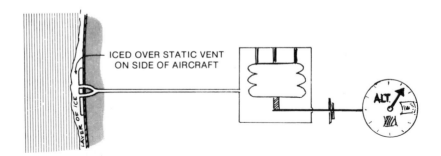

ICED OVER STATIC VENT
ON SIDE OF AIRCRAFT

ALT.

Fig.25-12. A Blocked Static Vent – Altimeter Reads Constant Irrespective of Aircraft Altitude.

THE UNIT OF PRESSURE.

The Unit of Pressure used in aviation in the United Kingdom is still **the millibar (mb),** however a new term – **the 'hectoPascal' (hPa)** – has been adopted in many countries. At the time of writing, the millibar is the unit to be used for the immediate future in the United Kingdom however 'hectoPascals' will be encountered internationally.

The two units, millibars (mb) and hectoPascals (hPa), are equivalent and so the change of unit has no operational significance other than the name change itself. In the **Air Pilot's Manual** the unit of pressure will be shown as 'mb(hPa)', however, for the UK, using 'mb' will be sufficient for examination and other purposes.

In the United States yet another unit of pressure is standard in aviation – the 'inch of mercury' (abbreviated 'Hg'). Altimeter subscales are graduated in this unit, commonly called **inches** but which always refers to the amount of pressure required to support a specific column of the element Mercury (Hg).

THE INTERNATIONAL STANDARD ATMOSPHERE (ISA).

Conditions in the actual atmosphere change from place to place and time to time. To have some sort of 'measuring stick' an International Standard Atmosphere (abbreviated 'ISA') has been defined as having:

- A mean sea level pressure of 1013·2 millibars (hectoPascals), which, in the lower levels of the atmosphere, decreases by 1 mb(hPa) for every 30 ft gained (approximately). For practical purposes, 1013 mb(hPa) for ISA MSL pressure is sufficiently accurate. (If you fly in the U.S.A., standard pressure is 29·92 inches, which is the same as 1013·2 millibars.)

- A mean sea level temperature of 15 degrees Celsius, that decreases by 2 degrees Celsius (approximately) for every 1,000 ft gained, i.e. at 3000 ft altitude in the ISA, the temperature should have fallen by 6 degrees to be 9 degrees Celsius.

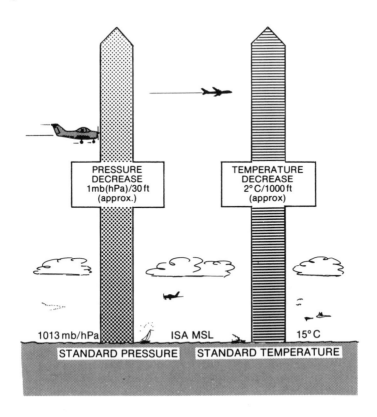

Fig.25-13. The International Standard Atmosphere.

The Main Use Of The International Standard Atmosphere Is To Calibrate Altimeters.

PRESSURE ALTITUDE.

'Pressure Altitude' is the height in the International Standard Atmosphere above the 1013·2 mb(hPa) pressure level at which the pressure equals that of the aircraft or point under consideration (definition).

If the pressure in the vicinity of the aeroplane is the same as that at 6,800 ft in the ISA, then its 'Pressure Altitude' is 6,800 ft. If the altimeter in the aircraft has its subscale set to 1013·2 millibars, it will read height above the 1013 mb(hPa) pressure level.

With 1013·2 Millibars on the Subscale the Altimeter Reads Pressure Altitude.

ALTIMETER SUBSCALE SETTINGS.

If the mean sea level pressure differs from the ISA MSL pressure of 1013 mb(hPa), there is a small **subscale** on the altimeter that allows us to set this actual MSL pressure (known as QNH).

QNH is usually within 20 mb(hPa) either side of 1013. As the altimeter will read the altitude above whatever pressure level is set in the subscale – **with QNH set in the subscale, the altimeter will read altitude,** (i.e. height Above Mean Sea Level). This is very handy for checking the amount of vertical clearance above terrain, radio masts, etc., which are shown on maps and charts in height AMSL.

In the UK, there is also a term **'Regional QNH'** (or *'Regional Pressure Setting')* which is the lowest QNH in a defined region; its use is described in the 'Aviation Law' Section of Volume 2, under 'Altimeter Setting Procedures'.)

The Altimeter Reads Height Above Whatever Pressure Level is Set in the Subscale.

If **1013 mb(hPa) is set** in the altimeter subscale, the altimeter will indicate **pressure altitude,** i.e. the equivalent height in the ISA above the 1013 mb(hPa) pressure level. If **the aerodrome surface pressure (QFE)** is set in the altimeter subscale, (i.e. on the ground, the altimeter will indicate 0), then in-flight the altimeter will indicate height above the aerodrome (only useful if you are not flying away from that aerodrome). QFE will be different for each aerodrome.

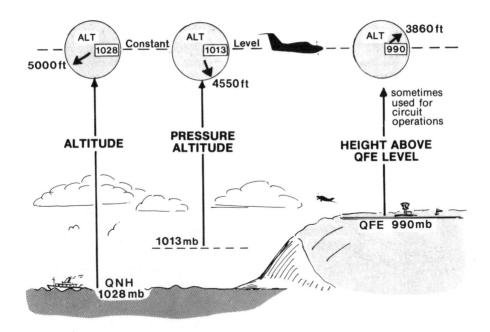

Fig.25-14. The Altimeter Reads Height Above Whatever Pressure Level Is Set in the Subscale.

Notice that, if your aeroplane stays at the same level, winding on millibars in the subscale will wind on more height, and vice versa.

Wind On Millibars, Wind On Height.

With 990 mb(hPa) set in the subscale in the above situation, the altimeter reads 3860 ft above the aerodrome level.

If you wind on millibars until 1013 mb(hPa) is set in the subscale, you also wind on height to 4550 ft – an increase of 23 mb(hPa) and 690 ft, i.e. 30 ft for each millibar (hectoPascal) – yet the aeroplane has not changed its level. If you then rotate the subscale (with the setting knob) until the current QNH of 1028 mb(hPa) is set, you also wind on height to 5000 ft – yet the aeroplane has still not changed its level.

NOTE: When the aeroplane in the above illustration lands on the runway, its altimeter should read:
• zero if the aerodrome QFE is set;
• aerodrome elevation if the Aerodrome QNH is set.

THE VERTICAL SPEED INDICATOR (VSI).

Whilst a Pilot could form some idea of how fast he is changing altitude by comparing the altimeter against a stopwatch (a somewhat tedious process), the Vertical Speed Indicator can provide a direct readout of the **rate of change of altitude.**

The VSI is a pressure instrument based, like the altimeter, on the fact that air pressure decreases with altitude. The VSI converts a rate of change of static pressure to a rate of change of altitude, which is expressed in hundreds (or thousands) of **feet per minute (fpm).** The VSI is also called the **Rate of Climb Indicator.**

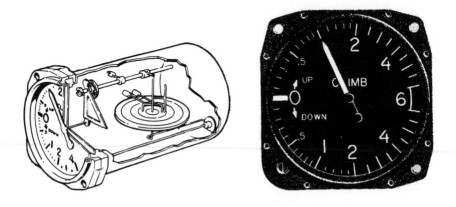

Fig.25-15. The Vertical Speed Indicator.

If the aeroplane commences a descent, the new and higher pressure is conducted straight into the capsule. Because there is some delay in the new pressure being conducted through the capillary or 'choke' to the surrounding area, the capsule will expand. This drives the pointer around the scale (graduated in fpm) to indicate a rate of descent, e.g. 500 fpm.

A Pilot (being very good at arithmetic) would know that when flying at a rate of descent of 500 fpm he will take 3 minutes to descend 1500 ft.

If the **static vent became iced over or blocked,** then the two pressure areas (inside the capsule and surrounding it) would equalise and the VSI would read zero, even though the aeroplane's height might be changing.

THE ALTERNATE STATIC SOURCE.

The static pressure is vital to the functioning of the Air Speed Indicator, the Altimeter and the Vertical Speed Indicator. Many aircraft have an alternate source of static pressure that can be fed to the instruments in the event of the primary source not providing correct static pressure for some reason.

The alternate static source (in unpressurised aircraft) often taps static pressure from within the cockpit, which is slightly less than the outside pressure.

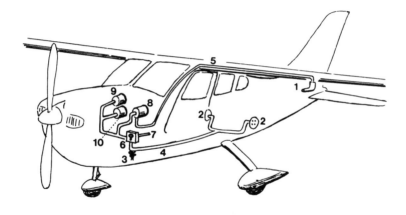

1. PITOT TUBE	6. ALTERNATIVE STATIC SELECTOR
2. STATIC PRESSURE SOURCES	7. ALTERNATIVE STATIC PRESSURE
3. STATIC DRAIN	8. AIRSPEED INDICATOR
4. STATIC DRAIN	9. ALTIMETER
5. PITOT LINE	10. VERTICAL SPEED INDICATOR

Fig.25-16. Typical Pitot-Static System Installation.

The instruments will then indicate slightly in error:
- the altimeter will indicate an altitude higher than actual.
- the difference between total pressure and static pressure will be greater than actual, and so the Air Speed Indicator (which measures this difference) will show an IAS greater than the actual IAS.
- the VSI will initially indicate a climb when first connected to the alternate static source, but will then settle down and read correctly – the VSI reads the rate of change of static pressure.

☐ **Exercises 25 — Pressure Instruments.**

26

GYROSCOPIC INSTRUMENTS

A gyroscope is a rotating wheel (or *'rotor'*), mounted so that its axis can turn freely in one or more directions. A rotating mass is capable of maintaining the same absolute direction in space despite what goes on around it – this property is called **'rigidity in space'**. Therefore, the gyroscope is useful as an indicator of direction and attitude. Due to the property of *'rigidity in space'* the gyro is able to remain stable in space whilst the aeroplane moves around it.

The degree of rigidity of a gyroscope depends upon the mass of the rotor, the speed at which it is rotating, and the radius at which the mass is concentrated. A large mass concentrated near the rim and rotating at high speed provides the greatest directional rigidity.

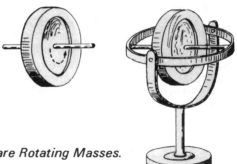

Fig.26-1. Gyroscopes are Rotating Masses.

A gyroscope has a second property called **'precession'**. If a force is applied to the gyroscope, the change in direction brought about by the force is not in line with the force, but is displaced 90 degrees further on in the direction of rotation.

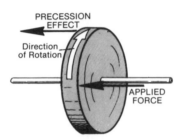

Fig.26-2. Gyroscopic Precession.

242

A Simple Demonstration Of Gyroscopic Effect.

The 'gyroscopic effect' is quite common (you use it every time you lean your bicycle over to turn a corner), but difficult to understand. Cleaning up in our office (at 2 am, after a hard day's work on this manual), we discovered an excellent demonstration of gyroscopic precession, which we now refer to (privately) as the *'Electrolux'* effect.

Take a *'barrel-type'* vacuum cleaner (we used an Electrolux, model 720, hose removed) and balance it by the handle so that its nose is free to move vertically. The demonstration consists of applying a force to move the nose of the cleaner horizontally, and seeing the effect in the vertical plane.

1. With **the motor not running,** sharp movements of the nose left or right have no vertical effect.
2. With **the motor running** (the rotating mass acting as a gyro rotor):
   - a sharp movement of the nose horizontally to the right causes the nose to drop vertically.
   - a sharp movement of the nose horizontally to the left causes the nose to rise vertically.

There are various ways of mounting the gyroscope on one or more axes of rotation (Gimbals), depending upon the information required from that gyroscopic instrument. Gyroscopes are used in the Turn Co-ordinator / Turn Indicator, the Artificial Horizon and the Directional Indicator.

THE TURN CO-ORDINATOR AND THE TURN INDICATOR.

These instruments use *'rate gyros'.* The rotating mass has freedom to move about two of its three axes and is designed to show the rate of movement of the aircraft about the third axis (in this case the turning or normal axis). This rate of movement is indicated to the Pilot in the cockpit on one of two possible types of presentation – either a **'Turn Indicator'** (which has a vertical needle or 'bat') or a **'Turn Co-ordinator'** (which has a symbolic aeroplane).

Fig.26-3. The Turn Co-ordinator and the Turn Indicator.

NOTE: Both these instruments indicate the aircraft's *'rate of turn'* and **not** *'angle of bank',* however, because the gyro in the Turn Co-ordinator is mounted slightly differently to that in the Turn Indicator, the Turn Co-ordinator will also show **'rate of bank'.** It will respond when an aeroplane banks, even before the turn actually commences. Also note that the symbolic aeroplane on the Turn Co-ordinator (even though it resembles that on an Attitude Indicator) does not give pitch information.

If the aeroplane is turning to the left, this turning force is passed to the gyroscope as shown, **the spin axis of the turn indicator being horizontal.** The applied force causes the gyro to change its direction a further 90 degrees in the direction of rotation, i.e. it will cause the gyro to tilt (or *precess*). The greater the turning force, the greater the tendency to tilt. That is, the Turn Indicator derives its turning information from the precession of a gyro which has its spin axis horizontal, as seen below. **The spin axis of a Turn Co-ordinator,** however, is tilted slightly to the horizontal, which provides a reaction not only to turning but also to rate-of-roll.

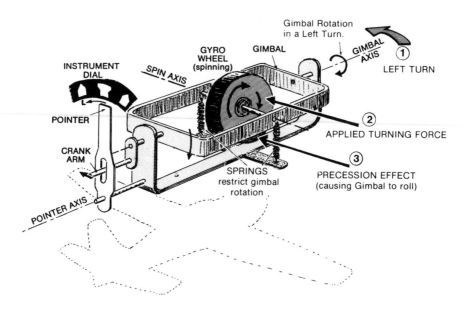

Fig.26-4. Workings of the Turn Indicator.

This tilting of the gyroscope stretches a spring, which makes the gyro precess with the aircraft turn until the rates match up, when further tilt ceases. A pointer moved by the gimbal tilting indicates the rate of turn against a scale, i.e. a turn indicator.

The scale is graduated to show a *'Rate 1 turn'* (3 degrees a second, therefore 180 degrees in one minute, 360 degrees in 2 minutes), a *'Rate 2 turn'* (6 degrees a second) and so on. This is a means of checking the accuracy of the turn indicator – time yourself through a steady turn of say 90 or 180 degrees and see if the number of degrees/second matches up with the turn indicator.

The gyroscope may be rotated electrically or it may be spun by a small jet of air directed at small *'buckets'* cut into the edge of the gyro wheel.

In the latter case, you should check that the vacuum system is providing sufficient air (a *'suction'* of 2·5 inches of mercury is usually adequate), otherwise the gyro rpm will be low, its rigidity in space less than desired, causing less pointer movement for a particular rate of turn to occur. That is, with a low vacuum – the turn indicator under-reads (i.e. the rate of turn will be greater than the rate indicated).

THE BALANCE INDICATOR.

A small curved glass cylinder containing a ball can be used to indicate the balance of the aeroplane. If no yawing forces are present, the ball will be at the bottom centre position. If there is a yawing force, the ball will be driven to one side – the greater the yaw, the greater its movement up the curved glass cylinder.

Right Rudder
required

IN BALANCE   **OUT OF BALANCE**

Fig.26-5. The Balance Indicator,
(at base of Turn Co-ordinator and Turn Indicator.)

In a balanced turn, the ball will still be in the central position and the Pilot will not feel thrown to one side.

If the aircraft is **'slipping'** into the turn, the ball will be on the low side and the Pilot will feel as though he is falling down in the direction of turn. A bit of rudder on the low side will put the ball back into the centre and the Pilot will feel comfortable in his seat. **'Ball to the Left, Use Left Rudder'.**

If the aircraft is **'skidding'** out of the turn, the ball and the Pilot will be thrown to the outside of the turn. A bit of rudder on the high side will balance the turn.

Whilst the balance indicator is not a gyroscopic instrument, but purely a mechanical indicator of balance, we present it here because it is found in a combined Turn and Balance indicator in most aeroplanes.

TURN AND BALANCE INDICATOR.

The correct use of this combined instrument is to bank the aeroplane to get the desired angle of bank and rate of turn, and then to balance the turn with the rudder so that the ball is central.

If the ball is to the left, use left rudder — if the ball is to the right, use right rudder. In days gone by, instructors said *"kick the ball back into the centre"*. *"Pressure the ball back into the centre"* is preferable.

Pilot checks for the serviceability of this instrument should include:

- a check of the gyro rotation speed (whirring sound and no failure flags if electrically-driven, correct vacuum if pressure-driven),

- correct indications in a turn whilst taxiing *("turning left, skidding right – turning right, skidding left"),* and, if in any doubt, a timed turn in flight (clock versus a turn through a known number of degrees).

245

THE ATTITUDE INDICATOR (ARTIFICIAL HORIZON, GYRO HORIZON).

As the aircraft changes its attitude, the *'earth gyro'* that is the basis of the Attitude Indicator retains its rigidity relative to the Earth's vertical. This means that the aeroplane moves around the gyro rotor of the Attitude Indicator which, as can be seen in *Fig. 26-6,* has a vertical spin axis.

Attached to the gyroscope is a picture of the horizon, around which the aeroplane (and the instrument panel) moves. The attitude of the aeroplane to the real horizon is symbolised by the artificial horizon line attached to the gyro and a small symbolic aeroplane attached to the instrument dial.

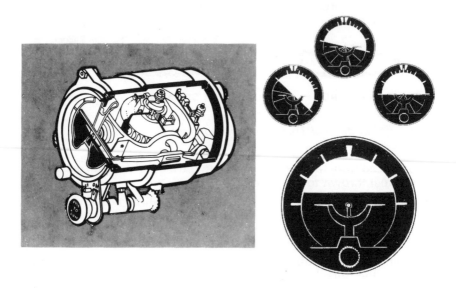

Fig.26-6. The Attitude Indicator Shows Pitch Attitude and Bank Angle.

The Attitude Indicator shows pitch (attitude) and roll (angle of bank). It shows a picture of the aircraft's attitude, but tells the Pilot nothing about the performance of the aeroplane.

The same nose-high attitude could occur in a steep climb or in a stalled descent – to know the performance of the aeroplane, the Pilot needs to refer to other instruments (Air Speed Indicator, Altimeter, Vertical Speed Indicator).

The Pilot should check the power source of the attitude gyro (whether it is electrical, or vacuum – about 4·5"Hg). Some Indicators, especially the vacuum-driven ones, have limits of pitch and bank which, if exceeded, may cause the gyro to topple and give erroneous readings (your operating handbook may contain this information, otherwise refer to your Instructor).

Some gyros are caged when not being used. If caged, it should be uncaged when the aeroplane is straight and level and the gyro is up to speed. This should be done shortly before take-off or in straight and level unaccelerated cruising flight. Also, the small model or index aeroplane should be aligned with the artificial horizon on the instrument when the gyro is up to speed and the aeroplane is straight and level (in-flight or on the ground).

The Attitude Indicator is subject to small errors when the aircraft accelerates or decelerates. This affects the pendulous gravity unit used to keep the axis of rotation vertical. Acceleration, as on take-off, may cause a small transient error in pitch and roll, but this is hardly visible in training aircraft with low acceleration.

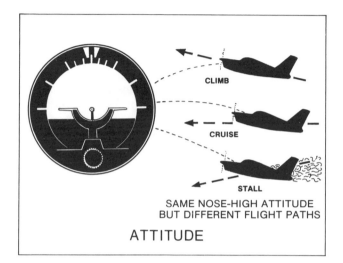

CLIMB

CRUISE

STALL

SAME NOSE-HIGH ATTITUDE
BUT DIFFERENT FLIGHT PATHS

ATTITUDE

LEFT HAND
TURN

BANK

Fig.26-7. The Attitude Indicator Displays Attitude and Bank Angle.

THE DIRECTION INDICATOR (DIRECTION GYRO, HEADING INDICATOR).

The magnetic compass is the primary indicator of direction in most aircraft. It is, however, difficult to read in turbulence and subject to acceleration and turning errors. It is a difficult instrument to fly accurately on.

The DI is a gyroscope that is aligned with the magnetic compass periodically in flight. It takes its direction from the compass, but is not subject to acceleration and turning errors (making accurate turns and heading-keeping possible) and is easy to read in turbulence.

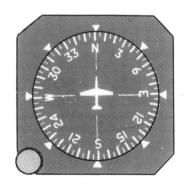

There are mechanical errors in the DI (friction) that will cause it to drift off accurate alignment with Magnetic North. This is called **'Mechanical Drift'.**

Fig.26-8. The Direction Indicator.

The *'perfect'* DI rotor will maintain its alignment precisely in space. However, due to the movement of the aeroplane through space, the line in space from the aeroplane to North will steadily change. This gives rise to **'Apparent Drift'** – a natural phenomenon caused, not by changes in the gyro's plane of rotation due to mechanical imperfections, but by motion of the earth through space and motion of the aircraft relative to the earth.

(This topic is pursued further at Commercial Pilot Licence level. Here at PPL level, all you need to remember is to re-align the DI with the Magnetic Compass every 10 or 15 minutes, following the suggested procedure described below.)

Checks on the Direction Indicator.

The Pilot should check the power source (the electrical system or the vacuum system, depending upon type), and when taxying, the correct turn indications on the DI *("turning right, heading increases – turning left, heading decreases")*.

The DI has a **'slaving knob'** that enables the Pilot to re-align the DI with the magnetic compass – correcting for both mechanical drift and apparent drift. This should be done every 10 or 15 minutes – about a 3 degree drift is acceptable in this time. Some older Direction Indicators have to be uncaged after re-aligning with the magnetic compass.

Procedure For Re-Aligning the DI with the Magnetic Compass.

- Choose a reference point directly ahead of the aircraft, aim for it and fly steadily straight and level;
- Keeping the nose precisely on the reference point, read the Magnetic Compass Heading (when the compass is steady);
- Maintain the aeroplane towards the reference point and then refer to the DI, adjusting its reading (if necessary) to that taken from the Magnetic Compass;
- Check that the aircraft has remained steadily heading towards the reference point during the operation – (if not, repeat the procedure).

VACUUM-DRIVEN GYROSCOPES.

Many gyroscopes are operated by a vacuum system which draws high-speed air through a nozzle and directs it at the gyro rotor blades. A vacuum pump that draws air through is generally preferable to a pressure pump that blows air through, since the air may pick up contaminants such as oil from the pump which could affect the very sensitive rotor.

The suction is shown on a gauge in the cockpit and, typically, is of the order of 3–5"Hg (5 inches of mercury below atmospheric pressure). If the vacuum reading is too low, the air flow will be low, the rotor(s) will not be up to speed and the gyros will be unstable or only respond slowly; if it is too high, the gyro rotors may spin too fast and be damaged.

The vacuum in most aeroplanes is provided by an **engine-driven Vacuum Pump,** but some older aeroplanes may have the vacuum provided by an **externally-mounted Venturi-tube** (making the gyroscopic instruments unusable until after several minutes at flying speed following take-off).

ELECTRICALLY-DRIVEN GYROSCOPES.

When the electrical Master Switch first goes on, you will probably hear the gyroscopes start to spin up. They should self-erect and red power-failure warning flags (if fitted) should disappear.

If the engine is shut down on the ground and the master switch is left on, these instruments will be drawing power from the battery and the battery may become *'flat'*. Not a very desirable situation, so ensure that there is no power to the electrically driven gyroscopes when leaving the aeroplane for any length of time.

Fig.26-9. Flight Instrument Panel of a Cessna 172.

ERRORS IN GYROSCOPIC INSTRUMENTS.

If the gyroscope is not up-to-speed, the instrument may indicate erratically, respond only slowly to changes in attitude and/or heading, or indicate incorrectly.

- Check for a red power-failure warning flag on electrically-driven instruments, and check for correct suction on vacuum-driven instruments.
- Check that the Direction Indicator is aligned with the Magnetic Compass during steady straight and level flight and that the Attitude Indicator, if it has a caging device, has been uncaged, also in steady straight and level flight or in a level attitude on the ground.

☐ Now complete **Exercises 26 — Gyroscopic Instruments.**

27

THE MAGNETIC COMPASS

The *'simple'* Magnetic Compass is one of the most poorly understood instruments in the cockpit. Since it is found in almost all aircraft – from Tiger Moths to Boeing 747s – we have decided to give it the full treatment.

In most light aircraft, the Magnetic Compass is the primary source of direction information, to which other directional indicators are aligned. In steady flight, the **lubber line** of the Magnetic Compass indicates the **magnetic heading** of the aeroplane.

If you handle the compass incorrectly, then perhaps accurate directional information will not be available to you.

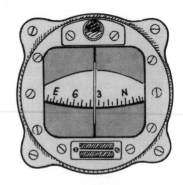

Heading 035° M

Fig.27-1a. The Magnetic Compass.

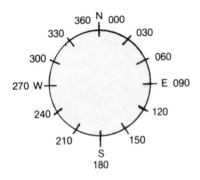

Fig.27-1b. Direction

DIRECTION.

There are two common ways to describe direction – using the cardinal points (the four chief directions) of North, South, East and West, or by using a circle of 360 degrees going clockwise from North (True or Magnetic as the case may be).

Direction is almost always expressed as a three-figure group (e.g. 251, 340, 020, etc.), the only exception being runway direction where the numbers are rounded-off to the nearest 10°. A runway bearing 247°M would be referred to as RWY 25.

These notes go a little beyond what is required in the
examination, but they will help to save you flight
time as you learn about turning onto compass headings.

A bar magnet that is freely suspended horizontally will swing so that its axis points roughly North-South. The end of the magnet that points towards the Earth's North Magnetic Pole is called **'the North-seeking Pole'** of the magnet.

The magnet is an ancient means of determining direction and it is still used in almost every aeroplane flying.

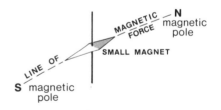

Fig.27-2.
A Simple Bar Magnet.

THE EARTH'S MAGNETIC FIELD (or TERRESTRIAL MAGNETISM).

The Earth acts like a very large and weak magnet. The surface of the Earth is covered by a weak magnetic field – lines of magnetic force that begin deep within the Earth near Hudson Bay in Canada and flow towards a point deep within the Earth near South Victoria Land in Antarctica.

Because of their proximity to the North and South Geographical Poles (which are known as True North and True South on the Earth's axis of rotation), the magnetic poles are referred to as the North Magnetic Pole and the South Magnetic Pole.

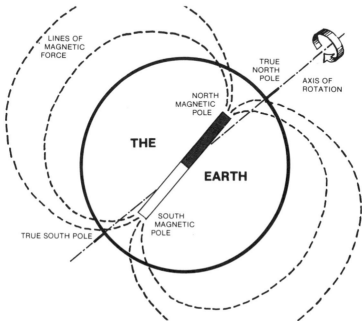

Fig.27-3. The Earth Has A Magnetic Field.

VARIATION.

The Latitude-Longitude grid shown on maps is based on the geographical poles – True North and True South. Our small compass magnet, however, does not point exactly at True North and True South. The perfect compass magnet points at the North Magnetic Pole.

The angular difference between True North and Magnetic North at any particular point on the Earth is called **Variation** – if the magnet points slightly East of True North, then the Variation is said to be East. If the compass points to the West of True North, then the Variation is West.

Isogonals.

On maps, as well as the lines forming the latitude-longitude grid, are dashed-lines joining places that have the same Magnetic Variation, known as **Isogonals.**

For example, the Four Degrees West isogonal is drawn through all the places having a Variation of 4°W. If you are anywhere on this line, then you can relate the message your Compass is giving you about Magnetic North to True North – your compass will point at Magnetic North, which will be 4 degrees West of True North.

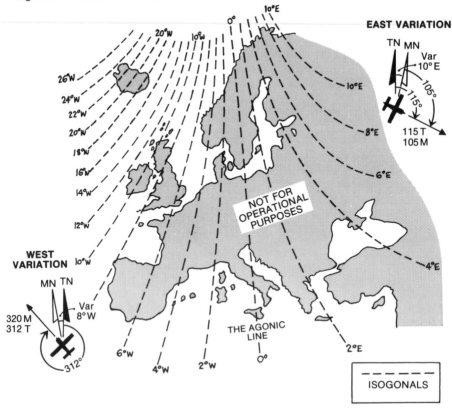

*Fig.27-4. Variation is the Angle Between True and Magnetic;
Isogonals Join Places of Equal Magnetic Variation.*

Example 1: If your compass indicates due East, i.e. 090 degrees Magnetic, and the Magnetic Variation where you are is 4 degrees West, then your heading related to True North is 090 – 4 = 086 degrees True.

An easy way to remember the relationship between True and Magnetic is:

VARIATION WEST, MAGNETIC BEST,

VARIATION EAST, MAGNETIC LEAST.

Example 2: If the Magnetic Variation in your area is 10 degrees East and your aeroplane is heading 295 on the Magnetic Compass, what is your true heading?

Variation East, Magnetic Least –

so 295°M is 295 + 10 = 305°T.

DEVIATION.

Unfortunately, the magnet in the compass is affected not only by the magnetic field of the Earth, but by any magnetic field. The aeroplane is made up of metal, rotating parts of an engine, radios, etc., all of which can generate their own magnetic field.

The effect that these fields in a particular aeroplane have on its magnetic compass is called **Deviation,** and they cause the compass to deviate or deflect from precisely indicating Magnetic North.

In each aeroplane is a small placard, known as the **Deviation Card,** which shows the Pilot the corrections to be made to the compass reading to obtain the magnetic direction. This correction usually involves only a few degrees and is an easy mental calculation to do in flight.

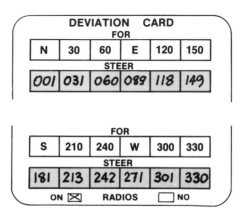

Fig.27-5. Deviation Card.

PRECAUTIONS WHEN CARRYING MAGNETIC OR METAL GOODS.

The deviation card is written out by an engineer who has actually checked the compass in that particular aeroplane. This deviation correction card allows only for the magnetic influences in the aeroplane that were present when he tested the compass.

Common Items in the Cockpit NOT to leave near the Magnetic Compass:
- Headphones;
- Ferrous Metals;
- Transistor Radios, etc;
- Calculators;
- Books with Metal Binders.

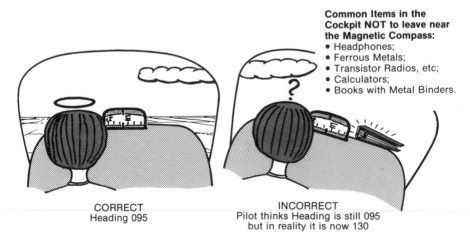

CORRECT
Heading 095

INCORRECT
Pilot thinks Heading is still 095
but in reality it is now 130

Fig.27-6. Keep Foreign Objects Away From The Magnetic Compass.

Any other magnetic influences introduced into the aeroplane will not be allowed for, even though they can significantly affect the compass. Therefore, as Pilot, ensure that no metal or magnetic materials, such as metal pens, clipboards, books with metal binders, key rings, headphones, electronic calculators, transistor radios, etc. are placed anywhere near the compass.

Magnetic or metal materials placed near the compass may introduce large and unpredictable errors. Many Pilots have been lost – or should we say more politely *'temporarily uncertain of their position'* – as a result of random deviations in the compass readings caused by these extraneous magnetic fields.

CONSTRUCTION OF THE AIRCRAFT COMPASS.

The modern aeroplane has a direct-reading compass, usually filled with a liquid in which a *'float'* supporting a bar magnet is pivoted. The liquid supports some of the weight, decreases the friction on the pivot and, most importantly, dampens (decreases) the oscillations of the magnet and float during flight. This allows the compass to give a steadier indication and makes it easier to read.

Attached to the pivot assembly and the float is a compass card graduated in degrees. This can be read by the Pilot against a reference marker attached to the bowl of the compass, and therefore attached to the rest of the aeroplane. Remember that it is the aeroplane that turns around the magnet inside the compass. Ideally, the compass magnet points due (magnetic) North and South at all times. As the aeroplane changes direction, the compass magnet should not.

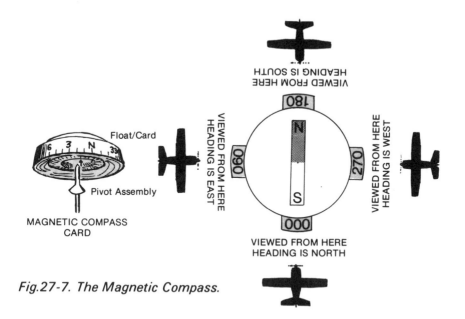

Fig.27-7. The Magnetic Compass.

PILOT SERVICEABILITY CHECKS ON THE COMPASS.

Pre-flight, check that the compass is securely installed and can be easily read. The liquid in which the magnet is suspended should be free of bubbles and should not be discoloured. The glass should not be broken, cracked or dis-coloured, and it should be secure.

Check the position of the compass deviation card in the cockpit.

Check that the compass indication is at least approximately correct.

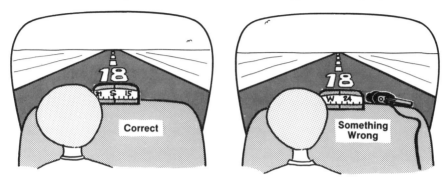

Fig.27-8. Always Cross-Check Compass Direction.

Runways are named according to their magnetic direction, e.g. a runway pointing 243 degrees magnetic is called *'Runway 24',* so when pointing in the same direction as this runway, your compass should indicate approximately the same.

When you are taxying out prior to take-off, turn the aircraft left and right and check that the response of the magnet is correct. Remember that the magnet should remain in the same direction and the aeroplane turn around it.

SWINGING THE COMPASS.

This is the engineering procedure to check and adjust the aeroplane compass. The aeroplane is taken to a special area on the aerodrome and aligned precisely with known directions. The compass is adjusted as accurately as possible and any remaining errors entered on the deviation card.

A Pilot does not usually perform this function – but he can advise when he thinks that it should be done.

The compass should be *'swung'* when it is new, when any electrical circuit or magnetic influence in its vicinity has been altered, after a considerable change in magnetic latitude, (i.e. if you have flown several thousand miles North or South), after passing through a severe magnetic storm, after major and minor inspections, and whenever the Pilot has grounds for suspecting the accuracy of the compass.

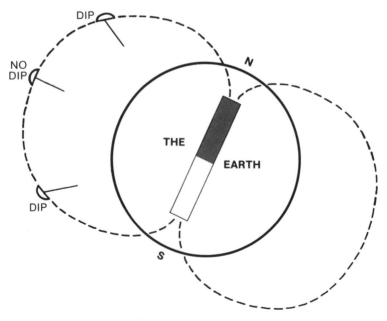

*Fig.27-9. Magnetic Dip is Strongest
Nearest the Poles.*

MAGNETIC DIP.

Near the magnetic equator, the lines of magnetic force are parallel to the surface of the Earth. As the magnetic poles are approached, the lines of magnetic force dip towards them and any magnet bar will also try to dip down and align itself with them.

In the northern areas of the United Kingdom, for example, a freely suspended magnet would dip down towards the North at about 65–70 degrees to the horizontal. In the South of Australia, the angle of dip is approximately 60 degrees down towards the South. This is known as the angle of **Magnetic Dip.**

Magnetic Dip is zero at the magnetic equator and increases to 90 degrees at the magnetic poles – (i.e. a magnet would point straight down).

The strength of the magnetic field is fairly constant over the whole surface of the Earth. Its strength can be resolved into two components – a horizontal one parallel to the surface of the Earth, which is used to align the compass with magnetic North, and a vertical component, which causes the magnetic needle to dip down.

At the magnetic equator, the horizontal component of the Earth's magnetic field is at its strongest and so the Magnetic Compass is very stable and accurate.

At the higher latitudes near the magnetic poles, the vertical component of the Earth's magnetic field causing dip is stronger, and the horizontal component parallel to the surface of the Earth is weaker – making the compass magnet less effective as an indicator of horizontal direction. At latitudes higher than 60 degrees North or South, the Magnetic Compass is not very reliable.

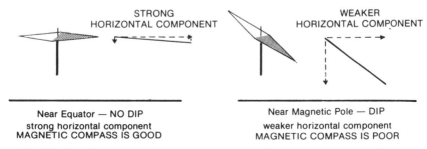

| STRONG | WEAKER |
| HORIZONTAL COMPONENT | HORIZONTAL COMPONENT |

Near Equator — NO DIP
strong horizontal component
MAGNETIC COMPASS IS GOOD

Near Magnetic Pole — DIP
weaker horizontal component
MAGNETIC COMPASS IS POOR

Fig.27-10. Dip is Caused by the Vertical Component of the Earth's Magnetic Field.

A freely-swinging compass needle allowed to point down at the angle of dip would not be very satisfactory in an aeroplane. To keep the magnet at least approximately horizontal, the pivot point is designed to be high, with the magnet suspended below – like a pendulum.

As the magnet tries to align itself with the field, the more it tries to dip down, the further out its centre of gravity moves. Its weight, acting through the CG, will try to move back into a position directly under the point of support, which is the pivot. Some sort of balancing couple will be set up – a couple formed by the supporting force of the pivot and the weight force acting through the CG.

The arm of the couple is the horizontal distance between the line of action of the pivot and the line of action of the magnet weight. This couple will act against the magnetic dip and, by finding an angle where the moment arm is sufficiently long for the pivot/magnet couple, will balance the magnetic dip. The result is a reasonably horizontal compass needle with only a small amount of **'residual dip'** (usually less than 3 degrees from the horizontal).

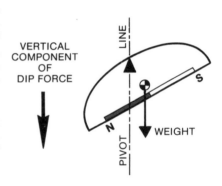

Fig.27-11. Pendulous Suspension.

Wherever the compass is located on (or above, as in the case of aircraft) the Earth's surface, the magnet will find a level of residual dip where the pivot.magnet couple automatically balances the magnetic dip. Note that the CG is not directly under the pivot but is displaced slightly away from the nearer pole.

In the northern hemisphere, the CG of the magnet will be displaced South of the pivot. This displacement of the magnet's CG from directly under the pivot away from the nearer pole leads to transient indication errors in the compass when the aeroplane is accelerated in a straight line – (i.e. speed increase or decrease) or turned – (i.e. accelerated by changing the direction).

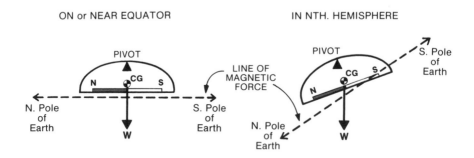

Fig.27-12. The Magnet's CG is South of the Pivot in the N-Hemisphere.

The pivot is attached firmly to the aeroplane – if the aeroplane accelerates or turns, so does the pivot. The magnet, however, is not attached firmly to the aeroplane structure, but is suspended from the pivot – any motion of the magnet depends upon this *'swinging'* effect under the pivot, which is slightly more complicated by the fact that the magnet's CG (in the northern hemisphere) is displaced South of the pivot.

ACCELERATION ERRORS OF THE MAGNETIC COMPASS.

If you change the airspeed, either accelerating or decelerating, transient indication errors occur with a Magnetic Compass, especially on easterly and westerly headings.

As the aeroplane accelerates, it takes the compass and the pivot along with it. The compass magnet, being suspended like a pendulum, is left behind due to its inertia. Its weight, not being directly under the pivot, will cause the needle to swing away from the correct magnetic direction as the pivot accelerates away. The compass card attached to the magnet rotates a little and indicates a new direction, even though there has been no change in direction.

Once a new steady speed is maintained, the magnet will settle down and the compass will read correctly.

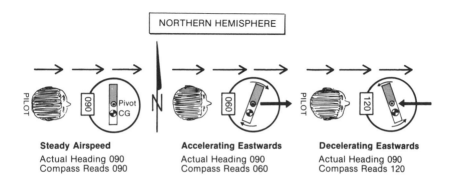

NORTHERN HEMISPHERE

Steady Airspeed
Actual Heading 090
Compass Reads 090

Accelerating Eastwards
Actual Heading 090
Compass Reads 060

Decelerating Eastwards
Actual Heading 090
Compass Reads 120

Fig.27-13. Acceleration and Deceleration On An Easterly Heading.

Accelerating towards the East, the CG (near the south-seeking end of the magnet) is left behind. This swings the compass card so that it indicates an **'apparent' turn to the North.** During the acceleration, the Pilot will read a compass heading more Northerly than the actual magnetic heading. He should allow the compass to settle down after the acceleration is completed before adjusting the aircraft heading.

Decelerating towards the East, the pivot slows down with the rest of the aeroplane and the CG of the magnet, due to its inertia, tries to advance. The compass card rotates to indicate an **'apparent' turn to the South.**

Accelerating towards the West, the CG of the magnet and compass card (near the south-seeking end of the magnet) is left behind. This swings the compass card so that it indicates an 'apparent' turn to the North. The compass will indicate a **more northerly heading** than the aeroplane is actually on.

Heading West, a deceleration will cause the CG to advance ahead of the pivot, and the compass will indicate an 'apparent' turn to the South, i.e. it will appear, according to the compass, that the aeroplane has turned to a **more southerly heading.** After the speed has settled down, the compass will return to a more correct indication.

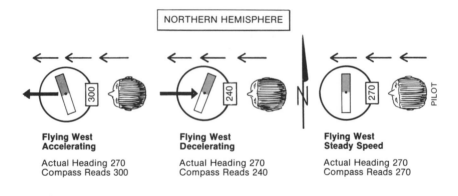

Fig.27-14. Accelerating and Decelerating on a Westerly Heading.

Accelerating and decelerating on Northerly or Southerly headings will not cause 'apparent turns', because the pivot and the CG of the magnet will lie in the same N–S line as the acceleration or deceleration. **On other headings,** the acceleration errors will be greater the closer you are to due East or West.

Acceleration Errors of the Magnetic Compass can be summarised in a small table:

Heading	Acceleration Error	Deceleration Error
Northerly	–	–
Easterly	Apparent Turn to N	Apparent Turn to S
Southerly	–	–
Westerly	Apparent Turn to N	Apparent Turn to S

These results are valid only for the northern hemisphere, where the magnetic dip is down towards the North Magnetic Pole and the compass's magnet CG is displaced from directly under the pivot towards the South.

The Acceleration and Deceleration errors in the northern hemisphere can be remembered with the mnemonic *'A N D S'* –

Acceleration gives an apparent turn North;

Deceleration gives an apparent turn South.

The situation in the **southern hemisphere** is reversed. Also, **the closer to the pole you are, the greater the effect** because the dip is greater. **Magnetic Dip** is the major source of Magnetic Compass indication errors.

TURNING ERRORS OF THE MAGNETIC COMPASS.

Turning is also an acceleration due to the change in direction.

The aircraft has a centripetal force acting on it directed at the centre of the turn – i.e. in a turn, the centripetal force acts towards the centre of the turn and is therefore at right angles to the velocity. This force also acts on the pivot, which is attached to the aeroplane, and accelerates it towards the centre of the turn. The compass magnet (and compass card), being suspended like a pendulum, is left behind due to inertia. This leads to a transient error in the direction indicated by the compass.

Turning Through A Northerly Heading.

When the aeroplane is turning through a Northerly heading the acceleration is at right angles – Easterly or Westerly, depending upon which way you are turning. If you are turning **right** through North, the acceleration is towards the East, the CG is left behind so that the compass indicates less of a turn than is actually occurring.

Once the aeroplane takes up a steady heading, the compass will catch up with the turn and settle down. For this reason, **undershoot when turning through North.** For example, turning from 340 to 040, level the wings before 040 is reached on the compass (say at an indicated 020), after which the compass will catch up and settle down on approximately 040.

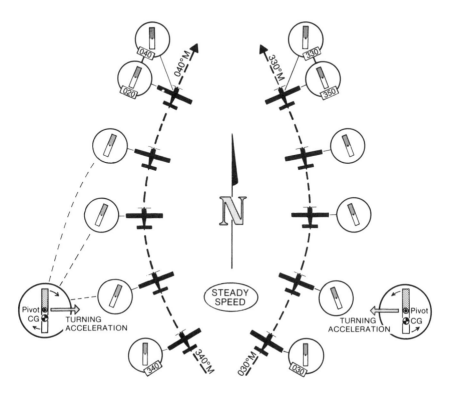

Fig.27-15. Undershoot the Heading When Turning Through North.

If you are turning left through North, the acceleration is towards the West, the CG gets left behind and the compass will again lag behind. Therefore, **undershoot when turning through North.** For example, when turning from 030 to 330, level the wings when the compass indicates approximately 350, after which it should gradually settle down on about 330.

When turning left through South, the acceleration is towards the East and the CG is left behind so that the aeroplane appears to have turned further than what it really has. Therefore, you should **overshoot the heading** because, once the compass settles down, it will return to a more accurate reading. For example, turning from 200 to 140, do not level the wings until the compass indicates about 120. Once the compass settles down, it should indicate about 140.

When turning right through South, the acceleration is towards the West and the CG is left behind so that the aeroplane appears to have turned further than what it really has. Again, you should **overshoot the heading.** For example, turning from 160 to 230, do not level the wings until the compass indicates about 250. After it settles down, it should indicate about 230.

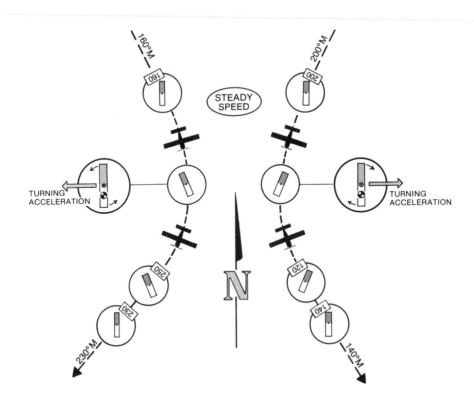

Fig.27-16. Overshoot the Heading When Turning through South.

These turning and acceleration errors are a result of the CG of the compass magnet being displaced South of the pivot point (in the northern hemisphere) – the amount of displacement being greater the greater the magnetic dip, i.e. the nearer the magnetic pole you are, the more pronounced are these errors.

NOTE: Turning errors in the southern hemisphere are reversed.

PRECAUTIONS WHEN ALIGNING THE 'DIRECTION INDICATOR' WITH THE MAGNETIC COMPASS.

The Direction Indicator is a Gyroscopic Instrument (described in the previous chapter on *Gyroscopic Flight Instruments)*.

Do not align the DI (or DG) with the Magnetic Compass if you are changing speed or direction, as the Magnetic Compass will be experiencing acceleration or turning errors, i.e. keep the wings level and maintain a constant speed when aligning the DI with the compass.

One of the advantages of a Direction Indicator is that it is not subject to turning or acceleration errors. Its accuracy depends upon it being aligned with Magnetic North correctly, so this must be done when the Magnetic Compass is indicating correctly.

☐ Now work through **Exercises 27 — The Magnetic Compass.**

Intentionally Blank

4

AIRWORTHINESS AND PERFORMANCE

28

AIRWORTHINESS

The Airworthiness requirements for aircraft in the United Kingdom are specified in the Air Navigation Order (Articles 7-16). The airworthiness documents that are of most importance to the individual Pilot are the:
• Maintenance Documents;
• Flight Manual;
• Certificate of Airworthiness.

TYPE CERTIFICATE.

When a new type or model of aircraft is designed and built, the manufacturer applies for and, after suitable tests on the original test aeroplanes have been passed, is granted a *'Certificate of Type Approval'*. This document is issued to the manufacturer by the Aviation Authority in the country of manufacture.

Engineering and safety requirements, reliability and many other factors are considered in detail, with many inspections and flight tests being carried out prior to the issue of a Type Certificate. Once it is obtained, the Manufacturer commences production and a new aeroplane type comes onto the market.

The Pilot does not see the Type Certificate, which is retained by the Manufacturer.

THE CERTIFICATE OF REGISTRATION.

It is required that UK-owned or operated aircraft be registered with the Civil Aviation Authority (CAA). When this is done for an individual aircraft, the CAA issues a Certificate of Registration to the owner.

Fig.28-1.

**United Kingdom
Civil Aviation Authority**

Certificate of Registration of Aircraft

Certificate Number G-KILT/R1

1 Nationality or Common Mark and Registration Mark	2 Manufacturer and Manufacturer's Designation of Aircraft	3 Aircraft Constructor's Serial Number
G- K I L T	Gulfstream American Aviation Corporation, USA Gulfstream AA5A	AA5A-0893
4 Name of Registered Owner or Charterer		

The aircraft is given a registration number of four letters to follow the UK nationality marking **'G'** (e.g. G-AESE) and this must be displayed prominently on the aircraft in specific sizes and positions. The aeroplane may be identified in-flight by its registration, which in the above case is 'Golf Alfa Echo Sierra Echo'. The Pilot should verify that the aircraft is registered – hiring from a reputable organisation or owner is usually sufficient.

Other nationality markings are: 'D-' for West Germany (Deutschland), 'N-' for the USA, 'F-' for France and 'VH-' for Australia.

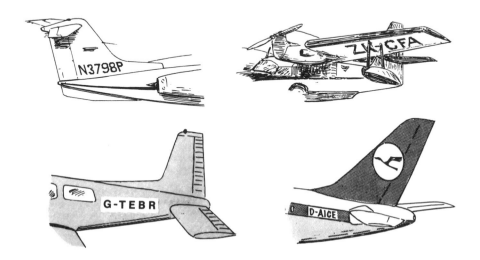

Fig.28-2. Examples of Aircraft Registrations.

CERTIFICATE OF AIRWORTHINESS (CofA).

The Certificate of Airworthiness is issued by the CAA for an individual aircraft for a specified period and an aircraft shall not fly unless it has **a valid CofA.** (Note: there are some exceptions to this, such as during test flights or whenever an aeroplane has a Permit to Fly, but for a Private Pilot the rule generally holds.)

Part of the CofA for each individual aeroplane is the **Flight Manual** – the two documents being linked with an identification number.

The Certificate of Airworthiness is issued by the CAA for an individual aeroplane to operate in a particular **category**, provided it complies with the appropriate airworthiness requirements. Categories and their authorised purposes include:
- Transport (Passengers) – any purpose;
- Transport (Cargo) – any purpose except the public transport of passengers;
- Aerial Work – any purpose other than public transport;
- Private – any purpose other than public transport or aerial work;
- Special.

United Kingdom
Civil Aviation Authority

CERTIFICATE OF AIRWORTHINESS

No. ......SR-991-1..

Nationality and Registration Marks	Constructor and Constructor's Designation of Aircraft	Aircraft Serial No. (Constructor's No.)
G-KILT	Grumman American Aviation Corporation USA AA-5A	AA5A-0893

CATEGORY   Transport Category (Passenger)

This Certificate of Airworthiness is issued pursuant to the Convention on International Civil Aviation dated 7 December 1944, and to the Civil Aviation Act, 1949, and the Orders and Regulations made thereunder, in respect of the above-mentioned aircraft which is considered to be airworthy when maintained and operated in accordance with the foregoing and the pertinent operating limitations. A Flight Manual forms part of this Certificate.   (1977/1978/1979 Pilots Operating Handbook including Gulfstream American United Kingdom Supplement).

This Certificate is issued subject to the Condition(s) shown overleaf.

Date ......26th March 1982....................................

for the Civil Aviation Authority

This certificate is valid for the period(s) shown below		Official Stamp and Date
From 26th March 1982	to 15th September 1984	
From 1st October 1984	to 30th September 1987	C.A.A.
From	to	
From	to	
From	to	
From	to	
From	to	

Fig.28-3. A Certificate of Airworthiness.

Note that the sample CofA expires on the stated date (30th September 1987 in this case) and would normally be renewed prior to this date.

Aeroplanes are further categorised in a different manner acording to the manoeuvres that they are permitted to perform:

- a **Normal** category aeroplane (below 5700 kg and non-acrobatic: manoeuvres limited to stalls and steep turns of 60 degrees – typical limit load factors +2.5g and –1.0g.)
- a **Utility** category aeroplane (as for a Normal category, plus limited aerobatics. Typical limit load factors are +4.5g and –1.8g.)
- an **Acrobatic** category aeroplane. An aeroplane in this category is fully-aerobatic. (Typical limit load factors are +6.0g and –3.0g.)

Do not intentionally carry out inappropriate manoeuvres for the category of your aeroplane – structural damage or destruction is a very real possibility. Some aircraft in the **normal** category may be allowed to operate in the utility category within certain specified weight limits – usually with fuel/passenger restrictions – and these will be seen on the Weight and Balance Schedule as limits on the weight and position of the CG.

As well as being a physical piece of paper, **The Certificate of Airworthiness,** has other documents associated with it – in particular, the **Flight Manual** and the **Certificate of Maintenance Review.** A very important part of the latter is the **Certificate of Release to Service.** It is stated on the CofA (see *Fig.28-3)* that the aeroplane must be maintained and operated correctly for the CofA to remain valid. If the aeroplane is not maintained according to the approved maintenance schedule, the CofA becomes invalid until the required maintenance has been completed.

THE FLIGHT MANUAL.

The Flight Manual must be approved by the CAA and it forms part of the CofA for a particular aeroplane. The CofA and the Flight manual for a particular aeroplane carry the same identification number.

Since requirements in the country of manufacture, (where the aeroplane and the Flight Manual originate), may differ to those in the United Kingdom, the CAA will often issue a **Flight Manual Supplement** that amends the original. This supplement may contain additional limitations, which **must be observed even if in conflict with the manufacturer's Flight Manual. Performance information and operating limitations** for a particular aeroplane are found in its Flight Manual and these are often areas which the CAA Supplement amends.

A Pilot must comply with all the requirements, procedures and limitations with respect to the operation of the aeroplane as set out in its approved Flight Manual, as amended by the CAA Supplement. Placards placed in the cockpit reflect the Flight Manual and have the same status, i.e. the instructions should be adhered to.

The Flight Manual (and its CAA Supplement if there is one) must be carried in the aeroplane, which means that a Pilot cannot take it home for reference. An easy-to-follow booklet derived from the Flight Manual and other operational documents is the **Pilot's Operating Handbook,** which a Pilot should have for each type of aeroplane that he flies and which does not have to remain with the aeroplane. The Pilot's Operating Handbook does not have the same legal standing as the Flight Manual.

THE MAINTENANCE SCHEDULE.

Each aeroplane must have a maintenance schedule approved by the CAA, the usual one being the **Light Aircraft Maintenance Schedule (LAMS)**. This requires a system of regular checks and inspections by licensed and approved people. Logbooks must be kept for the airframe, the engine and the propeller if it has a Constant Speed Unit. Instrument Flight Rules aircraft will have a Radio and Navigation Aids Logbook.

A typical maintenance schedule will include:
- scheduled *'major inspections'*;
- inspections to be carried out every 100 (or 150) hours;
- (there may be) 25 or 50 hour inspections;
- the **daily inspection** (or **check A**) carried out by the Pilot.

The Certificate of Maintenance Review is issued periodically by a licensed engineer following major inspections to certify that the aeroplane has been maintained and operated properly from an airworthiness point of view. Inspection of this document enables a Pilot to determine the time (in flying hours or calender months) remaining until the next maintenance inspection is due.

A Certificate of Release to Service is issued by a licensed engineer following maintenance or an inspection.

A Technical Log may be kept for an aeroplane, in which the Pilot can record any defect immediately following the completion of his flight, and the ground engineer can record the maintenance performed to correct that defect. Take-off and landing times will also be recorded in the Technical Log and there may be a small pocket to hold the Certificate of Maintenance Review and the Certificate of Release to Service. Each Pilot should review these documents prior to flight.

An aeroplane structure subjected to severe turbulence in flight and/or a heavy landing may result in the aeroplane becoming unairworthy. Following such events, and prior to the next flight, the airframe should be checked for distortion, popped or sheared rivets, cracks, skin wrinkles, etc. Appropriate entries should be made on the Technical Log.

MAINTENANCE ALLOWED BY PILOTS.

The Owner or Operator who holds a Private Pilot's Licence or higher (i.e. Student Pilots are excluded) are permitted to carry out minor repairs and services on his aircraft not exceeding 2730 kg (6000 lb) and which are in a category other than Public Transport. This permission is granted by Air Navigation Order, Article 11(3).

These minor repairs or replacements are listed in the **Air Navigation (General) Regulations,** number 16, which is reproduced below.

Pilot maintenance—prescribed repairs or replacements

16. With reference to Article ~~10(2)~~ of the Order the following repairs or replacements are hereby prescribed— ➤ became 11(3) in 1985 ANO (Author's note)

   (1) Replacement of landing gear tyres, landing skids or skid shoes;

   (2) Replacement of elastic shock absorber cord units on landing gear where special tools are not required;

(3) Replacement of defective safety wiring or split pins excluding those in engine, transmission, flight control and rotor systems;

(4) Patch-repairs to fabric not requiring rib stitching or the removal of structural parts or control surfaces, if the repairs do not cover up structural damage and do not include repairs to rotor blades;

(5) Repairs to upholstery and decorative furnishing of the cabin or cockpit interior when repair does not require dismantling of any structure or operating system or interfere with an operating system or affect the structure of the aircraft;

(6) Repairs, not requiring welding, to fairings, non-structural cover plates and cowlings;

(7) Replacement of side windows where that work does not interfere with the structure or with any operating system;

(8) Replacement of safety belts or safety harness;

(9) Replacement of seats or seat parts not involving dismantling of any structure or of any operating system;

(10) Replacement of bulbs, reflectors, glasses, lenses or lights;

(11) Replacement of any cowling not requiring removal of the propeller, rotors or disconnection of engine or flight controls;

(12) Replacement of unserviceable sparking plugs;

(13) Replacement of batteries;

(14) Replacement of wings and tail surfaces and controls, the attachments of which are designed to provide for assembly immediately before each flight and dismantling after each flight;

(15) Replacement of main rotor blades that are designed for removal where special tools are not required;

(16) Replacement of generator and fan belts designed for removal where special tools are not required;

(17) Replacement of VHF communications equipment, being equipment which is not combined with navigation equipment.

Fig.28-4. Air Navigation (General) Regulation 16, listing Maintenance (Repairs or Replacements) permitted for a Private Pilot.

The Pilot should record any minor work that he carries out in the appropriate logbook and certify it with his signature and licence number.

The 50 Hour Check of an aircraft in the Private category may be carried out and signed for by a Licensed Pilot who is the owner or operator of the aeroplane. A Pilot may only sign for the actual 50 Hour Check and for rectification work within the scope of Air Navigation (General) 16 Regulation as discussed above, with the provisio that any CAA mandatory requirements due at that time must be certified by a Licensed or Authorised Engineer.

THE DAILY INSPECTION or CHECK A.

A Daily Inspection, which is known as *Check A* in the UK, must be carried out prior to the first flight of the day, and can be performed by the Pilot. Each flying training organisation or operator will have a specific Daily Inspection procedure to follow. It will be available in written form and contain items closely resembling the list below.

CHECK A

General
Remove frost, snow or ice, if present.
Check that the aircraft documents are available and in order.
Ensure all loose equipment is correctly stowed and the aircraft is free of extraneous items.
If the aircraft has not been regularly used, ensure before resumption of flying that:

(a) Either (i) the engine has been turned weekly or run fortnightly,
or (ii) the manufacturer's recommendations have been complied with.

(b) Compression appears normal when engine turned by hand.

(c) Previously reported defects have been rectified.

Power-plant/ Engine
Check – oil level; security of filler cap and dipstick.
Inspect – engine, as visible, for leaks, signs of overheating, and security of all items.
Inspect – air filter/air intake for cleanliness.
Check – security of cowlings, access doors and cowl flaps.

Propeller
Inspect – blades and spinner for damage and security.

Windscreen
Inspect – for damage and for cleanliness.

Fuel System
Check visually that quantities are compatible with indicator readings.
Drain fuel sample from each drain point into a transparent container and check for water, foreign matter and correct colour.

Wings
Inspect – skin/covering, bracing wires, struts and flying control surfaces for damage and security of all items.
Inspect – pitot/static vents, fuel vents and drain holes for freedom from obstruction.
Test operation of stall warning device.

Landing Gear
Check – shock-absorber struts for leaks and that extension appears normal.
Check – tyres for inflation, damage and creep.
Inspect – brake installation for external evidence of leaks, and for damage and security.

Fuselage and Empennage
Inspect – skin/covering, bracing wires, struts and flying control surfaces for damage and security of all items.
Inspect – drain holes and vents for freedom from obstruction.
Inspect – radio aerials for damage and security.

Cabin Area
Check – flying and engine controls, including trimmers and flaps, for full and free movement in the correct sense.
Check – brake operation is normal.
Check – instrument readings are consistent with ambient conditions.
Perform manual override and disengagement check on auto-pilot.
Check – avionic equipment operation, using self-test facilities where provided.
Inspect – seats, belts and harnesses for satisfactory condition, locking and release.
Check – emergency equipment properly stowed and inspection dates valid.
Test operation of electrical circuits.
Inspect – cabin and baggage doors for damage, security, and for correct operation and locking.
Check that markings and full complement of placards are correctly positioned and legible.

Fig.28-5. 'Check A' Items (from Light Aircraft Maintenance Schedule).

DUPLICATE INSPECTION.

Any adjustments that are made to either **the flight controls and/or the engine controls** of an aeroplane are normally required to be **checked by two licensed personnel,** either engineers or inspectors, before it is considered to be airworthy again.

The Airworthiness Requirements (specifically **BCAR*** Section A, Chapter 5-3) do, however, state that, should a **minor adjustment** of a vital point or control system be necessary when the aircraft is away from base, the second part of the Duplicate Inspection may be completed by a Pilot licensed for the type of aircraft concerned.

* British Civil Airworthiness Requirements

THE INSURANCE DOCUMENT.

Whilst the Certificate of Insurance has no standing as an airworthiness document, it is commonsense that a Pilot confirms that the aeroplane he is about to fly is covered by adequate insurance.

OTHER DOCUMENTS.

Other documents associated with a particular aeroplane may include a:
• Noise Certificate;
• Certificate of Approval of Radio Installation;
• Aircraft Radio Licence;
• Weight and Centre of Gravity Schedule.

□ You should now attempt **Exercises 28 — Airworthiness.**

29

AIRFRAME LIMITATIONS

WEIGHT LIMITATIONS.

The **Gross Weight or All-Up Weight** of the aeroplane is subject to certain limitations. Some of the limitations are **Structural** in nature, as the aeroplane is designed and built to perform certain tasks and carry certain loads, up to a maximum. Other limitations are due to the **Performance** limitations of the aeroplane – certain conditons of temperature and pressure, runway conditions, etc., may limit allowable weights for take-off, landing and so on.

The Maximum Take-Off Weight (MTOW).

This is a structural limitation. The MTOW is the maximum gross weight, according to the Certificate of Airworthiness or approved Flight Manual, at which that aeroplane is permitted to take-off. (It is sometimes referred to as the Maximum Brakes Release Weight MBRW.)

NOTE: The TOW for a particular take-off may not exceed the structural MTOW or the TOW as limited by aeroplane performance and runway considerations.

The Maximum Landing Weight (MLW).

This is also a structural limitation. The MLW is the maximum gross weight, according to the Certificate of Airworthiness or approved Flight Manual, at which that aeroplane is permitted to land.

NOTE: The LW for a particular landing should not exceed the structural MLW or the LW as limited by aeroplane performance and runway considerations. The MLW is usually less than the MTOW because of the greater stresses expected in landing compared to taking-off.

Maximum Zero Fuel Weight (MZFW).

This may be specified (but is not for many light aircraft). MZFW is the maximum allowable gross weight with no usable fuel in the wing tanks.

The wings provide the upwards Lift force to balance the Weight of the aeroplane. This upwards force tends to bend the wings upwards, which it will do, especially if there is no fuel in the wing tanks whose weight will tend to bend the wings down. The greatest upward bending of the wings will occur when the aeroplane is heavy and there is little fuel in the wing tanks – the Maximum Zero Fuel Weight places a structural limit on this.

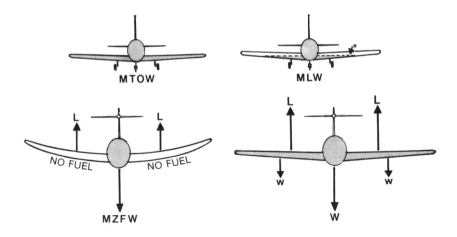

Fig.29-1. MTOW, MLW, MZFW.

SPEED LIMITATIONS.

The aeroplane should only be flown in a specific operating speed range, limited by certain high and low speeds. Sometimes aerodynamic considerations provide the reason for the limit, (e.g. stalling speed is the lower speed limit) and sometimes power considerations limit the speeds, (e.g. maximum speed on the cruise is limited by the amount of power available to overcome the increasing parasite drag).

More important are the **structural limitations**. There might be sufficient power available for a very high speed cruise or dive, but the airframe may not be designed to withstand these stresses.

The airframe is subjected to forces of 1g in calm straight-and-level flight, i.e. the aeroplane and the Pilot experience a force equal to their own weight. As you read this, sitting (half asleep) in your chair, you will be experiencing a force provided by the chair equal and opposite to your weight, i.e. 1g.

We already know that the important speed for **aerodynamic** considerations is the **Indicated Air Speed** (IAS) as shown on the Air Speed Indicator (ASI). The IAS is related to the dynamic pressure '½ Rho V-squared' which governs the generation of aerodynamic forces like Lift and Drag. Therefore all of these aerodynamically limiting speeds are Indicated Air Speeds.

NOTE: You will find that advanced texts refer to a *'Calibrated Air Speed'* or *'Rectified Air Speed'*. This is simply Indicated Air Speed read off the ASI in the cockpit, corrected for any errors in the instrument reading, say due to imperfect positioning of the pitot tube and static vent. In most light aircraft this error is only a knot or two at the speeds we are considering and so we can assume that IAS and RAS/CAS are the same. There is no need for you to remember this for the examination.

The airframe is subjected to forces of 1g in calm, straight and level flight; the Pilot also experiences a force of 1g exerted on his body by the chair, equal and opposite to his weight. This force, both on the airframe and on the Pilot, will change in manoeuvres.

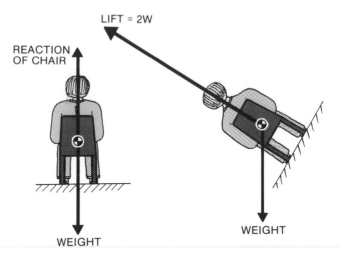

Fig.29-2. Experiencing 1g and Experiencing 2g.

Any manoeuvring, such as turning, diving, performing aerobatics etc., will increase or decrease this load on the structure and on the Pilot, e.g. a perfect 60 degrees banked turn increases the structural load to 2g. The Pilot will experience a force (exerted on him by the seat) equal to double his weight, i.e. double the force of gravity – hence the expression '2g'.

Turbulence and gusts provide almost instantaneous changes in the local angle of attack between the aerofoils and the relative airflow, causing immense changes in the lift produced and placing great stresses on the aeroplane structure. These stresses are described in terms of the **load factor** or 'g-forces' – how many times greater than g, the force of Gravity, they are.

$$\text{LOAD FACTOR (n)} = \frac{\text{(LIFT produced by wing)}}{\text{(WEIGHT of aeroplane)}}$$

It is important **when recovering from the more unusual attitudes of flight** (steep turns, steep dives, spiral dives) that the Pilot **avoids pulling excessive 'g',** because this may overstress the airframe, causing distortion, skin wrinkles, cracks, and popped or sheared rivets.

An aerobatic category aeroplane will be certificated for higher load factors than a normal or utility category aeroplane of course.

As well as the static load factor or 'g-forces', there are **dynamic strength considerations,** such as dynamic instability of the aeroplane in high speed flight, 'flutter' in the control panels, which, if allowed to develop, can lead to structural failure.

There are **absolute limit speeds,** such as the 'never-exceed speed' (VNE) on the high side and the stalling speed (Vs) on the low side. Within these extreme limits are other more cautious limits, such as the 'normal operating limit speed' (VNO) on the high side, and the stall buffet on the low side.

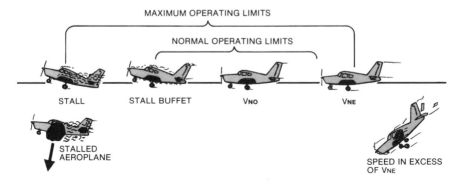

Fig.29-3. The Speed Range of an Aeroplane.

The Never-Exceed Speed (VNE).

VNE is the absolute speed at which the aeroplane should be flown by the Pilot. It is indicated on the Air Speed Indicator (ASI) by a red line. **Any gusts or manoeuvring at speeds higher than VNE can cause unacceptable load factors.** A sensible Pilot would not allow the aeroplane to approach this speed under normal operations.

The Normal Operating Limit Speed (VNO).

VNO is **the maximum speed at which the aeroplane should be flown under normal operating conditions.** The normal operating speed range is indicated on the ASI by a green arc. Above VNO (normal operating limit speed) is a yellow or orange caution arc, extending to the limiting red line at VNE.

Flight should not occur in the speed range above VNO – whilst it may be 'safe' in smooth air, any gusts could over-stress the airframe.

Fig.29-4. Colour Coding on the Air Speed Indicator.

The Manoeuvring Speed (VA or VMAN) (or Speed for Maximum Control Deflection).

When the Pilot is manoeuvring the aeroplane, the control surfaces (ailerons, elevators and rudder), the wings and the tailplane are all subjected to increased loading. The Manoeuvring Speed (VA) is the limiting speed at which, if a control is fully deflected during any manoeuvre, overstressing of the airframe will not occur.

Manoeuvring Speed (VA) is the maximum speed for manoeuvres at which full application of the primary flight controls will not overstress the airframe.

NOTE: The Aeroplane Flight Manual may specify varying speeds for VA because, at light weights, VA is lower than at higher weights.

FLYING IN TURBULENCE

Turbulent air or gusts can change the direction of the local relative airflow and the angle of attack almost instantaneously. Flying slowly (at a high angle of attack), an upwards gust could increase the angle of attack and the wing-loading (g-forces) such that the wing stalls. Flying slowly through gusts decreases the stresses on the aeroplane, but exposes it to the possibility of a stall.

Flying fast through turbulence gives a bumpier ride and puts more stress (higher load factors) on the structure than at low speeds.

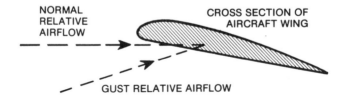

Fig.29-5. Gusts can Increase or Decrease the Angle of Attack, cause High Wing Loadings, or cause the Wing's Critical Angle of Attack to be Exceeded (Stall).

The Turbulence Penetration Speed (VB or VTURB), or the **Rough Air Speed** (VRA), are the recommended target speeds for flying through turbulence. They are **compromise speeds** to avoid 'high g' stalls on the low speed side and excessive wing loading on the high speed side. **If no VB or VRA is specified (often the case for light aircraft), then use the Manoeuvring Speed (VA) to avoid structural damage.**

There are special techniques for flying in turbulence that your Flight Instructor will pass on to you.

Some general comments on flying in turbulence are:

- Turbulence Penetration Speed is a 'target' speed. In turbulence the airspeed may fluctuate rapidly and any attempt to chase a constant airspeed with elevator control and power changes may over-stress the aeroplane. Allow the airspeed to fluctuate around the V_{TURB}. If V_{TURB} is not specified then Manoeuvring Speed V_A is a good 'target speed' for turbulence penetration. V_{NO} should **not** be exceeded in turbulence.

- Maintain wings level with ailerons, but be gentle with the elevators. Due to their long moment arm from the Centre of Gravity, the elevators can easily over-stress the structure if they are moved too violently or too far in turbulence.

- Do not chase altitude – allow the aeroplane to rise and fall with the air currents (provided terrain clearance and clearance from other aircraft is adequate).

- Ensure that any power changes are made **smoothly.**

There may be other maximum speeds specified:

V_{FE}. As the flaps are lowered, the airframe is subjected to extra stresses and so a **Maximum Flaps Extended Speed** (V_{FE}) is usually specified.

V_{LO}, V_{LE}. For aeroplanes with **retractable landing gear** (also known as retractable undercarriage) one or two speed limitations will be specified according to system design. **The maximum speed for operating** (extending or retracting) **the landing gear** (V_{LO}) may be lower than the airspeed at which you may fly with the gear extended (V_{LE}).

This is because, while the landing gear is extending and retracting, some gear doors may open out into the airstream and be subjected to air loads. With those systems in which the doors close again once the gear is extended, the higher airspeed V_{LE} is permitted (although not as high as when the gear is retracted and the gear doors are closed). Also, small locking devices may be fitted to strengthen the landing gear structure when it is fully extended.

THE 'VELOCITY/LOAD FACTOR' (or V-n) DIAGRAM.

The **V-n** diagram illustrates the flight operating strength of an aeroplane. Limit load factors and limit speeds are specified by the CAA for different aeroplane categories, within which the aeroplane must be operated. Taken beyond these limits, the aeroplane may suffer structural damage or even structural failure.

The high speed limit is V_{NE}, the never-exceed speed, and speed on the low side is limited by the stall. The stalling speed is affected by the load factor, occurring at higher speeds when 'g' is being pulled. V_{S1g} is the 1g stalling speed, i.e. when flying straight and level.

Full backward movement of the control column will increase the g-loading and cause a stall to occur, at low speeds the stall occurring before the limit load factor is reached. At high speeds, however, the limit load factor may be reached before the stall occurs and so the Pilot must not apply full back stick. The manoeuvring speed V_A is the speed above which this is a consideration and full back control column should not be applied. In fact, **above VA the Pilot should avoid making any abrupt or large control movements**

Gusts also cause changes in the load factor and care should be taken when flying in turbulence. VNO, the normal operations limit speed, should not be exceeded except in very smooth air, when VNE becomes the absolute limit. In strong turbulence, consideration should be given to flying at the turbulence penetration speed (if specified), otherwise at the manoeuvring speed VA, to avoid excessive flight loads causing damage to the aeroplane structure.

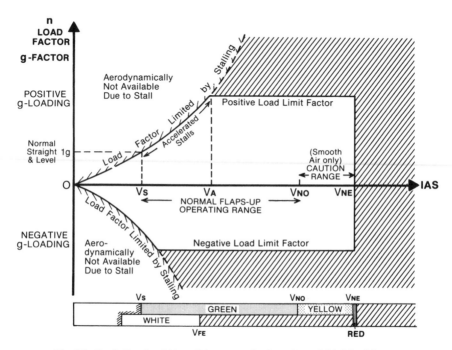

Fig.29-6. A Typical V-n Diagram Related to ASI Markings.

CHECKS FOLLOWING EXCESSIVE STRESS ON THE AIRFRAME.

While the Pilot must not knowingly exceed the airframe limitations, excessive stress can be caused by unexpected severe turbulence or a particularly heavy landing. In both cases, the wing structure may be heavily loaded and, in the case of a heavy landing, the landing gear and the areas to which it is attached to the airframe will be heavily loaded.

One of the responsibilities of being a Pilot is to ensure that following Pilots will be presented with an airworthy aeroplane. The occurrence of heavy stress should cause a Pilot to refer to an Engineer. There could be damage not immediately apparent to the Pilot during an inspection, quite apart from those items already listed. For this reason, **if an aeroplane has been overstressed, the Pilot should ensure that a qualified Engineer carries out an inspection prior to the next flight.**

Many light aircraft are of *semi-monocoque* construction, where the loads are carried, not only by the internal structure, but also by the skin. Damage to any of these will weaken the overall structure.

In carrying out an inspection the Engineer will look for indications of stress on the airframe, the main external items being:
• distortion of the structure;
• cracks;
• popped or sheared rivets; and
• wrinkles in the skin –
especially in the areas surrounding the main structural attachments for the engine, wing, wing struts and tailplane.

Severe overload can distort or break the wings and associated struts or braces. In the case of a **heavy landing**, checks of the landing gear and the areas surrounding its attachment points would be made (e.g. the engine firewall to which a nosewheel may be attached).

NOTE: Structural damage can exist even without external indications, hence the importance of consulting qualified personnel.

☐ **Exercises 29 — Airframe Limitations** please.

30

THE ATMOSPHERE

For a safe take-off to be achieved, the Pilot must first of all have the skills to handle the aeroplane in flight. Then he, or she, must learn the skills involved in taking the aeroplane from one medium (the ground) to another (the atmosphere). Of course, even whilst on the ground the aeroplane is immersed in the air and so wind effects and pressure/temperature (i.e. density) play a role.

Pressure and temperature play an extremely important role in the performance of aeroplanes (both the performance of the airframe and the performance of the engine). The critical element is **Air Density** (Rho), which decreases as pressure falls and temperature rises. On a **hot** day, the air is less dense and the aeroplane performance capabilities will also be less. If the pressure is low, (e.g. for take-off at an aerodrome of **high** elevation), then the air is less dense, lowering the performance capabilities of the aeroplane.

The **power** delivered by the **engine** depends upon the weight of the fuel/air charge – the less dense the air, the lower the power-producing capability of the engine.

The **Aerodynamic Qualities** of the **airframe** depend upon air density (Rho). *'Dynamic Pressure'* is '$\frac{1}{2}$ Rho V-squared' and this appears in the vital aerodynamic relationship: Lift = C$_{Lift}$ x $\frac{1}{2}$ Rho V-squared x S.

If air density (Rho) decreases, then aerodynamic qualities decrease. High temperatures and low pressures (at altitude) cause a decrease in air density, as does high humidity (moisture content).

COMPOSITION OF THE ATMOSPHERE.

The atmosphere consists of a mixture of gases that surround the Earth and are held to it by the force of gravity. For this reason, the atmosphere is densest near the earth's surface and the air density decreases as height is gained. Since both engine and aerodynamic performance depends on air density, they also decrease with altitude.

The pressure that the air exerts at any point depends upon the weight of air pressing down from above, therefore pressure also decreases with altitude. If the pressure is reduced, then the air expands and becomes less dense. **Performance is poorer at high altitudes.**

Heating of an air mass causes it to expand and decreases its density, therefore decreasing both engine and aerodynamic performance of an aeroplane, i.e. **performance is poorer on hot days.** Temperature generally decreases with altitude (the nominal standard rate being 2°C/1000 ft).

Cooling of an air mass increases its density, although this effect is not as great as height is gained as that of the decreased pressure, the overall effect being a decrease of density at higher altitudes.

The mixture of gases that we call 'air' consists mainly of:
- nitrogen (78%);
- oxygen (21%); and
- water vapour.

The other 1% consists of argon, carbon di-oxide and other gases.

The amount of water vapour in the air is called **humidity.** Because water molecules are very light, a high humidity will cause the air density to be slightly less, but no account of this effect is taken in performance charts.

Just how much water a parcel of air is capable of holding depends upon its temperature – warm air being able to hold more water than cold air. If a parcel of air is holding 70% of its maximum capacity of water vapour, then it has a **relative humidity** of 70%. If it cools, its capacity to hold water vapour is less and, even though the actual amount of water does not change, the relative humidity increases.

If the parcel of air cools until its capacity to hold water vapour is equal to that which it is actually holding, then its relative humidity is 100% and the parcel of air is said to be **saturated.** Any further cooling will cause some of the water vapour to condense out as water droplets and form cloud, fog or dew.

Relative Humidity is defined as the amount of water vapour present in a parcel of air compared to the maximum amount that it can support (i.e. when it is *'saturated'*) at the same temperature.

A very rough measure of humidity is what happens to perspiration. If it evaporates, the air is *'dry'* (low relative humidity) and can absorb more water vapour. If the perspiration remains as 'beads of sweat', the relative humidity is high and the air cannot absorb the extra moisture.

THE INTERNATIONAL STANDARD ATMOSPHERE (ISA).

Because the pressure and temperature in the real atmosphere are continually changing, a theoretical International Standard Atmosphere (the ISA, or the ICAO Standard Atmosphere) has been defined as a *'measuring stick'* by the International Civil Aviation Organisation (ICAO).

NOTE: as mentioned earlier, a unit of pressure for aviation purposes known as the **'hectoPascal'** has recently been adopted by ICAO, however, in the UK, the unit **'millibar'** has been retained for the forseeable future. 1 millibar of pressure is equal to 1 hectoPascal. Other countries also differ from the ICAO standard – a notable example being the U.S.A. where atmospheric pressure for aviation purposes is calibrated in 'inches of mercury', usually abbreviated to 'inches'.

The International Standard Atmosphere has a Mean Sea Level (MSL) pressure of 1013·2 hPa(mb), and an MSL Temperature of 15 degrees Celsius. They decrease at specified rates as altitude is gained.

The real and ever-changing atmosphere will differ from the ISA, and we can compare the real and actual atmosphere existing at the point under consideration with the conditions one would expect in the ISA.

PRESSURE ALTITUDE.

The standard ISA Mean Sea Level **pressure** is 1013·2 mb(hPa) (in practice we use 1013 mb or hPa), and this decreases at about 1 mb(hPa) per 30 feet increase in height.

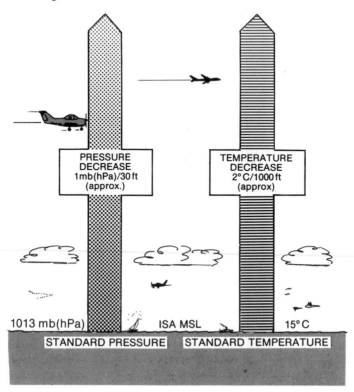

Fig.30-1. The I.S.A.

At 600 ft in the ISA, the pressure will have decreased by approx (600/30) = 20 mb, i.e. from 1013 mb it will have decreased to 993 mb. If the point where your aeroplane is has a pressure of 993 mb, then we say it has a *'pressure altitude'* of 600 ft, i.e. it is the equivalent of 600 ft above the 1013 mb(hPa) pressure level in the ISA.

Pressure Altitude is the height in the International Standard Atmosphere above the 1013·2 mb(hPa) Pressure Level at which the Pressure equals that of the Aircraft or Point Under Consideration.

The easiest way to read pressure altitude in the cockpit is to set 1013 mb(hPa) in the altimeter subscale – the altimeter will then indicate pressure altitude. Knowing the pressure altitude allows us to compare the aeroplane performance against a known standard.

Pressure altitude can be calculated mathematically (using a decrease of 1 mb per 30 ft gain in height) or on your navigational computer.

Example 1: QNH is 1005 mb and the aeroplane is on the ground at an aerodrome, elevation 20 ft. Find the pressure altitude.

Discussion: QNH (MSL) is 1005 mb.

Since pressure decreases with height, the standard pressure level of 1013 mb will occur (theoretically) below sea level.

To find pressure altitude (height above the standard 1013 mb level), we first find the height between MSL (QNH) and 1013. The 8 mb difference is equivalent to (8 x 30) = 240 ft.

The aeroplane is a further 20 ft above this, i.e. 260 ft above the 1013 mb pressure level. The **Pressure Altitude** is 260 ft.

Fig.30-2. Example 1.

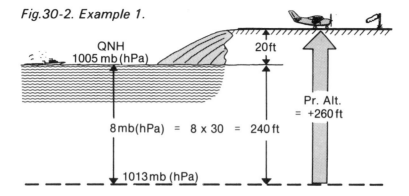

Example 2: QNH is 1030 mb, and the aeroplane is on the ground at an aerodrome whose elevation is 20 ft. Find the pressure altitude.

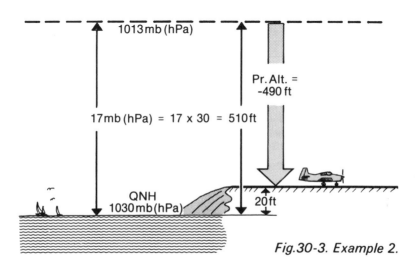

Fig.30-3. Example 2.

Discussion: Pressure decreases with altitude. Since MSL pressure is 1030 mb, the standard pressure level of 1013 mb, being less, must be higher than MSL on this particular day. The 17 mb pressure difference means that the height difference is about (17 x 30)= 510 ft.

From our diagram we can see that the aeroplane is 490 ft below the standard 1013 mb pressure level. Thus, its pressure altitude is –490 ft or 490 ft **Below** Mean Sea Level (BMSL).

Example 3: An aircraft is cruising at 5000 ft with QNH (actual MSL pressure) 1027 mb set in the subscale. Find the pressure altitude.

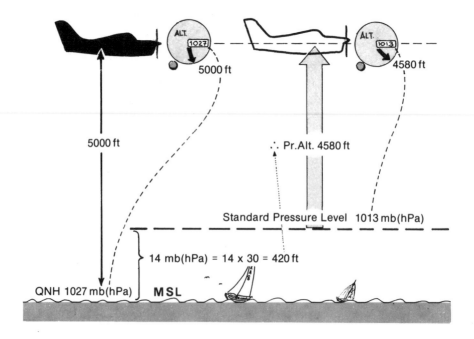

Fig.30-4. Example 3; A Good Approach to Pressure Altitude Problems.

The altimeter measures the height it is from the pressure level set in the subscale. A quick means of estimating pressure altitude (height in the ISA above the 1013 mb/hPa) pressure level is simply to wind the subscale around so that 1013 is set there.

From the above example you can see:

WIND OFF MILLIBARS (HECTOPASCALS) —

WIND OFF HEIGHT.

TEMPERATURE.

The higher the temperature the lower the air density — and the lower the aeroplane performance.

The *'measuring stick'* for temperature in the atmosphere is the International Standard Atmosphere (the ISA). Standard sea level temperature is +15 degrees Celsius and it falls at approximately 2°C per 1,000 feet gain in altitude.

- At 1000 ft in the ISA, the temperature will have fallen to +13 degrees C.
- At 2000 ft in the ISA, the temperature will have fallen to +11 degrees C.
- At 3000 ft in the ISA, the temperature will have fallen to +9 degrees C.

Now if the actual temperature at a pressure altitude of 3000 ft is +16 degrees C, i.e. 7 degrees warmer than that expected in the ISA, we refer to it as 'ISA+7'. The *temperature deviation* from ISA is +7.

If the actual temperature at 2,000 ft is +7 degrees C, (i.e. 4 degrees cooler than in the ISA), we refer to that as 'ISA–4'. The temperature deviation from ISA is –4.

Aeroplane and engine performance depends upon air Density. It is impractical for the Pilot to have the equipment necessary to measure air density, so we use two pieces of information already available in the cockpit and upon which air' density depends – **Pressure Altitude and Temperature.**

DENSITY ALTITUDE.

By considering pressure altitude (related to height in the International Standard Atmosphere that is our measuring stick) and temperature, we are really considering density (Rho). Most performance charts allow us to enter with these two, therefore there is usually no need to directly calculate density. On the rare occasion that it is, there is a quick method of doing it.

We already know that in the ISA, temperature is +15 degrees Celsius at ISA MSL (i.e. pressure altitude 0 ft), and decreases at 2 degrees Celsius for every 1,000 ft gained in height. Therefore, at a pressure altitude of 3000 ft, the ISA temperature should have dropped by 6 degrees to be +9°C.

If the temperature at pressure altitude 3000 feet exceeds this – (say it is +13°C), the air will be less dense than in the ISA and the aeroplane will perform as if it were higher than the 3,000 ft in the ISA – by an amount equal to:

'120 ft for each 1 degree deviation from the ISA temperature'.

In this case, it is 4 degrees warmer than ISA and so the aeroplane will perform as if it were (4 x 120) = 480 ft higher than the 3,000 ft pressure altitude. We say it has a **Density Altitude** of 3480 ft. Performance will be poorer.

Reminder: Navigation Computers have the facility for finding Density Altitude.

TO CONVERT BETWEEN FAHRENHEIT AND CELSIUS.

There are various temperature scales in use and, if you are flying in foreign countries, it may be necessary to convert from one to the other. The Celsius (Centigrade) and Fahrenheit scales both use the boiling point and freezing point of water as standard temperatures – the difference between them being 100°C or 180°F as shown below.

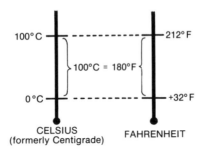

Fig.30-5. Comparing the Celsius and Fahrenheit Temperature Scales.

Each 1°C is larger than 1°F by a ratio of 180/100 or 9/5. The starting point of both scales is the freezing point of water, 0°C or 32°F. These can be combined into the one relationship connecting °F and °C:

Degrees F = 9/5 Degrees C + 32.

Example 4: Convert 20°C to °F.
°F = 9/5 x 20°C + 32 = 36 + 32 = 68°F.

To reverse the relationship, simply subtract 32 from both sides and then multiply both sides by 5/9 to obtain:
°C = 5/9 (°F – 32).

Example 5: Convert 68°F to °C.
°C = 5/9 (68°F – 32) = 5/9 x 36 = 20°C.

NOTE: You may be required to supply these formulae in the examination but, in practice, the easiest method of converting temperatures is to use the navigation computer.

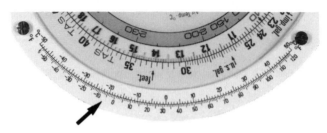

Fig.30-6. Temperature Conversion Scale on the CRP-1.

☐ Now complete **Exercises 30 — The Atmosphere.**

31

TAKE-OFF AND LANDING PERFORMANCE

Take-Offs and Landings involve much more than smooth Piloting Skills. They involve careful prior consideration (planning) to ensure that the aeroplane is capable of the task asked of it. A very smooth take-off is of little value if the aeroplane, once airborne, is faced with obstacles impossible to avoid. The Take-Off Performance of the aeroplane needs to be compared to the runway and surrounding obstacles in the existing conditions **prior to actually taking-off.** Similarly, each landing must be carefully planned. A smooth touchdown is of little value if the aeroplane runs into the fence at the far end of a 'too-short' landing strip.

Aeroplane take-off and landing performance is **subject to many variables,** including:
- **Aeroplane weight;**
- **Aerodrome pressure altitude;**
- **Temperature** (which, together with pressure altitude, gives **density altitude**);
- **Wind;**
- **Runway length;**
- **Runway slope;**
- **Runway surface;**
- **Flap setting;**
- **Humidity.**

The supplied performance data for the aeroplane will usually allow adjustments to be made for these variables. Later in this chapter, typical percentage effects on the Take-Off and Landing Distances due to these variables are considered.

A competent Pilot will know approximate take-off and landing distances required at maximum weight on a level, hard, dry surface for his particular aeroplane. If a runway is particularly long, say at Manchester International, and the conditions are good, then obviously sufficient distance will be available for a light aircraft and no precise performance calculation is needed. If, however, the strip is short, or conditions are poor (mud, snow, wet grass, tailwind etc.), or some marginal situation exists (say a request to make an intersection departure using only part of a runway at a busy aerodrome), then the performance data should be checked carefully.

WHERE TO FIND PERFORMANCE INFORMATION.

Performance figures may be given in a variety of publications and it is important for Pilots to know where to find the data needed to predict the performance in the expected flight conditions. The appropriate documents are specified in the Certificate of Airworthiness and may be any one of the following:

- The UK Flight Manual for the aircraft;
- The Owner's Manual or Pilot's Operating Handbook, which may contain a CAA supplement giving additional performance data either supplementing or overriding data in the main document (the case for many light aeroplanes);
- The Performance Schedule (applicable to some older aeroplanes);
- For some imported aeroplanes, an English Language Flight Manual approved by the Airworthiness Authority in the country of origin, but with a UK supplement containing performance data approved by the CAA.

The Use of Performance Data.

The majority of modern light aeroplanes in the UK are certified in *Performance Group E.* The CAA-approved performance charts or tables for these aeroplanes enable the Pilot to obtain **'Measured Take-Off Distance'** and **'Measured Landing Distance'**. This is **unfactored** performance data, usually representing the measured performance achieved by the Manufacturer using a new aeroplane flown by a Test Pilot in ideal conditions.

For **some** aeroplane types, the CAA has imposed a **mandatory limitation** (or *'Performance Writedown'*) on the Manufacturer's performance data that requires certain corrections to be made to this data. For instance, one commonly-used trainer has the following 'Writedown' applied by the CAA.

> The corrections listed below must be applied to the P.O.H. performance information whenever it is used, in addition to any other corrections which may be applicable, as indicated by the text.
>
> Rate of Climb - subtract 40ft/min. *(applicable graph quoted);*
> Take-off Field lengths - add 5% *(applicable graph quoted).*

The performance figures extracted from the Manual or Handbook (with any CAA-imposed limitation applied) **are the absolute minimum figures that may legally be used by a Private Pilot.** They are, however, considered **inadequate** for normal operations. Since it is most unlikely that an average Pilot in a well-used aeroplane in less favourable conditions will be able to achieve the certificated performance, the CAA **strongly recommends** that a **Safety Factor of 1·33 for Take-Off** and **1·43 for Landing** be applied to the performance data obtained from the Manual or Handbook.

(Whilst these safety factors are 'strongly recommended' for Private flights, they are in fact 'mandatory' for Public Transport flights. **A Private Pilot conscious of safety should always apply these factors,** even though it is not a legal requirement, and maintain the same level of safety as a Public Transport flight.)

NOTE: Performance data in manuals for aeroplanes certified in the other light-aircraft Performance Groups (C and D) already includes factoring, and the Manuals and Handbooks should clearly indicate this. If in any doubt, the pilot should consult the Airworthiness Division of the CAA.

Each Pilot should be aware that it is his or her **legal obligation** to ensure that the aeroplane has adequate performance to carry out the proposed flight **safely** (ANO Article 35), and one of the aims of this chapter is to remind pilots to:

- carefully read the published performance data and allow for the variables;
- apply any mandatory CAA-imposed limitations; and
- consider adding the strongly recommended safety factor.

AEROPLANE TAKE-OFF PERFORMANCE

The '**Measured Take-Off Distance**' for a particular weight and flap setting is the measured distance to accelerate on a dry, hard surface with (all) engine(s) operating at maximum power from the Starting Point, to effect a transition to climbing flight and attain a 'Screen Height' of 50 ft (15.2 metres) at a speed not less than the *Take-Off Safety Speed – TOSS* (or V_2).

Whilst it is the '**Take-Off Distance**' and '**Take-Off Safety Speed**' at 50 ft which are the vital performance figures for a pilot, some tables also make available the actual '**Ground Run**' from the Starting Point on the Runway to the Point of Lift-Off (or 'unstick') where the aeroplane's wheels leave the ground, as well as the '**Lift-Off Speed**'.

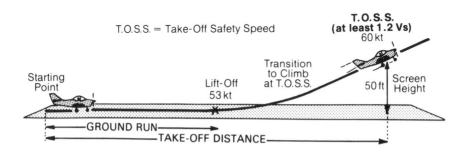

Fig.31-1. Take-Off Distance.

There are various presentations of **Take-Off Performance tables** and graphs. Each pilot must become familiar with those in the aeroplane's Manual or Handbook, since it is the starting point for the calculation of *Take-Off Distance Required.*

A TYPICAL TAKE-OFF PERFORMANCE CHART

UNITED KINGDOM
SUPPLEMENT

GULFSTREAM AMERICAN
MODEL AA-5A CHEETAH

TAKEOFF DISTANCE (AA-5A United Kingdom)

ASSOCIATED CONDITIONS:
POWER – MAXIMUM
FLAPS – UP
RUNWAY – HARD SURFACE (LEVEL & DRY)
FUEL MIXTURE – FULL THROTTLE CLIMB, MIXTURE LEANED ABOVE 5000
FT TO SMOOTH ENGINE OPERATION.

NOTES:
1. DECREASE DISTANCE 4% FOR EACH 5 KNOTS HEADWIND. FOR OPERATION
   WITH TAILWINDS UP TO 10 KNOTS, INCREASE DISTANCE BY 10% FOR EACH
   2.5 KNOTS.
2. IF TAKEOFF POWER IS SET WITHOUT BRAKES APPLIED, THEN DISTANCES
   APPLY FROM POINT WHERE FULL POWER IS ATTAINED.
3. FOR TAKEOFF FROM A DRY, GRASS RUNWAY, INCREASE GROUND RUN
   AND TOTAL DISTANCE TO CLEAR A 50 FT OBSTACLE BY 12.5% OF THE
   HARD SURFACE RUNWAY TOTAL TO CLEAR 50 FT OBSTACLE.

WEIGHT KGS	TAKEOFF SPEED KIAS LIFT OFF	TAKEOFF SPEED (MPH) CLEAR 50 FT	PRESS. ALT FT	0°C (32°F) METRES GND RUN	0°C (32°F) METRES 50 FT	10°C (40°F) METRES GND RUN	10°C (40°F) METRES 50 FT	20°C (68°F) METRES GND RUN	20°C (68°F) METRES 50 FT	30°C (86°F) METRES GND RUN	30°C (86°F) METRES 50 FT	40°C (104°F) METRES GND RUN	40°C (104°F) METRES 50 FT
998	56 (64)	63 (73)	SL	230	419	255	464	282	512	311	564	341	618
			2000	273	495	304	549	336	606	370	667	407	732
			4000	326	587	362	651	401	719	442	791	485	868
			6000	391	698	434	774	479	854	529	940	581	1031
			8000	469	832	520	922	575	1018	634	1120	697	1229
907	53 (61)	60 (69)	SL	183	336	203	372	224	411	247	452	272	496
			2000	218	397	241	440	267	486	294	535	323	587
			4000	260	471	288	522	319	576	351	635	386	696
			6000	311	560	345	621	382	685	420	754	462	828
			8000	373	668	414	740	458	817	504	899	554	983
816	50 (58)	57 (66)	SL	142	263	158	292	174	322	192	355	211	389
			2000	169	312	187	345	207	381	229	419	251	460
			4000	202	369	221	409	247	452	273	497	300	546
			6000	241	439	268	486	296	537	326	591	359	649
			8000	290	523	321	580	355	640	392	704	430	773

SAMPLE ONLY
Not to be used in conjunction
with Flight Operations or
Flight Planning

Fig.31-2. Gulfstream AA-5A Cheetah Take-off Performance Tables.

There is no mandatory *Performance Writedown* to be applied to these
particular figures by the CAA, (because it is not mentioned in the Flight
Manual or P.O.H. for this aeroplane).

Example 1: From the table it can be seen that, for an aeroplane weighing 907 kg at a sea level aerodrome with a temperature of +10°C (and in nil-wind conditions), the measured Take-Off Distance to 50 ft above the level of the runway for a zero-flap take-off is 372 metres.

Lift-off should occur at 53 kt, and a Take-Off Safety Speed of 60 kt should be achieved by the 50 ft point. The ground run will be 203 metres, but it is the *Take-Off Distance to 50 ft* that is more important to the Pilot.

The aeroplane should be lifted-off at 53 kt which should take a ground run of 203 metres, and then be flown so that it reaches the Take-Off Safety Speed of 60 kt by the 50 ft Screen Height which should occur approximately 372 metres from the Starting Point on the Runway **under the stated conditions.**

The speeds are those which should be flown, but it is strongly recommended by the CAA that the Take-Off Distance be factored by 1·33 to increase the level of safety, as well as the variables which must be allowed for (explained shortly). This means there should be more Take-Off Distance **Available** than the minimum required by the chart.

THE CHOICE OF FLAP SETTING.

Some aeroplanes offer a choice of flap setting for take-off.

The Use of Small Flap Settings Decreases the Ground Run. Flap has the effect of lowering the stalling speed making the appropriate lift-off speed and take-off safety speed less. Provided that the flap setting used for take-off is small (so that the Drag is **not** greatly increased), the aeroplane will reach lift-off speed after a shorter ground run. Hence a shorter runway may be used. If the ground surface is rough, using flap for take-off will allow you to leave the ground sooner.

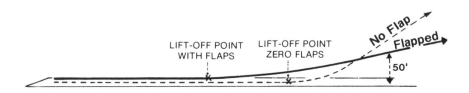

Fig.31-3. Flaps Reduce Take-Off Ground Run.

While the ground-run (also known as the *take-off run*) may be less with flap, the take-off distance (to 50 feet) may not be reduced significantly, because, as well as increasing Lift, flap usually increases Drag, thus reducing the Lift/Drag ratio, and thereby **reducing both the rate and angle of climb.**

This is the reason for only using **small flap settings for take-off.** A larger flap setting, even though it might reduce the stalling speed, would increase the aerodynamic Drag during the ground run, causing a slower acceleration, and then, once airborne, would significantly degrade the climb performance due to the poor Lift/Drag ratio.

We cannot generalise too much in our statements here, as the precise effect of the use of flap on the take-off of a particular aeroplane depends upon many things, including the flap setting, the engine/propeller combination, the airspeed flown, etc. You must become familiar with your own type of aeroplane and this is the job of your flying instructor.

Remember, large flap settings are good for landing, but bad news for take-off.

THE VARIABLES THAT SHOULD BE CONSIDERED FOR TAKE-OFF.

Many CAA-approved performance tables and charts allow the Pilot to account for weight, flap setting, wind effect, etc. An estimate of the effect that these variables have on Take-off Distance follows.

Increased WEIGHT Means A Greater 'Take-off Distance'. A higher weight has a number of effects each increasing the 'take-off distance':

(a) **In the Air.** With increased weight, the **Stalling Speed is Increased.** The lift-off speed is related to the stalling speed and so any increase in stalling speed must mean an increase in lift-off speed and in 'take-off safety speed'.

After lift-off, the increased weight will degrade the aeroplane's climb performance (rate of climb and angle of climb) and so the distance to reach 50 feet above the runway will be greater. This is still part of the 'take-off distance', hence more distance is consumed.

(b) **On the Ground.** The greater mass means a slower acceleration by the Thrust force from the engine/propeller, hence more distance is consumed. The greater Weight on the wheels during the ground-run increases the frictional forces resisting acceleration, hence more distance is consumed.

The overall effect of a 10% increase in weight is to increase the Take-Off Distance by 20%, i.e. a factor of 1·2. Most performance tables or graphs allow the Pilot to extract the performance figures applicable to the aeroplane's actual gross weight.

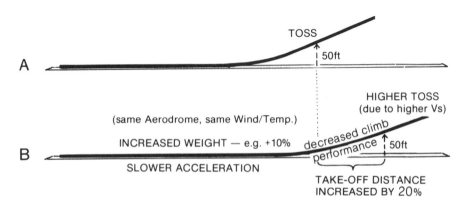

Fig.31-4. A 10% Increase in Weight Increases Take-Off Distance by 20%.

294

An Increased DENSITY ALTITUDE (i.e. lower air density *'Rho'*) **means a longer 'Take-Off Distance'.**

There are a number of things that will cause a **decrease in air Density:**

- A lower air pressure will decrease the density and this can occur as a result of a different ground level pressure or as a result of a higher aerodrome elevation. This effect is covered by **'pressure altitude'**, which relates the actual pressure experienced by the aeroplane to a level in the International Standard Atmosphere (ISA) that has an identical pressure. High aerodromes lead to longer take-off distances.

A High Aerodrome Elevation Decreases Aeroplane Performance.

- A higher **air temperature** will decrease the density, so:

High Temperatures Decrease Aeroplane Performance.

The effect of decreased density (high pressure altitude and/or high temperature) on aeroplane performance is allowed for in one of two ways:

(1) By adjusting the pressure altitude to allow for a temperature deviation from the standard ISA temperature at that particular pressure altitude (120 ft per 1 degree Celsius deviation from ISA), thereby giving **'density altitude'** (the height in the ISA with an identical density); or

(2) By having a graph that allows for the effects of both pressure and temperature separately.

If the air density (*Rho*) decreases, the engine/propeller combination will not produce as much power and so the take-off distance will increase.

As well as the deterioration in power/thrust from engine/propeller combination, the aerodynamic performance of the aeroplane will also decrease as air density becomes less. To produce the required Lift force (L = C_{Lift} x ½ Rho V-squared x S), a decrease in air density (Rho) means an increase in the velocity (True Air Speed V), hence a longer *Take-Off Distance*. The Indicated Air Speed shown in the cockpit will not alter, as it is a function of the dynamic pressure (½ Rho V-squared).

This is a little tricky to understand, but it is **extremely important** and worthwhile stating again. **The lift-off speed you see in the cockpit is the IAS and it will remain the same irrespective of air density.** (What does change with a low air density (Rho) is the True Air Speed (V), which will be greater for a lower air density, hence a longer take-off distance.)

Not only does a lower air density (Rho) affect the aerodynamic performance of the airframe (controlled by ½ Rho V-squared), it also decreases the mass of the fuel/air mixture in the engine cylinders, causing a decrease in engine power. **'Hot and High' penalises you both in terms of Aero-dynamics and Engine Power.**

Many Take-Off Performance tables or graphs allow for variations in the **pressure altitude** and the **ambient temperature** of the aerodrome (i.e. the *'density altitude'*). The pressure altitude is easily determined in the cockpit by winding the altimeter subscale to 1013 mb and noting the altimeter reading.

In approximate terms:

- a 1000 ft increase in pressure altitude will increase Take-Off Distance by 10%, i.e. a factor of 1·1; and
- a 10°C increase in ambient temperature will increase Take-Off Distance by 10%, also a factor of 1·1.

HUMIDITY.

Air is a mixture of gases, mainly oxygen and nitrogen whose molecules are reasonably heavy. When the humidity is high, some of these heavier molecules are replaced by very light water molecules, which has the effect of lowering the air density.

Humidity Decreases Aeroplane and Engine Performance. This effect is usually taken into account during certification, however there may be a correction factor applicable to your aircraft. (Check the Flight Manual or Pilot's Operating Handbook.)

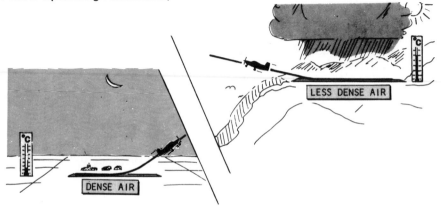

Fig.31-5. Hot, High and Humid Means Decreased Performance.

WIND Effect in Performance Charts.

A Headwind reduces the Take-Off Distance. For flight, the aeroplane requires a certain speed relative to the air it is flying through. An aeroplane stopped at the end of the runway and facing into a 20 kt headwind is already 20 kt closer to the lift-off speed compared to the nil-wind situation. Of course a 10 kt tailwind would worsen the situation considerably, the aircraft having to accelerate to a Ground Speed (GS) of 10 kt before it had an airspeed of zero.

In a headwind take-off, the aeroplane reaches lift-off airspeed at a lower ground speed, and so less ground run is required. Once in the air, the angle or gradient relative to the ground is increased by a headwind, giving better obstacle clearance.

With a tailwind, the effect is to lengthen the ground run and to flatten the climb-out over obstacles. As a guideline factor, the Take-Off Distance will be increased by 20% for a tailwind component of 10% of the lift-off speed, i.e. a factor of 1·2. Tailwinds in excess of 5 kt should not normally be considered suitable for take-off. Obviously, **a take-off into-wind shows better airmanship.**

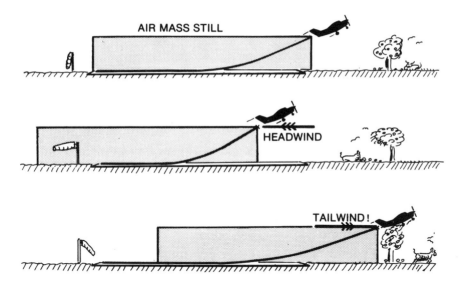

Fig.31-6. A Headwind Reduces Take-Off Distance.

NOTE: Where the published data allows adjustment for wind, it is recommended that not more than 50% of the headwind component and not less than 150% of the tailwind component of the reported wind be assumed. This allows for some variations in the wind effect during take-off – the headwind not being as strong or the tailwind being stronger than expected. In some Manuals this factoring is already included (indicated, for instance, by different spacing on graphs or different percentage corrections on tables for the headwinds and tailwinds), and it is necessary to check the performance section of the Manual. A sound briefing by a Flying Instructor on the performance data in the Manual to be used is highly recommended.

Windshear. A further wind effect that was not often considered in earlier days is that of **Windshear,** a term which means **a wind that differs in strength or direction from place to place.** Windshear is a complex subject and is still not fully understood, however some of the basics should be considered by even the Student Pilot.

We have already discussed Windshear briefly and there is a well-illustrated chapter on it later in this Section – Chapter 36. The following points are mentioned here in relation to the effect of Windshear on Take-Off and Landing Performance.

The wind usually increases in strength as you move further from the ground. This is a result of the friction forces between the ground and the wind causing the wind to slow down near the surface.

Taking-off into a headwind would normally mean that you would climb into an increasing headwind, which tends to increase your airspeed (the speed of the aeroplane relative to the air) and increase the gradient of climb-out over obstacles on the ground. **An increasing headwind leads to increased performance.**

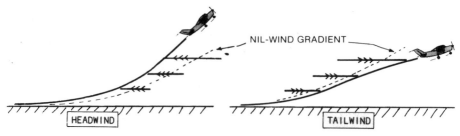

Fig.31-7. Increasing Headwind Assists Performance.

Taking-off downwind would normally mean that you would climb into an increasing tailwind and the effect is a little like trying to catch a bus that is accelerating away from you. It tends to decrease your airspeed, hence the nose must be lowered to retain the desired IAS, and the climb-out angle over obstacles on the ground is degraded.

The effect of a tailwind in degrading climb-out angle or gradient relative to the ground is not considered in take-off charts. **Once again, a take-off into-wind shows good airmanship.**

Crosswind. The aeroplane must not be taken-off in a Crosswind that exceeds the maximum crosswind limitation for the aeroplane.

Directional control is one problem – the aerodynamic Lift force from the rudder having to overcome the effect of the keel surfaces wanting to weathercock the aeroplane into wind – as well as **lateral control,** the crosswind generally trying to lift the into-wind wing, which then has to be held down with aileron. The deflected ailerons and rudder will cause a slight increase in Drag with a consequent decrease in acceleration.

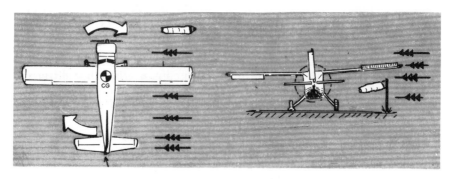

Fig.31-8. Crosswind Take-Off.

To estimate the strength of a crosswind component it will pay us to consider a 10 kt wind blowing from various directions:

- If the wind is 30 degrees off the runway heading, then the crosswind component is ½ the wind strength.
- If the wind is 45 degrees off the runway heading, then the crosswind component is ⅔rd the wind strength.

- If the wind is 60 degrees off the runway heading, then the crosswind component is $\frac{9}{10}$th the wind strength.

- If the wind is 90 degrees off the runway heading, then it is all crosswind.

When calculating the crosswind angle, be sure to work in common units – usually °**M**. Wind from the tower or ATIS is in °**M**, as is runway direction.

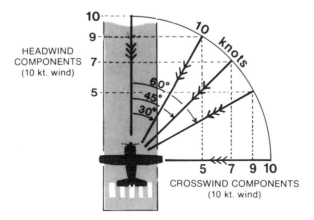

Fig.31-9. Estimating Crosswind and Headwind Components.

In crosswind conditions, the headwind or tailwind component has to be calculated to enter the performance charts or tables.

NOTE: Navigation Computers have the facility for calculating crosswind (and head/tail wind components). The method is explained in Volume 3 on Navigation.

Runway Surface.

Take-off performance information in the UK is based on a hard surface that is level and dry. Other surfaces, such as grass, will retard the acceleration on the ground and therefore lengthen the Take-off Distance.

The rolling resistance or friction can seriously degrade the take-off acceleration:

- Short, dry grass increases the take-off distance by 20%;
- Long, dry grass or short, wet grass increases it by 25%; and
- Long wet grass by 30%;
- Soft ground or snow may increase the take-off distance by 25% or more, i.e. a factor of at least 1·25; (such a surface may in fact make acceleration to the lift-off speed impossible, no matter how much length is available).

It is recommended that a take-off not be attempted if the grass is more than 10 inches long (wet or dry).

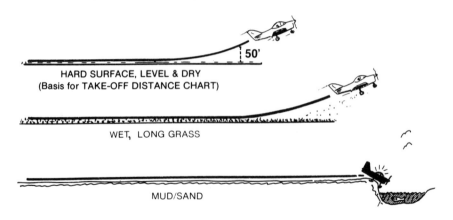

Fig.31-10. Poor Surfaces May Increase Take-Off Distance.

Runway Slope.

Take-off distance is calculated for a level runway, so the take-off chart must allow for the effect of runway slope. A down-slope of 2 in 100 – (i.e. 2% down) will allow the aeroplane to accelerate faster and so will decrease the take-off distance. An up-slope of 2 in 100 (i.e. 2%) will make it more difficult for the aeroplane to accelerate and so the Take-Off Distance will be greater.

Some charts allow for slope and others do not. In general terms, a 2% upslope will increase the Take-Off Distance by 10%.

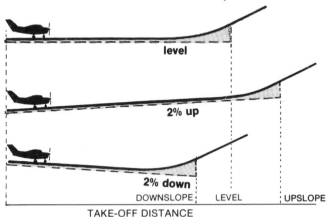

Fig.31-11. An Upward Sloping Runway Will Increase The Take-Off Distance.

NOTE: The corrections are for Take-Off Distance from the Starting Point to the Screen Height of 50 ft. For the surface and slope factors the correction to the Ground Run will be greater.

Runway slope is calculated using the elevations at either end of the Take-Off Run Available (TORA), therefore a runway with downslope may have a hump (involving upslope) somewhere along its length (and vice versa).

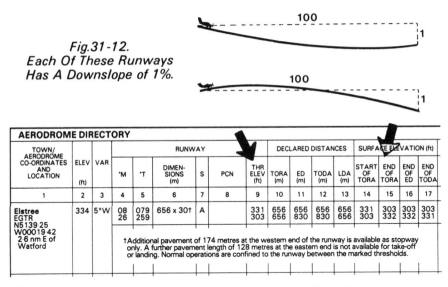

Fig.31-12.
Each Of These Runways
Has A Downslope of 1%.

AERODROME DIRECTORY																
TOWN/ AERODROME CO-ORDINATES AND LOCATION	ELEV (ft)	VAR	RUNWAY						DECLARED DISTANCES					SURFACE ELEVATION (ft)		
			°M	°T	DIMEN- SIONS (m)	S	PCN	THR ELEV (ft)	TORA (m)	ED (m)	TODA (m)	LDA (m)	START OF TORA	END OF TORA	END OF ED	END OF TODA
1	2	3	4	5	6	7	8	9	10	11	12	13	14	15	16	17
Elstree EGTR N5139·25 W00019·42 2·6 nm E of Watford	334	5°W	08 26	079 259	656 x 30†	A		331 303	656 656	656 830	656 830	656 656	331 303	303 332	303 332	303 331
			†Additional pavement of 174 metres at the western end of the runway is available as stopway only. A further pavement length of 128 metres at the eastern end is not available for take-off or landing. Normal operations are confined to the runway between the marked thresholds.													

Fig.31-13. AIP-AGA contains Runway Threshold Elevations, necessary for Calculating Slope.

THE RECOMMENDED SAFETY FACTOR.

After taking account of the above variables and their **cumulative** effect, the CAA strongly recommends that a safety factor of 1·33 be used for take-off for all Group E aeroplanes – the majority of light general aviation aircraft. (It is necessary to check the Manual or Handbook of Performance Groups C and D aeroplanes to see if this factor is already included.)

Example 1: Suppose the base figure for 'Measured Take-Off Distance' is 400 metres for a take-off at a sea level aerodrome at +10°C at the particular aeroplane weight, and there is no CAA-imposed mandatory performance writedown for this type.

Situation A: A sea level aerodrome, a hard dry runway with no slope, nil wind, temp 10°C.
Mandatory CAA Writedown: Nil
Correction factors: nil
Safety factor for take-off: 1·33

Recommended Take-Off Distance = 400 × 1·33 = 532 metres.

Situation B: Aerodrome elevation 1000 ft, a wet long-grass strip with 2% upslope, temp 20°C, tailwind component 5 kt (lift-off speed 50 kt).
Mandatory CAA Writedown: nil
Correction factors: (elevation) 1·1 ×; (10°C temp increase) 1·1 ×; (long wet grass) 1·3 ×; (2% upslope) 1·1 ×; (tailwind 10% of lift-off speed) 1·2 ×
Safety factor for take-off: 1·33
Recommended Take-Off Distance = 400 × 1·1 × 1·1 × 1·3 × 1·1 × 1·2 × 1·33 = 1105 metres.

Note the significant increase in distance. Good airmanship would suggest that a take-off in the opposite direction would be preferable, taking advantage of a downslope and a headwind.

USE OF TAKE-OFF PERFORMANCE CHARTS:

There are various presentations of these performance charts and tables. They are presented logically and allow you to enter with known data such as **Temperature** and **Pressure Altitude** and proceed through the chart or table, to end up with an answer for **Take-off Distance,** or the highest **Weight** in the conditions.

UNITED KINGDOM
SUPPLEMENT

GULFSTREAM AMERICAN
MODEL AA-5A CHEETAH

TAKEOFF DISTANCE (AA-5A United Kingdom)

ASSOCIATED CONDITIONS:
POWER – MAXIMUM
FLAPS – UP
RUNWAY – HARD SURFACE (LEVEL & DRY)
FUEL MIXTURE – FULL THROTTLE CLIMB, MIXTURE LEANED ABOVE 5000 FT TO SMOOTH ENGINE OPERATION.

NOTES:
1. DECREASE DISTANCE 4% FOR EACH 5 KNOTS HEADWIND. FOR OPERATION WITH TAILWINDS UP TO 10 KNOTS, INCREASE DISTANCE BY 10% FOR EACH 2.5 KNOTS.
2. IF TAKEOFF POWER IS SET WITHOUT BRAKES APPLIED, THEN DISTANCES APPLY FROM POINT WHERE FULL POWER IS ATTAINED.
3. FOR TAKEOFF FROM A DRY, GRASS RUNWAY, INCREASE GROUND RUN AND TOTAL DISTANCE TO CLEAR A 50 FT OBSTACLE BY 12.5% OF THE HARD SURFACE RUNWAY TOTAL TO CLEAR 50 FT OBSTACLE.

WEIGHT KGS	TAKEOFF SPEED KIAS (MPH) LIFT OFF	TAKEOFF SPEED CLEAR 50 FT	PRESS. ALT FT	0°C (32°F) METRES GND RUN	0°C 50 FT	10°C (40°F) METRES GND RUN	10°C 50 FT	20°C (68°F) METRES GND RUN	20°C 50 FT	30°C (86°F) METRES GND RUN	30°C 50 FT	40°C (104°F) METRES GND RUN	40°C 50 FT
998	56 (64)	63 (73)	SL	230	419	255	464	282	512	311	564	341	618
			2000	273	495	304	549	336	606	370	667	407	732
			4000	326	587	362	651	401	719	442	791	485	868
			6000	391	698	434	774	479	854	529	940	581	1031
			8000	469	832	520	922	575	1018	634	1120	697	1229
907	53 (61)	60 (69)	SL	183	336	203	372	224	411	247	452	272	496
			2000	218	397	241	440	267	486	294	535	323	587
			4000	260	471	288	522	319	576	351	635	386	696
			6000	311	560	345	621	382	685	420	754	462	828
			8000	373	668	414	740	458	817	504	899	554	983
816	50 (58)	57 (66)	SL	142	263	158	292	174	322	192	355	211	389
			2000	169	312	187	345	207	381	229	419	251	460
			4000	202	369	221	409	247	452	273	497	300	546
			6000	241	439	268	486	296	537	326	591	359	649
			8000	290	523	321	580	355	640	392	704	430	773

SAMPLE ONLY
Not to be used in conjunction
with Flight Operations or
Flight Planning

Fig.31-14a. Tabular Performance Chart for Take-Off.

The tabular style of Performance Chart has been seen in *Fig.31-14a*. Below is an example of the graphical approach – the Piper Tomahawk (PA-38).

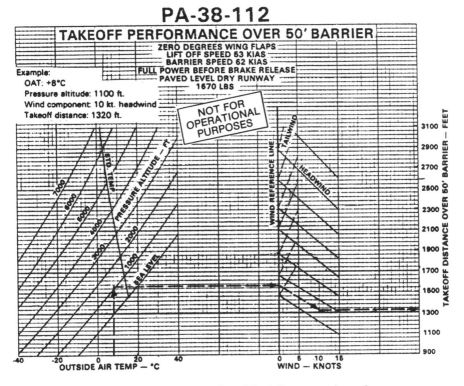

Fig.31-14b. Typical Graphical Presentation of a Take-Off Performance Chart.

Notice that this chart is for a fixed weight (1670 lb.) and that zero degrees of wing flaps is used. Ensure that you use the Chart or Table for the **Flap Setting that you will be using for the particular Take-Off.**

The next example uses a chart which is already factored for take-off surface and runway slope, (unlike the previous Figure).

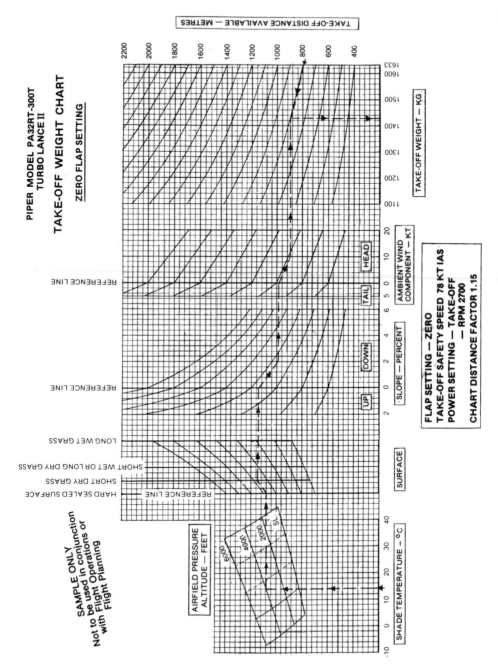

Fig.31-15. A Typical Take-Off Weight Chart (Zero Degrees Flap).

304

Example 2:
- Take-Off Distance Available 800 metres;
- Pressure Altitude 4,000 ft;
- Temperature +14°C;
- 2% down slope;
- Short dry grass;
- 10 kt head wind.

Using a flap setting of 0 degrees for take-off and the procedures recommended on the chart (take-off power setting 2700 rpm, which should be applied prior to rolling to achieve the chart distance), Take-Off Safety Speed 78 kt, find the **highest** Take-Off Weight.

Method: as shown on the chart opposite, we enter with a temperature of +14°C and proceeded vertically up to the airfield pressure altitude of 4000 ft.

Proceed horizontally to the 'surface' reference line, following the guide lines up from it to the 'short dry grass' line (as we will be taking off this time on short dry grass). Then proceed horizontally to the 'slope' reference line, and since our surface has a 2% down slope, we follow the guide lines down to the '2% down' line.

Continue across to the wind reference line and follow the guide lines down to the '10 kt headwind' line. (If you had a 5 kt tailwind, you would go horizontally to the reference line and then back up the guide lines until intercepting the 5 kt tailwind line. You will see later that this tailwind has the effect of lengthening the take-off distance required, whereas the headwind shortens it.)

Proceed horizontally until you intercept the 800 metre TODA line (Take-Off Distance Available), and then drop vertically to determine the **highest Take-Off Weight** allowable for this take-off. **It is 1430 kg.**

ENSURE THAT SUFFICIENT TAKE-OFF DISTANCE IS AVAILABLE.

The Pilot should always ensure that, having applied all the relevant factors, including the safety factor, to obtain the Recommended Take-Off Distance, there is sufficient **Take-Off Distance AVAILABLE (TODA)**. This is covered shortly.

THE CLIMB-AWAY AFTER TAKE-OFF.

So that aeroplane climb performance does not fall below the prescribed minimum, some Manuals give take-off and landing **W**eights that should not be exceeded at specific combinations of **A**ltitude and **T**emperature, known as '**WAT' limits** (pronounced *'wott'*). Unless included in the Limitations section of the Manual, these weight restrictions are only mandatory for Public Transport flights. They are, however, **recommended** for Private flights and are calculated using the pressure altitude and temperature (i.e. density altitude) at the relevant aerodrome.

Where WAT limits are not given, it is recommended that a single-engine, fixed-undercarriage aeroplane should be capable of a 500 ft/min rate of climb in the en route configuration at the en route climb speed and using Maximum Continuous Power.

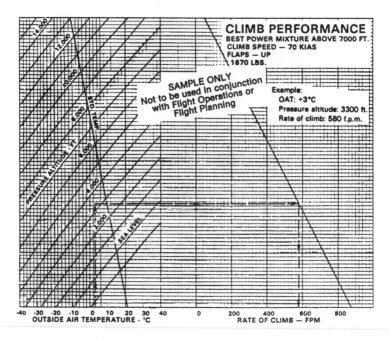

Fig.31-16. Example of a Maximum Rate of Climb Performance Chart.

PHYSICAL CHARACTERISTICS OF RUNWAYS

A **Runway** is a defined rectangular area on a land aerodrome prepared for the landing and taking-off of aircraft. The surface of a runway may be sealed (e.g. bitumen, concrete) or natural (e.g. grass, clay).

The **Take-Off Run Available (TORA)** is the length of runway which is available and suitable for the ground run of an aeroplane taking-off. In most cases this corresponds to the physical length of the runway.

Fig.31-17. Take-Off Run Available.

The take-off is not completed at lift-off when the wheels leave the runway. Take-off considerations apply until you are at least at the *Take-Off Safety Speed* at 50 feet above the take-off surface. There is no need for all of this air distance to be above an actual runway surface – some of the air distance from lift-off to 50 ft can be above an obstacle-free zone, called a *'Clearway'*.

A Clearway is a defined rectangular area on the ground or water at the end of a runway in the direction of take-off and under the control of the Competent Authority, selected or prepared as a suitable area over which an aircraft may make a portion of its initial climb to a specified height (50 ft in our case).

This means that the *Take-Off Distance Available* may exceed the *Take-Off Run Available* by the distance provided by the *Clearway*. Thus, the **Take-Off Distance Available (TODA)** is the length of the runway available plus the length of clearway available (if clearway is provided). TODA is not to exceed 1·5 times TORA.

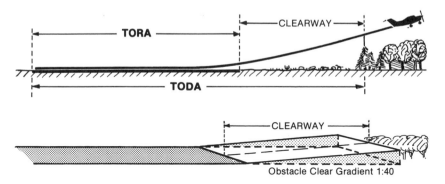

Fig.31-18. Clearway.

Occasionally a take-off is rejected, say due to an engine failure. A Rejected Take-Off (RTO) is also known as an *'accelerate-stop'*, because the aeroplane first accelerates as in every take-off and then, for some reason, the take-off manoeuvre is aborted and the aeroplane is stopped. The distance required for such a manoeuvre is called the *'Accelerate-Stop Distance'* or the *'Emergency Distance' (ED)*.

The **Emergency Distance (ED)** on the runway is the *take-off run available* (usually the physical length of the runway) plus the length of any *'Stopway'* available (if stopway is provided).

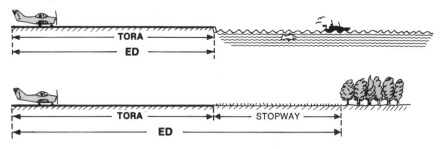

Fig.31-19. Emergency Distance (ED).

A Stopway is a defined rectangular area on the ground at the end of a runway in the direction of take-off, designated and prepared by the Competent Authority as a suitable area in which an aircraft can be stopped in the case of an interrupted take-off.

Note that a *Stopway* must be on the ground, as the aeroplane will be braked and stopped on it, whereas a *Clearway* is provided as an obstacle-free zone over which the aeroplane can fly, hence can be ground or water.

The Landing Distance Available (LDA) is the length of runway available for landing, taking into account any obstacles in the approach path.

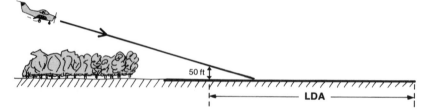

Fig.31-20. Landing Distance Available (LDA).

The above lengths available are vital distances when calculating the performance limitations on an aeroplane for take-off or landing on a particular runway. **TORA, ED, TODA** and **LDA** are known as the **Declared Distances** for that runway.

THE AGA SECTION OF THE AIP.

The **Declared Distances** and other important information regarding particular runways at certain aerodromes are obtainable from the Aerodrome and Ground Aids (AGA) section of the UK Aeronautical Information Publication (AIP) – (formerly known as the 'UK Air Pilot'). Any changes will be notified by NOTAM.

Emergency Distance — Take-Off Run Available — Take-Off Distance Available — Landing Distance Available

AERODROME DIRECTORY

TOWN/AERODROME CO-ORDINATES AND LOCATION	ELEV (ft)	VAR	RUNWAY					THR ELEV (ft)	DECLARED DISTANCES				SURFACE ELEVATION (ft)			
			°M	°T	DIMEN-SIONS (m)	S	PCN		TORA (m)	ED (m)	TODA (m)	LDA (m)	START OF TORA	END OF TORA	END OF ED	END OF TODA
1	2	3	4	5	6	7	8	9	10	11	12	13	14	15	16	17
Blackbushe EGLK N5119.43 W00050.74 8.5 nm SE by S of Reading	329	5°W	08 26	072 252	1 352 x 46	A		321 324	1 262 1 287	1 262 1 287	1 262 1 287	1 112 1 062	321 325	323 321	323 321	323 321
			08 26	072 252	550 x 18	G		321 323	550 550	550 550	550 550	550 550	321 323	323 321	323 321	323 321
Blackpool	*See* AGA 2-6															
Bodmin EGLA N5029.50 W00440.42 3.5 nm NE of Bodmin	625	7°W	03 21	022 202	480 x 18	G		610 600	480 480	480 480	480 480	480 480	610 600	600 610	600 610	600 610
			14 32	129 309	610 x 18	G		625 605	598 610	598 610	598 610	598 540	625 600	600 625	600 625	600 625
Bourn EGSN N5212.59 W00002.47 7 nm W of Cambridge	220	5°W	01 19	007 187	633 x 18	B		207 225	633 633	633 633	633 633	633 633	220 218	218 220	218 220	218 220

NOT FOR OPERATIONAL PURPOSES

Fig.31-21a. Example of Distances Available as Published in AIP-AGA.

Another source of Runway Information is *Pooley's Flight Guide* which lists Take-Off Run Available (TORA) and Landing Distance Available (LDA) for UK aerodromes. If using this guide, be sure your information is up-to-date, and, if in doubt, refer to AIP AGA.

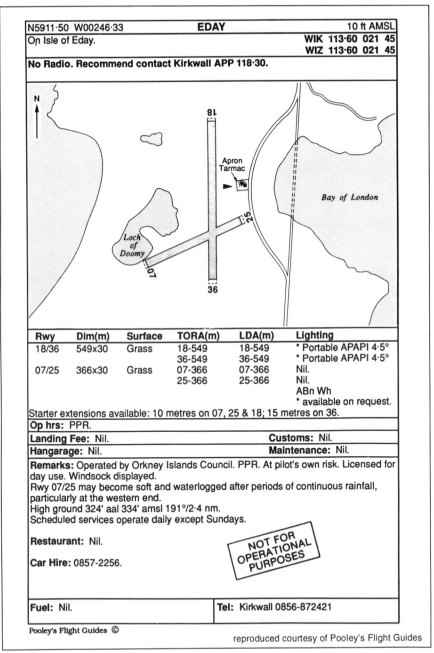

Fig.31-21b. Extract of Runway Information as shown in Pooley's Guide.

AEROPLANE LANDING PERFORMANCE

The **Measured Landing Distance** is the distance established from a point where the aircraft is 50 ft over the runway (assumed to be a hard, level, dry surface) at a speed not less than '1·3 V-stall' to the point where the aeroplane reaches a full stop, following a steady, full flap, no power approach and maximum braking.

The '1·3 V-stall' provides a 30% safety margin over stalling speed in the landing configuration. If the stalling speed is 50 kt, then the minimum approach speed should be 30% up on this at 65 kt.

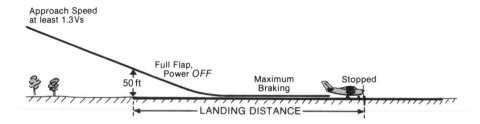

Fig.31-22. Landing Distance.

PERFORMANCE DATA FOR LANDING.

The aeroplane's Flight Manual or Pilot's Operating Handbook will contain performance data for landing in the form of a graph or table.

For example, using the Chart opposite, the Landing Distance from 50 ft for a Cheetah at Landing Weight 907 kg on a hard, dry, level surface at a sea level aerodrome and +10°C in nil wind conditions is 392 metres. The Approach Speed is 65 kt and the Ground Run will be 118 metres.

The actual Landing Performance from 50 ft to a Stop will be affected by a number of variables which the Pilot must take into account.

Increased Weight means a Greater 'Landing Distance'. A higher weight has a number of effects:

- The stalling speed is increased, so the minimum approach speed of 1·3 V-stall must be greater. A higher speed requires more distance to land and stop.

- The higher weight means that the kinetic energy (½ m V-squared) is higher and the brakes have to absorb this greater energy, increasing the landing run. (There will be a slight increase in the retarding friction force due to the extra weight on the wheels).

As a guideline, the Landing Distance will be increased by 10% for each 10% increase in aeroplane weight, i.e. a factor of 1·1.

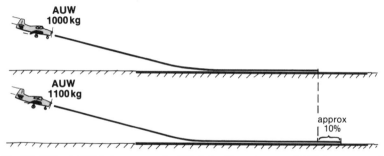

Fig.31-23. A 10% Increase in Weight Requires a 10% Increase in Landing Distance (approximately).

┌A TYPICAL LANDING PERFORMANCE CHART┐

GULFSTREAM AMERICAN
MODEL AA-5A CHEETAH

UNITED KINGDOM
SUPPLEMENT

LANDING DISTANCE (AA-5A United Kingdom)

ASSOCIATED CONDITIONS:
POWER – OFF
FLAPS – DOWN
RUNWAY – HARD SURFACE (LEVEL & DRY)
BRAKING – MAXIMUM

SAMPLE ONLY
Not to be used in conjunction
with Flight Operations or
Flight Planning

NOTES:
1. DECREASE DISTANCE 4% FOR EACH 5 KNOTS HEADWIND.
2. FOR OPERATIONS WITH TAILWINDS UP TO 10 KNOTS, INCREASE DISTANCE BY 9% FOR EACH 2.5 KNOTS.
3. WHEN LANDING ON A DRY GRASS RUNWAY, INCREASE GROUND RUN AND TOTAL DISTANCE OVER 50 FT. OBSTACLE BY 20% OF THE HARD SURFACE RUNWAY TOTAL DISTANCE OVER A 50 FT OBSTACLE.

WEIGHT KGS	SPEED AT 50 FT		PRESS ALT FT.	0°C (32°F) METRES		10°C (40°F) METRES		20°C (68°F) METRES		30°C (86°F) METRES		40°C (104°F) METRES	
	KIAS	MPH		GND RUN	CLEAR 50 FT	GND RUN	CLEAR 50 FT	GND RUN	CLEAR 50 FT	GND RUN	CLEAR 50 FT	GND RUN	CLEAR 50 FT
998	68	78	SL	123	410	127	422	130	434	133	445	137	458
			2000	130	434	134	447	138	460	141	473	145	487
			4000	138	461	142	476	146	490	150	504	155	519
			6000	147	492	151	507	156	523	161	539	165	555
			8000	157	526	162	543	167	560	172	578	177	595
907	65	75	SL	115	362	118	392	121	402	124	413	127	424
			2000	121	403	125	414	128	426	131	438	135	449
			4000	128	427	132	440	135	452	139	465	143	478
			6000	136	454	140	468	144	482	148	496	152	511
			8000	145	484	149	500	154	515	158	531	163	547
816	61	71	SL	107	353	110	362	112	371	115	380	118	390
			2000	112	371	115	381	118	392	121	402	121	412
			4000	118	393	122	404	125	415	128	426	131	438
			6000	125	416	129	429	132	441	136	454	140	467
			8000	133	443	137	457	141	471	145	485	149	499

Fig.31-24. A Typical Landing Distance Table (Gulfstream Cheetah).

An Increased Density Altitude means a Longer 'Landing Distance Required'. Low pressure, high elevation and high temperatures can decrease the air density (Rho), giving what we call a higher Density Altitude (the height in the International Standard Atmosphere that has the same density as the point under consideration).

A decreased Rho means an increased V (TAS) to provide the same Lift force. Even though the Pilot sees the same Indicated Air Speed in the cockpit, the True Air Speed is higher in air of lower density.

Therefore, at high density altitudes the True Air Speed will be greater than for lower density altitudes, the touchdown ground speed will be higher, and therefore the amount of kinetic energy to be dissipated in the stop is greater – hence a longer landing distance.

In approximate terms, an increase in pressure altitude of 1000 ft *or* an increase of 10°C will increase the Landing Distance by 5%, i.e. a factor of 1·05.

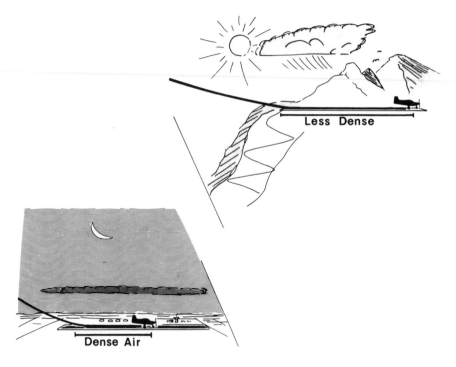

Less Dense

Dense Air

Fig.31-25. 'High Temperature and High Altitude' Requires More Landing Distance.

A Headwind Reduces the Landing Distance because the ground speed (GS) is reduced by the headwind for the same TAS (V).

A tailwind means that the GS will exceed the TAS, and so the touchdown speed relative to the ground is higher and a longer landing distance will be required.

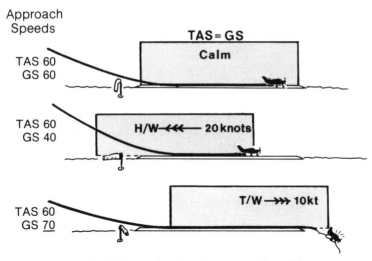

Approach
Speeds

TAS 60
GS 60

TAS = GS
Calm

TAS 60
GS 40

H/W ◀◀◀ 20 knots

TAS 60
GS 70

T/W ⟩⟩⟩ 10kt

Fig.31-26. A Headwind Reduces Landing Distance.

As for take-off, further wind effect to consider is **Windshear** (discussed in detail in Chapter 36). If the headwind component increases, then the aircraft experiences a **transient** increase in performance.

There are advantages in approaching into wind (lower ground speed, shorter landing distance required), however, as you near the ground, if the headwind decreases, then the aircraft will experience a loss of performance and tend to sink and possibly undershoot the aiming point.

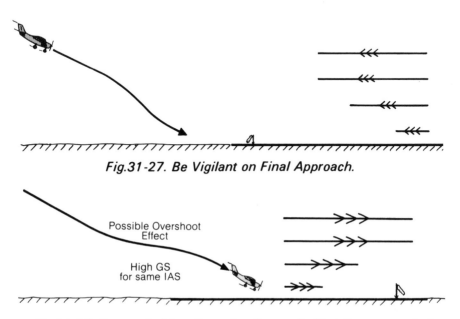

Fig.31-27. Be Vigilant on Final Approach.

Possible Overshoot
Effect

High GS
for same IAS

*Fig.31-28. Downwind Landings Are Generally **Not** Recommended. .*

It is disadvantageous to approach in a tailwind due to the high touchdown ground speeds and longer landing distances required. Approaching the ground, the reducing tailwind has the same effect as an increasing headwind – the aircraft may experience an increase in performance and tend to float further down the runway.

As a guideline, a tailwind wind component of 10% of the Landing Speed will increase the Landing Distance by 20%, i.e. a factor of 1·2.

NOTE: Where the published data allows adjustment for wind, it is recommended that not more than 50% of the headwind component and not less than 150% of the tailwind component of the reported wind be assumed. This allows for some variations in the wind effect during the approach and landing – the headwind not being as strong or the tailwind being stronger than expected. In some Manuals this factoring is already included (indicated, for instance, by different spacing on graphs or different percentage corrections on tables for the headwinds and tailwinds), and it is necessary to check the performance section of the Manual. A sound briefing by a Flying Instructor on the performance data in the Manual to be used is highly recommended.

RUNWAY SURFACE.

A low-friction runway surface (wet, slick, icy, etc.) will not allow good braking to occur and so the landing distance required will be longer. **Aquaplaning** on a wet surface may occur and this can give extraordinary increases in the stopping distances.

Aquaplaning is the phenomenon of a tyre skating along on a thin film of water and not rotating, even though it is free to do so. **Wheel braking therefore has no effect when aquaplaning and directional control can easily be lost.** Friction forces are practically zero.

As **aquaplaning is more likely to occur at higher ground speeds,** landing into-wind on a wet runway (which keeps the GS to a minimum) is recommended.

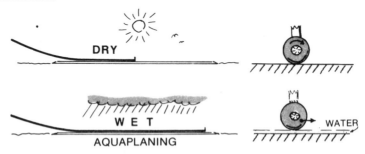

Fig.31-29. Low Friction Surfaces Increase Landing Distance.

Typical increases in Landing Distance are:

- for short dry grass (under 5 inches) 20%, a factor of 1·2;
- for long dry grass (over 5 inches) 30%, a factor 1·3;
- for short wet grass (under 5 inches) 30%, a factor of 1·3;
- for long wet grass (over 5 inches) 40%, a factor 1·4;
- for snow 25% or more, a factor of at least 1·25.

RUNWAY SLOPE.

A down-slope will require a longer landing distance. It will take longer for the aeroplane to touch down from 50 ft above the runway threshold, as the runway is falling away beneath the aeroplane, and of course braking whilst going downhill is not as effective as on a level or upwards sloping runway. A 2% downhill slope will increase Landing Distance by 10%, a factor of 1·1.

NOTE: For surface and slope factors, the guideline factors are for Landing Distance from 50 ft. The correction to the Ground Roll will be greater.

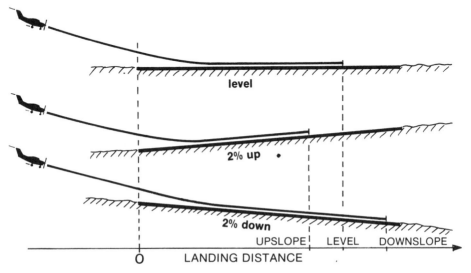

Fig.31-30. Downslope Increases Landing Distance.

INCREASED FLAP SETTINGS DECREASE LANDING DISTANCE.

Higher flap settings reduce the stalling speed and therefore the approach speed (1·3 Vs) is less. High flap settings also give additional aerodynamic drag that helps to slow the aeroplane down, as well as allowing a steeper approach path.

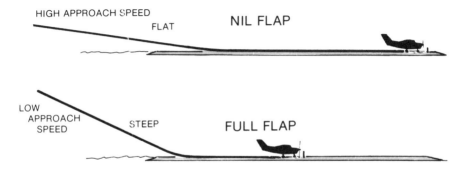

Fig.31-31. Increased Flap – Slower and Steeper Approach.

THE RECOMMENDED SAFETY FACTOR FOR LANDING.

The CAA recommends that a **Landing Safety Factor of 1·43** be applied for Private flights (it is mandatory for Public Transport flights) in Group E aeroplanes. It is necessary to check the Manual of Performance Groups C and D aeroplanes to see if it is already included.

THE LANDING FACTORS ARE CUMULATIVE AND SHOULD BE MULTIPLIED.

The above factors are cumulative and, where several factors are relevant, they must be multiplied. The resulting distance can sometimes be surprisingly high.

Example 3: In still air on a level dry runway with an ambient temperature of 10°C an aeroplane has a Measured Landing Distance from a Height of 50 ft of 400 metres.

Situation A: The Recommended Landing Distance in the above situation is 400 × 1·43 = 572 metres.

Situation B: The landing strip is long wet grass with a downslope of 2% and a tailwind of 5kt (Landing Speed 50 kt), +20°C, elevation 2000 ft.

Recommended Landing Distance = 400 × 1·4 (surface); × 1·1 (slope); × 1·05 (temp); × 1·1 (elev); × 1·2 (tailwind); × 1·43 (safety factor) = 1221 metres. Good airmanship might lead the Pilot to consider landing in the opposite direction, taking advantage of a headwind and an upslope.

ENSURE THAT THE LANDING DISTANCE AVAILABLE IS SUFFICIENT.

Having calculated the Landing Distance from 50 ft, the Pilot must ensure that the landing field chosen has sufficient Landing Distance **Available** (LDA). This is obtained from AIP-AGA, as shown earlier. (Also, *Pooley's Flight Guide* provides values for LDA.)

PRESENTATIONS OF LANDING DATA.

Similar to take-off charts, there are various ways of presenting the performance data. *Fig.31-24* showed the tabular method of presentation; the next examples show the graphical style.

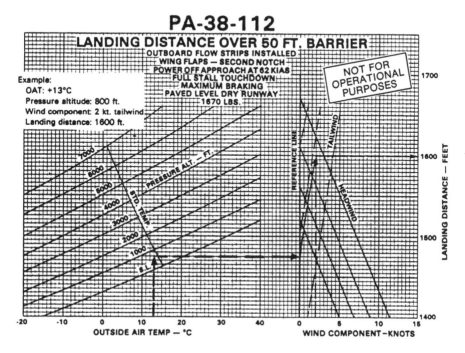

Fig.31-32. Graphical Presentation – Piper Tomahawk Landing Chart.

The next Figure (31-33) shows another type of landing performance chart. It is for a 40 degree **Flap** landing approaching at 76 kt Indicated Air Speed and is based on power-off at 50 ft.

(Note that, although this is the method used for certification, it does not mean that you must take the power *OFF* at 50 ft in every landing – it is used simply as a standard method of determining landing distances.)

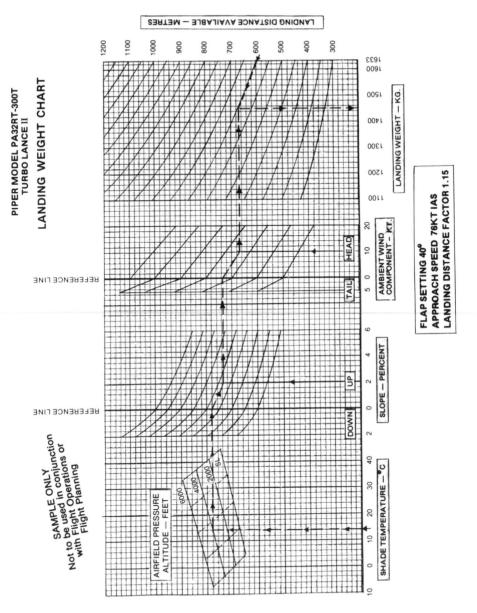

Fig.31-33. Another Type of Landing Performance Chart.

In the next example we could be faced with the problem of finding the Maximum Landing Weight possible on a 600 metre runway at a pressure altitude of 4,000 ft, temperature +14°C, 2% up-slope, 10 kt headwind.

Enter with +14°C and move vertically to intercept the pressure altitude 4,000 ft line.

Move horizontally to the slope reference line and from there follow the guide lines down to the '2% up' line (notice by a quick glance to the landing distance scale on the right hand side that this has the effect of reducing it).

Next, proceed to the wind reference line – the 10 kt headwind being favourable.

Now move across to meet the 600m landing distance available line, dropping vertically to a Maximum Landing Weight of 1450 kg.

Suppose your weight was 1500 kg. Under the same meteorological conditions, the 1500 kg line proceeding up the graph would intersect the horizontal line from the left at about 620m landing distance, and this is what you then legally require to land.

If you were limited by the landing distance available being only 600m, then you could look at the wind situation (by proceeding left from where the 1500 kg line intersects the 600m line). To be able to land legally, the headwind component would have to be at least 14 kt.

Notice that:

- **Higher Temperatures** mean More Landing Distance or Lower Landing Weight;

- a **Higher Pressure Altitude** means More Landing Distance or Lower Landing Weight;

- a **Down-Slope** means More Landing Distance or Lower Landing Weight;

- a **Tailwind** means More Landing Distance or Lower Landing Weight.

FAST APPROACH SPEEDS.

The landing performance charts are based on **Specified Approach Speeds**. If you approach for a landing at a speed higher than that specified, the landing distance may exceed that predicted by the chart.

An important point to note in *'too-fast'* approaches is that the aeroplane is reluctant to settle onto the ground due to **'Ground Effect'**. This is the *'cushioning'* of the aeroplane on the air between it and the ground when the aeroplane is close to the ground as during the flare to land.

Ground Effect is caused by the reduction in the amount of downwash behind the wings, and by the tendency of the aeroplane not to slow down (decreased drag) resulting from the reduction in the formation of wingtip vortices. (Chapter 35 later in this section covers Ground Effect in detail.)

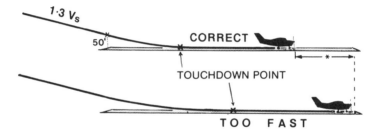

Fig.31-34. High Approach Speeds Increase Landing Distance.

SOME PERFORMANCE CONSIDERATIONS

Incorrect performance calculations (or none at all!) can result in aeroplanes failing to get airborne on take-off in the distance available, or colliding with obstacles owing to an inadequate climb-out, or overrunning the Landing Distance Available on landing. Contributing factors are often short strips, tailwind, slope, poor surfaces, poor airmanship and lack of recent experience.

The Pilot has a legal obligation to check that aeroplane performance is adequate for all aspects of the proposed flight – take-off, climb-out, approach and landing. What has gone before in this chapter, plus sound consideration of the performance charts of the aeroplane to be flown, should prepare a Pilot to undertake this responsiblity prior to each flight. Some runways in certain weather conditions will obviously be more than adequate for a particular operation in a light aircraft, in which case no precise calculations are necessary. In doubtful situations, the charts should definitely be referred to.

If there is no published information for the airfield to be used, then the distances should be paced out. The pace length can be established accurately or assumed to be no more than 2·5 ft. A crude method of establishing slope is to taxi the aeroplane from one end of the strip to the other and note the difference in readings. An altitude difference of 50 ft on a 1000 metre strip (3280 ft) gives a slope of 50/3280 × 100/1 = 1·53%. (Do not mix feet and metres.)

The Pilot should **always bear in mind the possibility of engine failure,** which can occur at any stage in flight (although less frequently now than in years gone by). For a single-engined aeroplane, considerations are the gliding performance of the aeroplane and the availability of a field for forced landing. For instance, all other things being equal, a take-off over open fields is preferable to a take-off over a built-up area.

For normal operations, the aeroplane must have sufficient performance and be flown so that it clears any obstacles in the take-off or landing path by a safe margin.

If any doubt exists on the source of data to be used or its application in given circumstances, advice may be sought from the CAA's Performance Section in the Airworthiness Division.

☐ You should now find **Exercises 31 — Take-Off and Landing Performance** straightforward.

32

EN ROUTE PERFORMANCE

The Total Drag generated by an aeroplane is high at both high and low speeds – at high speeds because of the large amount of parasite drag and at low speeds because of the large amount of induced drag. Minimum drag occurs at an intermediate airspeed.

For the aeroplane to maintain straight and level flight at a constant airspeed, the Thrust must balance this Drag. Thrust is produced by the propeller's use of engine power – high power being required, therefore, to maintain both high and low airspeeds. The **Power Required** to maintain speed straight and level is illustrated on the graph below.

The engine has a certain maximum power capability at various airspeeds and this is shown as the **Power Available** curve. The excess power available over that required at any speed can be used, if desired, to accelerate or to climb. If there is no excess power available, then neither a climb at that speed nor acceleration in level flight is possible. If there is a deficiency of power, the aeroplane will decelerate or descend.

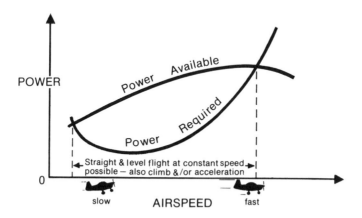

Fig.32-1. The 'Power Required' and 'Power Available' Curves.

The greatest rate of climb, (i.e. to achieve height in the shortest **time),** can be achieved at the airspeed at which excess power is maximum. This speed is usually specified in the Flight Manual.

The speed for the **maximum angle** or **maximum gradient** climb, (i.e. to achieve height in the shortest **distance),** is also specified and is usually some 5–10 kt less than that for maximum rate.

321

Aircraft weight, aircraft configuration and density altitude affect the power curves.

A heavily-laden aeroplane requires more Lift to balance the Weight, hence needs to be flown at a higher angle of attack to maintain a given airspeed. This means more Drag, and an increased power requirement. Inefficient in-flight aircraft configuration (such as landing gear extended when it could be retracted, or even partial flap extended) increases the drag, especially at high speeds, thereby decreasing the acceleration and rate of climb capabilities of the aeroplane. **High density altitudes** (i.e. high altitudes and/or temperatures) increase the power required and decrease the power available.

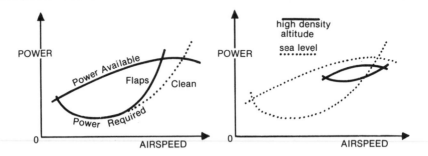

Fig.32-2. Flaps and High Density Altitudes Affect the Power Curves.

RANGE AND ENDURANCE.

En route performance is a very important consideration, especially in high-performance aeroplanes where incorrect selection of power settings, cruising speeds and altitudes can significantly affect the efficiency and economics of the operation.

Fuel consumption is a function of the **power used,** so minimum fuel straight and level will be used at the airspeed for minimum power. This airspeed is known as the **endurance airspeed,** since it allows the longest time of flight for the minimum amount of fuel burn. This speed is used for delaying action, for instance holding whilst waiting for a fog to lift at the destination aerodrome.

It is more common to want to cover the **maximum distance** for a given amount of fuel, and the speed at which this can be achieved is the **best range speed.**

Since the *rate of covering distance* is airspeed, and the *rate of burning fuel* depends upon power, the **maximum range airspeed** will be that where the 'power/airspeed' ratio is least. This occurs where the line from the origin is a tangent to the curve. At all other airspeeds, the line from the origin to the point on the curve will be steeper and the 'power/speed' ratio greater, causing more fuel per mile to be burnt.

In strong headwind conditions, the best range speed will be a little faster – the increased fuel flow being compensated for by a higher speed allowing less time en route for the headwind to act. Conversely, the best range airspeed will be a little slower when there is tailwind assistance. Wind will not affect endurance speed, since time and not distance is the important factor.

It·must be emphasised that **the manufacturer's cruise performance .figures assume correct leaning of the mixture.**

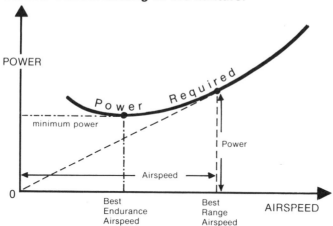

Fig.32-3. Best Endurance and Best Range Speeds.

The graphical analysis above is a theoretical approach. In practice, the Flight Manual should be referred to, since it will contain tables of cruise performance figures. By comparing the Ground Speed and the Fuel Flow, the speed and altitude for best range can be calculated.

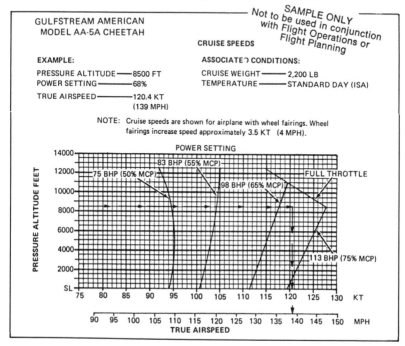

Fig.32-4. Example of Cruise Speeds Table.

GULFSTREAM AMERICAN
MODEL AA-5A CHEETAH   CRUISE PERFORMANCE

Not to be used in conjunction
with Flight Operations or
Flight Planning
SAMPLE ONLY

CONDITIONS:
Recommended lean mixture, weight 2200 pounds.

NOTE:
Shaded area represents operation with full throttle. (F.T.)

RPM	PRESSURE ALTITUDE 8000 FEET											
	20°C BELOW STD. TEMP				STANDARD TEMP				20°C ABOVE STD. TEMP			
	% BHP	TAS KT	TAS MPH	FUEL GPH	% BHP	TAS KT	TAS MPH	FUEL GPH	% BHP	TAS KT	TAS MPH	FUEL GPH
	21°C (−6°F)				−1°C (31°F)				19°C (67°F)			
2700	79	128	147	9.1	75	128	147	8.6	72	126	145	8.2
2600	73	123	142	8.3	69	121	140	7.9	65	119	137	7.4
2500	66	117	134	7.5	63	114	132	7.1	59	111	128	6.7
2400	60	110	126	6.8	67	107	123	6.5	55	104	120	6.2
2300	54	102	118	6.1	52	99	114	5.9	51	96	110	5.7
	PRESSURE ALTITUDE 9000 FEET											
	−23°C (−9°F)				−3°C (27°F)				17°C (63°F)			
2700	75	126	145	8.7	73	126	145	8.3	70	125	144	8.0
2600	71	122	141	8.1	67	120	138	7.7	64	118	136	7.3
2500	64	116	133	7.3	61	113	130	7.0	59	111	128	6.6
2400	58	108	125	6.6	56	106	122	6.3	54	108	118	6.1
2300	53	101	116	6.0	51	98	112	5.8	50	93	107	5.7
	PRESSURE ALTITUDE 10,000 FEET											
	−25° (−13°F)				−5°C (23°F)				15°C (59°F)			
F.T.	71	123	142	8.1	69	123	142	7.9	68	123	142	7.7
2600	70	122	140	8.0	66	119	137	7.5	62	116	134	7.1
2500	63	115	132	7.2	60	111	128	6.8	58	107	126	6.5
2400	57	107	123	6.5	55	105	120	6.2	53	101	116	6.0
2300	52	100	115	5.9	51	96	110	5.7	49	91	105	5.6
	PRESSURE ALTITUDE 11,000 FEET											
	−27°C (−16°F)				−7°C (20°F)				13°C (45°F)			
F.T.	—	—	—	—	65	119	137	7.4	64	119	137	7.3
2600	57	119	137	7.6	64	118	136	7.3	61	116	133	7.0
2500	62	114	131	7.0	59	111	129	6.7	57	108	124	6.4
2400	56	107	123	6.4	54	108	118	6.1	53	99	114	6.0

Fig.32-5. Example of a Cruise Performance Chart.

□ **Exercises 32 — En Route Performance.**

33

WEIGHT AND BALANCE

AIRCRAFT WEIGHT.

Aircraft weights that we use in calculating the Gross Weight (or All-Up Weight) are as follows:

1. The Basic Empty Weight.
This includes the airframe, engine, fixed equipment (which is used for all operations), unusable fuel, but **full** oil and other items necessary for all flights. The Basic Empty Weight does **not** include:
- Pilot;
- payload (Passengers and freight);
- any ballast (for balance); or
- usable fuel.

Fig.33-1. We Use 'Basic Empty Weight' For All Our Load Sheet Calculations.

BASIC EMPTY WEIGHT

2. The Empty Weight.
The Empty Weight is the same as the above except that it includes only the undrainable oil rather than full oil. The Empty Weight and its Centre of Gravity are determined by a licensed-weighing of the aeroplane and are specified in the Flight Manual.

For our purposes, since one normally flies with full oil, we will use Basic Empty Weight in our problems, as this is simpler.

---

3. The Operating Weight.
Some operators will determine an 'Operating Weight' for a particular aeroplane. The operator can nominate what is included in Operating Weight – it may or may not include all items necessary for the flight (Pilots, special equipment, etc., etc.), but it will **not** include the usable fuel.

Different operators may define different Operating Weights for the same aeroplane depending upon what they choose to include. If you use Operating Weight, then be sure you know exactly what is included and what is not.

If the Operating Weight is used then it will appear on the Load Sheet in place of the Basic Empty Weight. Because Basic Empty Weight is a more clearly defined quantity than Operating Weight is not, we will use Basic Empty Weight for our calculations on the Load Sheet.

4. The Zero Fuel Weight.

This is the gross weight of the aeroplane excluding the usable fuel in the wing fuel tanks – (i.e. it includes the Pilot, payload and ballast, but none of the usable fuel).

ZERO FUEL WEIGHT

Fig.33-2. Zero Fuel Weight.

ZFW includes the Basic Empty Weight of the aeroplane plus the Pilot plus Passengers plus baggage and cargo. Usable fuel is not included – (unusable fuel which* is always in the tanks is included). The Zero Fuel Weight is used along the way in your Weight and Balance calculations, although in reality (hopefully) the aeroplane would never be in the zero fuel situation of having everything on board except usable fuel.

5. The Gross Weight.

This is the total weight of the aircraft (and its contents) at that particular time. It is the Basic Weight plus Pilot plus Payload (Passengers and cargo), plus Ballast (if any), plus Fuel.

USABLE FUEL ADDED

GROSS WEIGHT

Fig.33-3. The Gross Weight.

The Gross Weight should not exceed the maximum weight permissible for that manoeuvre. On take-off, GW must not exceed MTOW (structural) or the performance-limited TOW. On landing, GW must not exceed MLW (structural) or the performance-limited LW.

Each aircraft has **Weight Limitations** placed upon it. They depend upon the structural strength of the aircraft, the operations for which it is designed, and the manoeuvre being considered.

6. Maximum Ramp Weight.

This is the maximum gross weight permitted prior to taxying. It may exceed the Maximum Take-Off Weight by the taxi fuel allowance. Whilst this is not specified for many light aircraft, it is specified for some, and so you should be aware of Ramp Weight.

The Cessna 172 (which we consider later) has a 3 kg taxi allowance (fuel burn-off during the taxi), so the Ramp Weight may exceed the Maximum Allowable Take-Off Weight by this amount.

7. Maximum Take-Off Weight (MTOW) — Structural.

This is the maximum allowable gross weight permitted for take-off.

8. Performance-Limited Take-Off Weight.

Sometimes a performance limitation (short runway, high obstacle in the take-off path, unfavourable wind or slope, high temperature, high pressure altitude, i.e. high density altitude) will limit that particular take-off to a weight less than the structural MTOW. The Pilot should refer to the performance charts in the aircraft's Flight Manual.

9. Maximum Landing Weight — Structural.

The MLW is the maximum permitted gross weight for landing. For many light aircraft the MLW is the same as the MTOW, and you can take-off at maximum weight and return for an immediate landing without exceeding the limitations. The MLW of other aircraft may, for structural reasons, be less than the MTOW. In this case, the fuel burn-off must be sufficient to reduce the actual Take-Off Gross Weight to a figure less than the Maximum Landing Weight.

NOTE: **The Basic Empty Weight** (and **moment arm** – which we consider later) will be different for each individual aeroplane, and is always specified in that particular aeroplane's **Flight Manual.**

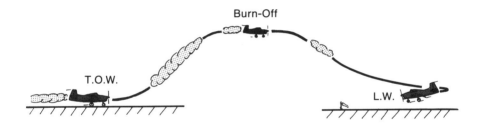

Fig.33-4. Landing Weight Equals Take-Off Weight Minus Burn-Off.

10. Performance Limited Landing Weight.

Sometimes a performance limitation (short runway, high obstacle in the approach path making a long touchdown necessary, unfavourable wind or slope, high density altitude) may limit that particular landing to a weight less than the structural MLW.

WHY THE WEIGHT OF AN AEROPLANE IS RESTRICTED.

The main force generated to balance the **Weight** is the **Lift** force. Its magnitude (size) depends upon the wing, the airspeed and the air density (Rho).

The airspeed is limited by the power available from the engine/propeller, the wing is fixed by the designer and the air density is outside the control of the Pilot. If Lift cannot be made to equal the Weight, then the aircraft cannot maintain level flight.

An overweight aeroplane will perform badly, handle badly and may suffer **structural damage** if flown. From the **performance** point of view, an overweight aeroplane will have:

- a higher stalling speed;
- a higher take-off speed;
- poorer climb performance (angle and rate);
- a lower service ceiling;
- less endurance;
- a higher landing speed;
- greater braking requirements.
- less manoeuvrability;
- a longer take-off run;
- higher fuel consumption;
- shorter range;
- a longer landing distance;

THE LOADING OF AN AEROPLANE.

The Air Navigation Order specifies the operational requirements for the **Loading** of aircraft. The items that must be weighed in determining the loading of an aircraft are:

- all cargo;
- removable equipment;
- baggage;
- occupants, including their personal effects.

Knowing the exact weight of Passengers is, of course, best, but approximate weights that can be used are:

- an infant 8 kg (17 lb) (under 2 years);
- a child 48 kg (105 lb) (under 15 yrs);
- an adult 77 kg (170 lb).

> NOTE: 1 kg = 2·2 lb (approximately);
> - to convert **kg to lb,** multiply by 2·2
> - to convert **lb to kg,** divide by 2·2.

OTHER WEIGHT RESTRICTIONS.

There may be other weight restrictions, such as maximum baggage compartment loads, maximum floor loads (per unit area), etc., specified in the Flight Manual and on placards in the aircraft.

THE WEIGHT OF FUEL.

- Fuel has a specific gravity of 0·72 AVGAS (100/130);
- Oil has a specific gravity of 0·96 (synthetic), 0·90 (mineral).

A specific gravity of 0·72 means that 100/130 AVGAS weighs only 0·72 times much as an equal volume of water. 1 litre of water weighs 1 kg, therefore **1 litre of 100/130 AVGAS weighs 0·72 kg.**

1 Imperial Gallon of water weighs 10 lb, therefore:
- **1 Imperial Gallon of AVGAS weighs 7·2 lb; and**
- **1 US Gallon of AVGAS weighs 6·0 lb.**

It is the Pilot's Responsibility to Ensure Weight Limitations are Not Exceeded. In many Light Aeroplanes it is **not** possible to carry both a full Fuel load and a full Passenger and Baggage load.

BALANCE OF THE AEROPLANE.

The turning **Moment** of a force depends upon two things:
1. The size of the force;
2. Its moment arm.

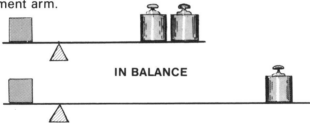

IN BALANCE

Fig.33-5. Balancing (or Turning) Moment Depends Upon Weight and Moment Arm.

If a body does not turn, then the moments wanting to turn it clockwise must be perfectly balanced by the moments wanting to turn it anticlockwise.

Fig.33-6. A Balanced Beam Experiences No Resultant Turning Moment.

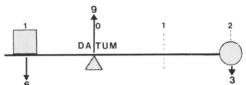

Using the pivot as the datum:
• Clockwise moments = 3 x 2 = 6
• Anticlockwise moments = 6 x 1 = 6

Because they balance, there is no resultant turning moment.

We can calculate turning moments about any **Datum Point.** Suppose we choose the left hand side of the beam as our **Datum.**

Fig.33-7. Choice of Datum Point Does Not Affect The Balance.

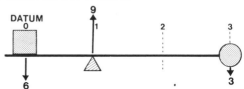

• Clockwise moments = 3 x 3 = 9
• Anticlockwise moments = 9 x 1 = 9, i.e. no resultant turning moment.

Suppose we choose a point 1 unit to the left of the beam as the **Datum.**

Fig.33-8. An 'External' Datum Is Also Acceptable.

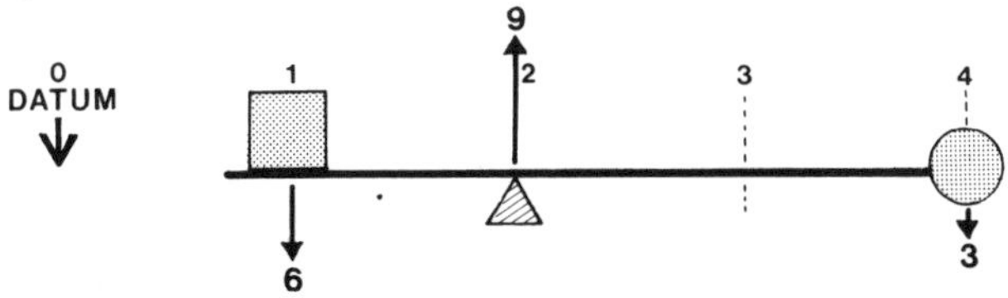

• Clockwise moments = (6 x 1) + (3 x 4) = 18
• Anticlockwise moments = 9 x 2 = 18

You can see that the choice of a datum point makes no difference to the results. If the system is in balance, the moments taken about **any** datum point will have a zero resultant.

In the same sense, when considering the **Balance** of an aeroplane it does not matter where the datum point is chosen to be. The designer nominates one, specifies it in the Flight Manual, and bases all his charts on it.

The units of a *turning moment* are those of 'force x distance' and may be *pound.inch* or *kilogram.millimetre*. For a force of say 200 kg acting 300 mm from the datum, its moment is (200 kg x 300 mm =) 60,000 kilogram.mm. Since large numbers often result, it is quite usual to divide them by 1,000 and instead of 60,000 kg.mm, we have 60 **Index Units** (where 1 IU = 1,000 kg.mm).

WHY AN AEROPLANE MUST HAVE ITS CENTRE OF GRAVITY WITHIN LIMITS.

In straight and level flight: LIFT = WEIGHT and THRUST = DRAG.

These four main forces provide two couples which have turning moments that are not always perfectly in balance. Extra forces are provided by the **Tailplane** to make up for this. The tailplane force has a turning moment in the pitching plane (nose-up or nose-down) about the centre of gravity. Its effectiveness depends on its magnitude (size) and the length of its moment arm from the CG.

Any movement of the Centre of Pressure on the mainplanes (through which the Lift force acts), or of the Centre of Gravity (through which the Weight acts), will require a different balancing force from the tailplane.

The Lift force that the tailplane can produce depends upon its airspeed. Its effectiveness at low speeds, therefore, determines just how much the length of its moment arm to the CG can change, by movement of the CG. **The reasons for limiting the forward and aft movement of the CG** were discussed earlier in the chapter on Stability (Principles of Flight section). Briefly, they are:

- **If the CG is forward,** the tailplane has a long moment arm and the aeroplane is very stable in the pitching plane, i.e. naturally resistant to any pitching motion. The forward position of the CG is limited to ensure that the elevator has a sufficient turning moment available to overcome the natural stability and flare the nose-heavy aeroplane for take-off and landing, which occur at relatively low speeds when the elevator is less-effective.
- **With an aft CG,** the aeroplane is less stable in the pitching plane. The aft position of the CG is limited so that the static stability of the aeroplane (its ability to retain a steady nose attitude) and the elevator 'feel' experienced through the control column by the Pilot both remain satisfactory.

The CG Must Remain within Specified Limits throughout a Flight.

Since fuel is burned in the course of a flight, this will affect both the **Gross Weight** and the **CG position.** Prior to flight, a Pilot should consider these two items at both:

- **Take-Off Weight** (the highest gross weight of the flight); and
- **Zero Fuel Weight** (as if all usable fuel had been burned-off; – not that you will reach this point in flight – hopefully!)

CG position at Landing Weight may also be found if desired.

Fuel tanks are normally designed to be near the CG, so that as the weight burns down, the CG will not move greatly. In aeroplanes with swept-back wings there will be some difficulties in achieving this. Of course, movement of Passengers and cargo will change the position of the CG.

The actual forward and aft limits of the CG will be different for different Gross Weights of the aeroplane. The manufacturer usually shows this in the Flight Manual with a graph of **'Gross Weight vs CG Position'**. It is often labelled **'Centre of Gravity Moment Envelope'**.

The aircraft manufacturer will specify a **Datum Point** on which his graph is based and from which all the moment arms are measured. If we can calculate the turning moment for a particular gross weight about this datum, calculate the position of the CG and plot it on the manufacturer's graph, we can see if he guarantees the balance of the aeroplane or not.

If our **'CG vs GW'** point falls within the envelope, then all is fine. If it does not fall within the envelope, then we must alter the loading of the aeroplane – shift the load, reduce it, add ballast – until the Weight and Balance requirements are satisfied.

Following an aircraft accident, two of the first things investigated are that the Pilot was licensed and that the aircraft was being operated within correct Weight and Balance limitations.

MATHEMATICAL APPROACH TO WEIGHT AND BALANCE.

We obtain the **Gross Weight** by adding up the various component weights – in this case, 2200 lb.

We obtain the **Total Moment** by adding up the various component moments. The various component weights act at known positions relative to the fixed datum. Each of these has a moment, which we can calculate by multiplying the individual weight by its arm from the datum, e.g 222 lb of fuel x 90·9 inches = 20,180 lb.in (or 20·18 lb.in/1000 or 20·18 IU). We obtain the total moment by summing (adding up) all of the moments due to these component weights. It adds up to 202·72 lb.in/1000.

Referring to the loading graph, we see that 2200 lb and 202·72 lb.in/1000 lies within the Normal Category Envelope.

If we wish to calculate the **Position of the CG** through which all of these weights, combined into the **Gross Weight,** may be considered to act, we do a small sum:

Sum of Individual Moments = Total Moment
                               = Gross Weight x its Moment Arm.
      202,720 lb.in = 2200 lb x Moment Arm
        Moment Arm = 202,720/2200 = 92·17 in.

Carrying out the 'Weight and Balance' calculations for an aircraft is fairly straightforward, especially after a bit of practice.

1. Total-up the Weights and ensure no weight limitation is exceeded.
2. Total-up the Moments and divide this total by the Gross Weight to find the position of the Centre of Gravity.
3. Verify that the CG vs GW point lies within the approved envelope.

SAMPLE LOADING PROBLEM	SAMPLE AIRPLANE			YOUR AIRPLANE		
	WEIGHT (LBS.)	ARM (IN.)	MOMENT (LB.-IN. /1000)	WEIGHT (LBS.)	ARM (IN.)	MOMENT (LB.-IN. /1000)
*1. Licensed Empty Weight (Typical)	1262	83.4	105.25	———	———	———
2. Oil (8 qts.) 1 qt. = 1.875 lbs.	15	32.0	.48	———	32.0	
3. Fuel (in excess of unuseable) Standard Tanks (37 gal.) Long Range Tanks (51 gal.)	222	90.9 94.81	20.18	———	90.9 94.81	———
4. Pilot and Co-Pilot	340	90.6	30.80	———	90.6	———
5. Rear Seat Passengers	340	126.0	42.84	———	126.0	———
*6. Baggage (in baggage compartment) Max. allowable 120 lbs.	21	151.0	3.17	———	151.0	———
7. Cargo Area Max. allowable 340 lbs.		116.4		———	116.4	———
8. Total Airplane Weight (loaded)	2200	92.17	202.72			
9. Usable Fuel	222	90.9	20.18			
10. Zero Fuel Weight	1978		182.54			

NOTE: If desired, the **Landing Weight and CG position** can be calculated by subtracting from the Take-Off Weight values the weight and moment of the fuel consumed.

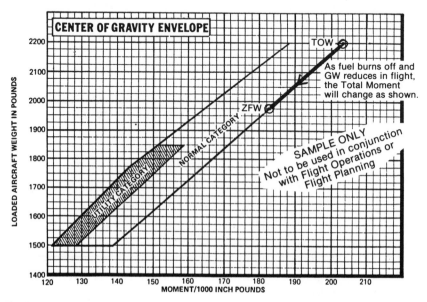

Fig.33-9. Mathematical Approach to Weight and Balance Calculations.

GRAPHICAL APPROACH (quite common and easy to use).

Some (thoughtful) manufacturers provide a small loading graph that allows us to enter with weight, take it across horizontally to the appropriate guide line, travel vertically and read off the moment (in Index Units).

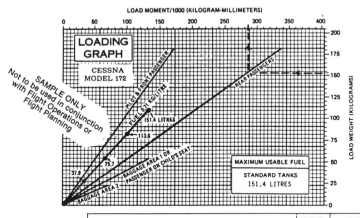

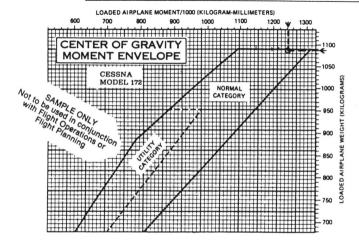

Fig.33-10.
The Graphical
Approach.

SAMPLE LOADING PROBLEM	WEIGHT (kg)	MOMENT (kg.mm/1000)
1. BASIC EMPTY WEIGHT (INCLUDES UNUSABLE FUEL AND FULL OIL)	665	660
2. USABLE FUEL - STANDARD TANKS (151.4 l max) . . .	107	132
3. PILOT AND FRONT PASSENGERS (STATION 34 to 46) . .	154	145
4. REAR PASSENGERS	154	286
5. BAGGAGE AREA 1 or PASSENGER ON CHILD'S SEAT (STATION 82 to 108, 54 kg max)	11	21
6. BAGGAGE AREA 2 (STATION 108 to 142, 22 kg max)		
7. RAMP WEIGHT AND MOMENT	1091	1244
8. FUEL ALLOWANCE FOR ENGINE START, TAXI & RUNUP . .	3	-3
9. TAKE-OFF WEIGHT AND MOMENT (SUBTRACT STEP 8 FROM STEP 7)	1088	1241
10. LOCATE THIS POINT (1088 at 1241) ON THE CENTRE OF GRAVITY MOMENT ENVELOPE. SINCE THIS POINT FALLS WITHIN THE ENVELOPE THE LOADING IS ACCEPTABLE.		

AN EVEN EASIER METHOD — THE LOAD SHEET.

Example of a Load Sheet Weight and Balance Calculation.

Data: Basic Weight of aircraft 830 kg, –270 Index Units,
1 Pilot; 4 Passengers;
Maximum Baggage allowed in lockers: 90 kg (45 kg in each);
Maximum Fuel: 356 litres (252 kg).

Basic Empty Weight	830 kg
Row 1 – Pilot, 1 Passenger	154
Row 2 – 1 Passenger	77
Row 3 – 2 Passengers	154
Forward baggage	45
Rear baggage	45
ZFW	1305
Fuel	252
Take-Off Weight	1557 kg

NOTE: We have done the weight calculation above separate to the load sheet, to make it a little clearer for you. There is no need for you to do this, as space is available down the right hand side of the aircraft loading system sheet and you can enter the figures directly onto it.

With the above Passenger arrangement, the CG position is just inside the rear limit. A better arrangement would be to have two Passengers in Row 2, 1 Passenger in Row 3, as this would move the CG position well into the envelope and provide you with a more stable aeroplane to fly.

You must be very careful that the correct figures, especially for **Basic Empty Weight** and its **Index Unit,** are entered onto the load sheet. This is the starting point for the whole thing. Always check this.

We have used the 77 kg **Standard Weight** for an adult. The designer of the chart has made our task easier by dividing the scale line into 77 kg divisions along the bottom, each 1 division representing 1 adult person. 2 adults in the one row of course gives us 154 kg for the weight column and 2 divisions on the Index Unit (moment) scale.

Along the top of the scale line he has placed 50 kg divisions to ease our task if we are carrying baggage or other items in the seat rows. Notice that loading Row 1 (R1) and loading the forward baggage compartment both have the effect of moving the CG forward.

Loading Row 2 and aft of it, including the rear baggage locker, will move the CG rearwards. **In this aeroplane**, the fuel has an IU of zero, i.e. the tanks are on the datum, so, as fuel is consumed in flight, the moment will remain unchanged.

LOAD DATA SHEET

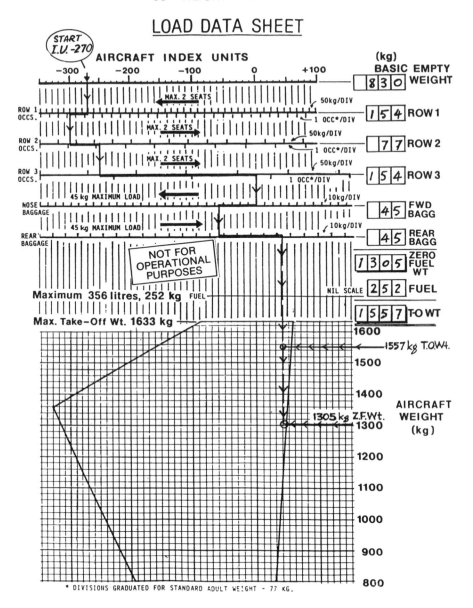

Fig.33-11. Example of Load Sheet Weight and Balance Calculation.

DO NOT CARRY DANGEROUS GOODS.

There are many goods which should not be carried in an aeroplane. There are some items which are illegal to carry and others which, whilst legal, are better not carried. The Pilot must show responsibility and common sense in accepting or rejecting particular items. The following are some of the Dangerous Goods that are hazardous to aviation:

- explosives;
- flammable goods (including chemicals which may evaporate as altitude is gained, cigarette lighters, books of matches, alcohol etc);
- radioactive materials;
- infectious substances;
- corrosive substances (e.g. the weak sulphuric acid in a spare battery);
- magnetic substances (that could affect the Magnetic Compass – so do not place a transistor radio near it).

RESTRAIN BAGGAGE AND OTHER ITEMS.

Baggage should be restrained so that it cannot move in flight and cause a shift in the Centre of Gravity which, in extreme cases, could lead to loss of control, or, if it is thrown around the cabin in turbulence, cause personal injury, damage to the aeroplane or obstruction of the controls. The same applies to other heavy items such as a fire extinguisher.

Most baggage compartments have tie-down points to which the load may be secured by ropes or a security net. If baggage is loaded onto a seat, restraining it by passing a seat belt through it may be sufficient. If not, use additional tie-downs. Do not leave loose parcels or suitcases on the seats. Similarly, ensure that everyone has their selt belt on for take-off, landing and in turbulence.

☐ **Exercises 33 — Weight and Balance** please.

34

WAKE TURBULENCE

As the wing produces Lift, the higher static pressure area beneath the wing forces an airflow around the wingtip into the lower pressure area above. The greater the pressure differential, the greater is this flow around the wingtips.

At the high angles of attack necessary to produce the required Lift force at low speeds, very large and strong trailing vortices are formed. As the aeroplane is moving forward, a trail of wingtip vortices is left behind. This effect was discussed under *'Induced Drag'* – the drag generated by the production of Lift.

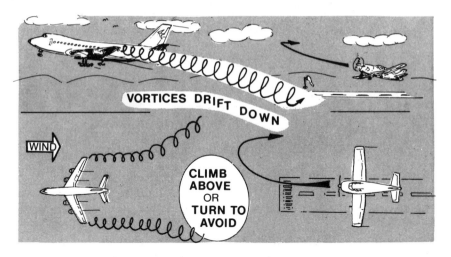

Fig.34-1. Wake Turbulence From A Large, Slow-Flying Airliner.

As a large and heavy aircraft is rotated for take-off or flared for landing, the angle of attack is large. The trailing wingtip vortices formed can be strong enough to upset a following aeroplane if it flies into them. They are **invisible** but **real.** This effect is known as **Wake Turbulence.**

The **Wake Turbulence** behind a Boeing 747 can significantly affect, for example, a 737 or a DC-9, and can cause a lighter aeroplane to become uncontrollable.

To avoid Wake Turbulence accidents and incidents, Air Traffic Control delays the operation of light aircraft on runways behind heavy jets for up to five minutes to allow the vortices to drift away and dissipate.

Every Pilot should have an awareness of Wake Turbulence because even the Air Traffic Control procedures occasionally provide insufficient separation from the wingtip vortices behind another aircraft. An Air Traffic Controller is an expert at his job – do not expect him to be an expert at yours as well. The Pilot has the ultimate responsibility for the safety of his or her aeroplane – so learn to visualise the formation and movement of **invisible** wingtip vortices.

Heavy aircraft will also leave vortices in their wake in flight, especially in the circuit area where they are flying slowly at high angles of attack – make sure that you provide your own separation in the circuit.

The vortices will tend to lose height slowly (i.e. drift downwards) and drift downwind. To be able to avoid these invisible danger areas, you, as a Pilot following a much heavier aeroplane, must be able to visualise the movement of the vortices and take steps to avoid them.

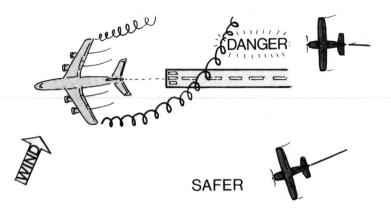

Fig.34-2. Wingtip Vortices Drift Downwind (as well as backwards).

A **crosswind** will cause the vortices to drift off the downwind side of the runway.

A **headwind** or a **tailwind** will carry them down the runway in the direction of the wind.

In **nil wind** or **light and variable** conditions, the vortices will just 'hang around'. These latter conditions can be very dangerous – delaying your take-off or changing runway is worthwhile considering.

HOW TO AVOID WAKE TURBULENCE.

The main aim of Wake Turbulence avoidance is to avoid passing through it at all, especially in flight.

Avoiding Wake Turbulence on Take-Off.

When taking-off behind a large aircraft which has itself just taken-off, commence your take-off at the end of the runway so that you will become airborne in an area well before where the 'heavy' rotated or to where its vortices may have drifted. If doubtful, delay your take-off.

Do not use an intersection departure (less than the full length of the runway) behind a 'heavy', as this may bring your flight path closer to his wake turbulence.

Manoeuvre to avoid the vortices in flight by climbing steeply (but not too slowly, as speed is a safety factor if you strike Wake Turbulence) or turning away from where you think the Wake Turbulence is.

MANOEUVRE TO AVOID VORTICES

Fig.34-3. Avoid Wake Turbulence on Your Take-Off.

When taking-off after a heavy aircraft has landed, plan to become airborne well past the point where it flared and landed.

If a 'heavy' has taken-off on a different runway and you expect to be airborne prior to the intersection of the runways, observe that the 'heavy' was still on the ground until well past the intersection, before you commence your take-off.

Always avoid flying through the wake of a 'heavy', especially at low speed near the ground.

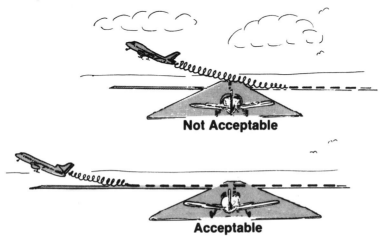

Fig.34-4. Awareness of Wake Turbulence For Your Take-Off.

Avoiding Wake Turbulence in the Circuit.

Avoid flying below and behind large aircraft. Fly a few hundred feet above them, a thousand feet below them or to windward of them. Calm days where there is no turbulence to break up the vortices are perhaps the most dangerous.

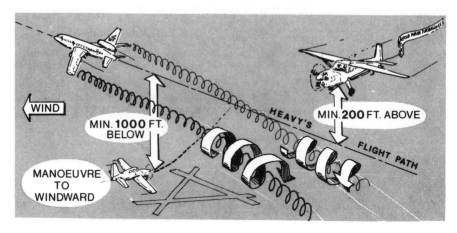

Fig.34-5. Avoidance of Wake Turbulence in the Circuit Area.

Avoiding Wake Turbulence on Approach.

When following a preceding landing aircraft, fly above the approach path of the 'heavy' and land well beyond his touch-down point. This is usually possible in a light aircraft landing on a long runway where heavy aircraft are landing.

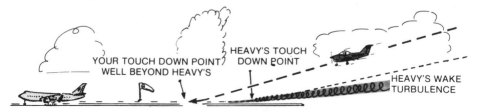

Fig.34-6. Avoidance of Wake Turbulence on Your Approach.

When landing on a runway where a 'heavy' has just taken-off, touch down well short of his lift-off point or where you think the vortices may have drifted to. The normal touchdown zone will probably ensure this.

Fig.34-7. Landing Behind a 'Heavy' That Has Taken-Off.

If a preceding 'heavy' has discontinued his approach and gone around, his turbulent wake will be a hazard to a following aircraft. You should consider changing your flight path in these circumstances.

NOTE ACCENTUATED WAKE TURBULENCE ON GO-AROUND

Fig.34-8. Making an Approach behind a 'Heavy' that has Gone Around.

WAKE TURBULENCE IS DIFFERENT TO *JET BLAST*

Do not confuse *Wake Turbulence* (wingtip vortices) with *jet blast* (sometimes referred to as *thrust stream)*, which is the high-velocity air exhausted from a jet engine or a large propeller-driven aircraft, especially a turbo-prop. Jet Blast can be dangerous to a light aircraft taxying on the ground behind a jet or large propeller-driven aircraft.

JET BLAST

WAKE TURBULENCE

Fig.34-9. Wake Turbulence is different from Jet Blast (or Thrust Stream).

❏ Now we suggest you tackle **Exercises 34 – Wake Turbulence**.

35

GROUND EFFECT

An aeroplane's flight characteristics change when it is very close to the ground or any other surface, as:
- it can fly at a slower speed than when it is at altitude, and
- it can fly at the same speed using less Thrust than when it is at altitude.

The better 'flyability' of an aeroplane when it is just above a surface is known as **'Ground Effect'**.

Birds know all about Ground Effect and it is quite common to see large water-birds, for example, skimming leisurely just above the waves. Birds may not understand the physics of Ground Effect but they certainly know how to use it. Many Pilots fall into the same category – of knowing that the Effect is there but not really understanding why. These few pages will explain Ground Effect in simple terms.

In our chapters on Lift and Drag (in section One) we considered the aeroplane to be flying well away from the ground. There was no restriction to the downwash of the airflow behind the wings, nor to the upwash ahead of the wings. There was also no restriction to the formation of wingtip vortices.

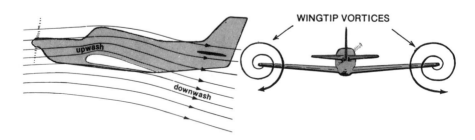

Fig.35-1. In 'Free Air', The Upwash and Downwash Are Not Restricted and the Formation of Wingtip Vortices Is Not Restricted.

When an aeroplane is flying close to the ground the ground surface interferes with the airflow around the wings, restricting it in a number of ways. A nearby surface:
- restricts the upwash and downwash, and
- restricts the formation of wingtip and line vortices.

When an aeroplane is *'in'* Ground Effect, the **Total Reaction** on the wing is more perpendicular to the remote free airstream and the **Induced Drag** is less, compared to when *'out of'* Ground Effect.

'Ground Effect' becomes noticeable when the aeroplane is at a height above the surface of less than one wingspan. The effect is greater the closer the wing is to the surface.

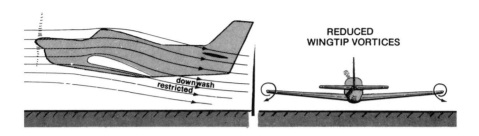

Fig.35-2. Near The Ground, the Upwash and Downwash Are Restricted and the Formation of Wingtip Vortices Is Restricted.

The term *'Ground Effect'* covers the general aerodynamic influence on an aeroplane when it is in proximity to a surface. (This can be considered as a definition.)

The wing, the fuselage and the tailplane will all be affected by Ground Effect, but by far the most significant effect is on the wing.

'Ground Effect' Reduces Upwash And Downwash Of The Airflow, And The 'Cushioning' Effect Produces More Lift.

By reducing the upwash in front of the wing and the downwash behind the wing the ground surface acts like a cushion, causing the wing to develop more Lift (i.e. a higher Coefficient of Lift or greater 'Lifting Ability'), even though the actual pitch attitude of the aircraft may not have changed.

'Ground Effect' Causes Reduced Wingtip and Line Vortices And Less Induced Drag Than In 'Free Air'.

You will recall from the chapter on Drag that we break up the Total Drag on an aeroplane into two main types – Induced Drag that is a by-product of the production of Lift, and Parasite Drag that is not directly associated with the production of Lift.

Wingtip Vortices, and Line Vortices behind the trailing edge, are a major cause of Induced Drag. So when a nearby surface restricts their formation the induced Drag will be less and therefore the Total Drag on the aeroplane will be less.

You are aware that, in level flight, Drag is balanced by Thrust. The reduction in Drag when near the ground or water means that the same airspeed can be maintained using less Thrust. Therefore, underpowered aircraft may be able to maintain flying speed whilst in Ground Effect, even if they cannot maintain that speed in 'free air' well away from the ground.

There are many 'Biggles' stories of multi-engined aircraft having lost power from one or more of their engines and, flying on severely limited power, not being able to climb away from the ground or water, but relying on Ground Effect to maintain flight.

Induced drag is greatest at high angles of attack and so is very significant at the high angles of attack and slow speeds common in take-offs and landings. The ground (hopefully) is reasonably close in these particular manoeuvres and so Ground Effect will play a significant role.

At one wingspan height above the ground there is about a 1% reduction in induced drag and this reduction becomes more significant the closer the aeroplane is to the ground. At a height equal to only $\frac{1}{10}$th of a wingspan, the induced drag is reduced by about 50%. (There is no need to remember these figures – they are included here just to give you an idea of how significant Ground Effect can be.)

'GROUND EFFECT' DURING LANDING.

On an approach to land, as the aeroplane enters 'Ground Effect' at about one wingspan high, the Pilot will experience a 'floating' sensation – a result of the extra lift (from the increased Coefficient of Lift) and the slower deceleration (due to less drag).

In most landings there is no desire to maintain speed – indeed the aim is to lose speed. It is therefore usually important at flare height and in ground effect to ensure that the power is throttled back, especially considering the reduction of drag due to Ground Effect.

Excess speed at the commencement of the landing flare and the better 'flyability' of an aeroplane in Ground Effect may incur a considerable 'float distance' prior to touchdown. This is not desirable, especially on landing strips of the minimum required length.

'GROUND EFFECT' ON TAKE-OFF.

As the aeroplane climbs out of Ground Effect on take-off, the Lift Coefficient will decrease for the same aeroplane pitch attitude (i.e. the 'lifting ability' of the wing will be less) and the induced drag will increase due to the greater wingtip vortices and line vortices, and the fact the Total Reaction now 'leans' further back from the perpendicular to the remote free airstream. With this increase in drag, airspeed will tend to decrease for the same thrust.

Thus the aeroplane will not perform as well in free air as it will in ground effect. The Pilot will feel a 'sagging' in climb-out performance as the aircraft flies out of 'Ground Effect'.

It pays to bear this in mind if ever you are operating on very short strips or strips which finish on the edge of a cliff (or aircraft carrier). Once away from the take-off surface the climb performance will be less – a very good reason for not forcing the aeroplane to become airborne at too low a speed because, whilst it might manage to fly in Ground Effect, it will be unable to climb out of it, possibly even settling back onto the ground. Some Pilots have found this a little embarrassing, especially if they have retracted the landing gear!

344

In summary, the two main results of Ground Effect are:

1. An increased 'Lifting Ability' of the wing, (i.e. increased C_{Lift}).

2. A reduction in Drag, (less formation of vortices and less induced drag).

Both of these cause a *floating* effect near the ground.

There are two further points for a Pilot to note about Ground Effect:

3. The disturbance in airflow may cause the Air Speed Indicator (ASI) and the Altimeter to read inaccurately when flying near the ground; and

4. The disturbance of normal airflow as compared to 'free air' may cause a change in the stability characteristics of the aeroplane near the ground.

☐ Now tackle **Exercises 35 — Ground Effect.**

36

WINDSHEAR

This chapter goes beyond the syllabus requirements for the Aeroplane – Technical Examination, however the information which follows is of very practical use. It helps explain why alterations of pitch attitude and/or power by the Pilot are continually required to maintain a desired flight path, just as changes in heading are required to maintain a steady track.

Severe Windshears have caused the loss of a number of aircraft, some of them large passenger aircraft.

The study of Windshear and its effect on aeroplanes and what protective measures can be taken to avoid unpleasant results is still in its infancy and much still remains to be learned. What is certain is that every aeroplane and every Pilot will be affected by Windshear – usually the light Windshears that occur in everyday flying, but occasionally a moderate Windshear that requires positive action from the Pilot and, on rare occasions, severe Windshears that can put an aeroplane out of control.

A little knowledge can help you to understand how to handle Windshear and how to avoid unnecessary problems with it.

EXPLANATION OF WINDSHEAR TERMS.

A **'Windshear'** is defined as a change in wind direction and/or wind speed, including updrafts and downdrafts, in space. Any change in the wind velocity (be it a change in speed or in direction) as you move from one point to another is a Windshear. The stronger the change and the shorter the distance within which it occurs, the stronger the Windshear.

'Updrafts' and **'Downdrafts'** are the vertical components of wind. The most hazardous updrafts and downdrafts are usually those associated with a thunderstorm.

The term **'Low Level Windshear'** is used to specify the Windshear, if any, along the final approach path prior to landing, along the runway and along the take-off/initial climb-out flight path. Windshear near the ground (i.e. below about 3,000 ft) is often the most critical in terms of safety for the aeroplane.

'Turbulence' is eddy motions in the atmosphere which vary both with time and from place to place.

THE EFFECTS OF WINDSHEAR ON AN AIRCRAFT.

Most of our studies have considered an aeroplane flying in a reasonably stable air mass which has a steady motion relative to the ground, i.e. in a steady wind situation. We have seen how an aeroplane climbing out in a steady headwind will have a better climb gradient over the ground compared to the tailwind situation, and how an aeroplane will glide further over the ground downwind compared to into wind, etc.

Of course in reality an air mass does not move in a totally steady manner – there will be gusts and updrafts and changes of wind speed and direction etc. which the aeroplane will encounter as it flies through the air mass. In this chapter, we look at the **transient** effects that these Windshears have on the flight path of an aeroplane.

AN EXAMPLE OF WINDSHEAR.

Often when the wind is relatively calm on the ground, at several hundred feet above the ground the light and variable wind conditions suddenly change into a strong and steady wind. If we consider an aeroplane making an approach to land in these conditions, we can see the effect the Windshear has as the aeroplane passes through the shear.

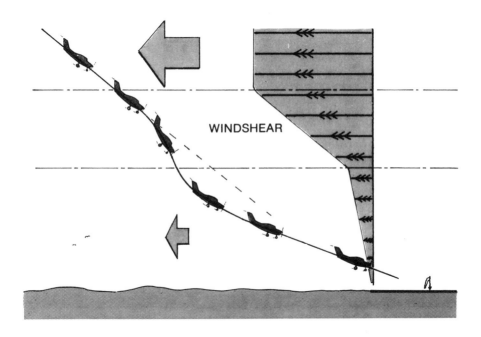

Fig.36-1. A Typical Windshear Situation – Calm On The Ground With A Wind At Altitude.

An aeroplane flying through the air will have a certain inertia depending upon its mass and its velocity relative to the ground. If the aeroplane has a True Air Speed of 80 knots and the headwind component is 30 knots, then the inertial speed of the aeroplane over the ground is (80 – 30 =) 50 knots.

When the aeroplane flies down into the calm air, the headwind component drops off reasonably quickly to (let us say) 5 knots. The inertial speed of the aeroplane over the ground is still 50 knots, but the new headwind of only 5 knots will mean that its True Air Speed has suddenly dropped back to 55 knots.

The Pilot would observe a sudden drop in Indicated Air Speed and a change in the performance of the aeroplane – at 55 knots airspeed the performance will be quite different to when it is at 80 knots airspeed. The normal Pilot reaction would be to add power or to lower the nose to regain airspeed, and to avoid undershooting the desired flight path.

The Pilot can accelerate the aeroplane and return it to the desired flight path by changes in attitude and power. The more the Windshear, the more these changes in power and attitude will be required. Any fluctuations in wind will require adjustments by the Pilot, and this is why you have to work so hard sometimes, especially when approaching to land.

THE EFFECTS OF WINDSHEAR ON AN AIRCRAFT'S FLIGHT PATH.

The effects of Windshear on an aeroplane's flight path depend on the nature and location of the Shear, as follows:

- **'Overshoot Effect'** is caused by a Windshear which results in the aeroplane flying above the desired flight path and/or an increase in Indicated Air Speed.

  The nose of the aircraft may also tend to rise. Overshoot Effect may result from flying into an increasing headwind, a decreasing tailwind, from a tailwind into a headwind, or an updraft.

- **'Undershoot Effect'** is caused by a Windshear which results in an aircraft flying below the desired flight path and/or a decrease in Indicated Air Speed.

  The nose of the aircraft may also tend to drop. Undershoot Effect may result from flying into a decreasing headwind, an increasing tailwind, from a headwind into a tailwind, or into a downdraft.

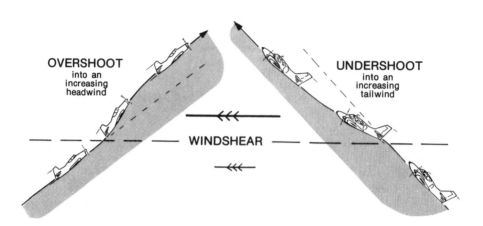

OVERSHOOT
into an
increasing
headwind

UNDERSHOOT
into an
increasing
tailwind

WINDSHEAR

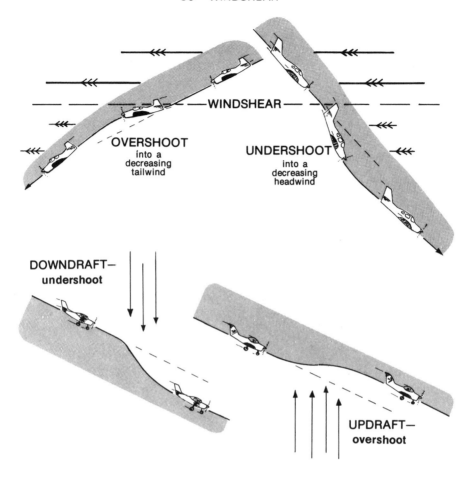

Fig.36-2. Six Common Windshear Situations.

Note that **the actual Windshear effect** depends on:
1. The nature of the Windshear.
2. Whether the aeroplane is climbing or descending through that particular Windshear.
3. In which direction the aeroplane is proceeding.

- **'Windshear Reversal Effect'** is caused by a Windshear which results in the initial effect on the aeroplane being reversed as the aircraft proceeds further along the flight path. It would be described as **'Overshoot Effect followed by Undershoot'**, or **'Undershoot followed by Overshoot Effect',** as appropriate.

Windshear Reversal Effect is a very common phenomenon that Pilots often experience on approach to land, when things are usually happening too fast to analyse exactly what is taking place in terms of wind. The Pilot can, of course, **observe** Undershoot and Overshoot Effect and react accordingly with changes in Attitude and/or Thrust.

349

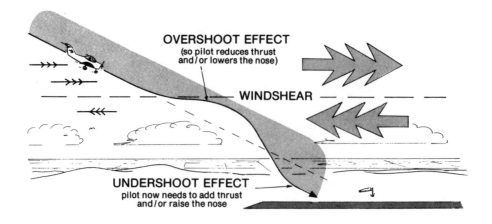

Fig.36-3. Windshear Reversal Effect.

- **'Crosswind Effect'** is caused by a Windshear which requires a rapid change of aircraft heading to maintain a desired track (not uncommon in a crosswind approach and landing because the crosswind component changes as the ground is neared).

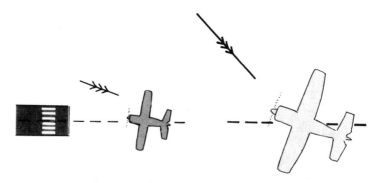

Fig.36-4. Crosswind Effect.

THE CAUSES OF WINDSHEAR.

These include the wind being slowed down by ground surface roughness, abrupt changes in terrain, thunderstorms, cumulonimbus clouds, large cumulus clouds (downbursts and gust fronts), low level jet streams, fronts, thermal activity, sea breezes, etc., etc.

As a particular warning to Pilots we strongly suggest that **thunderstorms and cumulonimbus clouds are best avoided.** A strong downburst out of the base of one of these clouds will spread out as it nears the ground. The initial effect may be an overshoot effect followed by what may be an **extremely severe undershoot.**

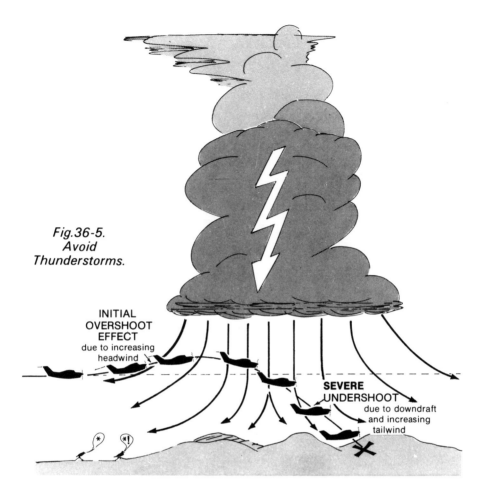

Fig.36-5.
Avoid
Thunderstorms.

INITIAL
OVERSHOOT
EFFECT
due to increasing
headwind

SEVERE
UNDERSHOOT
due to downdraft
and increasing
tailwind

Further reference reading on Windshear can be found in Part 7 of Pooley's *Pilot's Information Guide.*

☐ Now, finally, complete **Exercises 36 — Windshear.**

Intentionally Blank

APPENDIX

AIRCRAFT (TYPE)
— Aeroplanes

INTRODUCTION

The basic Principles of Flight, of Engines, of Systems and of Performance apply to all aeroplanes, but there are differences between one aeroplane type and another. It is a requirement that a Pilot be thoroughly familiar with the type of aeroplane that he or she is about to fly.

For this reason, the Applicant for a UK Private Pilot's Licence (Aeroplanes) must demonstrate a very sound knowledge of the specific aeroplane on which he or she has trained and which will be used during the flight test. This aeroplane will normally be a **Group A** Aeroplane (a single-engined aeroplane of 5700 kg or less).

The primary source of this specific knowledge is the CAA approved **Flight Manual**, which is associated with the aeroplane's Certificate of Airworthiness.

The Applicant should also have an understanding of what maintenance a Pilot is permitted to perform on the aeroplane, and what responsibility he can take in signing off the Duplicate Inspection form for adjustments made to *flight controls* and/or *engine controls.* These items are discussed in Chapter 28 of this volume and in Chapter L12 of Aviation Law, Flight Rules and Procedures in Volume 2 of this series. The primary source of the information is the Air Navigation Order (ANO) Article 10(3), the Air Navigation (General) Regulation (ANR) 16, and the British Civil Airworthiness Requirements (BCAR) Section A, Chapter 5-3.

Having learnt to fly one specific type of aeroplane, it is a relatively straightforward matter to be trained (or endorsed) onto another. Following an endorsement training programme, the Pilot must display not only an ability to fly the aeroplane but also a sound knowledge of it, along the same lines as described in this Appendix.

The PPL(A) *Aircraft (Type)* examination will normally take the form of an **oral** test, (usually combined with the General Flight Test for the Private Pilot's Licence itself), and will be confined to the type of aeroplane in which you are being flight tested.

You should be prepared to answer questions similar to those asked here. Since each specific type of aeroplane may require a different answer to the questions asked below, no answers are provided here. You should research them in the primary reference documents mentioned above, and discuss them with your flying instructor.

THE FLIGHT MANUAL.

1. The Flight Manual is for a (manufacturer's name and model) type of aeroplane.

2. This particular Flight Manual (has/does not have) a UK CAA Supplement.

3. A CAA Supplement (amends/does not amend) information contained in the original Flight Manual supplied by the manufacturer.

4. The Flight Manual (should/need not) remain with the particular aeroplane.

WEIGHT AND BALANCE LIMITATIONS.

1. The Maximum Take-Off Weight is ..... kg.

2. The Maximum Landing Weight is ..... kg.

3. The Maximum Passenger Load (excluding the Pilot) is ..... passengers.

4. The Maximum Number of Persons on Board (POB), including the Pilot, is ..... .

5. The Maximum Baggage Weight that can be carried is ..... kg.

6. The Empty Weight of the aeroplane is ..... kg.

7. In which Category (or Categories) is the aeroplane permitted to fly?

8. Do these weight limitations vary if the aeroplane is certificated to fly not only in the Normal Category but also in another category, such as the Utility Category, Semi-Aerobatic Category or Aerobatic Category? If so, what are their values?

9. Calculate the Weight and Balance situation (i.e. the Gross Weight and Centre of Gravity position), given certain requirements, e.g. a certain number of passengers, a given amount of fuel, a given amount of baggage, etc, using the Aeroplane Weight Schedule found in the Flight Manual.

AIRSPEED LIMITATIONS.

1. The Normal Operating airspeed range is marked on the Air Speed Indicator with a ..... arc.

2. The Caution airspeed range is marked on the Air Speed Indicator with a ..... arc.

3. The Flap Operating airspeed range is marked on the Air Speed Indicator with a ..... arc.

4. V_{NE} is known as the ..... airspeed and its value is ..... kt. It is marked on the Air Speed Indicator as a ..... .

5. V_{NO} is known as the ..... airspeed and its value is ..... kt. It is marked on the Air Speed Indicator as a ..... .

6. V_A is known as the ..... airspeed and its value is ..... kt. It (is/is not) marked on the Air Speed Indicator.

7. V_{RA}, if specified, is known as the ..... airspeed and its value is ..... kt. It (is/is not) marked on the Air Speed Indicator.

8. V_S is known as the ..... speed wings level and flaps up, and its value is ..... kt. It (is/is not) marked on the Air Speed Indicator as the (high/low) speed end of the ..... arc.

9. V_{FE} is known as the ..... airspeed and its value is ..... kt. It (is/is not) marked on the Air Speed Indicator as the (high/low) speed end of the ..... arc.

10. The Stalling Speed with full flap extended and the wings level is ..... kt.

11. The published stalling speeds are for when the aeroplane (is/is not) at maximum gross weight.

12. Stalling Speed (increases/decreases/does not change) if the aeroplane is at less than maximum weight.

13. Stalling Speed (increases/decreases/does not change) if the aeroplane is banked.

14. Stalling Speed (increases/decreases/does not change) if the aeroplane is manoeuvring, for instance pulling out of a dive.

15. In a 30° banked turn, the stalling speed will increase by ...%.

16. In a 60° banked turn, the stalling speed will increase by ...%.

17. The maximum airspeed at which you may use abrupt and full elevator travel is ..... kt.

AERODYNAMIC LOAD LIMITATIONS.

1. Maximum Load Factor (flaps up) is +... g and −... g.

2. Maximum Load Factor (flaps extended) is +... g and −... g.

3. Are there any other handling limitations if, for instance, the aeroplane has a full complement of passengers, maximum baggage, maximum fuel load, etc?

4. What precautions should be observed if recovering from a steep dive?

5. What precautions should be observed if recovering from a steep turn?

AUTHORISED OPERATIONS.

1. The aeroplane (is/is not) certificated to fly during the day.

2. The aeroplane (is/is not) certificated to fly at night.

3. The aeroplane (is/is not) certificated to fly under the Visual Flight Rules (VFR).

4. The aeroplane (is/is not) certificated to fly under the Instrument Flight Rules (IFR).

5. The aeroplane (is/is not) certificated to fly in icing conditions.

TAKE-OFF PERFORMANCE LIMITATIONS.

1. The Maximum Structural Take-Off Weight is ..... kg.

2. Be able to use the Take-Off Chart(s) in the Flight Manual to calculate the performance figures (performance-limited take-off weight, or runway length required) given a specific situation.

3. The runway length required, under ISA MSL conditions, for a take-off at maximum weight is ..... metres.

4. Compared to a take-off at a sea level aerodrome, the take-off at a high elevation aerodrome will require (the same/more/less) runway length.

5. Compared to a take-off at ISA temperature, the take-off at a higher temperature will require (the same/more/less) runway length.

LANDING PERFORMANCE LIMITATIONS.

1. The Maximum Structural Landing Weight is ..... kg.

2. Be able to use the Landing Chart(s) in the Flight Manual to calculate the performance figures (performance-limited landing weight, or runway length required) given a specific situation.

3. The runway length required, under ISA MSL conditions, for a landing at maximum weight is ..... metres.

4. Compared to a landing at a sea level aerodrome, landing at a high elevation aerodrome will require (the same/more/less) runway length.

5. Compared to a landing at ISA temperature, landing at a higher temperature will require (the same/more/less) runway length.

RANGE FLYING.

1. Be able to use any tables or graphs in the Flight Manual to calculate range, i.e. the **distance** that the aeroplane can fly under given conditions.

ENDURANCE FLYING.

1. Be able to use any tables or graphs in the Flight Manual to calculate endurance, i.e. the **time** that the aeroplane can remain airborne under given conditions.

FLYING CONTROLS.

1. Understand how the **Elevator** (or Stabilator) system works:
   e.g. moving the Control Column back will cause the nose of the aeroplane to (rise/drop) as a result of the elevator moving (up/down).

2. Understand how the **Aileron** system works:
   e.g. moving the Control Column to the left will cause the aeroplane, at normal flying speeds, to roll towards the (left/right) by moving the left aileron ..... and the right aileron ..... .

3. Understand how the **Rudder** system works:
   (a) Moving the left rudder pedal in will cause the right rudder pedal to move ..... .
   (b) Moving the left rudder pedal in will cause the nose of the aeroplane to yaw (left/right), as a result of the trailing edge of the rudder moving (left/right).
   (c) The main function of the rudder in normal flight is to (balance/yaw) the aeroplane.
   (d) There (is/is not) an interconnection between the rudder and the aileron systems.

4. Understand how the **Trim** system works:
   (a) Is there an Elevator Trim?
   (b) Is there a Rudder Trim?
   (c) Is there an Aileron Trim?
   (d) The Elevator Trim is a (servo/balance/anti-servo) type.
   (e) The main function of a trimming device is to (relieve steady pressures/manoeuvre the aeroplane).

5. Understand how the **Flap** system works:
   (a) The Flap system is (mechanical/electric/hydraulic).
   (b) The flaps are operated with a (switch/lever).
   (c) The Flap Indicating system is (mechanical/electric).
   (d) The Flap Range is from 0° to .....°.

6. The aeroplane (has/does not have) a Stall Warning Device.

7. The Stall Warning Device, if fitted, (is/is not) interconnected with the flap system.

THE PROPELLER.

1. The Propeller is a (fixed-pitch/contant speed unit) propeller.

2. Will nicks, mud, insects or other contamination affect the performance of the propeller?

3. Should new nicks or damage to the propeller be referred to an Engineer if possible prior to flight?

4. Most training aeroplanes used for initial PPL instruction have a fixed-pitch propeller, but if yours has a variable-pitch propeller controlled by a Constant Speed Unit (CSU), then you should know how it works, how to control the RPM/Manifold Pressure with the Pitch Lever and the Throttle, the RPM/MAP limits.

LANDING GEAR AND BRAKES.

1. The aeroplane is fitted with a (tricycle/tailwheel) type undercarriage.

2. The aeroplane (has/does not have) nosewheel steering.

3. The rudder and the nosewheel steering (are/are not) interconnected.

4. The rudder pedals on the ground (can/cannot) be used to provide directional control when taxying.

5. The undercarriage (is/is not) retractable.

6. Shocks on the nosewheel during taxying, take-off and landing are absorbed by a (leaf spring/bungee/oleo pneumatic strut).

7. Shocks on the main wheels during taxying, take-off and landing are absorbed by (leaf springs/bungees/oleo pneumatic struts).

8. The brakes are fitted to the (main wheels/nosewheel).

9. The brakes are operated from the cockpit using ..... .

10. The wheel brakes are operated (mechanically/hydraulically).

11. The wheel brakes are (disc/drum) type.

12. Normal tyre pressure is ..... .

13. Know what defects in the tyres are acceptable or unacceptable for flight, e.g. cuts, wear, bald spots, etc.

THE ELECTRICAL SYSTEM.

1. The DC electrical system operates at (12/24) volts.

2. The Battery is located ..... .

3. Once the engine is running, electrical power is supplied by (an alternator/a generator).

4. A serviceable battery (is/is not) required for the alternator (if fitted) to come on-line.

5. If a battery is fairly flat, a high charging rate following start-up (may/will not) cause 'boiling' within the battery.

6. Understand how to manage the electrical system, e.g. the indications and actions to take if the alternator (or generator) system fails or malfunctions.

7. If the alternator (or generator) fails in flight, then as much electrical load as possible (should/need not) be shed by switching non-essential services *OFF*.

8. A fully-charged battery should supply emergency power for a period of ..... if required.

9. Know the function and location of circuit breakers and fuses, and what to do if they *'pop'* or fail, as applicable.

10. Is it possible to use External Power to operate the electrical system whilst the aeroplane is parked and, if so, what is the procedure for connecting it?

11. The stall warning device, if fitted, operates (electrically/mechanically).

FLIGHT INSTRUMENTS.

1. Name the flight instruments operated by the pitot-static system and state whether they use pitot pressure, static pressure or both.

2. Know the position of the Pitot Tube(s) and Static Vent(s), and any associated drains to eliminate water from the lines.

3. Is there electric-powered pitot-heat to prevent ice forming on the pitot head and causing incorrect instrument indications?

4. Is there an alternate static source and, if so, where is it located? What is its purpose and what effect does it have on the instrument indications if the static source is changed by the Pilot from normal to the alternate?

5. Name the Gyroscopic Flight Instruments.

6. Name the Flight Instruments that are operated electrically.

7. Name the Flight Instruments that are operated by the vacuum system, if fitted, and know how the vacuum sytem works (venturi or vacuum pump) and the maximum/minimum suction required for correct operation.

8. The Air Speed Indicator is operated by ..... .

9. The Attitude Indicator (Artificial Horizon) is operated by ..... .

10. The Altimeter is operated by ..... .

11. The Vertical Speed Indicator is operated by ..... .

12. The Direction Indicator is operated by ..... .

13. The Turn Co-ordinator (or Turn Indicator) is operated by ..... .

14. The Flap Indicator is operated by ..... .

15. The Magnetic Compass is operated by ..... .

16. The Clock is operated by ..... .

FUEL.

1. The correct grade of fuel is ..... , which is coloured ..... .

2. Fuel fittings for AVGAS (which is used in piston engines) are usually coloured ....., whereas fuel fittings for AVTUR (which is used in turbine engines) are usually coloured ..... .

3. How many fuel tanks does the aeroplane have, where are they located, and what is their capacity in terms of usable fuel?

4. How can the aeroplane be refuelled? Where are the filler caps and what precautions need to be taken?

5. Is it advisable to fill the fuel tanks prior to parking the aeroplane overnight?

6. Where are the fuel drains located and why are they used? When should fuel be drained?

7. Where are the fuel tank vents located and why are they important?

8. How can fuel quantity be measured, both on the ground and in flight?

9. Does the engine have a carburettor or a fuel injection system? How does it work?

10. Does the engine require priming prior to start and, if so, how is it done?

11. Does the aeroplane have fuel pumps and, if so, where are they located, what is their function, are they electrical or engine-driven, what are their maximum and minimum acceptable operating pressures, and when should they be used?

12. Know the correct fuel management procedures, such as which tank(s) to use for take-off and landing, when to use fuel pumps if fitted, when and how to switch tanks, etc.

OIL.

1. The correct grade of oil is ..... .

2. The oil is stored in a tank or sump which is located ..... .

3. Explain how the oil quantity can be measured.

4. Minimum acceptable oil quantity prior to flight is ..... .

5. The maximum quantity of oil is ..... .

6. The oil is used to (lubricate/cool/both lubricate and cool) the engine.

THE ENGINE.

1. The engine has ..... cylinders, which are arranged (in-line/horizontally-opposed/.....).

2. The engine is (air-cooled/water-cooled).

3. Cooling of the engine can be increased by opening cowl flaps. (Yes/No.)

4. The cockpit gauges used to monitor engine operation are ..... , ... , ... , ...

5. Maximum engine RPM is ..... .

6. Normal RPM is ..... .

7. RPM is controlled with the ..... .

8. Maximum oil pressure is ..... .

9. Minimum oil pressure is ..... .

10. Normal oil pressure is approximately ..... .

11. Maximum oil temperature is ..... .

12. Minimum oil temperature is ..... .

13. Normal oil temperature is approximately ..... .

14. The aeroplane (is/is not) fitted with a Cylinder Head Temperature gauge and, if so, the CHT limits are ..... .

15. During ground operations of the engine, it is usual to perform a magneto check, which should be done according to procedures specified by your training organisation.
    (a) Specify the maximum acceptable RPM drop when one magneto is switched to *OFF*, the maximum difference between magnetos, and (if permitted) the significance of the 'dead-cut' check during which both magnetos are switched to *OFF* briefly.

(b) What is the probable cause if the engine keeps running even though the magneto switch has been placed to *OFF?*

16. Specify the action to be taken if an engine fire occurs in flight.

17. Specify the action to be taken if an engine fire occurs on the ground.

18. What services are no longer available if the engine fails in flight?

19. What instruments are rendered inoperative if the engine fails in flight?

20. Moving the throttle in will ..... .

21. Moving the throttle out will ..... .

22. Explain the functioning of the Mixture Control and how to operate it correctly. If an Exhaust Gas Temperature gauge (EGT) is fitted, explain how it may be of use.

23. Under what conditions is it permissible to lean the mixture?

24. To lean the mixture, the Mixture Control should be moved (in/out).

25. To enrichen the mixture, the Mixture Control should be moved (in/out).

26. Explain how to lean the mixture to obtain maximum power.

27. Explain how to lean the mixture to obtain maximum economy.

28. The fully-out position of the Mixture Control is called the .... position and is used to (stop/start) the engine.

29. What are the indications if ice forms in the carburettor?

30. How do you melt carburettor ice and prevent it forming again?

31. What effect does applying Carburettor Heat have on the mixture, i.e. does it lean, enrichen or not alter the mixture?

32. Does the hot air used to eliminate carburettor ice pass through a filter or not?

33. Why should you not use Carburettor Heat when taxying if it is not absolutely necessary?

VENTILATION AND HEATING.

1. Know how to ventilate the cockpit adequately.

2. Know how to heat the cockpit adequately.

3. Know how the Heating system works and where the heated air comes from, e.g. from exhaust muffs which allow air to circulate near the very hot exhaust system, thereby raising its temperature, before being channelled into the cabin.

4. The engine exhaust contains a poisonous gas (carbon dioxide/carbon monoxide), which is colourless and odourless and should be excluded from the cockpit.

5. The presence of carbon monoxide in the cabin (may/will not) give the Pilot a sense of well-being, even though it causes his performance to deteriorate and (may/will not) lead to unconsciousness.

6. What precautions would you take if you suspect the presence of carbon monoxide in the cabin?

7. What action would you take in the event of a fire occurring in the cabin?

INDEX